D1124658

THE EPISTEMOLOGY OF TESTIMONY

The Epistemology of Testimony

Edited by
JENNIFER LACKEY
and
ERNEST SOSA

CLARENDON PRESS · OXFORD

Contents

IV. TESTIMONY AND THE EXTENT OF OUR DEPENDENCE ON OTHERS

V. NEW AREAS AND NEW DIRECTIONS IN THE EPISTEMOLOGY OF TESTIMONY

List of Contributors

Robert Audi, Professor of Philosophy and David E. Gallo Professor of Business Ethics, University of Notre Dame

C. A. J. Coady, Professorial Fellow in Applied Philosophy at the Centre for Applied Philosophy and Public Ethics, University of Melbourne

Elizabeth Fricker, University Lecturer in Philosophy and Fellow, Magdalen College, Oxford University

Richard Fumerton, F. Wendell Miller Professor of Philosophy, University of Iowa

Sanford C. Goldberg, Associate Professor of Philosophy, University of Kentucky

Peter Graham, Assistant Professor of Philosophy, University of California, Riverside

Jennifer Lackey, Assistant Professor of Philosophy, Northern Illinois University

Keith Lehrer, Regents Professor of Philosophy, Emeritus, University of Arizona

Richard Moran, Professor of Philosophy, Harvard University

Frederick F. Schmitt, Professor of Philosophy, Indiana University

Ernest Sosa, Romeo Elton Professor of Natural Theology and Professor of Philosophy, Brown University; Distinguished Visiting Professor, Rutgers University

James Van Cleve, Professor of Philosophy, University of Southern California

Introduction

Jennifer Lackey

Our dependence on testimony is as deep as it is ubiquitous. We rely on the reports of others for our beliefs about the food we eat, the medicine we ingest, the products we buy, the geography of the world, discoveries in science, historical information, and many other areas that play crucial roles in both our practical and our intellectual lives. Even many of our most important beliefs about ourselves were learned at an earlier time from our parents and caretakers, such as the date of our birth, the identity of our parents, our ethnic backgrounds, and so on. Were we to refrain from accepting the testimony of others, our lives would be impoverished in startling and debilitating ways.

Despite the vital role that testimony occupies in our epistemic lives, traditional epistemological theories focused primarily on other sources, such as sense perception, memory, and reason, with relatively little attention devoted specifically to testimony. In recent years, however, the epistemic significance of testimony has been more fully appreciated, and the current literature has benefited from the publication of a considerable amount of interesting and innovative work in this area. *The Epistemology of Testimony* is intended to build on and further develop this work by bringing together new papers by some of the central figures in the field.

Most of the papers collected for this volume discuss issues in the epistemology of testimony from a contemporary point of view, though some offer treatments that are historically grounded in the work of Thomas Reid and, to a lesser extent, David Hume (Audi and Van Cleve). Some examine the similarities that testimony bears to other kinds of knowledge (Audi, Van Cleve, Sosa, and Schmitt), while others point to new areas of inquiry in the testimony literature (Coady) and new approaches to theorizing about these issues (Graham, Lackey, and Moran). Many of the papers address the debate between non-reductionist and reductionist theories of testimonial justification and knowledge, either directly (Goldberg, Lackey, and Lehrer) or indirectly (Fumerton, Graham, Sosa, Schmitt, Fricker, and Moran). This debate has rightly assumed a position of

For valuable assistance with this Introduction, I would like to thank Pete Nichols and, especially, Baron Reed and Ernie Sosa.

central importance in the literature on testimony. For at issue is a disagreement over the proper understanding of the relationship between epistemic agents and the broader social world: are the normative requirements for testimonial justification and knowledge a burden that falls primarily on individual knowers, or are they largely satisfied by features of the social interaction that takes place between speakers and hearers?

1. TESTIMONY AND TESTIMONIALLY-BASED BELIEF

One of the main questions in the epistemology of testimony is how we successfully acquire justified belief or knowledge on the basis of what other people tell us. This, rather than what testimony *is*, is often taken to be the issue of central import from an epistemological point of view. Because of this, those who are interested in the epistemic status of testimonial beliefs often embrace a very broad notion of what it is to testify, one that properly leaves the distinction between reliable and unreliable (or otherwise epistemically good and bad) testimony for epistemology to delineate. So, for instance, Elizabeth Fricker holds that the domain of testimony that is of epistemological interest is that of 'tellings generally' with 'no restrictions either on subject matter, or on the speaker's epistemic relation to it' (Fricker 1995: 396–7). Similarly, Robert Audi claims that in accounting for testimonial knowledge and justification, we must understand testimony as 'people's telling us things' (Audi 1997: 406). And Ernest Sosa embraces 'a broad sense of testimony that counts posthumous publications as examples . . . [it] requires only that it be a statement of someone's thoughts or beliefs, which they might direct to the world at large and to no one in particular' (Sosa 1991: 219).[1]

But not every expression of thought is appropriately regarded as an instance of testimony. For instance, suppose that we are walking down the street and I say, 'Ah, it is indeed a beautiful day'. Suppose further that such a statement, though it expresses my thought that it is indeed a beautiful day, is neither offered nor taken as conveying information for any proposition; it is simply a conversational filler, comparable to a sigh of contentedness. Or consider a case in which Ned tells a joke among a group of our friends and I casually say, 'He sure has a great sense of humor'. Again, though I am stating my thought that Ned has a great sense of humor, the context is such that we all know Ned and we all know that he has a great sense of humor; thus, my statement is simply a polite response to a friend's joke.[2] Since the concept of testimony is intimately connected with the notion of conveying information, either in terms of being offered as such or of being taken as such, it is arguable that both examples should fail to qualify as instances of testimony.[3]

An adequate account of testimony, therefore, should recognize the distinction between entirely *non-informational expressions of thought* and *testimony*.

Moreover, let us use the general term *act of communication* to include both verbal and written assertions as well as communicative physical gestures, such as nods, points, and so on. Given this, a rough characterization of testimony may be expressed in something like the following way:

> T: S testifies that *p* by making an act of communication *a* if and only if (in part) in virtue of *a*'s communicable content, (1) S reasonably intends to convey the information that *p*, or[4] (2) *a* is reasonably taken as conveying the information that *p*.[5]

The clause '(in part) in virtue of *a*'s communicable content' is intended to rule out cases such as the following: suppose that I sing 'La, la, la' in a soprano voice and I offer this as conveying the information that I have a soprano voice in virtue of its perceptual content.[6] Such an act of communication should not qualify as testimony because it was not offered as conveying information even in part in virtue of its communicable content; rather, it was offered as conveying information entirely in virtue of its perceptual content.[7] Furthermore, while there need not be a direct correspondence between the content of a proffered act of communication and the content of the proposition testified to—my saying that there are umbrellas in the closet, for instance, may properly be taken as conveying the information *both* that it is raining outside and that there are umbrellas in the closet—a *reasonable* connection must exist between such contents. For instance, my intending to convey the information that corn on the cob is yellow by virtue of saying that grass is green fails to satisfy (1) of T because, in the absence of rather unusual circumstances, there fails to be a reasonable connection between the contents of these two propositions. T, then, is broad enough to properly leave the distinction between instances of testimony that are truth-conducive and those that are not for epistemology to delineate while, at the same time, distinguishing between entirely non-informational expressions of thought and testimony.[8]

However, even if a speaker's assertion is properly connected with the conveying of information, not everything we learn from the testimony of others qualifies as *testimonially based* knowledge. For instance, suppose that I say that ten people have spoken in this room today and you, having counted the previous nine, come to know that ten people have spoken in this room today.[9] Here, my statement may certainly be causally relevant with respect to your forming this belief, but your knowledge is based on your having heard and counted the speakers in the room today, thereby rendering it perceptual in nature. What is of import for justification or knowledge that is distinctively testimonial is that a hearer form a given belief *on the basis of the content of a speaker's testimony*. This precludes cases—such as that above—where a belief is formed, either entirely or primarily, on the basis of features *about* the speaker's testimony from qualifying as instances of *testimonial* justification or knowledge.

There are also intermediate cases in which a hearer has relevant background information and uses it to derive knowledge from the statement of a speaker. For example, suppose that you know from past experience that I report that there is no milk in the refrigerator only when there is some. Now when I report to you that there is no milk in the refrigerator, you may supplement my testimony with your background information and hence derive knowledge that there is milk in the refrigerator. Because the epistemic status of beliefs formed in these types of cases relies so heavily on memory and inference, the resulting justification and knowledge are only partially testimonially based. Hence, such beliefs may fall outside the scope of theories purporting to capture only those beliefs that are entirely based on testimony.

2. NON-REDUCTIONISM AND REDUCTIONISM

Even if an expression of thought qualifies as testimony and the resulting belief formed is entirely testimonially based for the hearer, however, there is the further question of how precisely such a belief successfully counts as justified belief or an instance of knowledge. Indeed, this is the question at the center of the epistemology of testimony, and the current philosophical literature contains two central options for answering it: *non-reductionism* and *reductionism.*

According to non-reductionists—whose historical roots are standardly traced back to Reid—testimony is *just as basic* a source of justification (warrant, entitlement, knowledge, etc.) as sense perception, memory, inference, and the like. Accordingly, so long as there are no relevant defeaters, hearers can justifiedly accept the assertions of speakers *merely* on the basis of a speaker's testimony.[10] Otherwise put, so long as there is no available evidence *against* accepting a speaker's report, the hearer has no positive epistemic work to do in order to justifiedly accept the testimony in question.[11]

There are two different kinds of defeaters that are typically taken to be here relevant. First, there are what we might call *psychological defeaters.* A psychological defeater is an experience, doubt, or belief that is had by S, yet indicates that S's belief that *p* is either false or unreliably formed or sustained.[12] Defeaters in this sense function by virtue of being *had* by S, regardless of their truth value or justificatory status.[13] Second, there are what we might call *normative defeaters.* A normative defeater is a doubt or belief that S ought to have, yet indicates that S's belief that *p* is either false or unreliably formed or sustained.[14] Defeaters in this sense function by virtue of being doubts or beliefs that S *should have* (whether or not S does have them) given the presence of certain available evidence.[15] The underlying thought here is that certain kinds of experiences, doubts, and beliefs contribute epistemically unacceptable *irrationality* to doxastic systems and, accordingly, justification and knowledge can be defeated or undermined by their presence.

Moreover, a defeater may itself be either defeated or undefeated. Suppose, for instance, that Wendy believes that there is a hawk nesting in her backyard because she saw it there this afternoon, but Ted tells her, and she thereby comes to believe, that the bird is instead a falcon. Now, the justification Wendy had for believing that there is a hawk in her backyard has been defeated by her belief that the bird is a falcon. But since psychological defeaters can themselves be beliefs, they, too, are candidates for defeat. For instance, suppose that Wendy consults a bird guidebook to check whether the bird in her backyard is in fact a falcon and she discovers that it is a Cooper's hawk. In this case, the belief that she acquires from the bird book provides her with a psychological defeater for the belief that she acquired via Ted's testimony, and hence it provides her with a *defeater-defeater* for her original belief that there is a hawk nesting in her backyard. And, as should be suspected, defeater-defeaters can also be defeated by further experiences, doubts, and beliefs, which, in turn, can be defeated by further experiences, doubts, and beliefs, and so on. Similar considerations involving reasons, rather than experiences, doubts, and beliefs, apply in the case of normative defeaters. Now, when one has a defeater D for one's belief that *p* that is not itself defeated, one has what is called an *undefeated defeater* for one's belief that *p*. It is the presence of undefeated defeaters, not merely defeaters, that is incompatible with testimonial justification and knowledge.

In contrast to non-reductionism, reductionists—whose historical roots are typically traced back to Hume—maintain that in order to justifiedly accept the testimony of speakers, more is needed than the mere absence of undefeated defeaters. In particular, proponents of reductionism argue that hearers must have sufficiently good *positive reasons* for accepting a given report, reasons that are not themselves ineliminably based on the testimony of others. Typically, these reasons are the result of induction: for instance, we observe a general conformity between facts and reports and, with the aid of memory and reason, we inductively infer that certain speakers, contexts, or types of reports are reliable sources of information. In this way, the justification of testimony is *reduced* to the justification we have for sense perception, memory, and inductive inference.[16]

There are, however, at least two different answers given to what *relata* are involved in the relevant testimonial reductions. The first answer, and the stronger version of reductionism—a view sometimes called *global reductionism*—is that the justification of *testimony as a source of belief* reduces to the justification of sense perception, memory, and inductive inference. In particular, global reductionists maintain that in order to justifiedly accept a speaker's report, a hearer must have non-testimonially based positive reasons for believing that *testimony is generally reliable*. The second, and weaker, version of reductionism—often called *local reductionism*—is that the justification of *each particular report or instance of testimony* reduces to the justification of instances of sense perception, memory, and inductive inference. Specifically, local reductionists claim that in order to justifiedly accept a speaker's testimony, a hearer must have non-testimonially based positive reasons for accepting *the particular report in question*.[17]

Both non-reductionism and reductionism have been subject to various objections. For instance, because non-reductionists do not require any positive epistemic work from recipients of testimony in order to acquire justified belief or knowledge, such a view is often attacked for sanctioning gullibility, epistemic irrationality, and intellectual irresponsibility.[18] In addition, while non-reductionists maintain that testimony is an epistemically basic source, it has been argued that a source of epistemically basic beliefs must be an *a priori* source, and testimony is clearly not an *a priori* source.[19] On the other hand, because reductionists hold that testimony is ultimately reducible to other epistemic sources, such a view is frequently criticized for underestimating or devaluing the contributions made by testimony to our cognitive lives. Moreover, it is often claimed that the non-testimonial positive reasons required by reductionists simply cannot be possessed in all of those cases in which testimonial justification and knowledge are intuitively present, either because most (or all) of our knowledge is already indebted to testimony or because we simply lack the cognitive resources to acquire such reasons.[20] Some of these problems have recently led those working in the epistemology of testimony to develop qualified or hybrid views of either non-reductionism or reductionism, some of which can be found in this collection (Graham, Goldberg, Lehrer, and Lackey).[21]

3. TRANSMISSION

Despite the important differences between non-reductionists and reductionists, there is nonetheless surprising agreement between proponents of these two views regarding a central thesis about the epistemic status of testimony, which we may call the Transmission of Epistemic Properties thesis (hereafter, TEP). Roughly, the thought expressed by TEP is that a testimonial exchange involves a speaker's belief, along with the epistemic properties it possesses, being *transmitted* to a hearer. There are two dimensions to TEP; one is a necessity thesis and the other is a sufficiency thesis. More precisely,

TEP-N: For every speaker, A, and hearer, B, B's belief that p is warranted (justified, known) on the basis of A's testimony that p only if A's belief that p is warranted (justified, known).[22]

TEP-S: For every speaker, A, and hearer, B, if (1) A's belief that p is warranted (justified, known), (2) B comes to believe that p on the basis of the content of A's testimony that p, and (3) B has no undefeated defeaters for believing that p, then B's belief that p is warranted (justified, known).[23]

There is much that is intuitive about both of these theses. For, in many respects, a testimonial chain seems to be much like a bucket brigade: in order to give you a full bucket of water, I must have a full bucket of water to pass to you. Moreover, if I give you a full bucket of water, then—spills aside—the bucket of water you now possess as a result of our exchange will also be full. Similarly, in order to transmit to you a warranted belief, I must have a warranted belief to pass to you.

Moreover, if I transmit to you a warranted belief, then—defeaters aside—the belief that you now possess as a result of our exchange will also be warranted.

Further support for TEP, particularly for TEP-N, derives from the purported observation that testimony, unlike, for instance, sense perception and inference, is not a *generative* epistemic source. Indeed, in this respect, testimony is said to bear striking similarities to memory: while the former is capable of only *transmitting* knowledge from one speaker to another, the latter is capable of only *preserving* the epistemic status of beliefs from one time to another. In this way, just as I cannot know that *p* on the basis of memory unless I non-memorially knew that *p* at an earlier time, the thought underlying this picture of testimonial knowledge is that a hearer cannot know that *p* on the basis of testimony unless the speaker from whom it was acquired herself knows that *p*.

While this picture of testimony is widely accepted by both non-reductionists and reductionists (indeed, several papers in this volume include endorsements of different versions of TEP, such as Audi, Schmitt, and Fricker), various objections have been raised to both TEP-N and to TEP-S. For instance, it has been argued against TEP-N that *unreliable believers* may nonetheless be *reliable testifiers*—as, for example, may happen when a teacher who is a devout creationist nevertheless reliably teaches her students about evolutionary theory—and hence speaker-warrant or knowledge is not necessary for testimonial warrant or knowledge.[24] Against TEP-S, it has been argued that reliable believers may nonetheless be unreliable testifiers—as, for example, may happen when a speaker who knows and correctly reports that *p* is nevertheless such that she would have easily reported that *p* even if not-*p* had been the case—and hence speaker-warrant or knowledge combined with the absence of defeaters is not sufficient for testimonial warrant or knowledge.[25] These types of cases have led some either to qualify the relevant theses of TEP or to restrict their scope to certain kinds of testimonial knowledge only, such as that acquired through the particular mechanism of *trust*.[26]

4. SUMMARIES OF ESSAYS

In 'Testimony, Credulity, and Veracity', Robert Audi contrasts testimony-based belief—which is belief that arises naturally, non-inferentially, and typically unself-consciously to what someone says—with belief based on the other standard epistemic sources. Showing the ways in which his view of testimony bears striking similarities to Thomas Reid's, Audi argues that testimony is a source of basic knowledge—that is, knowledge not grounded in knowledge of some other proposition—though it is not a basic source of knowledge—that is, it cannot produce knowledge without the cooperation of another epistemic source.

Audi then compares testimonial knowledge with testimonial justification, arguing that in order for a hearer to acquire testimonial knowledge that *p*, the speaker from whom it was acquired must also know that *p*. In contrast, a hearer can acquire testimonially justified belief that *p* without the speaker from whom it was acquired herself being justified in believing that *p*. Moreover, Audi argues that while testimonial knowledge does not require that a hearer have knowledge or justification regarding the attester's credibility, justification concerning the attester's credibility is required in order for a hearer to acquire testimonially justified belief.

Finally, Audi discusses at least five ways in which testimony differs from the standard basic sources of perception, memory, and introspection. First, while the reliability of one of the basic sources cannot be tested without relying on that very source, the reliability of testimony can be tested without relying on it. Second, unlike the basic sources, there is no domain for which continued testimony is in principle necessary for a significant increase in knowledge or justification. Third, testimony-based belief, unlike that based on the basic sources, passes through the will. Fourth, because of the dependency on understanding an artificial language, testimony-based knowledge and justification must go through *convention*, while knowledge and justification based on the basic sources need only go through *nature*. Fifth, although testimony can increase the number of knowers in the world, it cannot, as the basic sources can, increase the number of propositions known.

In 'Reid on the Credit of Human Testimony', James Van Cleve explores the analogy between perception and the credit we give to human testimony as it is discussed in the work of Thomas Reid. He first attempts to properly understand the two principles Reid identifies as fundamental to the acquisition of testimonial knowledge: the principles of veracity and credulity. Van Cleve shows that there are two different ways to understand both the principle of veracity—i.e., as either V1: (It tends to be the case that) if A says *p*, *p* is true, or as V2: (It tends to be the case that) if A says *p*, A believes *p*—and the principle of credulity—i.e., as either C1: (It tends to be the case that) if A says *p*, B believes *p*, or as C2: (It tends to be the case that) if A says *p*, B believes that A believes *p*. Reid's writings suggest that the principle of veracity should be understood as V2 and the principle of credulity as C1. But this poses a problem, as Reid also claims that the two principles are meant to *tally* with each other. That is, the principles should combine with each other so as to imply that when a speaker says *p*, we tend to form true beliefs. The combinations that successfully achieve this, however, are V1 with C1 and V2 with C2, not Reid's V2 with C1. Van Cleve suggests that this problem can be solved, since a good Reidian case can be made for accepting all four of the principles. This results in two pairs of principles that tally with each other—V1 with C1 and V2 with C2.

Van Cleve then turns to Reid's discussion of the analogy between the testimony of nature given by the senses and the testimony of human beings given in language. According to Reid, there are four phenomena involved—original perception, natural language, acquired perception, and artificial language—which give rise to two analogies, one between acquired perception and artificial language and another between original perception and natural language. Acquired perception and artificial language are alike in that the connection between signs and what they signify is known by experience, but they differ in that the connection for artificial language, unlike acquired perception, holds by convention rather than by nature. The analogy between original perception and natural language, however, is even greater since in both cases nature has established the connection between sign and thing signified and taught us the interpretation of the sign prior to experience.

Finally, Van Cleve turns to Reid's view of the epistemology of testimony. Reid regards testimony as a source not merely of belief, but also of evident belief or knowledge. Moreover, this is true even if the hearer in question possesses no reason for accepting a given speaker's report. Testimony-based beliefs are, thus, epistemically basic on his view, thereby placing Reid clearly in the non-reductionist or fundamentalist camp in the epistemology of testimony. Van Cleve, however, finds this view implausible, since he argues that a source of epistemically basic belief must be an *a priori* source, and testimony is not an *a priori* source. Van Cleve therefore finds himself (uncharacteristically) on the side of Hume rather than Reid in defending a reductionist view of the epistemic status of testimonial beliefs.

In 'The Epistemic Role of Testimony: Internalist and Externalist Perspectives', Richard Fumerton contrasts the possible ways in which classical internalists and paradigm externalists might approach the question of how to characterize testimonial justification, focusing particularly on whether testimonial inference has a fundamental or a derivative place in our reasoning. He argues that the plausibility of countenancing a general and *sui generis* epistemic principle licensing testimonial inference is directly proportional to the plausibility of an externalist understanding of probability claims. Moreover, while much recent work in the epistemology of testimony focuses on whether testimonial inference is fundamental or derivative, Fumerton argues that the distinction itself is spurious since arguments that purportedly employ derivative epistemic principles are better thought of as enthymematic arguments governed by legitimate epistemic principles licensing inferences from premises to conclusion. Thus, derivative epistemic 'principles' aren't really epistemic *principles* at all.

In 'Liberal Fundamentalism and Its Rivals', Peter Graham argues on behalf of Liberal Fundamentalism, a view that holds that testimony-based beliefs, like perception, memory, and introspection-based beliefs, are epistemically direct. In particular, the Liberal Fundamentalist maintains that it is *a priori* necessary that understanding an attester's presentation-as-true that *p* confers justification on the hearer's belief that *p*. Such a view, according to Graham, includes two doctrines—it combines Liberal Foundationalism about *which* epistemic principles are true with Intuitionism about *why* they are true.

Graham then distinguishes between a strong and a weak version of Liberal Fundamentalism. The Strong version holds that, in the absence of defeat, the event or state of understanding the attester's presentation-as-true that p confers *on balance* justification for the belief that p, whereas the Weak version holds that the justification provided may fall short of on balance justification even if it is undefeated. Specifically, the Weak Liberal Fundamentalist—which is Graham's preferred view—maintains that no additional support of any kind (reductive or non-reductive) is required for *prima facie pro tanto* testimonial justification, while additional support (whether reductive or non-reductive) is often required for on balance testimonial justification. According to Graham, then, testimony is epistemically direct with respect to *pro tanto* justification, but it is epistemically inferential with respect to *on balance* justification. Finally, Graham argues that his view of the epistemology of testimony has notable advantages over its rivals, particularly over what he calls Strong Liberal Fundamentalism and Moderate Fundamentalism.

Ernest Sosa argues in 'Knowledge: Instrumental and Testimonial' that there are epistemically important similarities between testimonial knowledge and knowledge acquired through the use of instruments. In many cases of testimonial knowledge, for instance, the features that most saliently explain the truth of a given belief involve, not the individual competence of the subject holding such a belief but, rather, the testifiers in question and their cognitive accomplishments. But, according to Sosa, this is not distinctive of testimonial knowledge. For what carries the explanatory burden in cases of *instrumental knowledge* is not the individual competence of the subject possessing the knowledge but, rather, the *safety* of the deliverances of the instruments in question. When one knows the ambient temperature outside through the display of a given thermometer, for instance, this is explained primarily by the fact that the deliverances of the thermometer in question are systematically safe—that is, not easily would such deliverances be false.

Sosa argues, however, that if a responsiveness to a relevant field requires efficient causal input, then this systematic safety of reliable instruments does not always derive from such a responsiveness. For instance, the facts of arithmetic do not efficiently cause a calculator to display the correct answer when prompted, nor are cogito beliefs explained through any efficient causal responsiveness to the relevant field, yet both sets of deliverances are highly reliable. Moreover, though Sosa claims that there is a clear sense in which such deliverances are produced *because* they are true, this 'because' cannot be one of teleology or function, since an intelligent Swampman caused by lightning serendipitously hitting a swamp can exhibit epistemically efficient competence. Sosa's preferred explanation is one that is compatible with the relevance of evolution or theology to whether and how we have knowledge.

With respect to exchanges involving testimony, Sosa claims that hearers must interpret their speakers so as to discern the thoughts behind their oral or written displays, and hence this *interpretative knowledge*, in its use of the instrument of language, is itself a kind of instrumental knowledge. Because of this, testimonial knowledge not only shares important epistemic similarities with knowledge acquired through the use of instruments, it also presupposes instrumental knowledge.

Finally, while Sosa argues that direct bootstrapping is equally powerless to explain the justification we have for our senses as it is to explain the justification we have for trusting ordinary instruments, both our senses and human testimony, unlike instruments, enjoy a default rational justification. In particular, though we are default-justified in accepting the deliverances of our senses and of human testimony, we need a rational basis for justifiedly accepting the deliverances of instruments.

Sanford C. Goldberg argues in 'Reductionism and the Distinctiveness of Testimonial Knowledge' that testimonial knowledge is an epistemically unique kind of knowledge, regardless of whether there are epistemic principles that are unique to cases of testimony. In particular, only testimonial knowledge is associated with a characteristic expansion in the sorts of epistemically relevant moves that a subject can make when identifying the direct epistemic support for a given belief. According to Goldberg, the specific characteristic expansion in question is that testimonial knowledge—but no other—gives rise to the hearer's right to *pass the epistemic buck* after her own justificatory resources have been exhausted. Goldberg argues that this feature of testimonial knowledge reflects the epistemological distinctiveness of relying on the epistemic authority of another rational being. Moreover, Goldberg claims that the arguments on behalf of epistemic buck-passing do not depend on there being testimony-specific epistemic principles, and hence that the conclusion that testimonial knowledge is epistemically unique should be embraced by both reductionists and non-reductionists in the epistemology of testimony.

Keith Lehrer argues in 'Testimony and Trustworthiness' that testimonial knowledge requires trustworthiness on the part of both the speaker and the hearer involved in a given exchange. He begins by arguing against causal or transmission theories of testimonial knowledge, which maintain that knowledge can be transmitted from a speaker to a hearer in the absence of any evaluation of trustworthiness. Such theories, according to Lehrer, face what he calls the *opacity objection*—a subject may be completely unaware of whether a belief that she holds is worthy of her trust, that is, the epistemic merits of a belief may be *opaque* to the subject holding it, thereby rendering her unable to justify or defend her own belief. Moreover, because beliefs may be formed in evidentially defective ways, requiring that the causal relations in question have a reliable or otherwise appropriate etiology will not provide an adequate response to this objection.

In contrast, Lehrer argues that a speaker's testimony that *p* qualifies as *evidence* that *p* only when the speaker is found by the hearer in question to be trustworthy in what she accepts and what she conveys. In addition, the speaker's trustworthiness must be successfully truth-connected, and the hearer must be correct in her evaluation of the speaker's trustworthiness. The result, according to Lehrer, is that testimonial justification is neither reductive, as reductionists would have it, nor foundational, as non-reductionists would have it, since there is an essential loop in the justification for accepting the testimony of others. In particular, the hearer must depend on the testimony of others to evaluate her own trustworthiness, but she must evaluate her own trustworthiness to evaluate the testimony of others. According to Lehrer, however, there are two reasons why this loop is a virtuous rather than a vicious one. First, any complete theory of justification must explain why the theory itself is justified, and hence an explanatory loop of this sort should not be regarded as a problem. Second, there is a mutual support between the particular beliefs one has accepted in the past on the basis of testimony and one's general trustworthiness in accepting such reports. Finally, Lehrer argues that what converts the acceptance of testimony into knowledge is that acceptance cannot be refuted or defeated by any errors in the evaluation—irrefutable or undefeated justified acceptance of testimony is knowledge.

Jennifer Lackey argues in 'It Takes Two to Tango: Beyond Reductionism and Non-Reductionism in the Epistemology of Testimony', that the current focus in the epistemology of testimony needs to move beyond the debate between reductionism and non-reductionism. In particular, while a testimonial exchange typically involves the transfer of information between two central participants—the speaker and the hearer—Lackey argues that reductionists and non-reductionists alike have placed all of the epistemic work on only one or the other of these participants and, in so doing, have ignored the positive justificatory contribution that needs to be made by the other. On the one hand, reductionists focus entirely on the *hearer* in a testimonial exchange, thereby failing to account for the fact that no matter how excellent a hearer's positive reasons are on behalf of an instance of testimony, a speaker may still offer a report that is thoroughly unreliable. Non-reductionists, on the other hand, focus entirely on the *speaker*, thereby failing to account for the fact that no matter how reliable a speaker's testimony is, this cannot by itself make it rationally acceptable for a hearer to accept her report. In contrast, Lackey argues on behalf of what she calls *dualism* in the epistemology of testimony, which gives proper credence to the dual nature of testimonial justification by requiring positive epistemic work from both the speaker and the hearer. Moreover, Lackey claims that this shows that testimonial justification is neither reducible to nor completely independent from sense perception, memory, and inductive inference, thereby moving the focus of the current debate beyond the reductionism and non-reductionism dichotomy.

In 'Testimonial Justification and Transindividual Reasons', Frederick F. Schmitt argues that testimonially justified belief, though not social in a strong sense, can nonetheless be legitimately regarded as social in a qualified sense. In support of this claim, he invokes what he calls the Transindividual Thesis, which consists of the following two parts: first, H's belief that p is justified on the basis of testimony only if it is justified on the basis of S's good reason to believe that p, unless on the basis of a good reason to believe that p that H possesses herself and, second, H's belief that p can be justified on the basis of testimony even though it is not justified on the basis of a good reason that H possesses to believe that p.

By way of defending this thesis, Schmitt's central strategy is to discuss what he calls the Transtemporal Thesis, a similar though far more intuitively plausible thesis regarding memorial justification, which consists of the following two parts: first, a subject, A's, belief that p is justified on the basis of memory only if it is justified on the basis of A's original good reasons to believe that p, unless on the basis of a current good reason to believe that p and, second, A's belief that p can be justified on the basis of memory even though it is not justified on the basis of a current reason to believe that p that A possesses. Schmitt then argues that if the intuitively plausible Transtemporal Thesis is accepted, then an analogous case can be made showing that the Transindividual Thesis is nearly as strong. To this end, he relies on the intuitively plausible assumption that if A has a justified belief that p, then it is justified on the basis of a good reason to believe that p suitably related to A. This assumption, according to Schmitt, equally supports the first part of both the Transindividual and the Transtemporal Theses. He then focuses on the second part of these theses. Regarding the Transtemporal Thesis, he provides examples of memorially justified beliefs that are supported by neither good current reductive nor good current non-reductive reasons, thereby showing that no good current reasons exist for these justified beliefs. With respect to the second part of the Transindividual Thesis, Schmitt employs a similar argumentative strategy by providing examples of testimonially justified beliefs that are supported by neither an ultimately coherentist nor an ultimately foundationalist justification, thereby showing that these beliefs are not justified by good reasons possessed by the cognizer in question. Finally, Schmitt considers and rejects various attempts to locate an asymmetry between memorial and testimonial justification, including a counterfactual dependency sensitivity requirement, a constraint on the role of reasons in the process of reasoning, and a responsibilist conception of belief. He then concludes that the case for the Transindividual Thesis is nearly as strong as that for the Transtemporal Thesis and, accordingly, that those who accept the latter should similarly endorse the former.

In 'Testimony and Epistemic Autonomy', Elizabeth Fricker examines the ideal of the epistemically autonomous knower—that is, one who believes only where she herself possesses all of the (non-testimonial) evidence for what is believed, trusting no one else's work on any matter—and shows that the subtle and ubiquitous dependence each of us has on the testimony of others renders this ideal practically impossible. She then asks whether there is reason to regret this conclusion. By way of answering this question, Fricker focuses on the circumstances and topics in which one may properly accept and learn from another's testimony. She argues on behalf of the following Testimony Deferential Principle: A hearer, H, properly accepts that P on the basis of trust in a speaker, S's, testimony that P if and only if S speaks sincerely, and S is epistemically well enough placed with respect to P to be in a position to know that P, and S is better epistemically placed with respect to P than H, and there is no equally well-qualified contrary testimony regarding P, and H recognizes all these things to be so. She then further distinguishes between *weak deferential acceptance*, which occurs when H forms the belief that P on the basis of trust in S's testimony that P, when H has no firm pre-existing belief regarding P, nor would H form a firm belief regarding P were H to consider the question whether P using only H's current epistemic resources (apart from the testimony that P), and *strong deferential acceptance*, which occurs when H allows S's trusted testimony to override H's own previous firm belief, or disposition to form a firm belief, regarding P. The former, weaker kind of deferential acceptance, according to Fricker, is often appropriate when a speaker has no superior expertise regarding the topic in question but, rather, is merely contingently more expert than a hearer, such as when S but not H knows what happened at a concert because S but not H attended it. In contrast, Fricker claims that the latter, stronger kind of deferential acceptance is appropriate only when a speaker has an expertise—that is, an intrinsic epistemic power—superior to a hearer, such as when S but not H knows what is happening on the stage of a concert because S but not H has excellent distance vision. With respect to both kinds of expertise, Fricker argues that when H appreciates that S is an expert relative to H, it is not merely rationally permissible, but rationally mandatory, for S to defer to H regarding the domain in question.

After examining the various ways in which another person is sometimes better placed epistemically than oneself to make judgments regarding a certain domain, Fricker turns to a consideration of the way one's epistemic self-governances can be maintained in the face of one's practically inevitable dependence on the testimony of others. She first shows that our reliance on testimony *does* result in an important loss of autonomy, for if H knows that P through being told that P and trusting S, there is or was someone who knows that P in some other non-testimonial way. This second-hand nature of testimonial knowledge reveals its epistemic inferiority, since the hearer does not directly possess the evidence for the belief in question and, accordingly, is less able to monitor for defeaters relative to such a belief. Nevertheless, Fricker argues that epistemic self-governance can be maintained in spite of our dependence on others by critically assessing the sincerity and competence of those whom we trust and by discriminatingly, rather than blindly and universally, accepting what we are told.

In 'Pathologies of Testimony', C. A. J. Coady discusses three forms of telling things to others that are either morally or epistemically suspect—gossip, rumor, and urban myth—and evaluates the extent to which these suspicions are legitimate. He begins with gossip, some necessary features of which are that it is typically conveyed by those who believe it to be true, its subject matter is personal, there must be something unwelcome to the gossipee about the conveying of the information in question, and it can involve the transmission of justified beliefs. He then proceeds to evaluate both the moral and the epistemic status of gossip. With respect to the former, Coady claims that gossip can both reinforce positive existing norms and break down negative social norms, it need not violate the respect of the gossipee, and it can be quite enjoyable. Regarding the epistemic status of gossip, Coady considers two objections: first, since gossip is inspired, not by a consideration of the truth but by malice, it is epistemically defective and, second, it excludes the gossipee's falsification or correction of the report in question, which is an important epistemic source. He responds that gossip need not be malicious—one may gossip about a person's upcoming promotion simply out of interest in the topic—and, even if it is not inspired by the purest or loftiest of intentions, it need not be disconnected from a concern for the truth. To the second objection, Coady argues that there is often little reason to suppose that the gossipee will be a reliable source for confirming or disconfirming the report in question. Hence, Coady argues that gossip is not in fact a pathology of testimony at all but, rather, it is a perfectly normal form of testimony whose moral status is less problematic than is typically thought and whose epistemic status is actually quite epistemically reasonable.

Coady then turns to rumor and urban myth. Though similar to gossip in some respects, rumor differs in that it has no strong justificatory base, its subject matter is not necessarily personal, and it is not restricted in its circulation. Though rumor may have some epistemic merits, such as prompting the creation of hypotheses for further exploration, Coady argues that it is nonetheless a pathology of testimony. For unlike cases of normal testimony, many cases of rumor involve neither an original source of the information being conveyed nor a speaker who has competence with respect to this information. More precisely, Coady argues that rumor is what J. L. Austin calls a 'misfire' rather than an 'abuse' of the speech act of testifying. Whereas misfires simply involve speech acts that have gone wrong in a way that nullifies them, abuses constitute genuine but irregular performances of these acts. In this way, the lack of credentials on the part of the person who spreads rumor renders her assertion void as testimony, thereby resulting in rumor being a pathological form of testimony. Urban myths, however, differ from rumors in that they have much higher levels of complexity, are presented in the form of fully fledged stories, have an abiding nature, and are invariably false and ill-founded, though commonly believed to be true. Coady then argues that whether urban myths are pathologies of testimony depends on the degree to which they are presented as testimony or as fiction.

Coady concludes by pointing out two general lessons that should be drawn from his discussion. First, whether a certain communication is a pathology of testimony cannot simply be read off from the form or content of its telling and, second, pathologies of testimony need not be either morally or epistemically worthless.

In 'Getting Told and Being Believed', Richard Moran focuses on the reciprocal relations of a speaker's telling his audience something and his audience's believing him, where 'telling' is distinct from but includes asserting, and believing the *person* is distinct from but includes believing the proposition asserted. He approaches this through a contrast between what he calls the Evidential view and the Assurance view of testimony. The Assurance view is developed through a discussion of an earlier paper by Angus Ross (1986), where Ross claims that it is inconsistent with the spirit in which testimony is offered that the speaker present his utterance as evidence for the truth in question. One advantage Moran sees in the Assurance view is that it provides a way of understanding how the recognition of the intentional character of the utterance can contribute positively to the reason-providing force of the speaker's words, rather than being seen as evidence that has been deliberately tampered with. Investigating the nature of the audience's dependence on the speaker's free assurance leads to a discussion of Grice's formulation of non-natural meaning in an epistemological light, concentrating on just how the recognition of the speaker's self-reflexive intention is supposed to count for his audience as a reason to believe P. This is understood as the speaker's explicitly assuming responsibility for P's being true, and thereby constituting his utterance as a reason to believe.

Moran claims that several features of testimony are better understood in terms of the Assurance view than the Evidential view. These include the fact that for something a speaker does to be evidence for something else, it doesn't matter whether the speaker knows or understands that it is evidence, whereas this is crucial to the reason-giving force of testimony; the contrast between our epistemic relations to photographs and speech; the fact that something only counts as an assertion if it is something done freely and consciously; and the speaker's role in determining the epistemic import of his utterance, as contrasted with the absence of any authority he has with respect to the evidential significance of his actions, including his verbal ones.

REFERENCES

Adler, Jonathan E. (1994), 'Testimony, Trust, Knowing', *Journal of Philosophy*, 91: 264–75.

_____ (2002), *Belief's Own Ethics* (Cambridge, Mass.: MIT Press).

Alston, William P. (1989), *Epistemic Justification: Essays in the Theory of Knowledge* (Ithaca, NY: Cornell University Press).

Audi, Robert (1997), 'The Place of Testimony in the Fabric of Knowledge and Justification', *American Philosophical Quarterly*, 34: 405–22.

_____ (1998), *Epistemology: A Contemporary Introduction to the Theory of Knowledge* (London and New York: Routledge).

Austin, J. L. (1979), 'Other Minds', in his *Philosophical Papers*, 3rd edn. (Oxford: Oxford University Press).

Bergmann, Michael (1997), 'Internalism, Externalism and the No-Defeater Condition', *Synthese*, 110: 399–417.

_____ (2004), 'Epistemic Circularity: Malignant and Benign', *Philosophy and Phenomenological Research*, 69: 709–27.

BonJour, Laurence (1980), 'Externalist Theories of Epistemic Justification', *Midwest Studies in Philosophy*, 5: 53–73.

____ (1985), *The Structure of Empirical Knowledge* (Cambridge, Mass.: Harvard University Press).

____ and Sosa, Ernest (2003), *Epistemic Justification: Internalism vs. Externalism, Foundations vs. Virtues* (Oxford: Blackwell Publishing).

Burge, Tyler (1993), 'Content Preservation', *Philosophical Review*, 102: 457–88.

____ (1997), 'Interlocution, Perception, and Memory', *Philosophical Studies*, 86: 21–47.

Chisholm, Roderick M. (1989), *Theory of Knowledge*, 3rd edn. (Englewood Cliffs, NJ: Prentice-Hall).

Coady, C. A. J. (1992), *Testimony: A Philosophical Study* (Oxford: Clarendon Press).

____ (1994), 'Testimony, Observation and "Autonomous Knowledge" ', in Matilal and Chakrabarti (1994: 225–50).

Dummett, Michael (1994), 'Testimony and Memory', in Matilal and Chakrabarti (1994: 251–72).

Evans, Gareth (1982), *The Varieties of Reference* (Oxford: Clarendon Press).

Faulkner, Paul (2000), 'The Social Character of Testimonial Knowledge', *Journal of Philosophy*, 97: 581–601.

____ (2002), 'On the Rationality of our Response to Testimony', *Synthese*, 131: 353–70.

Foley, Richard (1994), 'Egoism in Epistemology', in Schmitt (1994: 53–73).

Fricker, Elizabeth (1987), 'The Epistemology of Testimony', *Proceedings of the Aristotelian Society*, suppl. vol. 61: 57–83.

____ (1994), 'Against Gullibility', in Matilal and Chakrabarti (1994: 125–61).

____ (1995), 'Telling and Trusting: Reductionism and Anti-Reductionism in the Epistemology of Testimony', *Mind*, 104: 393–411.

____ (2002), 'Trusting Others in the Sciences: A priori or Empirical Warrant?', *Studies in History and Philosophy of Science*, 33: 373–83.

____ (forthcoming), 'Knowledge from Trust in Testimony is Second-Hand Knowledge', *Philosophy and Phenomenological Research*.

Goldman, Alvin I. (1986), *Epistemology and Cognition* (Cambridge, Mass.: Harvard University Press).

____ (1999), *Knowledge in a Social World* (Oxford: Clarendon Press).

Graham, Peter J. (1997), 'What is Testimony?', *Philosophical Quarterly*, 47: 227–32.

____ (2000), 'Conveying Information', *Synthese*, 123: 365–92.

Greco, John and Sosa, Ernest (eds.) (1999), *The Blackwell Guide to Epistemology* (Oxford: Blackwell Publishers).

Hardwig, John (1985), 'Epistemic Dependence', *Journal of Philosophy*, 82: 335–49.

____ (1991), 'The Role of Trust in Knowledge', *Journal of Philosophy*, 88: 693–708.

Hawthorne, John (2004), *Knowledge and Lotteries* (Oxford: Oxford University Press).

Hume, David (1967), *An Enquiry Concerning Human Understanding*, in L. A. Selby-Bigge (ed.), *Hume's Enquiries* (Oxford: Oxford University Press).

Insole, Christopher J. (2000), 'Seeing Off the Local Threat to Irreducible Knowledge by Testimony', *Philosophical Quarterly*, 50: 44–56.

Lackey, Jennifer (1999), 'Testimonial Knowledge and Transmission', *Philosophical Quarterly*, 49: 471–90.

Lackey, Jennifer (2003), 'A Minimal Expression of Non-Reductionism in the Epistemology of Testimony', *Noûs* 37: 706–23.

——— (2005), 'Testimony and the Infant/Child Objection', *Philosophical Studies*, 126: 163–90.

——— (forthcoming *a*), 'Learning from Words', *Philosophy and Phenomenological Research*.

——— (forthcoming *b*), 'The Nature of Testimony', *Pacific Philosophical Quarterly*.

——— (forthcoming *c*), 'Knowing from Testimony', *Philosophy Compass*.

Lipton, Peter (1998), 'The Epistemology of Testimony', *Studies in History and Philosophy of Science*, 29: 1–31.

Lyons, Jack (1997), 'Testimony, Induction and Folk Psychology', *Australasian Journal of Philosophy*, 75: 163–78.

Matilal, Bimal Krishna and Chakrabarti, Arindam (eds.) (1994), *Knowing From Words* (Dordrecht: Kluwer Academic Publishers).

McDowell, John (1994), 'Knowledge By Hearsay', in Matilal and Chakrabarti (1994: 195–224).

Millgram, Elijah (1997), *Practical Induction* (Cambridge, Mass: Harvard University Press).

Nozick, Robert (1981), *Philosophical Explanations* (Cambridge, Mass: The Belknap Press).

Owens, David (2000), *Reason without Freedom: The Problem of Epistemic Normativity* (London and New York: Routledge).

Plantinga, Alvin (1993), *Warrant and Proper Function* (Oxford: Oxford University Press).

Pollock, John (1986), *Contemporary Theories of Knowledge* (Totowa, NJ: Rowman and Littlefield).

Reed, Baron (forthcoming), 'Epistemic Circularity Squared? Skepticism about Common Sense', Philosophy and Phenomenological Research.

Reid, Thomas (1993), *The Works of Thomas Reid*, ed. Sir William Hamilton (Charlottesville, Va.: Lincoln-Rembrandt Publishing).

Reynolds, Steven L. (2002), 'Testimony, Knowledge, and Epistemic Goals', *Philosophical Studies*, 110: 139–61.

Root, Michael (2001), 'Hume on the Virtues of Testimony', *American Philosophical Quarterly*, 38: 19–35.

Ross, Angus (1986), 'Why Do We Believe What We Are Told?', *Ratio*, 28: 69–88.

Ross, James (1975), 'Testimonial Evidence', in Keith Lehrer (ed.), *Analysis and Metaphysics: Essays in Honor of R. M. Chisholm* (Dordrecht: Reidel).

Rysiew, Patrick (2002), 'Testimony, Simulation, and the Limits of Inductivism', *Australasian Journal of Philosophy*, 78: 269–74.

Schmitt, Frederick F. (ed.) (1994), *Socializing Epistemology: The Social Dimensions of Knowledge* (Lanham, Md.: Rowman and Littlefield).

——— (1999), 'Social Epistemology', in Greco and Sosa (1999: 354–82).

Sosa, Ernest (1991), *Knowledge in Perspective: Selected Essays in Epistemology* (Cambridge: Cambridge University Press).

Stevenson, Leslie (1993), 'Why Believe What People Say?', *Synthese*, 94: 429–51.

Strawson, P. F. (1994), 'Knowing From Words', in Matilal and Chakrabarti (1994: 23–7).

Webb, Mark Owen (1993), 'Why I Know About As Much As You: A Reply to Hardwig', *Journal of Philosophy*, 90: 260–70.

Weiner, Matthew (2003), 'Accepting Testimony', *Philosophical Quarterly*, 53: 256–64.

Welbourne, Michael (1979), 'The Transmission of Knowledge', *Philosophical Quarterly*, 29: 1–9.

—— (1981), 'The Community of Knowledge', *Philosophical Quarterly*, 31: 302–14.

—— (1986), *The Community of Knowledge* (Aberdeen: Aberdeen University Press).

—— (1994), 'Testimony, Knowledge and Belief', in Matilal and Chakrabarti (1994: 297–313).

Williams, Michael (1999), *Groundless Belief: An Essay on the Possibility of Epistemology*, 2nd edn. (Princeton: Princeton University Press).

Williamson, Timothy (1996), 'Knowing and Asserting', *Philosophical Review*, 105: 489–523.

—— (2000), *Knowledge and its Limits* (Oxford: Oxford University Press).

NOTES

1. For views of the nature of testimony with various additional restrictions, see Ross (1975), Coady (1992), Graham (1997), and Lackey (forthcoming *b*).
2. Similarly, Peter Graham says, 'it should be noted that mere statements are not testimony. Saying "It is a nice day" is not usually taken as testimony about the weather (though it is when said by the weatherman). Repeating what you have already said over and over does not count as testimony either, unless you have forgotten each previous utterance' (1997: 231).
3. Of course, the claim here is *not* that such conversational fillers and polite responses should *never* qualify as instances of testimony but, rather, that they should not *always* qualify as testimony. For instance, if I say to my blind companion, 'It is a beautiful day today', such a remark may qualify as testimony in this context since its function may be to convey information, not to merely fill a gap in the conversation.
4. This, of course, is not an exclusive 'or'; both (1) and (2) could be satisfied simultaneously.
5. Clause (2) of T may need to be modified in something like the following way:

   (2*) *a* is *or should be* reasonably taken as conveying the information that *p*.

   This modification would allow for the following type of case to qualify as testimony: Thelma, while engaged in a soliloquy, confesses to murdering her husband. Although I overhear her make this confession, I do not take her act of communication as conveying the information for any proposition since I think it is far too outlandish a possibility. Nevertheless, we may still wish to regard Thelma's statement as an instance of testimony because I *should have* reasonably taken it as conveying the information that she murdered her husband. If this is correct, then (2*) can be substituted for (2) in T.
6. This is a modified version of an example found in Audi (1997).
7. The 'in part' clause is included since an act of communication can, for instance, be reasonably offered as conveying information in virtue of *both* its perceptual and its

communicable content and yet still qualify as testimony, e.g., I reasonably offer as conveying the information that I have a soprano voice my saying, in a soprano voice, that I do.

8. For more on the account of testimony found in T, see Lackey (forthcoming *b*).

9. This type of example is found in Sosa (1991).

10. Proponents of various versions of non-reductionism include Austin (1979), Welbourne (1979, 1981, 1986, and 1994), Evans (1982), Ross (1986), Hardwig (1985 and 1991), Coady (1992 and 1994), Reid (1993), Burge (1993 and 1997), Plantinga (1993), Webb (1993), Dummett (1994), Foley (1994), McDowell (1994), Strawson (1994), Williamson (1996 and 2000), Goldman (1999), Schmitt (1999), Insole (2000), Owens (2000), Rysiew (2002), Weiner (2003), Sosa (Chapter 5 in this volume), and Goldberg (Chapter 6 in this volume). Some phrase their view in terms of knowledge, others in terms of justification or entitlement, still others in terms of warrant. Audi (1997, 1998, and Chapter 1 in this volume) embraces a non-reductionist view of testimonial knowledge, but not of testimonial justification. Stevenson (1993), Millgram (1997), and Graham (Chapter 4 in this volume) defend restricted versions of non-reductionism.

11. This is a broad characterization, with subtler versions of non-reductionism not always clearly subsumed by it. (See, for instance, Graham (Chapter 4 in this volume) and Goldberg (Chapter 6 in this volume).)

12. To be even more precise, there are two different kinds of psychological defeaters: *rebutting defeaters* are those that indicate the target belief is *false* while *undercutting defeaters* are those that indicate the target belief is *unreliably formed or sustained.* See Pollock (1986) for further development of the distinction between rebutting and undercutting defeaters.

13. For various discussions of what I call psychological defeaters see, for example, BonJour (1980 and 1985), Nozick (1981), Pollock (1986), Goldman (1986), Plantinga (1993), Lackey (1999, 2003, 2005, and Chapter 8 in this volume), Bergmann (1997 and 2004), and Reed (forthcoming).

14. Following the distinction in n. 12, there are rebutting and undercutting normative defeaters. The central difference is that while psychological defeaters are doubts or beliefs had by the subject, their normative counterparts are doubts or beliefs that the subject *should* have. For more on this, see Lackey (1999, 2003, 2005, and Chapter 8 in this volume) and Reed (forthcoming).

15. For discussions involving what I call normative defeaters, approached in a number of different ways, see BonJour (1980 and 1985), Goldman (1986), Fricker (1987 and 1994), Chisholm (1989), Burge (1993 and 1997), McDowell (1994), Audi (1997 and 1998), Williams (1999), Lackey (1999, 2003, 2005, and Chapter 8 in this volume), BonJour and Sosa (2003), Hawthorne (2004), and Reed (forthcoming). What all of these discussions have in common is simply the idea that evidence can defeat knowledge (warrant, justification) even when the subject does not form any corresponding beliefs from the evidence in question.

16. Proponents of different versions of reductionism include Hume (1967), Fricker (1987, 1994, 1995, 2002, and Chapter 10 in this volume), Adler (1994 and 2002), Lyons (1997), Lipton (1998), and Van Cleve (Chapter 2 in this volume). For a nice discussion of Hume's version of reductionism, see Root (2001). Faulkner (2000),

Lackey (Chapter 8 in this volume), and Lehrer (Chapter 7 in this volume) develop 'hybrid' or qualified reductionist/non-reductionist views of testimonial justification and knowledge.

17. 'My reliance on a particular piece of testimony *reduces locally* just if I have adequate grounds to take my informant to be trustworthy on this occasion independently of accepting as true her very utterance' (Fricker 1995: 404).

18. See, for instance, Fricker (1987, 1994, and 1995), Faulkner (2000 and 2002), and Lackey (2003, 2005, and Chapter 8 in this volume).

19. See Van Cleve (Chapter 2 in this volume).

20. See, for instance, Webb (1993), Foley (1994), Strawson (1994), and Schmitt (1999).

21. See also Faulkner (2000).

22. Proponents of different versions of the necessity thesis (TEP-N) include Welbourne (1979, 1981, 1986, and 1994), Hardwig (1985 and 1991), Ross (1986), Burge (1993 and 1997), Plantinga (1993), McDowell (1994), Williamson (1996 and 2000), Audi (1997, 1998, and Chapter 1 in this volume), Owens (2000), Reynolds (2002), and Schmitt (Chapter 9 in this volume). For slightly weaker versions of this thesis, see Dummett (1994) and Fricker (forthcoming and Chapter 10 in this volume).

23. Proponents of different versions of the sufficiency thesis (TEP-S) include Austin (1979), Evans (1982), Fricker (1987), Coady (1992), and Owens (2000). Burge (1993), Williamson (1996), and Audi (1997) endorse qualified versions of this thesis. For instance, Burge claims that '[i]f one has acquired one's belief from others in a *normal way*, and if the others know the proposition, one acquires knowledge' (1992: 477 n. 16; emphasis added). Timothy Williamson writes that '[i]n *normal circumstances*, a speaker who asserts that *P* thereby puts a hearer in a position to know that *P* if (and only if) the speaker knows that *P*' (1996: 520; emphasis added). Similarly, Audi writes, 'Concerning knowledge, we might say that at least *normally*, a belief that *p* based on testimony thereby constitutes knowledge . . . provided that the attester knows that *p* and the believer has no reason to doubt either *p* or the attester's credibility concerning it' (1997: 412; emphasis added).

24. See Lackey (1999, 2003, and forthcoming *a*) and Graham (2000).

25. See Lackey (forthcoming *a*).

26. See Fricker (forthcoming).

PART I
TESTIMONY AND THE LEGACY OF THOMAS REID

1

Testimony, Credulity, and Veracity

Robert Audi

The social aspects of knowledge and justification are an important dimension of epistemology, and in the history of epistemology they have often been neglected. Recent work in social epistemology has partially filled this gap,[1] and the literature of epistemology now contains much discussion of testimony and other aspects of the communication of knowledge and, if to a lesser extent, of the communicative sources of justification.[2] In the history of philosophy, Thomas Reid stands out among major philosophers both for his extensive treatment of testimony and for his distinctive conception of it. My main aim here is to extend my own account of testimony, but the extensions in question are best accomplished in the light of some of what we learn from Reid. I begin with a partial statement and brief defense of my account. I then proceed to describe some major elements in Reid's view of testimony and to compare the two positions. In that light, I make a number of points both about how testimony yields knowledge and justification and about its status as a source of each.

I. TESTIMONY-BASED BELIEF

When philosophers speak of testimony, they usually have in mind not the formal reporting of the court witness (which is what, in many societies, first comes to mind when testimony is spoken of), nor even the self-conscious delivery of information, but virtually any instance of someone's telling somebody something, where this is *telling that*—*propositional telling*—as opposed to *telling to*—*imperatival telling*.[3] *Telling that* is roughly a matter of saying the kind of thing from which we learn facts from other people. In this wide sense, 'testimony' applies to nearly everything we say to others. To be sure, there is the *expository saying* illustrated when, in setting out someone else's view, we drop ascriptive expressions like 'for her' and express the view from the inside. There is also the *theatrical saying* characteristic of acting and the *narrative saying* exemplified by reading a story aloud to others. What is said in these cases does not constitute

This paper has benefited much from discussions with William Alston, Elizabeth Fricker, Christopher Green, Thomas Kelly, Jennifer Lackey, Fritz Warfield, and, especially, Peter Graham.

testimony, at least in the full-blooded sense, as opposed to the kind illustrated by, say, testimony given in a play. For cases that do constitute testimony, the verb 'attest' often serves better than 'testify' (as do 'tell' and 'say', used with 'that'), and I will often speak of attesting, attesters, etc., as well as of testimony.

If the philosophically interesting notion of testimony is immensely wide, the philosophically most important notion of testimony-based belief is much less so. I take this to be the kind of belief that arises naturally, non-inferentially, and usually unselfconsciously in response to what someone says to us. I ask you the time; you tell me it is nine o'clock; and straightaway I believe this on the basis of your saying it. This basis relation which your testimony bears to my belief has a causal component, but that is not its only element. Thus, if I mishear you, your saying, not that it is nine, but that it is noon, could cause me to believe it is nine; but my belief is not then based on your *testimony that it is noon*. It is in fact not, properly speaking, based on your testimony at all, but only on your testimonial act. I hear and am affected by this, but misunderstand it. To be sure, I might still be said to believe that it is nine *because of* that testimony, as I certainly might believe that you have a cold because of your attesting to this in a nasal voice. The latter is possible even when I do not understand what you have said and so do not believe this on the basis of your testimony that you have a cold.

Another case in which belief is produced by testimony, but not based on it, is this. Suppose I believe something on the basis of *premises* supporting your testimony, as where the content seems implausible by itself but I judge you to be both highly competent and unassailably sincere, and for that reason I believe what you say. Here I may also be said to believe it from your testimony (which is a triggering causal basis of my forming the belief) and, if I come to know it, to know it (mainly) *through* that testimony. But this is not belief or knowledge on the *basis* of your testimony. My basis is a combination of your testimony and my beliefs about you. To be sure, what is believed on the basis of testimony is also believed *from* it; but the converse is false.

It is not only in the case of testimony that a mere causal relation between a source of knowledge and a belief based on that source is not sufficient to render that belief knowledge of the kind distinctive of the cognitive products of that source. A perceptual belief, for instance, is more than a belief caused by seeing, hearing, or otherwise perceiving a perceptible object. It must certainly be more if it is to constitute perceptual *knowledge* of the object. A machine that stimulates our brains in a certain way could cause us to believe (truly) that this machine is in a certain room; it can do so without providing us with any ground for believing this and without our perceiving it there or otherwise knowing that it is there. Here, as in further respects, testimony is like other sources of knowledge and justification.

Perception provides more than a source of analogies (and disanalogies) with testimony. To yield a testimony-based belief, an attestation must figure as a perceptual object, for instance as an assertion one hears or as a sentence one sees in a letter from a friend. It must be appropriately received, and the appropriate reception requires that it be a perceptual as well as a semantic object. That is why the belief that someone has a cold, formed only through noting the nasal tone of an attestation, is not testimony-based belief, but only a kind of belief *from testimony*. The content of what is said is irrelevant to its grounding. In a sense, then, testimony-based belief requires semantic interpretation or, at any rate, semantic construal. This is why misinterpreting an attestation can prevent the proper functioning of the testimony.

It would be a mistake to think that some conscious activity of interpretation is generally required for testimony-based knowledge. Typically, we simply understand what is said and believe it. There may be a kind of interpretation process accomplished by the mind (or perhaps just by the brain)—'construal' seems preferable to 'interpretation' here. This certainly seems to occur where, in the light of context, we avoid misinterpretation or see past an apparent ambiguity produced by syntax, intonation, multivocality, or some other source of potential misunderstanding. But for normal adults receiving testimony in their native language, no conscious activity of, say, parsing is invariably required.

Even where one must think about what is said and laboriously interpret it, as with a complex message or an utterance by certain non-fluent non-native speakers, it does not follow that one's belief finally arising from accepting the message one discerns is inferential. Indeed, testimony-based belief, as I construe it, and as I think it is normally understood, is never inferential. If, before taking your word for my student's having left a paper for me by yesterday's deadline, I must note that it could not have gotten in the mail room (which was locked at the end of the day) any later than the deadline, my belief is at most partly based on your testimony. And if, as a ground for believing what you say, I must infer your credibility from background information about you, my belief of your attestation, though acquired through your testimony, may not be said without qualification to be based on it. In the first case, I may have two or more independent grounds for *p* (the proposition in question). It is not easy to explicate such cases. As I conceive this example, both grounds are necessary for my forming the belief. But I can also have two independent sets of grounds, say one perceptual and the other testimonial, that are each sufficient (and hence neither by itself necessary) for my knowing that *p*. There are other aspects of what we might call *mixed grounds*, but we may here set them aside. It is quite enough if we can understand belief based *wholly* on testimony, as much belief surely is.

One further point is needed before we can proceed to epistemological aspects of testimony. To say that testimony-based belief is not inferential is not to imply that it is "uncritical" or even manifests a degree of credulity incompatible with a critical habit of mind. This seems to me to hold even for much testimony-based belief formed where one has no information about the attester beyond what the context provides, which is often very little. We all have background beliefs that constrain what we accept, for instance by preventing our accepting stock market forecasts without special evidence; and some people may have standards of plausibility that go beyond the constraints provided by these beliefs.

Consider, for instance, how one might be habituated to taking intonation and facial features into account. These elements are important constraints on acceptance of much oral testimony, but no specific beliefs need express fully the way such elements constrain the formation of testimony-based beliefs. At least for non-skeptics, a critical stance is possible without reasoning from any of its standards to the acceptability of the testimony, and indeed without inference at all. Our critical habits and even our critical standards need not all reside in propositions we believe. Even active monitoring of testimony is possible without making inferences: if nothing is noticed that requires raising questions or drawing inferences, no questioning or inference need arise even from attentive monitoring by a critical listener.

II. TESTIMONY AS A BASIS OF KNOWLEDGE AND JUSTIFICATION

If testimony-based belief is non-inferential, then if such belief can constitute knowledge, it might seem to follow that it constitutes non-inferential knowledge. This does not obviously follow, however. Perhaps it is possible for a belief's status as knowledge to *depend* on inference in certain ways even when the belief is not itself inferentially based on any other belief. From the perspective of a certain kind of epistemological coherentism, this is how it might be: even if I non-inferentially believe what you tell me, I do not know it except on the basis of either inferring it (perhaps unconsciously) from something else, or at least on the basis of having both a set of suitable premises as grounds for my believing it and an appropriate readiness to infer it from them. I have elsewhere argued against even the weaker of these inferentialist pictures of knowledge[4] and will assume the independently plausible view that we commonly acquire non-inferential knowledge from testimony.

I do not deny that there is here (as elsewhere) a *negative* dependence on inference: our knowledge can be defeated if we draw certain inferences, for instance infer from certain telltale signs that the attester is unreliable. But to treat testimony-based knowledge as inferential on that ground is rather like treating the absence of poisonous gas as a source of one's physical well-being because, if such gas were present, one would be ill. Vulnerability to defeat by inferences that could occur does not entail dependence in any positive sense. Quashing skeptical worries might require drawing certain self-protective inferences, but testimony-based knowledge is possible without the support of precautionary inference.[5]

It is one thing to say that testimony can be a source of non-inferential knowledge; it is quite another to say under what conditions it achieves this epistemic success in producing testimony-based belief. In earlier work I have suggested that the attester must know that p and that the recipient of testimony, in addition to acquiring a belief that is non-inferentially based on the testimony, must not have certain kinds of grounds for doubting or denying p. A great deal must be said to explicate all of these conditions, but much of that comes from general epistemology and can be presupposed here.[6]

One kind of case, however, should be considered now.[7] Imagine a teacher (Luke, let us say) who disbelieves the theory of evolution but teaches it conscientiously. He tells his students, on the basis of his correct reading of the theory and his knowledge of fossil discoveries, that there were *homo sapiens* in a certain place. Suppose he is giving his students correct information for which there is adequate evidence. May we not conclude that testimony-based belief (theirs) can constitute knowledge without Luke's knowing the proposition in question (which he disbelieves)? This is an interesting case, since the hearers do have a testimony-based true belief that seems adequately grounded. But is it adequately grounded, if the teacher would have taught a false theory in the same disbelieving way, had this been required by his job? Even if the theory *itself* is (an item of) "knowledge" (as one might say if it is known by someone), *he* isn't a reliable link in the chain from the fossil record through the theory, since he neither knows the theory nor even believes it, hence does not believe it on the kind of ground that would protect him from error in the way the (truth-conducive) grounding of knowledge does. By his lights, in fact, he is *deceiving the children*—a point important in itself for the epistemology of testimony. Moreover, it appears that he would have been as likely to state a false proposition if the school required his teaching a mistaken theory that seemed to him no more pernicious than this one. Such a person might well be teaching a false theory or one that is not well evidenced and just happens to be correct.

The case has more plausibility on the assumption that the school would not require anyone to teach a theory that is not well evidenced. Let us suppose so. But do the students perhaps believe or presuppose something to this effect? In any case, might an essential part of their basis for believing Luke, or for knowing on the basis of his testimony, be that background belief or presupposition? If so, either their belief that p would be bolstered by background elements in a way that implies that it is at most in part testimony-based and hence not what normally counts as a testimony-based belief or, on the other hand, their belief would not count as knowledge owing to the falsity of the presupposition in the case of Luke. In order to believe what (in this kind of case) Luke says—or at least in order to know its truth—they would presumably have to believe or presuppose something to the effect that this is what the school is teaching. If, on the other hand, they simply take his word, they are taking the word of someone who will deceive when job retention requires it and (let us charitably assume) there is a plausible rationale for the proposition in question. It is highly doubtful that this kind of testimonial origin would be an adequate basis of knowledge.

A related case (readily generalizable to other subject-matters) is more difficult for the thesis that in order for the recipient of testimony to acquire testimony-based knowledge that *p* from an attestation that *p*, the attester must know that *p*. Suppose Luke is fallibilist, but doxastically incontinent. He thus too readily forms beliefs which he takes to be unjustified on his evidence, particularly where he wants to believe the proposition in question, say for reasons of an emotional or religious kind. Again imagine that *p* is both true and well supported by the evidence he has. Imagine that in the light of his evidence he believes that *p* is very likely to be true (and considerably more likely to be true than any contrary), but (while realizing the good chance of his being in error), for religious reasons, he still *dis*believes *p*. We can even assume that in the case at hand he would *not* (perhaps for moral reasons) teach that *p* apart from believing that it is well supported by the evidence. It may now seem that it is in general *unlikely* that he would teach a false proposition.

One question raised by the case is whether the kind of cognitive malfunction in question makes Luke insufficiently reliable for his (true) attestation to ground knowledge. For to fail to believe on evidence one takes to be good (to the degree required by the case) is a kind of malfunction (Luke does not have to have highly specific beliefs about the evidence but his standard must be high enough to make it plausible to say that its role enables the students to know that *p*). A related problem is this. Given that Luke's beliefs may go against his evidence, why should we think that his assessments of the evidence (including probability-ascribing beliefs) are sound? We have to imagine a cognitive malfunction that occurs isolated from what is clearly a similar one—both malfunctions are matters of responsiveness to grounds, whether they are constituted by evidence itself or by a sense thereof, or by a belief, regarding some source, to the effect that it *is* evidence for *p*. If he fails to believe (or even disbelieves) *p* when he takes the evidence to give it strong support, what is to prevent his failing to take evidence to show what it does, either believing (say) that it does not support *p* when in fact it does or at least failing to believe this truth? If his cognitive response to evidence is unreliable, why should his belief that he has it (or sense of it) render his (unbelieving) testimony reliable?

A further problem is this. Given Luke's willingness to deceive the students, why should we view what he says when he has evidence as sufficiently representative of his testimonial communications to give his present testimony the epistemic (knowledge-grounding) status it is supposed to have? The problem here is not, as above, that there might be relevantly similar situations in which his evidence is inadequate and what he is saying (*p*) is false. The problem is that, given his willingness to deceive the students regarding *p*, there are relevantly similar cases in which he does so without even believing the evidence supports *p* and where it is false. Why, given that willingness, should we take his devotion to the existence of evidence to be adequately stable? Here one might point out that virtually anyone will lie on some occasions; perfect devotion to truth or evidence is not a requirement on generating testimony-based knowledge. Granted. But there are what we might call *credibility requirements* on testimony that seem pertinent here. Compare a case in which, at gunpoint, A commands B to tell us whether *p*. Should we believe B here? There is a good reason why B might lie, and we cannot in general acquire testimony-based knowledge regarding *p*. And what of a case in which we see that an attester stands to risk bankruptcy depending on what the person says? It may well be that a kind of sincerity on the part of the attester is a requirement on the recipient's gaining testimony-based knowledge and that this partly explains why in these and certain other cases testimony-based knowledge apparently cannot be acquired.[8] But credibility requirements are broader still, and we are surely entitled to ask whether it might not be largely good fortune that the students are being told something true rather than something false that Luke thinks is well evidenced and believes he can express without reprisals from authorities. If reasons of emotion can lead to his willingly deceiving his students regarding what he *believes*, we are invited to wonder whether a similar kind of insincerity might lead Luke to deceive them regarding what is *true*. To be sure, it is not clear how strong grounds of genuine knowledge must be, and more remains to be said for a full assessment of the kind of case we are imagining. But my tentative conclusion is that it seems doubtful that cases like Luke's show that testimony-based knowledge can arise from a basis with defects of the general kind in question.

If testimony is limited in that an attestation cannot ground testimony-based knowledge that *p* if the attester does not know that *p*, testimony is *unlimited* in the diversity of knowledge it can convey and in the ease with which it enables us to learn things straightaway. Two other limitations should be mentioned. First, the success of testimony depends on the operation of another source of knowledge, namely perception, broadly conceived. Second, what is known through testimony must apparently be not only known by the attester but, in addition, known (by the attester or someone earlier in the testimonial chain) at least in part on the basis of another source, such as perception or reflection. In order to receive your testimony about the time, I must hear you or otherwise perceive[9]—in some perhaps very broad sense of 'perceive'—what you say; and in order for me to know the time on the basis of your testimony, you or someone else must have read a clock or come to know the time on some other basis that is at least partly non-testimonial. If all this is right, testimony is, as a source of knowledge, both *operationally dependent* on perception and *epistemically dependent* on at least one non-testimonial source of knowledge.

The case with justification is different. I do not need any justification for believing *p* in order for my testimony to provide others with ample justification for believing it. The credibility of testimony may be objectively ill-grounded in this way without that fact's providing any reason for the recipient to doubt either what is said or the attester's credibility (where objective grounding of justification for a belief is the kind that counts, as does normal perceptual grounding, toward the belief's constituting knowledge). The crucial question is whether the recipient is justified in believing my testimony (something quite possible without the recipient's having any actual *belief,* as opposed to dispositions to form beliefs, concerning my credibility).

There is a related contrast: whereas we can acquire testimony-based knowledge that *p* from testimony that *p* without having any knowledge of (or even justification for affirming) the credibility of the attester, we apparently cannot acquire justified testimony-based belief that *p* without having any justification concerning that credibility. The former, positive point is amply illustrated by the acquisition of such knowledge on the part of tiny children who are too conceptually unsophisticated to have knowledge (or justification) concerning the credibility of attesters. The latter, negative point is controversial (and I return to it in the final section), but it is quite plausible once we note that *having* justification for a proposition does not entail believing it; hence, having justification for presupposing the attester's credibility does not entail the psychologically implausible requirement that the recipient must have *beliefs* about that credibility. The point is still more plausible if we assume, as I do here, that the *degree* of justification required on the recipient's part is only that degree we normally have regarding ordinary attesters speaking within a domain concerning which we have no reason to think they are either misinformed or motivated to deceive us. I take the position (which I grant sets skepticism aside) that much of what people say to us and around us meets this condition. I view normal people as very commonly, and in many kinds of situations quite typically, both veracious and competent in the matters on which they give testimony.

I certainly do not wish to imply that we acquire testimony-based justification only if, independently of the testimony, we need justification for *p* itself. Even inductivist reductionists can grant that this requirement would undermine our capacity to acquire much of the justification that, on a non-skeptical view, we do acquire from what we are told. Of both points—the common veracity and usual competence of attesters, and the absence of any need for justification regarding each attested item we are justified in believing—I consider Reid a persuasive proponent. Let us consider some of his main ideas concerning testimony.

III. SOME MAJOR ELEMENTS IN REID'S CONCEPTION OF TESTIMONY

Reid is well known to have taken humanity to have a "natural credulity": "I believed by instinct whatever they [my parents] told me, long before I had the idea of a lie, or thought of the possibility of their deceiving me. Afterwards, upon reflection, I found that they had acted like fair and honest people."[10] Later, he includes a principle of credulity with one of veracity. Speaking of God as intending that "we should be social creatures" and as implanting "in our natures two principles that tally with each other," he says:

The first of these principles is, a propensity to speak truth . . . Truth is always uppermost, and is the natural issue of the mind . . .

Another original principle implanted in us by the Supreme Being, is a disposition to confide in the veracity of others, and to believe what they tell us. This is the counterpart to the former; and, as that may be called *the principle of veracity*, we shall, for want of a more proper name, call this *the principle of credulity*. (pp. 94–5)

In short, Reid sees us as endowed by God with natural tendencies toward both truthfulness and trustfulness.

Developing the idea of credulity in relation to what he apparently views as reasonable belief-formation in situations in which one receives testimony, he continues:

It is evident that, in the matter of testimony, the balance of human judgment is by nature inclined to the side of belief; and turns to that side of itself when there is nothing put into the opposite scale. If it was not so, no proposition that is uttered in discourse would be believed, until it was examined and tried by reason; and most men would be unable to find reasons for believing the thousandth part of what is told them. Such distrust and incredulity would . . . place us in a worse condition than that of savages. (p. 95)

If one thinks of credulity as implying naivety, one has the wrong picture of Reid's view. As he says in comparing the inductive principle with that of credulity, "This principle, like that of credulity, is unlimited in infancy, and gradually restrained and regulated as we grow up" (p. 102).

If, however, Reid finds important similarities between testimony and other sources of knowledge and belief, he also sees differences:

There is, no doubt, an analogy between the evidence of sense and the evidence of testimony. Hence, we find, in all languages, the analogical expressions of the *testimony of sense* . . . and the like. But there is a real difference . . . In believing upon testimony, we rely upon the authority of a person who testifies; but we have no such authority for believing our senses. (*Essays on the Intellectual Powers*, p. 203)

It is interesting that in comparing memory with perception Reid does not draw this contrast:

If we compare the evidence of sense with that of memory, we find a great resemblance, but still some difference. I remember distinctly to have dined yesterday with such a company . . . I have a distinct conception and firm belief of this past event; not by reasoning, not by testimony, but from my constitution. And I give the name of memory to that part of my constitution by which I have this kind of conviction of past events.

I see a chair on my right hand. What is the meaning of this? It is, that I have, by my constitution, a distinct conception and firm belief of the present existence of the chair in such a place . . . (*Essays on the Intellectual Powers*, pp. 203–4)

Reid's view here seems to be that whereas our reliance on testimony is instinctual initially and regulated as we mature, our reliance on memory, like our reliance on perception, is *constitutional*. (What is constitutional can also be instinctual, and Reid's contrast between testimony and, on the other hand, perception and memory, is consistent with our having to rely on God's design in the latter cases, in the sense that—as Reid seemed to think—the reliability of all our faculties is dependent on the "Author of Nature.")

Our reliance on perception, moreover, is associated with its feeding directly into cognition: perception, for Reid, seems at least normally belief-entailing (a property he apparently does not attribute to memory impressions as such). Shortly after noting that "the perception of an object implies both a conception of its form, and a belief of its present existence" and that this belief "is the immediate effect of my constitution" (*An Inquiry*, p. 84), he says, "My belief is carried along by perception, as irresistibly as my body by the earth" (p. 85).

The irresistibility of belief-formation given certain perceptions and perhaps certain memory impressions does not preclude our regulating our responses to these two sources, say in how *strong* a belief we form or in our disposition to form related *higher-order* beliefs, such as the belief that we may be deceived in believing *p*. But, for what one might call *basic perceptions,* as opposed to the "acquired" ones that we have when we have learned to see the three-dimensional roundness of a globe rather than just its circularity, Reid does not emphasize any regulation.[11] He seems, moreover, to treat memory and perception as playing roles in the development of our knowledge that are quite different from the role of testimony.

It would be a mistake to think, on the basis of Reid's contrast between testimony and memory, that he took the importance of testimony as a source of knowledge to be a secondary matter. He describes as a first principle of contingent truths "*That there is a certain regard due to human testimony in matters of fact, and even to human authority in matters of opinion*" (*Essays on the Intellectual Powers*, p. 281). It is noteworthy, however, that what immediately follows this is not (as I read it) mainly an indication of why testimony should be considered worthy of regard, but something quite different though certainly closely related: an affirmation of its essential role in developing human knowledge: "Before we are capable of reasoning about testimony or authority, there are many things which it concerns us to know, for which we can have no other evidence" (p. 281). Perhaps he took the unavailability of other evidence here to indicate worthiness of belief, if only through the good grace of God. But the concepts in question—certainly that of knowledge—are connected with the domain of reliability as well as with worthiness of regard, and in a way that implies the possibility of justification of testimony-based beliefs by reasons.[12] This possibility is consistent with Reid's view that we do not normally *need* reasons to believe testimony. Not needing does not entail the impossibility—or even the abnormality—of *having*.

We might speculate regarding one reason why Reid might think that testimony is worthy of regard. (I am taking it that there *can* be a reason for this and indeed that one can have it, even if the principle that testimony is due a "certain regard" is self-evident and one rightly thinks it is.[13]) Consider the principle he introduces just prior to setting forth the principle of testimony just quoted:

Another first principle I take to be, *That certain features of the countenance, sounds of the voice, and gestures of the body, indicate certain thoughts and dispositions of the mind*. (*Essays on the Intellectual Powers*, p. 279)

It is important to see that these features, sounds, gestures, and presumably other expressive aspects of human behavior are "natural signs": "It seems to me incredible, that the notions men have of the expression of features, voice, and gesture, are entirely the fruit of experience" (p. 280). Now, suppose Reid took testimony to be characteristically accompanied by natural signs of believing what is attested to (roughly, of conviction); he might have thought of testimony as, if only in elementary or otherwise special cases, naturally *indicating*, not as just *reporting*, or linguistically expressing, *belief*. In that case, it is easy to see how he could regard as so natural the kind of credulity that enables one to form testimony-based beliefs non-inferentially and without either screening for insincerity or seeking some premise to support what is attested to. Moreover, the recipient's ground for taking the attester to be sincere could be considered to be characteristically more "direct" than it would be if one needed to infer sincerity; there would normally be no liability to interference by deceitfulness or misspeaking, for instance. Misspeaking occurs, of course, but usually it is corrected before the recipient forms the relevant belief or at least before that becomes in any sense fixed.

We have seen that Reid thinks of belief as an inevitable product of perception (recall the passage quoted from p. 85 in the *Inquiry)*, and it is plain that he takes perception as a major and reliable source of true belief. This is clear in connection with his principle 5, concerning perception; and the same holds for other major sources of belief as he sees them: he has "first principles" for consciousness and memory, for instance. Thus, even if, as it seems to me, he does not treat testimony as basic in the way perception, consciousness, and memory are—in part because we do not in those cases rely on someone else's authority—he may think of it as characteristically putting before us not just a verbal expression of a proposition but the attester's belief of it. We can sometimes "see that" one person believes another to be guilty of an offense, "feel" or sense a person's bigoted beliefs underlying a proposal, and the like. Granted, we see what a person believes *by* hearing what the person says or by some other indication; but we also see (or otherwise know) persons themselves by seeing (or otherwise perceiving) their behavior or bodily surfaces. In neither case is inference needed. From the possibility that appearances can deceive us, we must not infer—and certainly common-sense philosophers will not infer—that we are never non-inferentially acquainted with what they manifest.

Even apart from the possibility that belief can be somehow present in testimony, if my belief that *p* is non-inferentially (and in that sense directly)—and "reliably"—produced by your belief that *p*, is there any reason why my belief cannot inherit the strength, or at least a good proportion of the strength, of your own grounds? Those grounds might have to be ultimately at least in part non-testimonial, but that would not prevent my getting a kind of knowledge that is both non-inferential and not evidentially dependent on inductive grounds. (I return to this point in the last section.) My response to your belief is ultimately a response to your response to your grounds; and if, as seems plausible, the relevant knowledge-sustaining relation of *being a response to* is transitive, my belief is also a response to your grounds.[14] Such a chain may be long, either owing to the *number* of its essential links or to the *length* of some of them, say those constituted by memory connections. But, in relation to transmitting knowledge, if a chain can be no stronger than its weakest link, it also need not be weaker. (Justification functions differently here. For one thing, one attester may be only minimally credible to the recipient in question, who is thereby only minimally justified in the resulting testimony-based belief that *p*, while further down the line an attester is highly credible and gives the last recipient much better justification for *p* than that gained by the recipient of the minimally credible testimony that *p*.)

IV. TESTIMONY AS AN EPISTEMICALLY ESSENTIAL SOURCE

It will be obvious that much of what Reid says about testimony is highly consonant with the sketch of its psychological and epistemological aspects I have presented on the basis of my own work on the topic. Indeed, I am aware of nothing he says that is clearly inconsistent with my conception of testimony.

It may seem that my view that testimony is not a basic source of knowledge precludes treating it as an essential one, but this is not so. It need not be *basic*, in the sense that it can produce knowledge without the recipient's relying on some other source, even if it is epistemically *essential*, in the sense that what we think of as "our knowledge," in an overall sense, would collapse if the contribution to it made by testimony were eliminated: what remained would be at best fragmentary. Testimony is in this respect *globally essential* for human knowledge (and presumably also for our overall justification, which would also be fragmented if such elimination occurred). Indeed, I agree with Reid in the view that—in human life as we know it—one simply could not develop a body of knowledge at all apart from the instruction one receives in childhood, in which testimony is central.[15]

It is more difficult to see where Reid might stand on the matter of testimony-based justification. He speaks of reasons for believing testimony as well as of regard for it; both expressions suggest justification, and it seems quite possible that he takes testimony to be a source of justified belief much as it is of knowledge (though the term 'justified belief' is not one he regularly uses). He notes, however, that most of us cannot give reasons for a "thousandth part of what we are told," and I take it this is meant to indicate that for the vast majority of propositions we believe, we would also lack what might be called "independent evidence" (*a* justification, in one sense). He surely thought that for a huge proportion of these propositions that are objects of our knowledge, testimony, by contrast with the kinds of inductive grounds Hume believed to be required for testimony-based knowledge and justification, is a (focally) essential basis of our knowledge of them as well as of our justification for believing them.

Would Reid think, then, that it is a mistake to maintain that in order to acquire testimony-based justification one must have some justification either for taking the attester to be credible or for accepting *p*? I believe he need not. He *would* think that far more often than not we do not have independent sufficient reason for believing *p*; but that is utterly common in cases where we *do* have justification for taking the attester to be credible. Given his emphasis on the naturalness of veracity and on our utterly pervasive dependence on testimony in childhood, he at least leaves room for my view that—once we are mature enough to have justification at all—we do have (prima facie) justification for believing normal testimony (the kind we typically get from family and friends).

Similarly, there is no reason to think that Reid must deny another point supporting my view that in order to obtain testimony-based justification for *p* one needs a measure of justification: apart from perceptual justification for believing something to the effect that you attested to *p*, I cannot acquire justification for believing *p* on the basis of your testimony. I need perceptually-based justification for believing you said something and a related (semantic) justification for taking it to be *that p*; and again we find a contrast between testimony and an apparently more basic source. He says, for instance, that

In artificial language [what is now called 'natural language'] the signs are articulate sounds, whose connection with the things signified by them, is established by the will of men; and in learning our mother tongue, we discover this connection by experience . . . (*An Inquiry*, p. 91)

He would presumably hold that one could culpably fail to have or exercise this knowledge of the relevant connection, whereas one would be deficient, but not necessarily culpable, if one lacked the innate power of perceptual belief-formation. Misinterpreting the words of one's language would tend to be avoidable and blameworthy in a way that being congenitally deaf is not.

In suggesting that Reid's view of testimony provides for its playing a role in knowledge (and presumably justification as well) that is less basic than the role of the standard basic sources, I may appear to undercut the point that testimony is (for Reid as for me) an essential source of knowledge and indeed of justification. But nothing I have said about testimony in comparison with other sources undermines the point that without testimony we might not even acquire the concepts essential for so much as believing the propositions in question. In this way, testimony is globally essential in a genetic sense, as well as globally essential in the epistemic sense already noted: if we were deprived of all the knowledge and justification we have that arose from testimony, either directly or by inference (and is now memorially retained), we would be at best reduced to (as Reid put it) a condition worse than that of savages.

Moreover, everything I have said, and everything I am aware of in Reid's treatment of testimony, points to another aspect of the epistemological importance of testimony. It *is* a source of *basic knowledge*, i.e., (propositional) knowledge not grounded in knowledge (or in justified belief) of some other proposition (basic knowledge need not be propositional, but my concern here is propositional rather than objectual knowledge).[16] This is important. It distinguishes testimony from another non-basic source of knowledge—inference. Inferential knowledge is *premise-dependent* as well as *source-dependent*, in being dependent on a basic source; testimony-based knowledge has only source-dependence. (Even in the case of knowledge by virtue of an inferential operation of reason, as with mathematical proofs, the conclusion is known or believed on the basis of a premise. Hence it is not basically known or basically justified, though it may still be a priori.)

It might seem that testimony cannot be a source of basic knowledge if I am right in thinking that although one need not believe that the attester is giving testimony that *p*, one must have grounds adequate *for* knowing or justifiedly believing this. But there is no inconsistency here: having grounds for believing this does not entail believing it. Even if it did, the belief in question would not necessarily be needed as a basis for believing the testimony, nor are the grounds a basis of the belief. Surely we do not normally form such a belief. We may in some sense *presuppose* its truth, but that is a quite different matter.

The point that testimony is a source of basic knowledge helps to explain why it is natural to hold the stronger view that testimony is a basic source of knowledge. For it is typical of such sources that they yield non-inferential knowledge, and it is necessary for a source's being basic at all that it do this with respect to the kind of knowledge for which it is a basic source.[17] Moreover, testimony is one of the distinctive and (in my view) *irreducible* ways in which we acquire knowledge. Still, a distinctive and irreducible mode of knowledge acquisition may nonetheless be both epistemically and operationally dependent on some other source of knowledge.

V. TESTIMONY IN COMPARISON WITH OTHER SOURCES OF KNOWLEDGE AND JUSTIFICATION

There are at least five further points that distinguish testimony from what I shall call the standard basic sources: perception, introspection, memory, and reason (or reflection), with intuition, in one sense, as a special case of the operation of reason. I take these four basic sources in turn.

First, we cannot test the reliability of one of these basic sources or even confirm a deliverance of it without relying on that very source.[18] I refer to *externally* testing for reliability, roughly for reliability in yielding true beliefs in the appropriate domain *given* internal consistency. A source with inconsistent outputs is not even a candidate for external reliability.[19] One can of course *internally* test for reliability by ascertaining whether there is inconsistency or probabilistic incoherence among the cognitive outputs of the source (though such testing would be only *negative*—aimed at ruling out *un*reliability, since consistency and indeed even coherence, would not by themselves imply truth[20]). With perception, for instance, quite apart from any question of its overall reliability (which is not my concern here) one must, in a given case of mistrust, look again (or otherwise rely on perception). With memory, in order to overcome mistrust of a particular deliverance, one must try harder to recall or must consult other memories—and one must remember the original belief being examined, lest the target of confirmation be lost from view. With testimony, one can, in principle, check reliability using any of the standard basic sources.

The qualification 'in principle' is important. Even apart from the point that in normal human life one cannot acquire concepts without reliance on testimony, there may be certain facets of its reliability that we are in no position to check without dependence on its deliverances. Consider, for instance, testimony about technical matters on which, apart from relying on other testimony by colleagues or teachers, even experts do not know all one needs to know in order to understand these matters. It remains true, however, that important aspects of testimonial reliability can be checked without counting on specific knowledge grounded essentially in testimony, and the counterpart of this point does not seem to hold for the basic sources.

The second point about the standard basic sources in comparison with testimony concerns memory in particular and has already been suggested. Memory is central, in a way testimony is not, for both our retaining and our extending of knowledge at any given moment—at least if extension of knowledge, as where inference adds to what we know, is conceived as adding to knowledge we *retain*, as opposed to simply increasing the number of propositions we know. We could speak here of *additive extension* to distinguish this (standard) case from *mere quantitative extension* ('increase' might be a better term), the case in which one simply gets new knowledge that increases the number of propositions one knows. That could occur where our brains are so affected that, without our memories' playing any role in the process, new knowledge of wider scope than our present knowledge (or of a larger number of propositions) supplants the knowledge we now have. But given the power of memory, even if knowledge could not be acquired at all without at least the amount and kind of testimony needed to learn a language (a process in which what parents or others attest to is crucial for acquiring a vocabulary), once we climb that linguistic ladder, we can discard it and still retain what we know.

As to significantly extending our knowledge, if we could not remember our premises after inferring our conclusion, then even if rehearsing them had sufficed for causing us to believe it, we would either not come to know it at all, or might be unjustified in (or at least unable to justify) our believing it.

The epistemic role of memory can be better understood in relation to the other standard basic sources. These differ from memory in a way that adds to their contrast with testimony. They are basic with respect to knowledge as well as justification, whereas memory is basic only with respect to justification—assuming that what we *know* from memory we must have come to know on the basis of some other source. Reason in some minimal form is indispensable to possessing any knowledge (at least in protecting us from pervasive inconsistency), and certainly to inferential extension of our knowledge, which depends on our being at least implicitly guided by deductive or inductive logic. Consciousness and perception are essential for development of new knowledge in their domains. There is, however, no domain (except possibly that of other minds) for which continued testimony is *in principle* needed for significant increase of knowledge. Similar (but not entirely parallel) points hold for justification.

The third point is of a rather different sort. There is a sense in which testimony-based belief passes through the will—or at least through agency. There are at least two cases here. Consider the side of the attester. The attester must in *some* sense, though not necessarily by conscious choice, select what to attest to, and in doing so can also lie or, in a certain way, mislead, and in these cases the testimony-based belief does not constitute knowledge[21] (and the justification the recipient may get is, in a certain way we need not pursue here, objectively deficient in a sense that goes with the notion of misleading evidence). For the basic sources, there is no comparable analogue of such voluntary representation of information. Now consider the side of the recipient. The recipient commonly can withhold belief, if not at will then indirectly, by taking on a highly cautionary frame of mind (I am taking withholding to be *roughly* a kind of blocking of belief formation when a proposition is presented).

In many cases, then, testimony-based beliefs commonly pass through agency twice over. This passage does not entail an *exercise* of agency. The point is that testimony is subject to its power. The attester can falsify it, and the recipient commonly has both a monitoring system and the voluntary capacity to withhold belief of a huge range of propositions even if not of just any belief. To be sure, the contrast with the basic sources can be exaggerated. But we commonly can, and sometimes do, withhold belief from attested propositions in a way we cannot withhold belief from propositions strongly supported directly by experience or by reason.

What, then, of a case of double epistemic support, as where someone attests to a plainly self-evident proposition one had not thought of but intuitively sees to be true directly upon hearing it asserted? What is attested may be irresistibly obvious. Here withholding the proposition is not possible. It is usually not possible where we already believe what we hear—though some people's attesting to certain propositions could even give us reason to *disbelieve* them! In that case, withholding may result.

I would also stress that the common possibility of withholding belief of testimony does not imply that in each case we must *consider* whether to believe the testimony, though we often do consider this. The point is that, commonly, whether we withhold belief is "up to us." For many cases, we may also have more voluntary control over how we *interpret* testimony than we have regarding normal deliverances of the standard basic sources. The unreasonable exercise of this control could lead to our forming a testimony-based belief that is either not justified or does not constitute knowledge. In our voluntary control over our interpretation of testimony, as perhaps concerning withholdability of believing it, I grant that the contrast between testimony and standard basic sources is probably more one of degree than of kind.

The conditions under which a person can withhold belief are a contingent matter. Some people may be able to learn to withhold—even if not to reject—the natural belief that those speaking to them are people as opposed to robots.[22] Moreover, the possibility of withholding belief of what is plausibly and truly attested to would not show that testimony is not a basic source, but only that it is not an irresistible one. Still, it is significant that the normal level of control for the standard sources is different from that applicable to testimony. Reid seems to have seen something like this. For one thing, he considered both receptivity to testimony and our use of induction to be "regulated" as we gain experience. He also contrasted testimony with memory and, especially, perception, on this score, as in the passage quoted above comparing memory and perception.

In addition, with respect to testimony, appraisal of credibility may always involve *both* the kinds of doubts we may have about basic sources and any we may have about the attester's response to them. To be sure, we sometimes speak of the "testimony of the senses." But this is metaphor, at least insofar as it suggests that the senses derive knowledge from another source, as attesters must ultimately do, since knowledge that *p* cannot derive from an infinite or circular testimonial chain in which *no* person giving testimony that *p* knows it even in part on a non-testimonial basis.[23]

One might think that the contrast between testimony and the standard basic sources as regards the will is important in part because testimony is less reliable than those other sources of justification and knowledge. Whether this is so is a contingent matter. In any case, the point would have limited significance. It would at best indicate a difference of degree rather than of kind and might give misleading support to the idea that, *given* adequate reliability, testimony, or some kind of testimony, is a basic source.[24] As the case of valid inference shows, however, the conditional reliability of a source can be readily accounted for without taking it to be basic. Moreover, for justification as opposed to knowledge, I do not see that actual reliability is the crucial ground (as I have argued elsewhere[25]), but that issue is too large to pursue here.

A fourth point of contrast between testimony and the standard basic sources has already been suggested. It concerns the need for grounds for the semantic construal of what is said on the basis of which it is taken to be *that p*. This is not a justificatory or epistemic burden intrinsic to the standard basic sources. In Reidian terms, we might say that testimony-based knowledge and justification must go *through convention,* since they depend on our understanding an "artificial" language; knowledge and justification grounded in the standard basic sources need only go *through nature*. The point is not that no kind of interpretation is ever needed in order for (say) perception to yield knowledge or justification. It is that testimony-based knowledge that *p* arises only when we have both perceptual grounds for believing that the attester has said something *and* semantic grounds for believing that it is *the proposition that p* which is attested to; and testimony-based justification that *p* arises only if we have the corresponding perceptual and semantic justification. This point illustrates both the operational dependence of testimony on perception and the epistemic dependence of testimony-based beliefs on semantic considerations.

We might speculate that with Reidian natural language, such as the "threatening or angry tone of voice" by which "Children, almost as soon as born, may be frightened" (*Essays,* Essay 6, ch. 5), what makes the language natural is that something about its oral expression is a criterion, in a Wittgensteinian sense, of some element it conveys. Here, however, we have knowledge *from* testimony rather than *testimony-based* knowledge; for just as we can know that people have a cold from their nasal tone regardless of what they attest to, a child can know that Father is angry quite apart from what he is saying.[26]

Granted, much a priori knowledge and justification is acquired *through* consideration of linguistic expressions of propositions. But perception of such an expression is not required, nor is there a comparable need (if any) for semantic interpretation. On the most plausible account of the nature and basis of such knowledge and justification, its object is in principle accessible without reliance on semantic construal; the ground of justification or knowledge is in any case a kind of understanding of the proposition in question or, perhaps more directly, the concepts figuring in or essential to it. To be sure, one might think that testimony could somehow convey propositional content directly to another mind without using any semantic "vehicle." If this is possible, it would surely require at least a *symbolic* vehicle, such as an image produced in my mind that I can see to come from some other mind. If someone simply causes me to have an image that produces a belief that *p* or, especially, simply causes me, in a direct way, to believe that *p*, then there is no testimony-based belief, but only some kind of cognitive product of action by someone else. Even where testimony is not verbal, then, if it retains its essential character, the fourth point of contrast with the basic sources seems unlikely to disappear. The contrast might be thought to be somewhat attenuated, but this speculative possibility is not what is normally in question in the epistemology of testimony, and it would in any case not affect the first three points of contrast.

It should also be granted that a lack of semantic understanding will normally restrict the range propositions that are even candidates for one's a priori knowledge or justification, since one's comprehension of language will (for most of us, at least) limit the range of propositions we can get before our minds. Semantic *misunderstanding*—which is of course possible even in people of wide and deep semantic comprehension—may give us the wrong proposition or range of propositions. Nonetheless, neither of these defects need affect how good our grounds are once the right object is before us. To be sure, defeaters of knowledge or justification can come from semantically interpreted items and can afflict beliefs deriving from any of the standard sources; but none of those sources seems dependent on semantic grounds in the way that testimony is.

The fifth contrast I want to draw is of a quite different sort. It presupposes that testimony yields testimony-based knowledge in the recipient only if the attester knows that *p*. This point is controversial (in part owing to the kind of case illustrated by Luke, discussed in Section II), but the exceptions to it are at best rare and probably of special kinds that can be described in a way that enables us to set them to one side. In any case, given this presupposition, we can say that although testimony can increase the number of *knowers* in the world, it cannot increase the number of *propositions known*. Thus, in *one* sense it cannot increase the amount of knowledge in the world. This is an important limitation. It would be a mistake, however, to think that it detracts from the importance of testimony. Far from it: the indefinitely extensive testimonial communicability of knowledge is an incalculably valuable characteristic of testimony, and it is not paralleled by any of the standard basic sources. Moreover, in this limitation testimony is like memory: it, too, cannot (by itself) increase the amount of knowledge in the world.

Testimony-based justification works differently here. Testimony can *both* increase the number of justified beliefs in the world and contribute to the degree of their justification. It can thus add to the amount of justification in the world. This would not be so unless it could produce new justification. It can justify people not already justified in holding the relevant propositions and can enhance the justification of those who are already so justified. Indeed, as suggested already, there is much that we believe which we would not believe at all, much less justifiedly believe, apart from our reliance on testimony. Again, the comparison with memory is significant. For whereas concurring testimony from many people can increase the justification of a single belief, concurring memory impressions that *p* on the part of different people cannot—in the same way—increase the justification of a single belief. They can do so only indirectly, say by yielding testimony based on the several people's memories; but this is quite different.

These contrasts between testimony and the basic sources are not meant to impugn the importance of testimony. In addition to being a source of basic knowledge and an essential source of our overall knowledge, it is apparently an essential source of much of our justified belief as well. Our overall knowledge of the world, including even many things we know about ourselves, depends on it in far-reaching ways, though not perhaps as much as, and certainly not in quite the same ways as, it depends on memory. The most important thing memory and testimony have in common may be that they do not generate, as opposed to (respectively) preserving and transmitting, knowledge (the case with justification is different, since memory, unlike testimony, *is* a basic source of that).

In one way, however, testimony is a more far-reaching source than memory: although they share unlimited epistemic breadth, in the sense that in principle anything that can be known can be known at least in part on the basis of them, we can *learn* from testimony in a way we cannot learn, as opposed to *recovering,* from memory.[27] As to how testimony differs from both perception and memory, there is far more to say than can be said here. I have already stressed that the important differences are not a matter of reliability, either of the process by which these various cognitive sources produce belief or of their cognitive outputs. No matter how reliable testimony in fact is in either respect, the acquisition of knowledge or even of justified belief on the basis of testimony depends (as noted earlier) on the agency of another person. The attester must not lie, or (in certain ways) seek to deceive, in attesting to *p* if we are to come to know that *p* on the basis of the testimony. By contrast, our responses to the deliverances of the basic sources are not normally mediated by anyone else's action. Testimony may be unreliable—or fail to justify one's believing that *p*—both because of natural connections between the state(s) of affairs the testimony concerns *and* because of the person's exercise of agency. This is not normally so for the testimony of the senses or of memory or of reason. The point is not that the exercise of agency cannot be a purely "natural" phenomenon—though philosophers who think that freedom is incompatible with determinism may argue that it cannot—but that the concepts of knowledge and justification apparently presuppose that if it is a natural phenomenon, it is nonetheless special.[28]

Whether Reid could accept all these conclusions is not clear to me; but he does treat testimony differently from the standard basic sources, and I see no bar to his granting the specific differences I have noted. In any case, it should be plain that the contrasts I have drawn between, on the one hand, testimony-based knowledge and testimony-based justification and, on the other, knowledge and justification deriving from the basic sources, do not imply that testimony is inessential in a normal human life or that its authority in cognitive matters is only contingent and empirical. Testimony is both globally and focally essential in our lives. It is indeed of virtually unlimited breadth in its epistemic power: virtually anything that can be known firsthand can also be known on the basis of testimony. Testimony is a source of basic knowledge; it is normally the starting point of everyone's conceptual learning; for all I have said, it may even have a measure of a priori justificatory authority;[29] and it is, as Reid so vividly shows us, as natural a source of knowledge and justification as any of the others.

REFERENCES

Adler, Jonathan E. (1994), 'Testimony, Trust, Knowing', *Journal of Philosophy*, 91.

—— (2002), *Belief's Own Ethics* (Cambridge, Mass.: MIT Press).

Alston, William P. (1985), 'Thomas Reid on Epistemic Principles', *History of Philosophy Quarterly*, 2/4: 435–52.

Audi, Robert (1993*a*), 'The Foundationalism-Coherentism Controversy: Hardened Stereotypes and Overlapping Theories', in Audi (1993*b*: 117–64).

—— (1993*b*), *The Structure of Justification* (Cambridge and New York: Cambridge University Press).

—— (1997), 'The Place of Testimony in the Fabric of Knowledge and Justification', *American Philosophical Quarterly*, 34/4: 404–22.

—— (1999*a*), 'Doxastic Voluntarism and the Ethics of Belief', *Facta Philosophica*, 1: 87–102.

—— (1999*b*), 'Self-Evidence', *Philosophical Perspectives*, 13: 205–28.

—— (2001), *The Architecture of Reason* (Oxford and New York: Oxford University Press).

—— (2003), 'An Internalist Theory of Normative Grounds', *Philosophical Topics*, 29/1–2: 19–46.

—— (2004), 'The A Priori Authority of Testimony', *Philosophical Issues*, 14: 18–34.

Beanblossom, Ronald, and Lehrer, Keith (eds.) (1983), *Thomas Reid's Inquiry and Essays* (Indianapolis: Hackett).

Coady, C. A. J. (1992), *Testimony* (Oxford: Clarendon Press).

Corlett, J. Angelo (1996), *Analyzing Social Knowledge* (Lanham, Md.: Rowman and Littlefield).

Dretske, Fred (1981), *Knowledge and the Flow of Information* (Cambridge, Mass.: MIT Press).

Foley, Richard (2001), *Intellectual Trust in Oneself and Others* (Cambridge: Cambridge University Press).

Fricker, Elizabeth (1987), 'The Epistemology of Testimony', *Proceedings of the Aristotelian Society*, suppl. vol. 61.

—— (1994), 'Against Gullibility', in B. K. Matilal and A. Chakrabarti (eds.), *Knowing from Words* (Dordrecht: Kluwer), 125–61.

—— (2003), 'Trusting Others in the Sciences: A Priori or Empirical Warrant', *Studies in History and Philosophy of Science*, 33.

—— (2004), 'Testimony: Knowing Through Being Told', in I. Niinilouto, M. Sintonen, and J. Wolenski (eds.), *Handbook of Epistemology* (Dordrecht: Kluwer).

Goldman, Alvin I. (1999), *Knowledge and the Social World* (Oxford and New York: Oxford University Press).

Graham, Peter J. (2000*a*), 'Conveying Information', *Synthese*, 123: 365–92.

—— (2000*b*), 'The Reliability of Testimony', *Philosophy and Phenomenological Research*.

Graham, Peter J. (2000c), 'Transferring Knowledge', *Noûs*, 34.

Hardwig, John (1985), 'Epistemic Dependence', *Journal of Philosophy*, 82/7: 355–49.

Lackey, Jennifer (1999), 'Testimonial Knowledge and Transmission', *Philosophical Quarterly*, 49: 471–90.

Matilal, B. K. and Chakrabarti, A. (eds.) (1994), *Knowing from Words* (Dordrecht: Kluwer).

Plantinga, Alvin (1993), *Warrant and Proper Function* (Oxford: Oxford University Press).

Schmitt, Frederick (ed.) (1994), *Socializing Epistemology: The Social Dimensions of Knowledge* (Lanham, Md.: Rowman and Littlefield).

Sosa, Ernest (1991a), *Knowledge in Perspective* (Cambridge and New York: Cambridge University Press).

——— (1991b), 'Testimony and Coherence', in Sosa (1991a).

——— (forthcoming), *Knowledge in Focus, Skepticism Resolved.*

Van Cleve, James (1999), 'Reid on the First Principles of Contingent Truths', *Reid Studies*, 3/1: 3–30.

Webb, Mark Owen (1993), 'Why I Know about As Much as You', *Journal of Philosophy*, 90.

Wolterstorff, Nicholas (2001), *Thomas Reid and the Story of Epistemology* (Cambridge: Cambridge University Press).

NOTES

1. See, e.g., Schmitt (1994); Goldman (1999); and Corlett (1996).

2. Among the recent works on or treating testimony are Coady (1992); Matilal and Chakrabarti (1994); Fricker (1987); Hardwig, (1985); Sosa (1991a); Plantinga (1993); Webb (1993) in part a critique of Hardwig (1985); and Adler (1994) in part a critique of Webb (1993); Lackey (1999); and Graham (2000a, 2000b, and 2000c); Foley (2001); and Adler (2002).

3. Much space could be devoted to refining this idea, e.g. explaining why fictional cases do not count and ironic declarations can apparently tell us one thing when another is intended (in which case 'testimony' may be the wrong word for either reading, but certainly for the former).

4. In, e.g., "The Foundationalism-Coherentism Controversy," ch 4 in Audi (1993b).

5. It might be argued, however, that apart from a certain level of critical reflection on the grounds of our beliefs, we cannot arrive at something plausibly called *reflective knowledge*. This concept, and the requirements it imposes, have been explicated in detail by Ernest Sosa. See e.g., Sosa (1991b, and forthcoming).

6. For valuable recent discussion, see Lackey (1999) and Graham (2000a). In one example he brings against the requirement that the attester know that p if the recipient is to know it (fully) on the basis of testimony, a woman who cannot distinguish two twins, Judy and Trudy, says, on the basis of seeing her do it, that Judy broke a vase. She is right, but does not know, since she would have taken Trudy to be Judy if Trudy had been in the same position. Nonetheless, Bill, who sees Trudy before him and knows she *is* Trudy, but does not witness the vase-breaking, knows, from the testimony given just after the event, that it was indeed Judy. Graham grants that

Bill makes use of his background knowledge. On my view, however, Bill also does not have a testimony-based belief: rather, on the basis of what he is told *and* his knowledge that Trudy did not break the vase, he believes something to the effect that the person the attester knows to have broken it and takes to be Judy on the basis of appearing to be Judy, is indeed Judy. He knows Judy broke it by knowing what *grounded* the testimony, not on the basis of the testimony.

7. The case is from Lackey (1999). She presents others, but some of what I believe should be said about those may be implicit in this paper; further discussion must await another occasion.

8. I have emphasized the importance of sincerity for the epistemology of testimony in Audi (1997). The notion deserves more attention than it can be given here, but I take it as clear that a kind of insincerity is implied in telling someone that *p* when one believes it false and expects it to be believed by the recipient. If one simply does *not* believe *p* the case is less clear, but insincerity of a kind still seems implied. Peter Graham has noted that accepting *p*, which does not entail believing it, is a special case here. It is and deserves discussion not possible in this paper.

9. It may be that the sense is very broad indeed, since I might perhaps receive testimony by a telepathic reception of the attester's message. Perhaps the relation between testimony and perception is such that as our inclination to treat reception of stated information as non-perceptual increases, our inclination to regard it as testimonial decreases.

10. See Thomas Reid, in Beanblossom and Lehrer (1983: 87). Later references to Reid in this paper are to this edition.

11. Reid discusses acquired perceptions in Essay II, ch. 21 of the *Essays,* as well as in ch. 22. For discussion of his conception of such perception in relation to testimony, see Nicholas Wolterstorff's chapter on Reid's epistemological views on testimony in Wolterstorff (2001).

12. Justification by reasons does not, of course, exhaust justification *by reason*; and Reid may take it that the worthiness in question is self-evident. For extensive critical discussion of how he conceived his first principles see Alston (1985: 435–52), and Van Cleve (1999: 3–30), which explores the intriguing thesis that Reid's main first principles are not general epistemic principles such as those quoted, which are supposed to be self-evident indications of what conditions generate true belief (or knowledge or perhaps justification and knowledge) but the beliefs (of particular propositions) licensed by those propositions, say the belief that I just had Van Cleve's paper in my hands, grounded in my memory.

13. That the self-evident can be evidenced by something else, even though it does not stand in need of evidence, I have argued in some detail in Audi (1999*b*). Here, however, I depart from what Reid says in at least one place. At one point he speaks of things which, "though they admit of illustration yet, being self-evident, do not admit of proof" (*Essays on the Intellectual Powers,* p. 153).

14. In Audi (2001), I stress this element of responsiveness to experience in explicating the nature of belief and treat its formation as a *discriminative* response because of the way in which it is "selective" and alters with alteration in the relevant stimuli. Cf. Dretske's (1981) information-theoretical account of knowledge and its application to testimony in the papers by Peter Graham cited above.

15. In Audi (1997), I have described conceptual learning in relation to propositional learning and emphasized the importance of both in the development of justification and knowledge.

16. For a detailed account of the epistemology testimony that is in some ways inferentialist and in any event presupposes the formation of more beliefs on the part of the recipient as a condition for acquiring testimony-based knowledge, see Fricker, esp. (1994) and for a more recent rounded statement of her position (2004).

17. It may seem that a basic source never yields *inferential* knowledge; but that is perhaps not altogether clear. If we take reason as a basic source of knowledge and consider its application to judging a poem, its intuitive operation might produce non-inferential knowledge of such things as emotional tones in certain lines and its inferential operation might (indirectly) produce, on the basis of this knowledge and knowledge of criteria of interpretation, inferential knowledge constituting an interpretation of the poem. It may be, however, that the relevant intuitive knowledge should be considered quasi-perceptual—we do, after all, have aesthetic perception here—and that the case is better conceived as one in which rational perceptions serve as premises for reasoning, so that we have a combination of sources yielding inferential knowledge.

18. I do not take this feature of untestability for reliability without dependence on the source in question to be essential to a basic source; but it does seem to hold for the basic sources I am comparing with testimony.

19. If a source has inconsistent outputs, how can it be a candidate for reliability *at all*? Perhaps it can if the inconsistencies cause no trouble, e.g. because the subject recognizes them and can isolate them for scrutiny and elimination. It is not at all easy to say under what conditions inconsistencies are innocuous; this is one reason the preface paradox is difficult to resolve.

20. I argue for this limitation on coherence in Audi (1993*a*). It is true that coherence among the belief outputs of a source implies the truth that if the person believes these outputs to be mutually coherent, the belief is true. But this is trivial; the question is reliability of a general kind.

21. If we allow that a testimony-based belief may *also* be based on another source than the testimony in question—including other testimony—then lying testimony may not preclude knowing the proposition. I say 'may not' because it is not self-evident that a person is lying when attesting to a true proposition but *believing* the proposition false and intending to deceive the recipient in attesting to it. Unless otherwise indicated, however, I am making the natural assumption that calling a belief testimony-based implies that it is essentially based on the testimony in question, where this requires at least that the testimony is a necessary basis of it.

22. I discuss the issue of voluntary control of belief and cite much relevant literature in Audi (1999*a*: 87–102).

23. This point is explained and defended in Audi (1997).

24. Support for this point is provided in Peter Graham's informative paper (Chapter 4 in this volume), in which he argues that the point that testimony (as I would put it) goes through the will does not favor either the reductionist view of testimony or the view that it is an irreducibly credible source.

25. For a detailed defense of a moderate internalism concerning justification, see Audi (2003: 19–46).

26. It is noteworthy that the most relevant first principle is, "That certain features of the countenance, sounds of the voice, and gestures of the body, indicate certain thoughts and dispositions of the mind" (Essays, Essay VI, ch. 5). These natural signs do not even require making any assertions.

27. There are subtleties here that I cannot go into, but the need for 'at least in part' should be explained: for simple self-evident propositions it may be possible to know them only in part on the basis of testimony because an understanding of them sufficient to come to know them on the basis of testimony at all is such that given even the minimal kind of entertaining of them required for receiving testimony that they are true, one must know them on the basis of that understanding. Some detailed discussion of knowledge on the basis of understanding is given in Audi (1999*b*).

28. This point may support my view, defended in Audi (1997), that to acquire justification for *p* from testimony, one needs some degree of justification for taking the attester to be credible, though one can of course get it on the occasion of the testimony. (I do not think one needs a counterpart of this in order to acquire prima facie justification from one of the standard basic sources.)

29. The prospects for testimony's having a priori epistemic authority, and the difference between that and a kind of practical authority, are discussed in detail in Audi (2004).

2

Reid on the Credit of Human Testimony

James Van Cleve

Thomas Reid is perhaps the first philosopher to call attention to "the analogy between perception, and the credit we give to human testimony"—the topic of chapter 6, section 24 of his *Inquiry into the Human Mind* (hereinafter abbreviated as *IHM*). In this essay, I explore the extent of Reid's analogy. I begin by trying to arrive at a proper understanding of the two principles he identifies as fundamental to our acquiring knowledge from the information of others—the principles of veracity and credulity. Next, I investigate the similarities Reid finds between perception and testimony considered as mechanisms of belief formation. Finally, I consider whether the analogy between perception and testimony can be extended from psychology into epistemology. In particular, I discuss whether beliefs based on testimony, no less than beliefs based on sense perception, may be regarded as epistemically basic or foundational. This is the chief issue that divides Reid from Hume in the epistemology of testimony.

I. THE PRINCIPLES OF VERACITY AND CREDULITY

Reid introduces the two key principles of his theory of testimony in the *Inquiry* in the following passage:

The wise and beneficent Author of Nature, who intended that we should be social creatures, and that we should receive the greatest and most important part of our knowledge by the information of others, hath, for these purposes, implanted in our natures two principles that tally with each other.

The first of these principles is, a propensity to speak truth, and to use the signs of language, so as to convey our real sentiments. (*IHM*, p. 193)

Another original principle implanted in us by the Supreme Being, is a disposition to confide in the veracity of others, and to believe what they tell us. This is the counter-part to the former; and as that may be called *the principle of veracity*, we shall, for want of a more proper name, call this *the principle of credulity*. (*IHM*, p. 194)

Thanks to Albert Chan and Gideon Yaffe for helpful discussion of the issues in this paper.

These principles are the key elements in his account of how the words of others come to be signs conveying to us things we would not have come to know on our own.

Reid's formulation of the principle of veracity immediately prompts a vital question. By "a propensity to speak truth," does Reid mean a propensity to speak what is *in fact* the truth? Or does he mean a propensity to speak what the speaker *believes* to be the truth? His unqualified use of the expression "to speak truth" in the first clause suggests the former, but his use of "to convey our real sentiments" in the second clause suggests the latter.

It is possible that Reid's 'and' connecting the clauses is an 'and' of genuine conjunction, in which case he would mean *both* things. But it is also possible that his 'and' is an 'and' of explication, in which case by 'speaking the truth' Reid would simply *mean* speaking what you believe to be true.

Our question is whether Reid's principle of veracity should be understood as affirming the first, the second, or both of the following:

V1 (It tends to be the case that) if A says p, p is true.

V2 (It tends to be the case that) if A says p, A believes p.

(I use 'say' in a sense that includes writing as well as speaking, as was surely Reid's intent.)

As we read the ensuing paragraphs in which the principle is developed and defended, it becomes fairly clear that V2 is what Reid intends. Immediately after formulating the principle, he goes on to contrast speaking the truth with lying:

> This principle has a powerful operation, even in the greatest liars; for where they lie once, they speak truth a hundred times. Truth is always uppermost, and is the natural issue of the mind. It requires no art or training, no inducement or temptation, but only that we yield to a natural impulse. Lying, on the contrary, is doing violence to our nature; and is never practised, even by the worst men, without some temptation. (*IHM*, p. 193)

You are not a liar just because you say something false. Lying is saying what you *believe* false in an effort to deceive another, and that strongly suggests that the principle of veracity should be understood as V2: we tend to assert to others only what we believe to be true.

Further confirmation comes in the next paragraph. Reid defends his view that the tendency to speak truth is innate by arguing that moral and political considerations are insufficient to account for it. The tendency is present even in young children before such considerations can have any influence upon them. Well, moral and political considerations would not even be a *candidate* explanation for speaking the truth in the sense of *getting things right*; they could at best induce us to speak what we *believe* to be correct. So the fact that Reid sees the moral-political explanation as a rival to his own shows again that V2 is the principle he has in mind.

To clinch the point, I note these two comments that Reid makes on his principle:

By this instinct, a real connection is formed between our words and our thoughts. (*IHM*, p. 194)

If there were not a principle of veracity in the human mind, men's words would not be signs of their thoughts. (*IHM*, p. 197)

If what the principle of veracity brings about is a real connection or sign relation between our words and our *thoughts*, the principle must be understood as V2.

Let us turn now to the companion principle, *the principle of credulity*. Here is Reid's formulation of it again: "Another original principle implanted in us by the Supreme Being, is a disposition to confide in the veracity of others, and to believe what they tell us" (*IHM*, p. 194).

As we did with the first principle, we may distinguish two possible versions of this principle. Letting A be the speaker and B the hearer, we have

C1. (It tends to be the case that) if A says p, B believes p.
C2. (It tends to be the case that) if A says p, B believes that A believes p.

I let it go unstated in the antecedents of C1 and C2 that A's saying p is directed at B and that B hears his words. Which version of the principle is intended this time?

The evidence quickly mounts that C1 is the correct reading. In the very formulation of the principle, Reid speaks of a disposition to believe *what others tell us*. What they tell us is typically some fact about the wider world (that the fish are biting today or that the road through the pass is blocked), not merely an autobiographical fact to the effect that they believe this or that. A few lines later (*IHM*, p. 194, ll. 29–30), he says that this principle concerns "proposition[s] that [are] uttered in discourse," giving us further occasion to make the same point. Finally, and most tellingly, Reid observes that the principle of credulity confers enormous practical benefit on those who are regulated by it:

It is evident, that, in the matter of testimony, the balance of human judgment is by nature inclined to the side of belief; and turns to that side of itself, when there is nothing put into the opposite scale. If it was not so, no proposition that is uttered in discourse would be believed, until it was examined and tried by reason; and most men would be unable to find reason for believing the thousandth part of what is told them. Such distrust and incredulity would deprive us of the greatest benefits of society, and place us in a worse condition than that of savages. (*IHM*, p. 194)

The pragmatic advantage of credulity flows from believing what my informants report—for example, that the path to water lies in this direction. It does not flow simply from believing that they believe it themselves.[1]

Our preliminary finding, then, is that the principle of veracity should be understood as V2 and the principle of credulity as C1. But that finding immediately poses a problem. Reid tells us that the two principles are meant to *tally* with each other (*IHM*, p. 193). What does he mean by that? A plausible guess is that the principles are supposed to combine with each other to imply that when an informant says p, we tend to form true beliefs. But the combinations that yield that result are V1 with C1 and V2 with C2—not Reid's mixed combination of V2 with C1. So what is going on?

We can get at the problem in another way. One of Reid's objectives in his discussion of testimony in *Inquiry*, 6. 24 is to show how men's words come to be signs from which we gain knowledge of what they signify. He has explained earlier in 6. 21 that there are two requisites of knowledge from signs:

> But there are two things necessary to our knowing things by means of signs. First, That a real connection between the sign and the thing signified be established, either by the course of nature, or by the will and appointment of men. When they are connected by the course of nature, it is a natural sign; when by human appointment, it is an artificial sign. Thus, smoke is a natural sign of fire; certain features are natural signs of anger: but our words, whether expressed by articulate sounds or by writing, are artificial signs of our thoughts and purposes.
>
> Another requisite to our knowing things by signs is, that the appearance of the sign to the mind, be followed by the conception and belief of the thing signified. (*IHM*, p. 177)

In short, for X to be a sign on the basis of which we have knowledge of Y, (i) X must be a reliable indicator of Y, and (ii) the apprehension of X must produce in the mind of the subject a belief in Y. It seems clear that Reid intends the principles of veracity and credulity to ensure that these two requisites are satisfied in the case of human testimony: veracity brings about the reliable connection between sign and thing signified, and credulity produces our belief in the thing signified. But if veracity and credulity are to play these roles, veracity will have to be understood as V1 and credulity as C1 *or* veracity as V2 and credulity as C2. With Reid's V2–C1 mix, the principles do not tally with each other in the required way.

What are we to do about this? The best thing to say in Reid's defense, I think, is that he probably believes *all four* of the principles we have distinguished. As for credulity, when we hear someone say p, we normally believe p (as C1 says), but we also take for granted that the speaker believes p (as C2 says). As for veracity, we may note that an overarching principle of Reid's epistemology combines with V2 to yield V1. The principle I have in mind is Principle 7 in Reid's list in the *Essays on the Intellectual Powers of Man* (*EIP*) of the first principles of contingent truths—namely, the principle that our natural faculties are not fallacious (*EIP*, p. 480). By this principle Reid means to assert that the things we believe as deliverances of our natural faculties (perception, memory, inference, and so on) tend to be true. If we add this to V2, we arrive at something very close to V1 by means of the following argument: what people say, they normally believe (V2); what they believe is normally true (Principle 7); therefore, what people say is normally true (V1).[2]

To conclude this section: although there is an apparent disconnect in Reid's exposition of the content and functioning of his two principles, it is correctable given other materials he puts at our disposal. There is a good Reidian case to be made for all four of the principles we have discussed, as a result of which there are two pairs of principles that tally with each other: V1 with C1 and V2 with C2.[3]

II. THE ANALOGY BETWEEN PERCEPTION AND TESTIMONY

Reid announces at the beginning of *Inquiry*, 6. 24 that there is a remarkable analogy between the testimony of nature given by the senses and the testimony of our fellow human beings given in language—an analogy so great that it is natural to use the word 'testimony' in each case. He therefore undertakes to consider together the principles of the mind that are subservient to testimony of the two sorts. The analogy he sees is divided into two sets of similarities, as there are two varieties of perception and two varieties of language to be considered:

We have distinguished our perceptions into original and acquired; and language, into natural and artificial. Between acquired perception, and artificial language, there is a great analogy; but still a greater between original perception and natural language. (*IHM*, p. 190)

To appreciate the two analogies, we must first say a bit about each of the two distinctions.

Original versus acquired perception: "Our perceptions are of two kinds," Reid tells us; "some are natural and original, others acquired, and the fruit of experience" (*IHM*, p. 171). Our original perceptions are the perceptions we have prior to any learning. When I hold a hard, round ball in my hand, the tactile sensations I receive trigger an immediate belief in a hard, extended object. No learning is required; I am innately so constituted that on the appropriate sensory occasions, I conceive of and believe in the ball. Similarly, when a certain pattern of receptors on my retina is stimulated, I am presented with an object of a certain two-dimensional shape in a certain region of the space before me: I conceive of and believe in a square patch *there*. These are examples of original perception.

Others of our perceptions are acquired. By experience, I learn that a certain two-dimensional array of polygons presented to my eye will be attended by the tactile perception of a three-dimensional cube. A butcher learns that a sheep of a certain visual appearance will have a certain heft when he lifts it and places it on his scales. What was at first a matter of inductive inference or association based on accumulated experience becomes a matter of immediate, noninferential, quasi-perceptual belief: I see a cube in the pattern of lines, and the butcher sees the weight of the sheep. These are examples of acquired perception.

Natural versus artificial language: Reid first draws the distinction between natural and artificial language in *Inquiry*, 4. 2. By artificial language, he means any system of signs whose meaning is fixed by convention, or as he says, "by compact and agreement". By natural language, he means that small but indispensable body of signs that "previous to all compact or agreement, have a meaning which every man understands by the principles of his nature" (*IHM*, p. 51). For example, a smile is a natural language sign of approval. Reid argues that unless there were natural language, artificial language could never be invented, for artificial language requires compacts, and compacts could not be instituted by creatures who did not have a language of some sort. There must therefore be natural language to get things going. One could argue in similar fashion that artificial language, once invented, could not be learned by a novice unless there were natural language signs of reinforcement and dissent.[4]

We are now in a position to delineate the two analogies—the "great" analogy between acquired perception and artificial language and the "still greater" analogy between original perception and natural language. In all four of the phenomena to be considered—original perception, natural language, acquired perception, and artificial language—there are signs and things signified, and the mind passes from an apprehension of the sign to a belief in the thing signified. The various similarities and differences Reid notes all concern the origin of the relation between sign and thing signified and the means whereby we come to know of this relation.

Original perception: "The signs in original perception are sensations"—for example, the tactile sensations that trigger in us the conception of and belief in a hard, round ball in our hands. "Nature hath established a real connection between the signs and the things signified; and nature hath also taught us the interpretation of the signs; so that, previous to experience, the sign suggests the thing signified, and creates the belief of it" (*IHM*, p. 190). In other words, it is by an innate or hardwired principle that the mind passes from apprehension of the sign to belief in the thing signified.

Natural language: "The signs in natural language are features of the face, gestures of the body, and modulations of the voice" (*IHM*, p. 190). The things signified are the thoughts and dispositions of another's mind. As in the case of original perception, nature has both established the connection between sign and thing signified and taught us the interpretation of the sign previous to experience. An infant knows instinctively that a smile is a sign of approval and a frown of anger. As noted earlier, Reid holds that without a basic repertoire of such instinctively understood signs, artificial language could neither be devised nor learned.

A further point of similarity between original perception and natural language is this: in both cases, the signs "have the same signification in all climates and in all nations" (*IHM*, p. 191). Certain tactile sensations indicate hardness to any human being, and certain facial expressions indicate approval in all cultures.[5]

Acquired perception: "In acquired perception, the signs are either sensations, or things which we perceive by means of sensations" (*IHM*, p. 191). As in the other cases considered so far, the connection between sign and thing signified is *established* by nature. But in this case as not in the others, we must *discover* the connection by experience and induction. That a red glow in an iron bar signifies heat, or that the small size of a man on the beach signifies that he is a long way off, are things we must learn; they are not written into our constitution. Once the connection is learned, however, the sign automatically suggests the thing signified, and it is almost as though we *see* the heat of the bar or the distance of the man.

Artificial language: "In artificial language, the signs are articulate sounds, whose connection with the things signified by them is established by the will of men: and in learning our mother tongue, we discover this connection by experience" (*IHM*, p. 191). Artificial language is therefore like acquired perception in that the connection between signs and what they signify is known by experience; but it is unlike acquired perception in so far as the connection holds by convention rather than nature.

Reid notes a further respect in which acquired perception and artificial language are like one another, but different from original perception and natural language. "Our original perceptions, as well as the natural language of human features and gestures, must be resolved into particular principles of the human constitution". The emphasis here is on *particular*: it is by one particular principle that sensations of a certain sort signify hardness and by another particular principle that frowns express disapproval. By contrast, "our acquired perceptions, and the information we receive by means of artificial language, must be resolved into general principles of the human constitution" (*IHM*, p. 191). It may be objected that the interpretive principles we learn in the latter cases—for instance, that a red glow indicates heat, or that the word 'jaune' means yellow—are as particular as any. But Reid's point is that such particular principles are not programmed into our minds. The principles that are programmed into our minds are the general principles whereby we learn the particular principles. One of these general principles is the principle of induction; whether there are others we shall see presently.

The foregoing points of similarity and dissimilarity are summarized in Table 2.1. The table enables us to see at a glance in what respects the analogy between original perception and natural language is greater than the analogy between acquired perception and artificial language. In the first two columns, all four rows are filled in the same way, whereas in the second two columns, only two of the four rows are filled in the same way. Of course, in so far as the universal versus variable difference in row three is a corollary of the nature versus convention difference in row one, one may wish to say that at root there is only one difference in the right two columns. Nonetheless, the overall analogy is still not as great in the right columns as in the left.

We saw in Section I that Reid's formulation of the principle of veracity contains an ambiguity about the thing signified—is it the fact that p, or the speaker's belief in p? We must note now another blurred distinction that threatens to confuse his exposition. This time it is an ambiguity about the sign rather than the thing signified. What are the signs that figure in knowledge from testimony?

Table 2.1. Two Analogies.

	Greater analogy		Lesser analogy	
	OP	NL	AP	AL
How is the connection between sign and thing signified *established*—by nature or convention?	Nature	Nature	Nature	Convention
How is the connection between sign and thing signified *known*—innately or by experience?	Innately	Innately	By experience	By experience
Are the principles of signification universal or variable across cultures?	Universal	Universal	Universal	Variable
Are the principles of our constitution particular principles of signification or general principles enabling us to learn the particular principles?	Particular	Particular	General	General

Normally, they are signs belonging to artificial language,[6] and these, Reid tells us, are "articulate sounds" (or written signs, as he adds in another place). Are the signs to be construed simply as not-yet-interpreted sounds issuing from the mouths of our fellows? Or are they to be construed as sounds already interpreted as giving voice to propositions? Let me use in tandem the variables 'S' and 'p' in the following way: 'S' for a sentence, such as 'it is raining today' or 'il pleut aujourd'hui', and 'p' for a proposition expressed by that sentence, such as the proposition *it is raining today.* Then our question may be put thus: are the signs of concern to Reid in *Inquiry*, 6. 24 signs of the sort *A utters S* or signs of the sort *A says p*? I fear that the answer is sometimes one and sometimes the other, and that Reid does not mark the difference.[7]

Why do I say that Reid glosses over this distinction? In brief, it is because when he is discussing the principles of veracity and credulity, the signs he is concerned with must be assertions of propositions—items of the sort *A says p*. But when he is discussing the analogy between artificial language and acquired perception, the signs can only be utterances of words—items of the sort *A utters S*.

As noted above, Reid thinks there are two requisites for knowledge by signs—there must be a regular connection between the sign and the thing signified, and the appearance of the sign must induce a belief in the thing signified. It is always a matter of interest to Reid to ascertain how, in various cases of knowledge by signs, these requisites are satisfied. Is the sign conjoined with the thing signified by nature or by convention? Does the appearance of the sign produce belief in the thing signified by innate knowledge or by experience? In *Inquiry*, 6. 24, he advances the principles of veracity and credulity, two principles "implanted in our natures," as providing the answers to these questions in the case of testimony: by virtue of veracity there is a reliable connection between the sign and the thing signified, and by virtue of credulity we believe in the thing signified when we apprehend the sign. For these claims to be true, the signs must be assertions of propositions rather than utterings of words. There are no principles "implanted in our natures" whereby mere words signify a certain state of affairs or induce us to believe in it.

But now go back and look at the table delineating the various features Reid attributes to the sign-thing signified relation in artificial language. The connection holds by convention; it is known by experience; it varies from culture to culture. Here, obviously, the signs must be utterances of sentences, not assertions of propositions.

As far as I can see, the unmarked ambiguity in what counts as a sign causes only one mistake in what Reid tells us. In Reid's own order of exposition, the analogy between perception and language precedes his discussion of the principles of veracity and credulity. From the way in which Reid frames his discussion of these principles (beginning at lines 12–13 of *IHM*, p. 192 and closing at lines 35–7 of *IHM*, p. 195), it is clear that they are the principles he regards as "the general principles of the human mind which fit us for receiving information from our fellow-creatures". He then goes on (*IHM*, pp. 195–7) to consider "the general principles which fit us for receiving the information of nature by our acquired perceptions," which turn out to be the uniformity of nature and the inductive principle. In other words, he is suggesting that uniformity and induction are the general principles referred to in row four of our table under the heading 'acquired perception', while veracity and credulity are the general principles referred to under the heading 'artificial language'. But that is a mistake. If the signification of words is what is at issue, then induction is the relevant principle under both headings. It is induction that teaches me that a red glow signifies hotness, and it is also induction that teaches me what mama means by 'milk'.[8]

To summarize, Reid's exposition in *Inquiry*, 6. 24 of how signs signify what they do is clouded by two unmarked ambiguities. One is an ambiguity about the thing signified—is it a worldly fact or a fact about the speaker's state of mind? The other is an ambiguity about the sign—is it the utterance of a string of words or the assertion of a proposition? Fortunately, the ambiguities do not invalidate any of Reid's key contentions. Nearly everything he wants to say can still be said, but we need to take greater care in stating it. We can present the entire picture as shown in Fig. 2.1.

If we take *A says p* as the sign and *p* as the thing signified, the first requisite of knowledge by signs (reliable connection between sign and thing signified) is ensured by veracity principle V1 and the second requisite (belief in the thing signified upon belief in the sign) is ensured by credulity principle C1. If we take *A says p* as the sign and *A believes p* as the thing signified, the first requisite is ensured by V2 and the second by C2. If we take *A utters S* as the sign, things get more complicated, for there is now in effect an intermediate sign, *A says p*, signified

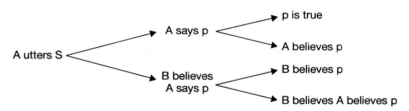

Figure 2.1. From Signs to Knowledge of what they signify.

by *A utters S* and signifying in turn either *p* or *A believes p*. When we consider *A utters S* as sign and *A says p* as (intermediate) thing signified, the first requisite is ensured by convention and the second by induction. When we consider *A utters S* as sign and *p* as (ultimate) thing signified, the first requisite is ensured by the logical product of convention and V1, the second by the product of induction and C1. Finally, when we consider *A utters S* as sign and *A believes p* as (ultimate) thing signified, the first requisite is ensured by convention and V2, the second by induction and C2. (The reader may wish to label the arrows in Fig. 2.1. On the left, the upper arrow should be labeled 'convention' and the lower arrow 'induction'. On the right, the arrows from top to bottom should be labeled as 'V1', 'V2', 'C1', and 'C2'.)

III. EXTENDING THE ANALOGY: ARE TESTIMONIAL BELIEFS EPISTEMICALLY BASIC?

The preceding sections have dealt mainly with Reid's views on the psychology of testimony—with the principles whereby we come to believe what we do when our fellows utter certain things. I turn now to matters more properly epistemological. What makes a belief acquired on the basis of testimony justified? What makes it knowledge?

It is not always clear in Reid where psychology stops and epistemology begins. When we have certain sensory experiences, Reid tells us, we instinctively and immediately believe in external objects, without any need of reasoning. Very well, his readers may ask, but is that just a piece of descriptive psychology (with which Hume could agree), or is it meant as normative epistemology?

In the case of sense perception, I believe it is meant as both. I shall take for granted here an interpretation of Reid's perceptual epistemology I have defended elsewhere (Van Cleve 1999). According to that interpretation, beliefs in physical objects prompted by sensory experiences are not only *psychologically immediate* (that is, triggered directly by the experiences without any reasoning or reliance on background information), but also *epistemically basic* (that is, justified without depending for their justification on any other justified beliefs). Beliefs about the observable features of things in our environment function as *first principles*—we appeal to them in justification of other things, but they are justified themselves without appeal to anything further. "First principles" may sound like too grand a name for such humble deliverances of perception as *there is a tree over there,* but Reid makes it clear that such propositions play the same role in our empirical knowledge as do axioms in mathematics (*IHM*, p. 172).

Can we extend Reid's analogy between the testimony of our fellows and the testimony of our senses one step further, maintaining that beliefs based on human testimony are like beliefs based on sense perception in being epistemically basic? In other words, can the mere fact that someone tells you p make you *prima facie* justified in believing p and (if p is true and there are no defeaters for your justification) thereby give you knowledge of p? On this question, Hume says no, but Reid says yes.

That Reid accords positive epistemic status, and perhaps even basic status, to testimonial beliefs can be argued on the basis of his discussion of testimony in the *Essays on the Intellectual Powers of Man.* His chapter on first principles includes the following principle relating to testimony: "Another first principle appears to me to be, That there is a certain regard due to human testimony in matters of fact, and even to human authority in matters of opinion" (EIP: 487). I reproduce here several of the sentences he offers in explanation of this principle, accompanying each with my own gloss.

"Before we are capable of reasoning about testimony or authority, there are many things which it concerns us to know, for which we can have no other evidence." "No *other* evidence:" so testimony is a source of evidence. This is confirmed in the chapter on probability (EIP: 557–58), where Reid discusses testimony as a species of probable evidence.

"The wise Author of nature hath planted in the human mind a propensity to rely upon this evidence before we can give a reason for doing so." That someone has usually told us the truth in the past would be a reason for believing what he says, but his say-so confers evidence even before I am capable of having this reason. Testimonial beliefs are evident even in the absence of reasons.

"If children were so framed, as to pay no regard to testimony or to authority, they must, in the literal sense, perish for lack of knowledge." This sentence reaffirms the immense practical advantage of credulity Reid had emphasized in the *Inquiry.* It also carries the further implication that what testimony bequeaths to children is *knowledge.*

When we put these three points together, it emerges that Reid regards testimony as a source not merely of belief, but also of evident belief or knowledge. Moreover, it plays this role even if the believer has no reason for his belief. Testimony-based beliefs therefore qualify for Reid as epistemically basic.[9]

Standing opposed to Reid on this question is Hume. Here is a well-known passage from his essay on miracles (section X of the *Enquiry Concerning Human Understanding*):

There is no species of reasoning more common, more useful, and even necessary to human life, than that which is derived from the testimony of men, and the reports of eye-witnesses and spectators. This species of reasoning, perhaps, one may deny to be founded on the relation of cause and effect. I shall not dispute about a word. It will be sufficient to observe, that our assurance in any argument of this kind is derived from no other principle than our observation of the veracity of human testimony, and of the usual conformity of facts to the reports of witnesses. It being a general maxim, that no objects have any discoverable connexion together, and that all the inferences, which we can draw from one to another, are founded merely on our experience of their constant and regular conjunction; it is evident, that we ought not to make an exception to this maxim in favour of human testimony, whose connexion with any event seems, in itself, as little necessary as any other. (Hume 1977: 74)

The reason, why we place any credit in witnesses and historians, is not derived from any *connexion*, which we perceive *a priori*, between testimony and reality, but because we are accustomed to find a conformity between them. (Hume 1977: 75)

Hume is nowadays regarded as the prototypical *reductionist* about the epistemological status of testimony. Reductionists hold that when B believes p because A says p, B's belief in p is justified only if B is justified in believing two further things: (i) that A did say p, and (ii) that most of the things said by A (or by the individuals in some wider relevant class of which A is a member) are true. Item (i) may be factored into the information that A produced certain signs and that these signs should be interpreted in a certain way. Item (ii) is what Hume refers to as the "usual conformity of facts to the reports of witnesses." It is clear that the reductionist position denies that beliefs based on testimony are epistemically basic—although they may be psychologically noninferential or immediate, they owe their justification to other justified beliefs B has about what A has said on this occasion and about his track record (or that of his cohort) in the past.[10]

Who is right—Reid or Hume? To answer this question, I shall set out the most formidable argument I know of against testimonial fundamentalism (as I shall call the anti-reductionist position, following Coady)[11] and then consider whether any good response to the argument is available to Reid.

The argument I have in mind consists of two premises and a conclusion:

Premise A: If a source S is a source of epistemically basic beliefs, then it must be an *a priori* matter that deliverances of S are *prima facie* warranted or likely to be true.[12]
Premise B: It is not an *a priori* matter that testimonial beliefs are *prima facie* warranted or likely to be true.
Conclusion: Testimony is not a source of epistemically basic beliefs.

Let me henceforth abbreviate 'it is *a priori* that deliverances of S are *prima facie* warranted or likely to be true' to 'S is an *a priori* source' and 'S is a source of epistemically basic beliefs' to 'S is a foundational source'. Then the argument can be put briefly as follows: a foundational source must be an *a priori* source, and testimony is not an *a priori* source.[13] But why should we accept the premises?

For premise A, there is a rationale that many traditional epistemologists would find compelling. This rationale is nicely laid out in the opening chapter of Pollock's *Knowledge and Justification* (Pollock 1974). Pollock begins by noting that basic beliefs about a given subject matter typically have a distinctive source. Beliefs about physical objects have perception as their source; beliefs about the past have memory as their source; beliefs about the future or the unobserved have induction as their source, and so on. It is part of Pollock's idea of a source that it is a way of knowing about its subject matter on which all other ways of knowing about that subject matter depend (Pollock 1974: 6). We can have knowledge of the physical world by means other than perception, such as memories and photographs, but if we couldn't have knowledge about the physical world through perception, we couldn't have it in these other ways, either. We might say that for Pollock, a source of basic beliefs is both autonomous (it gives knowledge or justification in its sphere without the help of other sources) and ultimate (no other sources give knowledge or justification about that subject matter without the help of it).

With this much assumed about sources, Pollock's argument may be set out (with some compression) as follows:

1. A putative source of knowledge is not a genuine source unless we can establish a connection between the source and the facts it is supposed to deliver.
2. Such a connection can be established only if (a) it can be established inductively, by showing that there is a reliable correlation between a belief's being delivered by the source and its being true, or (b) the connection holds *a priori*.
3. Since foundational sources are ultimate, alternative (a) is ruled out. We could establish the reliability of a foundational source only by relying on that very source and thus reasoning in a circle.
4. Therefore, a foundational source of knowledge must be an *a priori* source: if its deliverances are epistemically basic, it must be an *a priori* matter that its deliverances are warranted or likely to be true.

That, as I said, is a defense of premise A that many traditional epistemologists would find compelling.

Let us turn now to premise B, which tells us that there is no *a priori* connection between testimonial reports (or beliefs based thereon) and their truth or warrant. Why believe that? One reason would be that *a priori* connections must hold necessarily,[14] yet there seems to be no discernible necessary connection between a testimonial report and the truth or warrant of what is reported. That, indeed, was part of Hume's case for his stance on testimony as quoted above: he notes that the connection between human testimony and the event attested to "seems, in itself, as little necessary as any other."

In Pollock's scheme of things, there is an additional reason for denying an *a priori* connection between testimony and its deliverances. Pollock holds that an *a priori* connection "must arise from the meanings of the concepts or statements involved in the knowledge claims." Traditionally, this demand led to reductive analyses: for example, phenomenalist analyses of the truth conditions of external world statements in terms of the patterns of experience that serve as evidence for them. Pollock offers an alternative to the reductive tradition in which the meaning of a statement is given not by its truth conditions, but by its justification conditions. On his account, it is *part of the meaning* of 'x is red' that x's looking a certain way is a justification condition for it: one's understanding of what it is for something to be red is constituted in part by knowing that something's looking that way justifies you in believing it to be red. If we applied this strategy in the case of testimonial belief, we would say that one understands the meaning of a statement 'p' partly by knowing that 'A says p' is a justification condition for it. But 'A says p' has 'p' embedded within it! It is therefore out of the question that we understand 'p' in terms of 'A says p', since we can understand the latter only if we already understand the former. It is no accident that Pollock's book, which devotes a chapter to each of the traditional sources of justification, contains no chapter on testimony. His program of exhibiting the justification conditions of a statement as constitutive of its meaning cannot be carried out when the justification condition is a testimonial report.

Such, then, is the case against taking testimony as a foundational source: a source of basic beliefs must be an *a priori* source, and testimony is not an *a priori* source. How might a testimonial fundamentalist defend his position against this two-pronged attack? I shall discuss two strategies. One denies the first premise, invoking a reliability theory of justification to argue that a source of basic beliefs need not be an *a priori* source. The other denies the second premise, mobilizing some of the ideas in Wittgenstein's Private Language Argument to maintain that testimony is, after all, an *a priori* source. I discuss the second strategy first.

That testimony should qualify as an *a priori* source may seem surprising, but precisely that is an implication of some versions of the Private Language Argument. I focus on a version that was prevalent before considerations about rule-following took center stage. (I am indebted in what follows to Saunders and Henze 1967, especially ch. II.)

For present purposes, let a private language be a language whose terms refer to "private" data—to tickles and twinges and other inner states, regarded as having no conceptual ties to any manifestations in outward behavior. The argument to be reviewed maintains that a private language in this sense is impossible, because no one could know that he was employing its terms consistently and correctly.

Suppose I take myself to be using a term T to refer to the same type of private state that I have applied it to in the past. Since the referent of T is private, no one else can be in a position to correct or corroborate my use of T. I will have nothing but my own memory impressions to vouch for the fact that I am using T in the same way as before. But I am entitled to trust my memory impressions, it is insisted, only if there is some way other than memory of checking up on them. (Corroborating one memory by reference to another is disallowed on the alleged ground that it would be like buying two copies of the morning paper to verify that what it says is true [Wittgenstein 1953: para. 265].) The required independent check *is* available to speakers of a public language, for they may rely upon the testimony of their fellows that they are using T in the same way as before. The speaker of a private language, by contrast, cannot avail himself of any independent checks. His companions, having no outer criteria of his inner states, can provide no correction or corroboration. He can only be under the impression that he is following some semantic rule in the same way as before, but to *think* that you are obeying a rule is not the same thing as obeying it. You cannot obey a rule privately (Wittgenstein 1953: para. 202).

To the Private Language Argument in this incarnation, the traditionalist has a ready reply. He can say that his opponent's requirements would keep *anyone* from knowing he is using his terms correctly. For what entitles the speaker of a public language to rely upon the testimony of his fellows in corroboration of his memory impressions? In order for one to be justified in accepting something on someone else's say-so, one must know that the other person's testimony has been reliable in the past, and the only way one could know that is through reliance on one's own memory impressions. If the Wittgensteinian insists that memory can be relied upon only if backed up by testimony, he lands us in a vicious circle, because testimony in its turn can be relied upon only if backed up by memory.

It should be manifest that what the traditionalist's reply invokes is precisely a Humean reductionist position on testimony. In the next step in the dialectic—the crucial one for our purposes—the Wittgensteinian repudiates Hume. He says that it is a conceptual truth, knowable *a priori*, that an utterance by one of my fellows of a past-tense sentence that I would use to say p confers initial probability on p.[15] Thus there is no need to underwrite the deliverances of testimony by induction and memory, for such deliverances have their warrant *a priori*. QED.

The argument just given is, in effect, a transcendental argument for testimony as an *a priori* source. It proceeds from the premise that we know we are using the terms in our language correctly and argues it to be a necessary condition of this knowledge that the corroborative reports of our fellows have their evidential force *a priori*.

What verdict shall we pass on the argument? In my opinion, the argument can succeed in establishing the *a priori* credentials of one source of knowledge (testimony) only at the cost of destroying or downgrading the credentials of another (memory). If we allow that memory is an autonomous source of knowledge, capable of delivering knowledge and justified belief without corroboration by other sources, we can sidestep the argument entirely. I believe that memory is such an autonomous source, and I believe Reid would agree. For Reid, memory takes its place alongside perception as a source of first principles or basic beliefs. When we seem to perceive that there is a tree over there, we automatically believe there is a tree over there and are *prima facie* justified in so believing. Likewise, when we seem to remember some past event, we automatically believe that the event occurred and are *prima facie* justified in so believing (see EIP, pp. 253–5 and 474). One can gather what Reid's attitude would have been toward the thesis that memory stands in need of independent corroboration from the following remark: "When I remember a thing distinctly, I disdain equally to hear reasons for or against it" (EIP, p. 476). For better or for worse, then, Reid keeps the Private Language Argument from getting off the ground. The anti-fundamentalist premise that testimony is not an *a priori* source still stands.[16]

Let us turn, then, to the other strategy for avoiding the anti-fundamentalist's one-two punch. In this strategy we deny that a source of basic beliefs must be an *a priori* source. One basis for doing so is provided by the reliability theory of justification, which has come to prominence only in recent years, but which is sometimes discerned in the writings of Reid himself.

The tenets of the reliability theory may be set down in the following way, which is due to Goldman (1979). First, we distinguish two kinds of belief-forming processes: belief-independent processes, such as perception, which do not take other beliefs as inputs, and belief-dependent processes, such as reasoning, which do take other beliefs as inputs. Next, we say that a process of the first sort is reliable iff it tends to produce only true beliefs as outputs (this is "unconditional reliability"), and we say that a process of the second sort is reliable iff it tends to produce only true beliefs as outputs when it is given true beliefs as inputs (this is "conditional reliability"). Finally, we offer a recursive account of justification as follows: a belief is justified iff either (i) it results from an unconditionally reliable belief-independent process or (ii) it results from justified beliefs by way of a conditionally reliable belief-dependent process.

A reliability theory along these lines lets us counter the one-two punch in two ways. First, it undermines the case for premise A. The argument for that premise relied crucially on the following assumption: a putative source of knowledge is not a genuine source unless we can establish a connection between the source and the facts it is supposed to deliver. "Establishing" a connection in this context means knowing or verifying that it obtains. That is precisely what is *not* necessary according to the reliability theory: if the theory is correct, there need only *be* a connection, whether anyone knows it obtains or not. For the reliability theory, the mere fact that a belief has been formed by a reliable process is *sufficient* to make that belief justified. That implies that no knowledge by the subject or anyone else that the process is reliable is *necessary*. So the key assumption is false: a source is a source just so long as there *is* an appropriate connection between the source and its deliverances, whether anyone can establish it or not.

Second, the reliability theory not only undermines the case for premise A, but it also enables us to see directly that that premise is false. Suppose that when we hear others attest to some fact p, we automatically believe p. There is no drawing of inferences or weighing of reasons—we simply believe p. That, of course, is what Reid's principle C1 says. It implies that beliefs generated by the testimony of others are psychologically immediate, not based on reasons.[17] Suppose next that it is a contingent and *a posteriori* fact, but a fact nonetheless, that the things others attest tend to be true. That, of course, is what Reid's principle V1 says. It implies that believing what others say is a reliable method of belief formation, and thus that beliefs formed by this method are (by reliabilist standards) justified. Putting this all together, testimonial beliefs are immediate (by C1) and justified (by V1 and the reliability theory); therefore, they are justified immediate beliefs, which is another way of saying they are epistemically basic. So testimony is a source of epistemically basic beliefs, even though the fact that such beliefs are generally true is knowable only *a posteriori*.[18]

Could Reid avail himself of this way of avoiding the anti-fundamentalist argument? That depends on whether he is a reliabilist. The best case I know of for interpreting Reid as a reliabilist has been presented in a book by Philip de Bary (2002), whose main features I now sketch.

According to de Bary, when Reid draws up his list of first principles, he is in the first instance simply formulating psychological laws about human belief formation—laws specifying what sorts of things people instinctively believe in various circumstances. When I perceive a tree or a star, that is enough to make me believe one is there; when I remember walking on the beach yesterday, I believe that I did so; and when a friend or stranger tells me a tree has blocked the road, I believe forthwith that the road is indeed blocked. If Reid went no further than this, his list of first principles would "lack any epistemological bite" (de Bary 2002: 65). But Reid does go further (according to de Bary), embedding his principles in a framework of reliabilism. Reid believes that "the instinctive beliefs of healthy people . . . tend towards the truth" (de Bary 2002: 83) and further, that such a tendency towards truth (given a reliabilist view like Goldman's) is sufficient (in the absence of special reasons for doubting them) for their being justified and amounting to knowledge when true. So the various classes of belief marked out in Reid's list of first principles are not only psychologically immediate, but epistemically basic. When true, they are items of basic knowledge, and that goes for beliefs based on testimony just as much as for beliefs based on perception and memory.

I am not convinced that de Bary's interpretation of Reid is right. It is plausible, I admit, but I think there are alternatives at least equally plausible. I have sketched one such in "Reid on the First Principles of Contingent Truths" (Van Cleve 1999). According to my alternative, when Reid enunciates his first principles, he is giving generalizations that are epistemological principles as they stand, not just psychological laws that acquire epistemological significance only when supplemented with facts about reliability and the tenets of the reliability theory. They are principles according to which the deliverances of introspection, perception, memory, and credulity (if I may so name the "faculty" through which we believe testimony) are *prima facie* justified, regardless of whether they are true or false on a given occasion and possibly even regardless of whether they generally tend to be true.[19] On this interpretation, Reid's epistemology is more like Chisholm's than Goldman's. Chisholm provides a list of epistemic principles according to which the deliverances of introspection, perception, and memory have one or another positive epistemic status just in virtue of having those sources, not in virtue of any connection with truth (Chisholm 1977: ch. 4).

If Reid is taken in this way, he could perhaps still hold that testimony-based beliefs are epistemically basic. However, he would lack de Bary's reason for so regarding them: they would not be justified simply in virtue of their reliability, no matter how great that reliability is. They would be justified instead in virtue of ... what?

Here I think Reid would have no good answer. I do not think it entirely out of the question that perception and memory are *a priori* sources of justified belief,[20] but testimony just does not look to me like an *a priori* source, any more than the readings of a barometer do. If testimonial beliefs are not epistemically basic because they are deliverances of an *a priori* source, nor because they are deliverances of a reliable belief-independent source, then how they can they be epistemically basic at all? This question pushes me strongly in the direction of testimonial reductionism. I shall therefore conclude this essay by defending reductionism against what I take to be the most formidable objection to it. I shall also offer a sketch of what Reid's epistemology of testimony would look like if he were to join the reductionist camp.

The objection I have in mind is at least intimated if not explicitly articulated by several writers, including Anscombe (1979), BonJour (2002), Coady (1992), and Wolterstorff (2001). The key premise in it is that the vast majority (or perhaps even the totality) of what passes for corroboration of testimony *itself relies on other testimony*. "The guidebook was right," I say, "there is such a place as Piccadilly Circus"—but in so saying I rely on the street signs that someone has posted at the site. I cannot construct an inductive argument for the reliability of testimony because "the cases that I can investigate firsthand [without relying on further testimony to corroborate them] amount to only a vanishingly small proportion of either the persons and other sources that provide testimony or the subject matters to which such testimony pertains" (BonJour 2002: 172–3). An implausibly strong version of this argument would say that there is in principle *no* case in which I can corroborate testimony without relying on further testimony—in other words, that testimony is an ultimate source. A more plausible version would say that the proportion of cases I can corroborate firsthand is "vanishingly small," so that any inductive argument based on them must be *"extremely* weak" (BonJour 2002: 173). The first conclusion to be drawn from these premises would be that if reductionism is correct, I know little or nothing on the basis of testimony. The second conclusion would be that since I *do* know a great deal on the basis of testimony, reductionism is untenable—another transcendental argument.

In my opinion, this argument is far from decisive. To begin with, there is no plausibility at all in the strong version's contention that *any* corroboration of testimony *must* rely on further testimony. For many years of my life, I believed there were such wonders as the Grand Canyon and the Taj Mahal solely on the basis of books and postcards. Now I have verified the existence of those things with my own eyes. (More accurately: I have verified with my own eyes the existence of *such* things, that is, structures matching a certain general description, for I admittedly relied on the testimony of the locals to know *that building is the Taj Mahal*.) To these dramatic episodes of confirmation may be added thousands of more quotidian occurrences of finding beer in the fridge or a restroom down the hall on the right after being told where to look. To be sure, these myriad instances in which I have been able to check on the veracity of testimony firsthand are (as the weak version rightly points out) only a minuscule fraction of all the instances in which I have believed things on the basis of testimony. But does it follow that any inductive justification I have for believing testimony must be "extremely weak"? Not at all, for what matters is not the proportion of testimonial beliefs I have checked, but the proportion of checks undertaken that have had positive results. I have seen only a tiny fraction of the world's crows, but the ones I have seen have been overwhelmingly black, and that is enough to support my belief that nearly all crows are black. (Of course, the ratio of testimonies checked to testimonies that have proved true varies with different classes of testimony; I have found geography textbooks to be more reliable than presidential press conferences.[21])

How much of what Reid has to say about testimony can we still accept if we move into the reductionist camp? We can accept nearly everything he says about the psychology of testimonial belief, especially as regards the principle of credulity. We may also agree with what he says about the immense practical advantage of credulity. A viable reductionism had better not take the form of saying: believe no one whose track record you have not checked out for yourself. Children (fortunately for them and fortunately for all who were once children ourselves) go through a credulous phase during which they believe without reason nearly everything they are told. As reductionists, however, we must hold that these beliefs are justified only in a pragmatic sense, not in an epistemic sense. If they qualify as knowledge, it must be a kind of knowledge that does not require justification, but only a reliable connection with the truth, as in what Sosa calls "animal knowledge" (Sosa 1997; compare the view ascribed to Audi in n. 13).

As children grow into adulthood, their credulity diminishes and their ability to give inductive reasons for what they accept from others grows. As Reid notes,

[Credulity] will be strongest in childhood, and limited and restrained by experience. . . . When brought to maturity by proper culture, [reason] begins to feel her own strength, and leans less upon the reason of others; she learns to suspect testimony in some cases, and to disbelieve it in others; and sets bound to that authority to which she was at first entirely subject. But still, to the end of life, she finds a necessity of borrowing light from testimony, where she has none within herself, and of leaning in some degree upon the reason of others. . . . (*IHM*, p. 195)

In another passage, he tells us that adults are in a position to believe on the basis of experience and reflection things they originally believed only on instinct:

I believed by instinct whatever [my parents and tutors] told me, long before I had the idea of a lie, or thought of the possibility of their deceiving me. Afterwards, upon reflection, I found that they had acted like fair and honest people who wished me well. I found, that if I had not believed what they told me, before I could give a reason of my belief, I had to this day been little better than a changeling. And although this natural credulity hath sometimes occasioned my being imposed upon by deceivers, yet it hath been of infinite advantage to me upon the whole; therefore I consider it as another good gift of Nature. And I continue to give that credit, from reflection, to those of whose integrity and veracity I have had experience, which before I gave from instinct. (*IHM*, p. 170–1)

Things we accepted originally as a gift of nature we can give reasons for as we grow older. In this way, animal knowledge is replaced by reflective knowledge, and beliefs that were formerly justified only in a pragmatic or external sense become justified reflectively.[22]

My view, in conclusion, is that testimony gives us justified belief and reflective knowledge not because it shines by its own light, but because it has often enough been revealed true by our other lights. On this point, I find myself uncharacteristically on the side of Hume rather than Reid.

REFERENCES

Anscombe, Elizabeth (1979), 'What Is It to Believe Someone?', in C. F. Delaney (ed.), *Rationality and Religious Belief* (Notre Dame: University of Notre Dame Press), 141–51.

Audi, Robert (1997), 'The Place of Testimony in the Fabric of Knowledge and Justification', *American Philosophical Quarterly*, 34: 405–22.

BonJour, Laurence (2002), *Epistemology: Classic Problems and Contemporary Responses* (Lanham, Md: Rowman and Littlefield).

Burge, Tyler (1993), 'Content Preservation', *Philosophical Review*, 102: 457–88.

Chisholm, Roderick M. (1977), *Theory of Knowledge* (Englewood Cliffs, NJ: Prentice-Hall, 2nd edn.).

Coady, C. A. J. (1992), *Testimony: A Philosophical Study* (Oxford: Clarendon Press).

de Bary, Philip (2002), *Thomas Reid and Scepticism: His Reliabilist Response* (London: Routledge).

Ekman, Paul, Sorenson, E. Richard, and Friesen, Wallace V. (1969), 'Pan-Cultural Elements in Facial Displays of Emotion', *Science*, NS 164: 86–8.

Gilbert, Daniel T. (1993), 'The Assent of Man: Mental Representation and the Control of Belief', in Daniel M. Wegner and James W. Pennebaker (eds.), *Handbook of Mental Control* (Englewood Cliffs, NJ: Prentice-Hall), 57–87.

Goldman, Alvin (1979), 'What is Justified Belief?', in George S. Pappas (ed.), *Justification and Knowledge* (Dordrecht, Holland: D. Reidel), 1–23.

Hume, David (1977), *An Enquiry Concerning Human Understanding*, ed. Eric Steinberg (Indianapolis: Hackett) (first published in 1748).

Plantinga, Alvin (1993), *Warrant and Proper Function* (New York: Oxford University Press).

Pollock, John L. (1974), *Knowledge and Justification* (Princeton: Princeton University Press).

Reid, Thomas (1997), *An Inquiry into the Human Mind on the Principles of Common Sense*, ed. Derek R. Brookes (Edinburgh: Edinburgh University Press) (first published in 1764). It is abbreviated in the text as *IHM*, with '6. 24' indicating chapter 6, section 24.

____ (2002), *Essays on the Intellectual Powers of Man*, ed. Derek R. Brookes (University Park, Pa: Pennsylvania State University Press) (first published in 1785). It is abbreviated in the text as *EIP*.

Saunders, John Turk, and Henze, Donald F. (1967), *The Private Language Problem: A Philosophical Dialogue* (New York: Random House).

Shoemaker, Sydney (1963), *Self-Knowledge and Self-Identity* (Ithaca, NY: Cornell University Press).

Sosa, Ernest (1997), 'Reflective Knowledge in the Best Circles', *Journal of Philosophy*, 94: 410–30.

Van Cleve, James (1999), 'Reid on the First Principles of Contingent Truths', *Reid Studies*, 3: 3–30.

____ (2004), 'Reid's Theory of Perception', in Rene van Woudenberg and Terence Cuneo (eds.), *The Cambridge Companion to Reid* (Cambridge: Cambridge University Press), 101–33.

Wittgenstein, Ludwig (1953), *Philosophical Investigations*, trans. G. E. M. Anscombe (Oxford: Blackwell).

Wolterstorff, Nicholas (2001), *Thomas Reid and the Story of Epistemology* (Cambridge: Cambridge University Press).

NOTES

1. Interpreted as C1, the principle of credulity finds confirmation in the work of some contemporary cognitive psychologists. See Gilbert (1993) for descriptions of experiments in which the mere hearing or reading of a proposition tends to induce belief in it.

2. There is also a route leading from C2 to C1. Suppose B hears A say p; in accordance with C2, B thereupon believes that A believes p; drawing on Principle 7, he then draws the inference that p is probably true; in light of that, he commences believing p, just as C1 says. But this account would falsify what Reid regards as the psychology of the situation. C1 is meant to describe a mechanism whereby we forms beliefs immediately, not as the result of any reasoning

3. I am indebted in this section to Nicholas Wolterstorff's discussion of Reid's account of testimony in Wolterstorff (2001). Wolterstorff notes that Reid blurs the distinction between the consequents of the principles I have labeled C1 and C2 (2001: 172). He also observes that what Reid really needs by way of a veracity principle is V1—the disposition to assert only what one believes must be coupled with a tendency to get things right (2001: 176).

4. It may be helpful to relate Reid's discussion of natural language in *IHM* 4. 2 to his discussion of natural signs in *IHM* 5. 3. In the latter section, he distinguishes three classes of natural signs. The first class comprises signs "whose connection with the thing signified is established by nature, but discovered only by experience" (*IHM*, p. 59). For example, smoke is a class I natural sign of fire. The second class "is that wherein the connection between the sign and thing signified, is not only established by nature, but discovered to us by a natural principle, without reasoning or experience" (*IHM*, p. 60). For example, a smile is a class II natural sign of approval. The third class comprises those signs "which, though we never before had any notion or conception of the things signified, do suggest it, or conjure it up, as it were, by a natural kind of magic, and at once give us a conception, and create a belief of it" (*IHM*, p. 60). For example, certain tactile sensations are class III natural signs of hardness in bodies. The key difference between class II and class III natural signs is that although in both cases the *connection* between our apprehension of the sign and our conception of the thing signified is hardwired or innate, in the third class alone is our *conception* of the thing signified also innate.

What Reid calls "natural language" comprises natural signs of the second class. What he calls "artificial language" comprises signs whose connection with the thing signified is established by convention rather than nature and which therefore belong to none of the three classes of natural signs. His usage is obviously different from our own, as he would classify English as an artificial language rather than a natural language.

5. A smile's a smile the world around. That certain facial expressions are universal in their signification has been confirmed by contemporary research such as that of Ekman et al. (1969).

6. There are exceptions. Reid tells us that "two savages who have no common artificial language" (*IHM*, p. 52) could communicate with each other exclusively in the natural language of gesture, facial expression, and tone of voice. Presumably, they could exchange testimony.

7. I gloss over a further distinction myself. A speaker may utter a sentence S that means p without thereby saying p in the sense of *asserting* it (as contrasted with carrying out a speech act with some other illocutionary force). By 'saying p' I mean asserting p. For A's uttering S to amount to his saying p in this sense, it is required not only that S means p, but also that in uttering something that means p, A is asserting p (rather than reciting a line in a play, for instance). I ignore this second aspect of the difference between uttering S and saying p. It is discussed in Burge (1993) and Wolterstorff (2001).

8. Of course, once the language of one's elders has been learned, induction is no longer necessary; one simply hears S as saying *p*, attending to the sense rather than the sounds. Here is another similarity that Reid might have remarked between artificial language and acquired perception.

9. Here I am in agreement with Coady (1992: 23 and 123). It may also be the view of Plantinga (1993) that testimonial beliefs are epistemically basic for Reid.

10. Reductionism is so-called because it holds that testimonial knowledge can be "reduced to" or accounted for in terms of knowledge exclusively from other sources: B knows p because he knows by perception that A has said p, by memory that A

has said such-and-such other things in the past, by memory and a variety of other apposite sources that these things were true, and by induction based on the foregoing that A is probably right in what he says on the present occasion. I dislike the name 'reductionism' because of its misleading associations with "reductive" doctrines such as phenomenalism and behaviorism, in which there is a reduction not of one way of knowing to others, but of the subject matter known to facts belonging to some other class. Nonetheless, the label has become well entrenched, so I shall stick with it here.

11. Coady proposes 'fundamentalism' as a name for the view that testimony is a source of basic or foundational beliefs on a par with perception and memory (Coady 1992: 23).

Reductionism and the fundamentalism I ascribe to Reid do not exhaust the options, as Peter Graham makes clear (Chapter 4 in this volume). One of the other options is the position that Graham defends under the label 'weak fundamentalism'. In this view, a belief based on testimony is not thereby *prima facie* justified, that is, justified enough to qualify as knowledge if the belief is true and there are no defeaters. Instead, it is only *pro tanto* justified, that is, possessed of a modicum of justification, but not necessarily enough to qualify as knowledge. Coherence with other justified beliefs may be required to bring the justification of the belief up to the level required for knowledge. Graham's view about testimonial knowledge is thus analogous to C. I. Lewis's view about memory knowledge: ostensible memories have an initial level of justification or credibility just in virtue of being memory reports; this initial level can be brought up to the level required for knowledge through the coherence of the reports with one another and with other beliefs. I believe weak fundamentalism is a more plausible position than the strong fundamentalism I attribute to Reid. Nonetheless, I think the argument I am about to present, if cogent at all, would apply to weak fundamentalism as well as to strong. That would be so, at any rate, if *pro tanto* justification (no less than *prima facie* justification) must flow from an *a priori* source.

12. This is not to say, of course, that the deliverances themselves are *a priori*. What is *a priori* is the conditional: if a belief is delivered by S, then the belief is warranted or likely to be true.

13. I might have been tempted to abbreviate 'S is a source of epistemically basic beliefs' to 'S is a basic source', except that to do so would have been to ride roughshod over the nice set of distinctions developed by Robert Audi (1997). Audi distinguishes between 'source of basic X' and 'basic source of X', where X can be any of the commodities belief, knowledge, or justification. Roughly, S is a basic source of {belief, knowledge, justification} iff S can produce {belief, knowledge, justification} without the cooperation of another source of the relevant commodity. S is a source of basic {belief, knowledge, justification} iff S is a source of {beliefs not based on other beliefs, knowledge not derived from other knowledge, justification not dependent on other justified propositions}. In Audi's view, testimony is not a *basic source* of any of the three commodities. It is, however, a *source of basic belief* and a *source of basic knowledge*, though not a *source of basic justification*.

How is it possible for testimony to be a source of basic knowledge without being a source of basic justification? The answer is that Audi does not define basic knowledge as true belief with basic justification; in fact, he does not define knowledge as requiring justification at all. Reliably formed belief can count as knowledge for him, but reliability does not suffice for justification.

14. Kripkean reasons for believing that some propositions are both *a priori* and contingent are plainly not in play here.

15. In the exposition of the argument by Saunders and Henze, the thesis I have just mentioned is derived from two other theses, the Utterance Thesis and the Testimony Thesis. According to the Utterance Thesis, it is *a priori* that an utterance by A of a past-tense statement 'p' confers initial likelihood on the proposition that A is making a memory claim that p. According to the Testimony Thesis, it is *a priori* that A's testifying as to what he remembers (and thus his making the memory claim that p) confers initial probability on p. Saunders and Henze attribute versions of both theses to Shoemaker (1963).

Shoemaker maintains (1963: 249–50) that we do not make an inductive inference from *A uttered 'p'* to *A said p*. I suspect that in holding this, he is primarily concerned with the difference between uttering and the illocutionary act of saying. He seems to have lost sight of the need for induction that is surely involved in learning what 'p' means in the language of one's society.

16. I should acknowledge that Wittgensteinian worries about private languages are not the only reasons for regarding testimony as an *a priori* source. Tyler Burge advances the following as an *a priori* principle: "A person is entitled to accept as true something that is presented [by another person] as true and that is intelligible to him, unless there are stronger reasons not to do so." Burge argues for this principle by deriving it from two subsidiary principles, each of which he considers to be *a priori*: there is *prima facie* reason to regard a message one finds intelligible as coming from a rational source, and there is *prima facie* reason to regard a rational source as a source of truth. I lack the space to discuss Burge's case for the subsidiary principles here, but the interested reader may consult Burge (1993).

17. The following issue needs to be discussed: is believing testimony really a belief-independent process? When I believe a piece of testimony, I come to the belief only because I have heard (or otherwise perceived) someone say something. Audi points out that this indicates a dependency of testimonial belief on *perception*, but not necessarily a dependence on other *beliefs*, since I need not form the belief that A said p. For Reid, however, things may be otherwise. He sometimes (though not invariably) seems to define perception as involving belief, so that hearing A say p would include as an ingredient believing that A said p. (For discussion, see Van Cleve 2004: sect. III.) If that is so, believing what you hear others say would turn out to be a belief-dependent process rather than a belief-independent process. But I am going to assume for the sake of discussion here that testimonial beliefs for Reid are psychologically immediate, i.e., dependent on no other beliefs.

18. In Goldman's terms, any belief formed by a process that is both belief-independent and reliable is an epistemically basic belief, and testimonial beliefs are so formed.

19. It is these deliverances—particular propositions believed on the basis of perception, memory, and the like—that are the first principles on my interpretation, not the generalizations that single them out.

20. I have characterized an *a priori* source as a source S such that it is *a priori* that the deliverances of S are *prima facie* warranted or likely to be true. 'Likely to be true' is a statistical notion, implying that most of the deliverances of S are true. I cannot see that it is *a priori* that most deliverances of perception are likely to be true. However, '*prima facie* warranted' is a normative notion, not implying any statistics. Just conceivably, it is *a priori* that deliverances of perception are *prima facie* warranted.

21. Though skeptical about an inductive justification of testimony, BonJour notes the possibility of a coherentist justification of testimony, appealing to the agreement among one another of various authorities on matters I am unable to check on firsthand (2002: 173–7). I think such coherence can indeed boost the epistemic standing of testimony-based belief, but only provided there is some initial reason to believe the authorities. I also think such initial reason would have to derive from induction over some sample of authorities that I *have* been able to check on for myself. I do not, therefore, see a coherentist justification of testimony as an independent alternative to an inductivist justification.

22. As P. D. Magnus has pointed out to me, the view I am now recommending for Reid has the consequence that children's perceptual beliefs qualify as genuine knowledge, whereas their testimonial beliefs qualify only as animal knowledge. I am not altogether happy with this invidious distinction, but I think it may be pressed upon us *if* perception is an *a priori* source and testimony is not.

PART II
TESTIMONY AND ITS PLACE IN EPISTEMOLOGY

3

The Epistemic Role of Testimony: Internalist and Externalist Perspectives

Richard Fumerton

Setting aside radical skeptical concerns, it seems almost a truism that much of what we believe is based on the testimony of others. Beliefs about the distant past are based on the writings of historians. Beliefs about the microworld are based on the word of physicists. Beliefs about the names, ages, histories, habits, likes, and dislikes of friends are largely based on information those friends provide. There are important distinctions one can make between kinds of testimony.[1] Throughout this paper, however, I will be relying on a very broad understanding of the term. Any genuine assertion one person makes for the consumption of another will count, for these purposes, as that person's testifying to some putative fact. The assertion can be oral or written, formal and under oath, or casual in some familiar context of conversation. Again, understood this way, the road to much of what we believe travels through the testimony of other people.

Any plausible epistemology must distinguish questions about the genesis of belief from its epistemic justification.[2] If it is relatively uncontroversial from the perspective of commonsense that we very often rely on information provided by other people, it is far less clear how to construe the nature of the *evidential* path we need to travel in getting *justified* belief through reliance on testimony. The traditional view of testimony and the way in which it contributes to justi-fied belief makes the epistemic road long and winding. We hear sounds or see marks. We then must reasonably interpret those sounds and marks as meaningful assertions. Critically, we must have some reason to believe that the assertions in question are likely to be true. Only then are we in a position to reach a rational conclusion that takes into account what other people say. More recently, how-ever, philosophers have begun to challenge the idea that the epistemic contri-butions of testimony are so complex. Some have even seemed to suggest that reliance on testimony should be viewed as just as fundamental as reliance on inductive reasoning, memory, or perception.[3]

The attempt to determine how, if at all, testimony contributes to knowledge is made more difficult these days as the debate takes place in the shadow of the internalism/externalism controversy that dominates contemporary epistemology.

In this paper I want to contrast the way in which classical internalists and paradigm externalists might approach the question of how to construe the justification (if any) provided by testimony. In particular, I am interested in the question
of whether testimonial inference has a fundamental or a derivative place in our
reasoning. In the course of answering this question we will have occasion to
examine more closely this alleged distinction between fundamental and derivative principles of reasoning.

A CLASSICAL INTERNALIST FOUNDATIONALISM AND
A TRADITIONAL APPROACH TO TESTIMONY

On classical internalist foundationalist models of justification, the epistemic tasks
one must complete in order to justify belief based on testimony are intimidating
to say the least. There are, of course, radically different versions of internalism. I
have argued elsewhere (Fumerton 1985 and 1996) that one of the most demanding, but also one of the most plausible, takes S's foundationally justified beliefs
to be those justified by S's direct acquaintance with a correspondence between a
belief/thought and the fact that makes it true. That version of foundationalism
need not be a version of internal state internalism, at least if the *internal* states
of a subject are defined as those states that include as constituents only the self,
its nonrelational properties, and those relations it bears to itself and its nonrelational properties. According to Russell (1959), for example, we can be directly
acquainted with universals and relations that hold between them. Universals are
hardly mind-dependent entities. Also, direct realism as a theory of perception
is making a bit of a comeback. At least some philosophers hold that in veridical perception we are directly acquainted with mind-independent constituents of
physical objects.[4]

On a direct acquaintance theory, one's stock of foundationally justified beliefs
is a function of the class of facts with which one can be directly acquainted. The
radical empiricists, of course, were convinced that the only contingent truths one
knows noninferentially are descriptions of the current contents of one's mind.
They were convinced that one is directly acquainted only with one's own subjective states and the truth makers for necessary truths. *That* version of the acquaintance theory would take one's justification for believing contingent truths to be
constituted by one's internal states.

However the classical foundationalist construes foundational knowledge, that
foundationalist will also need an account of how one moves from foundational
knowledge to the rest of what one justifiably believes. This is another issue which
separates paradigm internalists and externalists. On the view that I call *inferential
internalism*, in order for S to be justified in believing P on the basis of some other
proposition justifiably believed E, S must be justified in believing that there is a
probabilistic connection between E and P (where entailment can be viewed as the
upper limit of making probable).[5]

Inferential internalism can be made at least initially attractive if we think about some commonplace epistemic criticisms of inferentially formed beliefs. The astrologer who forms beliefs about the future of human beings based on information he possesses concerning the positions of planets and stars has unjustified beliefs if he lacks reason to believe that there is some sort of probabilistic connection between the position of celestial bodies and the affairs of human beings. One who infers that a person will have a long life from the observation that the person has a long "life line" on the palm of her hand, forms an irrational belief in the absence of possessing good reason to think that a line on one's palm has some connection to the length of one's life.

One must be cautious, however, before one relies too heavily on the above intuitions to defend inferential internalism.[6] The problem is that we are promiscuous in our characterization of *the* evidence from which we infer conclusions. In casual conversation we often identify as our evidence for believing some proposition only a particularly interesting *part* of the entire body of knowledge upon which we rely in reaching our conclusion. I call the police and report that I have been robbed. If asked why I think that is so, I might cite as my evidence that my window has been broken and my valuables are missing. But it seems fairly clear on reflection that there is a vast array of unstated background information upon which I rely in reaching my conclusion. I know that I live in a culture in which it is not acceptable for friends and relatives to borrow my belongings with or without my permission and to use force if necessary to enter my home in order to achieve that end. I also know that glass does not typically break spontaneously causing valuables to disappear *in nihilo*. I also know (or at least think that I know) that I am not a psychotic prone to staging robberies which I subsequently can't remember having staged. To be sure, I probably don't consciously bring all these beliefs to mind in reaching the conclusion that I've been robbed, but it is perfectly plausible to suppose that their presence as dispositional beliefs plays a crucial role in my willingess to reach the conclusion that I've been robbed.

Once we realize that many, if not most, accounts of our reasoning are enthymematic, it is far less obvious what lesson we should learn from the fact that we reject astrological "reasoning" as illegitimate in the absence of justified belief concerning connections between celestial events and human affairs. It is more than likely that we, and for that matter the astrologers, view their reasoning as enthymematic. No one, not even an astrologer, is crazy enough to suppose that one can somehow legitimately infer that Susan is going to meet the love of her life from the fact that she was born in December and Jupiter is aligned with Mars. Everyone simply assumes that the information concerning birth dates and planets is only a *part* of a more complex array of premises which constitute the complete story of the alleged evidence justifying the astrological prediction. Furthermore, it is natural to assume that the unstated premises make assertions about correlations between celestial facts and human affairs. We reject the astrologer's conclusions as unjustified not because the astrologer lacks justification for believing that the premises of his argument make probable the conclusion, but because we are convinced that the astrologer lacks justification for believing a critical but unstated *premise* upon which he was relying.

Having said all this, I still think that inferential internalism is a plausible view. Deductively valid arguments are surely the paradigm of arguments whose premises bear an appropriate relation to their conclusion. And it still seems obvious to me that if someone infers a conclusion C from some known premise E when E entails C, it doesn't follow that the person has a justified belief in C based on E. If the person in question fails to "see" the connection—doesn't realize that the entailment holds—then the person lacks inferential knowledge.

THE STATUS OF TESTIMONIAL "INFERENCE" ON THE "TRADITIONAL" VIEW

My main concern here is not with the plausibility of inferential internalism. Rather, I want to see what lessons we can learn from the above discussion concerning the character of inferences that rely on testimony. And the first conclusion we *might* reach is that the whole idea of relying on testimony as a *kind of inference* is potentially misleading. Inferences from testimony might be like astrological "inferences". We do not, in fact, *ever* infer that P from the fact that some person tells us that P. To be sure we *talk* that way. We'll identify as our evidence for believing some proposition the testimony of another person. But a full and perspicuous representation of the reasoning will make explicit unstated premises upon which we critically rely in reaching our conclusion that P. The perspicuous representation of the argument we accept might be something like the following:

1) Jones said that P in conditions C (where C includes a description of Jones, his qualifications as an authority, and the circumstances under which he made the assertion).
2) People who make assertions like P in conditions C are usually saying something true.

Therefore,

3) P

That something like the above is the more perspicuous representation of the reasoning involved in reliance on testimony is also suggested by careful characterizations of the supposed fallacy of appealing to authority. I began this paper by observing that we rely on authority for much of what we believe. It would indeed be a bit unfortunate if this reliance involved some sort of fallacy. The writers of texts on informal fallacies understand clearly that they had better be careful in characterizing the fallacy in question. As a result, they typically describe it as the fallacy (better, mistake) of relying on the testimony of someone who is not in fact a reliable authority concerning the subject of his testimony. An *epistemically* more sensitive characterization of the mistake would presumably make reference instead to the epistemic position of the person relying on the testimony. An *epistemic* mistake is committed only if one relies on an authority when one has no reason to believe that the person in question is reliable. But if that's the mistake that constitutes the fallacy of appeal to authority, the clear implication is that when one is *not* making the mistake one *does* have some good reason to believe that the person is reliably testifying—that is, one has some good reason to believe our premises 1) and 2) above.

Earlier, I suggested that some recent work on testimony appears to focus on whether testimonial inference is fundamental or derivative. I'm now suggesting that this way of putting the controversy is needlessly confusing. *In general*, there may be no useful distinction between fundamental and derivative principles of reasoning. It's harmless enough to suggest that there is an epistemic rule permitting an inference from the litmus paper turning red in the solution to the conclusion that the solution is acidic, a rule which had to be learned from experience, and is in that sense derivative. But it is surely more perspicuous to suggest that there is no rule of inference *at all* sanctioning an inference from the proposition that the paper is red to the conclusion that the solution is acidic. Rather, the representation of the reasoning in question is enthymematic. It is only in conjunction with certain background information that the premise describing the litmus paper allows us to draw the conclusion. The most obvious unstated premise is one that describes a correlation between the change in the litmus paper and the character of the solution. The reasoning, when described fully, is either deductively valid (if the premise takes the form of a universal proposition describing the correlation) or inductive (if the premise describes merely observed or statistical correlations). Either way there is no need to recognize "secondary" epistemic principles sanctioning "litmus reasoning." We need only keep in mind that our descriptions of our reasoning are often (indeed, in ordinary discourse, almost always) enthymematic.

So the most perspicuous characterization of the *traditional* internalist's approach to understanding the role of testimony in acquiring justified belief is probably that strictly speaking there is no testimonial inference at all. When we make explicit critical unstated premises, we find that the *reasoning* that takes account of testimony is just some other familiar sort of deductive or nondeductive reasoning that employs at least one premise describing what other people say.

As we noted earlier, on the classical internalist/foundationalist model, the way in which information about what others say can legitimately be taken into account in reaching conclusions is complicated indeed. On a radical empiricism we first need to reach a justified belief that there are real mind-independent sounds and marks (based on what we seem to hear and see). I am not about to discuss the problem of perception here, so we'll just suppose for the sake of argument that we don't have any difficulty getting to knowledge of an external, mind-independent reality. But our work has just begun. We need some reason to believe that those sounds and marks are meaningful symbols.

What is involved in rationally believing that sounds or marks are representations of reality? That also is a question that would take us far afield. To answer it we'd need a general account of representation and intentionality. On classical views (which I think are almost obviously correct), we need to draw a distinction between signs that represent only by convention and signs that are in some sense "natural."[7] "Cat" represents a certain kind of animal but only because human beings *assigned* the mark or sound a certain task. If we collectively decided that we wanted that symbol to represent something else, we would need only to reach an alternative agreement. It used to seem obvious to almost all philosophers that not all symbols could represent by convention. Indeed, it seems plausible to suppose that unless we could independently think of both the symbol and what we use it to stand for, conventional representation would be impossible. But if that's right and thought itself represents only conventionally, we face a vicious regress. To assign thought its representational role we'd have to think of the thought and that for which it stands. To end the regress we need to recognize that there is a way of representing the world that does not rely on convention. On the traditional view, conventional representation presupposes a "language" of thought that represents naturally.

If the above is right, we now need an analysis of "natural" representation. In virtue of what does something X represent naturally something else Y? The internalism/externalism debate in epistemology is paralleled by a similar debate in philosophy of mind. Painting with a very broad stroke, most externalists are naturalists who attempt to understand representation employing causal analyses. X represents Y in virtue of the fact that X is nomologically tied to Y in certain ways. The devil is, of course, in the details. Information theoretic accounts have labored long and hard to tell us how we single out from among the vastly complex chain of causes and effects that produce some brain state the one that is represented by the brain state. Depending on just how the account goes, it *may* be possible to get *language* back on the side of natural representation. The import of much of Putnam's work (1975, 1978, 1988) (and before him Sellars (1954)) is to deny that one needs a radically different account of how thought represents from the account one gives of how language represents. The use of word tokens can stand at the end of causal chains just as surely as can images in the mind, or neurons firing in the brain, and if they occupy the right place in the right causal chains they can represent in precisely the same way that images or brain states can represent.

Waiting in the wings for the collapse of naturalistic accounts are "magical" theories—theories that maintain that certain states of mind (and *only* states of mind) have intrinsic and sui generis *content*.[8] Intentional states are unlike anything else simply in virtue of having the capacity to correspond to reality. That capacity to correspond defies any sort of reductive analysis. The view is derided as "magical" just because the critic is convinced that these peculiar states are dragged into the picture as a kind of *deus ex machina* to solve fundamental problems concerning intentionality. Of course, almost every philosopher who engages in analysis will admit that analysis must begin *somewhere*. There must be conceptual building blocks if we are to understand anything, and proponents of the magical theory should not apologize for the fact that something as mysterious as thought cannot be assimilated to any other natural phenomenon.

Again, we cannot expect to resolve the most fundamental questions concerning intentionality here. Our only concern is to point out that the nature of the epistemic task we need to complete in construing sounds or marks as testimony seems to depend directly on the account of intentionality one puts forth. The naturalists will suppose that the task of discovering that certain sounds or marks have the content they do is the task of discovering complex facts about their causal origin. The proponent of the magical theory who thinks that only thought represents naturally will be convinced that the key to correctly interpreting apparent language is to come up with the right hypothesis about what states of mind occur in the person (or people) who produce the relevant sounds or marks.

Suppose, for the sake of argument, that the internalist is right. The meanings of sounds or marks are to be found in the head, or better in the minds, of those who produce those sounds and marks. To interpret reasonably those sounds or marks we now need to solve the problem of other minds. We need to find some reason to suppose that those marks have the meaning we take them to have. That will minimally involve figuring out what conscious states were involved in their production. When the language we are interpreting is our own—without begging the question, when the sounds or marks appear to be of the same type as those we ourselves use to express thoughts—one might suppose that our best hope is to rely on some version of an argument from analogy or an argument to the best explanation. And indeed, I think that's probably right. The symbols "There's a mountain nearby" as used by me express a thought with which I am introspectively acquainted. Suppose I'm on the first expeditionary trip to Mars and upon setting foot on the planet immediately notice clearly etched on a rock face the symbols "There is a mountain nearby." While amazed and bewildered, I have no doubt that I would be irresistibly inclined to think that this was indeed a message, and that the message had the same content as the message in my language. I'd probably also think that there was a decent chance that the mountain was nearby. And notice that I'd probably think all this even if I had absolutely *no* further explanation of how the marks appeared. My thought would probably be that it would be such a bizarre coincidence that marks with that form and syntax appeared without having *some* connection to my own symbols with the meanings they have, that any other hypothesis is simply unbelievable. Note well that I don't have to be very clear at all about the connection in question. It could be that what I take to be our respective symbols acquired the meanings they have due to some unknown common cause. It could be that one of us somehow caused the other to adopt the relevant conventions. But the existence of some connection or other just seems more plausible than the detailed convergence of form and syntax that would otherwise be mysterious.

The above is not intended to be a very convincing argument. At the risk of setting aside all of the really difficult epistemological problems, I'll again simply beg off solving the difficult questions concerning arguments by analogy and arguments to the best explanation that would need to be explored in depth as part of any serious attempt to uncover the epistemic justification we possess for interpreting the familiar symbols we encounter. I will note in passing that the approach sketched above is committed to rejecting Davidsonian (1984) arguments (also embraced by Coady) for the idea that we must inevitably presuppose the *truth* of what people say (and also that what they say has a certain content) if we are to arrive at translations. If what is said above is correct, there may be a much cruder way of arriving at conclusions about meaning that are at least prima facie plausible.

On the traditional approach, reaching a rational conclusion about what symbols mean and that they are used as *assertions* is, of course, not the last step in the implicit reasoning involved in reliance on testimony. We need some reason to believe that the assertions are likely to be true. Given a radical empiricism, that reason will need to be traced again back to what we know about ourselves. Setting aside again some more extreme skeptical concerns,[9] we find ourselves in epistemic situations in which there are certain truths that it is pretty easy for us to come to know. When we have reason to believe that there is another person in a similar epistemic situation, we have reason to believe that that person would have similar access to those kinds of truths. For example, when conscious I know when I have a headache and when I don't. I expect that if you are remotely like me you are similarly positioned to know whether or not you have a headache. I also know of myself that I don't usually lie about such matters, and in the absence of any other information, therefore, I will, based on analogy, take what you say about your headache as a pretty good indicator of truth.

I deliberately started with testimony about the simplest of truths. Things get more complicated the more controversial the background assumptions about epistemic position get, and the more controversial background assumptions about motives to mislead are. All this mirrors precisely the controversies we encounter concerning whether or not to rely on testimony. Hume was quite right in suggesting that there are all kinds of live hypotheses as to why people might testify falsely concerning the occurrence of miracles. Alibis provided by mothers and lovers of the accused don't carry nearly as much weight as alibis provided by people the accused doesn't even know. The testimony of other philosophers concerning the truth of their philosophical views carries almost no epistemic weight at all for philosophers when it comes to evaluating those views.

None of this is very original. While I do think that the traditional approach to understanding the evidential role of testimony is quite right—indeed almost obviously right—my primary concern in this paper is to see what *alternatives* are available to both internalist and externalists. More specifically how might one try to find room within one's epistemology for genuine *fundamental* testimonial inference? The search for sui generis fundamental epistemic principles that sanction moves from hearing testimony to forming beliefs might be motivated partly by phenomenology. Classical foundationalists have often been accused of radically over-intellectualizing the processes by which we form beliefs. The view that we reach conclusions about the objective external world based on truths we discover about subjective and fleeting experience has often been criticized on the grounds that we rarely even pay attention to subjective appearance. There may be an appearance/reality distinction, but it takes a certain skill—the kind of skill acquired by painters, for example—to even notice the many and subtle ways in which appearance is constantly shifting. The person who actually wanders around *consciously* inferring truths about his physical environment from truths about appearance is probably not destined to stay that long in this world. If you can't react instinctively to sensory stimulation with the quick realization that the bus is bearing down on you, you've had it.

Just as it seems implausible to suppose that our beliefs about objects directly in front of us are produced through inference from truths we notice about appearance, so also it might seem implausible to suppose that in relying on testimony we travel anything like the long and winding road postulated by the radical empiricist. When I'm on the golf course and hear someone yell "Fore," I'd better duck. If I stand there trying to complete the steps of a rational reconstruction of my ultimate reliance on the "testimony" provided by that golfer's warning, I'm in serious danger.

It's not clear that the traditional approach need worry much about this alleged phenomenological data. Earlier, I suggested that there is no difficulty in supposing that dispositional beliefs can play a critical causal role in both producing and sustaining belief. I need not consciously rely on background information in forming some conclusion for my background beliefs to be playing the critical causal role. Just as I have background beliefs about truths that can serve as implicit premises, so also I may have background beliefs about inferential connections. Furthermore, those dispositional beliefs may concern particular inferences rather than general epistemic rules. If anything is obvious, it is that the mind is extraordinarily complex and it would surely not be surprising if much of the inference that takes place does not take place at the conscious level.

Still, one might worry about the fact that the traditional foundationalist's reconstruction of reliance on testimony requires so many problematic steps. Traditional foundationalism generally is fertile ground for skepticism. It might be a relief if we could understand the way in which testimony contributes to rational belief in a more straightforward way. But the world doesn't always cooperate to make life easy, and we need to figure out whether it is at all plausible to suppose that there is a more straightforward epistemic route from hearing testimony to forming rational beliefs. In what follows, I want to emphasize that the prospects for finding that more straightforward route are directly related to one's position on the internalism/externalism debate and one's corresponding position on the content and modal status of epistemic principles.

THE MODAL STATUS OF EPISTEMIC PRINCIPLES AND INTERNALIST AND EXTERNALIST PROSPECTS FOR RECOGNIZING INDEPENDENT TESTIMONIAL REASONING

We haven't said much about epistemic principles. I've hinted already that the distinction between fundamental and derivative epistemic principles might itself be spurious. Arguments that employ so-called derivative epistemic principles are probably better thought of as enthymematic arguments governed by legitimate epistemic principles that license the inference from premises to conclusion. Strictly speaking derivative epistemic "principles" aren't epistemic principles at all.

Epistemic principles can be thought of and described in a number of different ways. Consider the following:

1) If S has property X then S is justified in believing P.
2) S's having property X makes prima facie probable P for S.

Property X can be understood as broadly as you like. I don't want to prejudice any questions concerning what can justify a belief. So property X can be the property of having other beliefs, having other justified beliefs, being in a certain conscious state, having a brain state with a certain causal origin, or what have you. Principles governing inferential justification presumably license inference from believing one proposition justifiably to believing another. Principles governing noninferential justification license belief when one is in certain non-doxastic states. 1) and 2) might be just alternative ways of saying the same thing, but it is nevertheless important to be clear about which epistemic concept one takes to be conceptually fundamental. Chisholm and his followers, for example, clearly take as primitive certain epistemic properties of belief—specifically the comparative property of *being more reasonable to believe than.* Keynes (1921) and his followers took the most fundamental concept in epistemology to be the logical concept of probability. On Keynes's view there are relations of making probable holding between propositions that are directly analogous to relations of entailment holding between propositions.[10] When we make a reasonable inference, the rationality of belief in our conclusion is in part a function of our ability to "see" the relation of making probable holding between our premises and our conclusion. On Keynes's view, propositions asserting probability relations are *necessary* truths knowable *a priori.* Such a view would be a godsend to inferential internalists who are convinced that inferential justification requires awareness of probabilistic connections between premises and conclusions. The inferential internalists must obviously terminate a potential regress when it comes to getting justification for believing that the relevant inferential connections obtain. If propositions asserting those connections are necessary truths knowable a priori, it is plausible to suppose that knowledge of such connections can be foundational.

There are, of course, alternatives to construing the probability appealed to in 2) as Keynesean logical probability. One could hold that the relevant probability has something to do with frequency. Roughly, the idea is that we'd have to assign exemplifying the pair of properties, being X and believing P to a pair *kind*. We could then understand the probability claim as asserting that usually when the first member of the pair kind is instantiated by a subject, the second member (the belief) is true. The attempt to construe the probability appealed to in 2) in terms of frequency (or propensity) in effect makes 2) as a statement of an epistemic principle a version of reliabilism.[11] Any view that takes epistemic principles to be assertions of probability and then understands the relevant probability in terms of frequency will inevitably render epistemic principles *contingent* truths knowable only *a posteriori*. With such a view one would do well to eschew inferential internalism for there will be no plausible way to terminate a regress of justification that arises in connection with the possibility of justifying belief in inferential connections.

With the above as background, let us return to testimony. As we saw, on one rather natural understanding of the role of testimony in justifying belief there is no need to recognize epistemic principles taking the form of 1) or 2) that govern specifically testimony. Reasoning from testimony can easily be construed as a species of some other familiar sort of reasoning (inductive reasoning or reasoning to the best explanation), a form of reasoning which includes among its *premises* information about what other people assert. Is there an alternative to that view? The answer, of course, will depend in part on what one takes an epistemic principle to assert and on what one takes its modal status to be. Let's consider some candidates for an epistemic principle governing testimony.

T) When R hears a sentence "S" (e.g. the words "There is a dog outside") in the sort of conditions that characterize a context of genuine assertion, that makes probable for R that S (e.g. that there is a dog outside.)

T) certainly seems an unlikely candidate for the kind of synthetic necessary truth that a Keynesean would take a genuine epistemic principle to assert. Clearly there are all sorts of *possible* situations in which hearing those words would not make even prima facie probable (in any sense relevant to epistemology) the truth of the proposition that there is a dog outside. For one thing, there are all sorts of situations in which those words have an entirely different meaning.

Don't confuse the above with a quite different and clearly bad argument. One might suppose that *no* epistemic principle asserting a *probability* connection could be a necessary truth. After all, the fact that E only makes probable P suggests that E *can* be true while P is false. But if that is so then it can hardly be a necessary truth that E makes probable P. But that is to confuse the modal status of the conditional (If P then Q) with the modal status of the claim that P makes (prima facie) probable Q. The fact that I vividly seem to remember having a headache earlier might make it probable that I did have the headache. Can we imagine a world in which my seeming to remember that experience doesn't make it prima facie likely that I had the experience? Well, I can certainly imagine a world in which I seemed to remember having the experience when I didn't have it. I can probably even imagine a world in which the *conjunction* of my seeming to remember having the headache together with some other proposition (e.g. that my memory is hopelessly bad and I'm prone to "hallucinatory" memory states) doesn't make probable that I had the headache. But all that is perfectly consistent with its being true—indeed, *necessarily* true—that my seeming to remember having the headache makes it prima facie likely that I had the headache. Again, it is not the least bit plausible to suppose it is a necessary truth that my hearing the sounds "there is a dog outside" makes it likely for me that there is a dog outside and if genuine epistemic principles are necessary truths, T) isn't a genuine epistemic principle.

The situation is much more complicated if we adopt the position that the relevant epistemic principle simply asserts a statistical correlation of some sort between the processing of certain kinds of input and the truth of output beliefs. On most versions of reliabilism there is *no* a priori restriction on what can count as an unconditionally or a conditionally reliable belief-forming process. Plantinga (2000) points out, quite correctly, that there *might* be a Holy Spirit who is causally responsible for one's acquiring true belief in the existence of God. Should such a being exist and be causally active in producing true beliefs about God's existence, the resulting belief would be a prime candidate for a noninferentially justified belief (noninferentially, because the input, by hypothesis, involves no justified beliefs).

Have speakers evolved in such a way that when they take as input auditory experiences of certain symbols they immediately and unreflectively believe what they take the symbols to assert? And critically, does this process typically result in true beliefs? It is not perhaps wildly implausible to suppose that there may be such ways of forming beliefs that *are* generally reliable. A great deal (as always) depends on how the frequentist/reliabilist addresses the generality problem—how they specify in detail the relevant input–output mechanism. But if one includes enough mundane situations—situations in which people give you relatively unproblematic information about the time of day, the weather, their names, their ages, and the like—it may be plausible to suppose that something like T) is true when the probability is understood in terms of frequency. It is, of course, an empirical question. In fact, as I suggested earlier, I suspect that there are all sorts of background beliefs playing a critical causal role in the resulting "output" beliefs. I doubt therefore that T) accurately describes an actual process of forming beliefs that we employ. Even if T) were true, if we are never actually induced to believe a proposition based on the satisfaction of the conditions described in T)'s antecedent, we are not getting justified beliefs by implicitly "following" T).[12] But I'm a philosopher not a psychologist/sociologist/cognitive scientist. One can at least imagine our evolving in such a way that we are now so constituted that we skip whatever intermediate premises upon which the traditional foundationalist thought we needed to rely.

From the perspective of one who takes epistemic principles to state necessary truths, I said that T) above is a rather pathetic candidate for an epistemic principle concerning testimony. But there are, of course, others. One could, for example, modify T) as follows:

> T*) When S hears someone say "There is a dog outside" *and* rationally takes that sentence to be a sincere assertion that there is a dog outside, then it is prima facie reasonable for S to believe that there is a dog outside.

On one way of thinking about it, T*) isn't much more implausible than doxastic conservatism—the view that a proposition acquires a certain prima facie probability for S from the mere fact that S believes it. On T*) one takes the fact that someone believes P to make it prima facie probable that P is true. One must emphasize again that the proposition that someone's sincerely assenting to P makes probable P does not imply that P is probable relative to *everything* we know. As we saw earlier, one must take account of all sorts of other relevant truths in calculating the probability of P relative to one's *total* body of evidence. *Controversial* assertions automatically lose whatever probability is conferred on them from the fact that some person sincerely assents to the proposition asserted. What makes an assertion controversial, trivially, is that there isn't much agreement on its truth—some people assert the proposition while others assert its negation. So P might be made probable by the fact that S sincerely asserts it while not-P is made probable by the fact R asserts it. Relative to the fact that roughly equal numbers of people assent as dissent from P, and those facts alone, P is presumably no more likely than not-P. Relative to important information I might possess, P's probability might be 1 regardless of how many people believe not-P (if for example P is a proposition describing some obvious fact about my current conscious states).

Is T*) a candidate for the sort of fundamental epistemic principle to which a Keynesean would be committed? Well I suggested that it is not much more implausible than principles of epistemic conservatism. But then I've never found principles of epistemic conservatism very plausible. It has never seemed to be very plausible to suppose that the mere fact that someone believes a proposition (even if I am that person) confers the least likelihood on the proposition's being true (leaving aside those trivial cases in which the having of the belief entails its truth—e.g. the belief that there are beliefs). So I'm not inclined to think that the Keynesean inferential internalists should recognize T*) as a true epistemic probability principle having as much credibility as a principle of induction or a principle of memory. But the issue really now hinges on deep and difficult methodological issues in epistemology. In his famous discussion of the problem of the criterion Chisholm (1966) suggests that we simply have to decide whether or not we are going to take skepticism seriously. If we do not—if we take the fact that a philosophical view leads to skepticism as a *reductio* of that view—then we should adjust our epistemic principles until they allow us to achieve our non-skeptical conclusions. If one thinks that the traditional story of how to trust the testimony of others is fatally compromised by the need to rely on inductive arguments that proceed from the limited sample of one's own case, then one may simply need to supplement the epistemic principles that entitle us to form beliefs by adding to them a principle like T*). But we can't be Keyneseans (or Chisholmians, for that matter) and ignore the supposed modal status of the principles we add to our stock of epistemic principles in order to achieve desired epistemic ends. Though Chisholm is more coy than is Keynes, both will in the final analysis insist that epistemic principles state necessary truths knowable a priori. And it is an odd justification of commitment to a necessary truth that we "need" it to get where we want to go. The principle really should strike you as being necessary in precisely the same way that other synthetic necessary truths (What is red all over is not blue all over) strike you as necessary.

Once again T*) is a perfectly plausible candidate for a fundamental epistemic principle on an externalist/frequency understanding of the reference to probability. I'm not really interested in acquiring the empirical evidence that would be required in order to discover that people actually do process data to form beliefs where the processing would accord with such a principle. That's a task better left to cognitive scientists, psychologists, or perhaps evolutionary theorists.

CONCLUSION

The plausibility of recognizing a general and sui generis epistemic principle sanctioning testimonial inference is directly proportional to the plausibility of an externalist understanding of probability claims. Let reliabilism be a paradigm of externalism. Just as reliabilism places no a priori restrictions on what kinds of beliefs might be *noninferentially* justified (because there is no end of *possible* belief-independent unconditionally reliable belief-forming processes), so also reliabilism places no a priori restrictions on what interestingly different kinds of *inferentially* justified beliefs there are (because there is no end of possible belief-dependent reliable belief-producing processes). I have argued elsewhere (1995) that the very ease with which noninferential and inferential justification proliferates on most externalist views might give one pause. If one insists that inferential justification requires awareness of inferential connections, then the prospects for finding epistemic principles sanctioning sui generis testimony inferences are slim.

REFERENCES

Addis, Laird (1989), *Natural Signs* (Philadelphia: Temple University Press).

Bergmann, Gustav (1964), *Logic and Reality* (Madisons University of Wisconsin Press).

Brewer, Bill (1999), *Perception and Reason* (Oxford: Oxford University Press).

Coady, C. A. J. (1992), *Testimony* (Oxford: Oxford University Press).

Chisholm, Roderick (1966), *Theory of Knowledge* (Englewood Cliffs, NJ: Prentice-Hall).

Davidson, Donald (1984), *Inquiries into Truth and Interpretation* (Oxford: Clarendon Press).

Fumerton, Richard (1985), *Metaphysical and Epistemological Problems of Perception* (Lincoln, Nebr.: University of Nebraska Press).

—— (1995), *Metaepistemology and Skepticism* (Lanham, Md.: Rowman and Littlefield).

—— (2002), *Realism and the Correspondence Theory of Truth* (Lanham, Md.: Rowman and Littlefield).

—— (2004*a*), 'Inferential Internalism and the Presuppositions of Skeptical Argument', in Richard Schantz (ed.), *The Externalist Challenge* (De Gruyter).

—— (2004*b*), 'Epistemic Probability', *Philosophical Issues*, 14 (2004).

Goldman, Alvin (1979), 'What Is Justified Belief?', in George S. Pappas (ed.), *Justification and Knowledge* (Dordrech): D. Reidel Pub. Co.)

—— (1986), *Epistemology and Cognition* (Cambridge, Mass.: Harvard University Press).

—— (1988), 'Strong and Weak Justification', in James Tomberlin (ed.), *Philosophical Perspectives 2: Epistemology* (Ridgeview Publishing Co.).

Huemer, Mike (2002), 'Fumerton's Principle of Inferential Justification', *Journal of Philosophical Research*, 27: 329–40.

Keynes, John (1921), *A Treatise on Probability* (New York: MacMillan).

Plantinga, Alvin (2000), *Warranted Christian Belief* (Oxford: Oxford University Press).

Russell, Bertrand (1959), *The Problems of Philosophy* (Oxford: Oxford University Press).

Sellars, Wilfred (1957), 'Intentionality and the Mental', in Herbert Feigl, Michael Scriver, and Grover Maxwell (eds.), *Minnesota Studies in the Philosophy of Science*, vol. ii (University of Minnesota Press).

NOTES

1. See Coady (1992) for an extended discussion of different sorts of testimony and a definition (1992: 32, 42) of what testimony involves. Coady's definition is problematic in that he seems to argue that S's statement constitutes testimony only when that S has the competence, authority, or credentials to state truly that P. In order to evaluate the epistemic worth of testimony we surely need a way of characterizing it that leaves open the competency of the person who puts forth the testimony.

2. That the two are distinct doesn't mean that they aren't related in various ways. On most views a justified belief must be based on adequate justification, and the basing relation is often construed as causal.

3. See again Coady (1992). I'm not sure what precisely Coady's final view is. He sometimes seems to suggest that one can know a priori that testimony is generally reliable

or at least prima facie credible (1992: 96). In other places he seems only to suggest that testimony is a fundamental source of evidence on a par with perception and memory (1992: 145). I'll have more to say about the implicit distinction between fundamental and derivative sources of evidence in what follows.

4. See e.g. Brewer (1999).

5. See Fumerton (1995, 2004*a*, 2004*b*) for an extended discussion of inferential internalism.

6. I have profited enormously and been influenced heavily by Mike Huemer's (2002) thoughts on these matters.

7. The locution "natural sign" is used by Addis (1989). A version of the view defended by Addis was defended by Bergmann (1964). And variations of it are defended by Fumerton (1985, 1995, 2002).

8. The expression "magical" theory was coined by Putnam.

9. In characterizing the skepticism as extreme, I do not mean to diminish its threat.

10. With the emphasis on *analogous*. There are, of course, important differences between the quasi-logical relation of making probable that Keynes took to hold between propositions. From the fact that P entails Q it follows that the conjunction of P and any other proposition entails Q. From the fact that P makes probable Q it does not follow that the conjunction of P with any other proposition makes probable Q.

11. By far the most sophisticated versions of reliabilism were put forth by Goldman (1979, 1986, 1988). Note the discussion of justification rules in Goldman (1986) and the similarity between that view and the view that takes epistemic probability to be defined statistically.

12. Put another way, philosophers typically insist that for a belief that P to be justified by a belief that E, the belief that E must be based on the belief that E. If basing is to be understood, at least partially, in causal terms, then if that actual cause of my belief that P involves far more than my belief that E it is misleading to suggest that my belief that P is based on my belief that E.

4

Liberal Fundamentalism and Its Rivals

Peter Graham

Many hold that perception is a source of epistemically basic (direct) belief: for justification, perceptual beliefs do not need positive inferential support from other justified beliefs, especially from beliefs about one's current sensory episodes. Perceptual beliefs can, however, be defeated or undermined by other things one believes, and so to be justified in the end there must be no undefeated undermining grounds. Similarly for memory and introspection.[1]

Testimony-based beliefs are as indispensable as perception, memory, and introspection-based beliefs.[2] Many of our testimony-based beliefs are epistemically justified. Indeed, most of what we justifiably believe we believe, at least in part, on the basis of comprehending and accepting the word of others.

The testimony debate is largely over whether testimony-based beliefs are epistemically inferential or, like perception, memory, and introspection-based beliefs, epistemically direct. One side holds that a testimony-based belief is justified just in case the hearer has no reason to believe that the speaker is either insincere or unreliable. The other holds that a testimony-based belief is justified only if the hearer does possess positive reasons to think that the speaker is either sincere or reliable or both.[3] Advocates of the direct view include Burge (1993, 1997, 1999), Coady (1973, 1992), Dummett (1993), Goldberg (Chapter 6 in this volume), McDowell (1998), Quinton (1973), Ross (1986), Rysiew (2000), Stevenson (1993), Strawson (1994), and Weiner (2003) among others. It goes back to Reid. Those who reject the direct include Adler (2002), Audi (1997, 2002, 2004, Chapter 1 in this volume), Kusch (2002), Lackey (2003, Chapter 8 in this volume), Lehrer (1994), Lyons (1997), Faulkner (2000), Fricker (1987, 1994, 1995, 2002, Chapter 10 in this volume), and Root (1998, 2001), among others. It goes back to Hume.

An earlier version of this paper circulated under the title "Reductionism and Anti-Reductionism about Testimony". Another version circulated under the title "Fundamentalism and its Rivals". I have significantly altered the terminology from previous versions. I hope I have also made a number of improvements. For comments that led to changes, I am grateful to Jonathan Adler, Jennifer Lackey, Paul Hurley, Ted Hinchman, Brian Keely, Peter Thielke, Duncan Pritchard, and especially Peter Kung and Robert Audi. The two referees for this volume indirectly prompted substantial changes. I'm grateful to both.

In this essay I articulate and defend a version of the direct view. I shall call it 'Liberal Fundamentalism'. The Liberal Fundamentalist holds (to be qualified below) that it is a priori necessary that comprehending an attester's presentation-as-true that P confers justification on the recipient's belief that P. There is a Strong and a Weak version. The Strong version holds that (absent defeat) the event or state of comprehending the attester's presentation-as-true that P provides *on balance* justification for the belief that P, whereas the Weak version holds that the justification provided or conferred may fall short of on balance justification (even if undefeated).

This paper has two parts. The first articulates Liberal Fundamentalism and some of its central rivals. The second articulates and defends the Weak version.

The theme of the first part is that what one says about the testimony debate is driven in large part by one's overall theoretical orientation on the nature of epistemic justification, including one's epistemology of epistemology. The theme of the second is that one particular version of the direct view (Weak Liberal Fundamentalism) is more plausible than two of its immediate rivals (Strong Liberal Fundamentalism and Moderate Fundamentalism).

I use three new ideas. The first is a list of different versions of foundationalism. The second is a new taxonomy of theories of epistemic justification. The third is the distinction between *pro tanto* and on balance justification.

LIBERAL FUNDAMENTALISM

Four Versions of Foundationalism

Liberal *Fundamentalism* is a combination of two doctrines. The first is about *which* epistemic principles (given below) are true, and the second is about *why* they are true. The first doctrine I call 'Liberal *foundationalism*' and the second I call 'Intuitionism'. In the rest of this section I articulate Liberal foundationalism. In the next I explain Intuitionism.

Different versions of foundationalism are defined by which of the following epistemic principles they accept as true:

(AP)   If it seems to S upon understanding P that P is self-evident or necessary, then the belief that P is prima facie pro tanto justified.

(INT)   If it introspectively seems to S as if S is occurrently having a sensory, perceptual or otherwise conscious experience such and such, and this causes or sustains in the normal way the belief that S is experiencing such and such, then that confers justification on S's belief.

(DED)   If S believes P and believes (P entails Q) and believes Q on the basis of inferring Q from P and (P entails Q), then S's belief that Q is conditionally justified.

(MEM) If S seems to remember that P and this causes or sustains in the normal way S's belief that P, then that confers justification on S's belief that P.

(EIND) If S possesses a sufficiently large and representative (nonbiased) inductive base where all (most) Fs are Gs, then were S to infer that all (most) Fs are Gs on that basis, then S's belief that all (most) Fs are Gs would be conditionally justified by the inference.

(IBE) If S possesses one explanation that better explains S's evidence than any other available alternative explanation, then S is justified in believing that explanation on the basis of the evidence.

(PER) If S's perceptual system represents an object x as F (where F is a perceptible property), and this causes or sustains in the normal way S's belief of x that it is F, then that confers justification on S's belief that x is F.

(TEST) If a subject S (seemingly) comprehends a (seeming) presentation-as-true by a (seeming) speaker that P, and if that causes or sustains in the normal way S's belief that P, then that confers justification on S's belief that P.

One can find four versions of foundationalism embraced in the literature: Reactionary, Conservative, Moderate, and Liberal foundationalism (the labels are new, the positions are familiar). The Reactionary accepts the first three but no more, the Conservative the first five, the Moderate the first six, and the Liberal all seven.

Reactionary: **AP, INT, DED**
Conservative: **AP, INT, DED, MEM, EIND, IBE**
Moderate: **AP, INT, DED, MEM, EIND, IBE, PER**
Liberal: **AP, INT, DED, MEM, EIND, IBE, PER, TEST**

The Liberal foundationalist thus has three foundationalist rivals. The pure coherentist is a rival to *all* foundationalist views. The pure coherentist rejects the direct/inferential distinction altogether, and so rejects all of the principles listed above. The pure coherentist embraces only **COH**:

(COH) If the belief that P is a member of S's coherent set of beliefs R, then S's belief that P is justified to the degree that R is coherent.

I set aside coherentism about testimony in what follows. I intend to treat it elsewhere.

Liberal *Fundamentalists* are Liberal *foundationalists* that give one of four possible answers to *why* the epistemic principles they embrace are *true*. I characterize the four possible answers next.

Four Theoretical Perspectives

Elsewhere I have developed and defended a new taxonomy of theories of epistemic justification (forthcoming). On my new taxonomy, there are four different theories on the nature of epistemic justification. Each theory or perspective provides an answer to *why* any epistemic principle is true. I shall describe and make use of that taxonomy here.

The standard taxonomy relies upon two distinctions: foundationalism vs. coherentism and internalism vs. externalism. Though the standard taxonomy is useful and important, my new taxonomy relies on two different distinctions. The first concerns the relationship between justification and truth. The second concerns the epistemic (a priori or empirical) and modal (necessary or continent) status of the epistemic principles.

The first distinction involves the relation between justification and truth. Everyone agrees that epistemic justification is connected to truth (Audi 1988; BonJour 1999, 2002; Burge 2004). Disagreement emerges when one asks *how* it is connected to truth. There are two possible answers: either justification *makes* a belief objectively more likely to be true, or justification *properly aims* belief at the truth (Audi 1988). An "Actual Result" theorist holds the former, a "Proper Aim" theorist holds the latter. Actual Result theorists are like consequentialists about moral rightness where an act is right provided that it has good consequences, and Proper Aim theorists are like non-consequentialists. One way to get a grip on the distinction is to reflect on the demon-worlds objection to reliabilism. If you think a subject fooled by an evil demon may still enjoy justified perceptual, memorial, inductive, abductive, and other beliefs (even though they are not de facto reliably held), then you are more likely to be a Proper Aim theorist. If, on the contrary, you think those beliefs cannot be justified because not likely to be true, then you are more likely to be an Actual Result theorist. To telegraph, the Liberal Fundamentalist is a Proper Aim theorist.

The second distinction involves the epistemic and modal status of the epistemic principles. The "Fundamentalist" holds that the true epistemic principles are conceptually necessary, a priori knowable truths. The "Non-Fundamentalist" rejects this; the true epistemic principles are contingent, only empirically knowable truths. For example, if **PER** is true, the Fundamentalist thinks it is an a priori necessary, conceptual truth, whereas the Non-Fundamentalist thinks it is only a contingent, empirical truth. If **PER** is known to be true, the Fundamentalist thinks this is a piece of philosophical knowledge, whereas the Non-Fundamentalist thinks this is a piece of empirical knowledge, part of the subject-matter of the natural or social sciences.

The two distinctions are orthogonal; they determine four possible (and familiar) theories of justification: *Cartesianism, Reliabilism, Intuitionism*, and *Pragmatism* (see Fig. 4.1).

	Actual-Result	Proper-Aim
Fundamentalism	Cartesianism	Intuitionism
Non-Fundamentalism	Reliabilism	Pragmatism

Figure 4.1 Four Theoretical Perspectives on Justification.

Using our definitions of the two distinctions, we can define the four positions:

Cartesianism: a belief is justified only if held in a way which is a priori known or knowable to *either* necessarily make the belief true *or* make the belief true more likely than not in all worlds. The way held confers justification only if it is a priori knowable that it is *either* **every-instance** reliable *or* **all-worlds** reliable.

Reliabilism: a belief is justified only if held in a way that de facto makes the belief more likely than not to be true in the actual circumstances of use. The way held confers justification only if **de facto** reliable.

Intuitionism: a belief is justified only if held in a way that is a priori known or knowable to constitute properly aiming belief at truth, where "properly aiming belief at truth" means conformity to a priori necessary epistemic principles (listed above), and does not require de facto or all-worlds reliability.[4]

Pragmatism: a belief is justified only if held in a way that *de facto* constitutes properly aiming the belief at truth, where "properly aiming belief at truth" means conformity to our deepest held norms of proper belief formation (where "our" can mean the subject, the discipline, the community, the tradition, or the species).

Although each perspective, as stated, only places a necessary condition on justification, I shall, for the sake of illumination, treat each perspective as placing both a necessary and sufficient condition on justification.

Each perspective places conditions on what it takes for a belief held in a certain way to enjoy justification. Each perspective explains why an epistemic principle is true if true. It will also explain why a principle is false if false. It is easiest to see this in the case of the Cartesian. The Cartesian will only accept, at best, **AP**, **INT**, and **DED**, for only (some) a priori insight, introspection of one's current sensory episodes, and deductive reasoning, are likely candidates for ways of forming and holding beliefs that pass the Cartesian test; they are the only three ways of holding belief likely to be reliable in all worlds. The Cartesian will reject the other principles as false.

Which principles the other three theoretical perspectives would accept is much harder to determine. The Intuitionist accepts only those principles that are a priori, conceptually necessary truths, but it is not obvious right at the start which ones pass that test and which ones do not. One aim of this essay is to contribute to sorting out just which considerations are relevant and which ones are not to determining whether **TEST**, for example, is a priori necessary.[5]

The Reliabilist accepts only those principles that govern *de facto* reliable methods of belief acquisition and retention. It is not the job of the philosopher to figure out which ones are reliable, but rather the job of the cognitive scientist. Which ones will show up on the Reliabilist's list is an open question until the empirical inquiry is complete. It is the job of the philosopher to analyze justification and reliability; it is the job of the scientist to discover which processes are reliable.

The Pragmatist accepts only those principles that govern methods of belief acquisition and retention that are individually or socially embraced as the right methods. Which ones will show up on her list, is to be decided by the individual, the sociologist or the anthropologist.[6]

Liberal Fundamentalism and its Rivals

The two pieces are now in place to characterize both the Liberal Fundamentalist and certain rivals. The Liberal *Fundamentalist* is a Liberal *foundationalist* about *which* epistemic principles are true and an *Intuitionist* about *why* they are true; all seven epistemic principles are, for the Liberal Fundamentalist, a priori necessary truths.

The Liberal Fundamentalist has a number of rivals. Within the Intuitionist camp, the Reactionary, the Conservative, and the Moderate Fundamentalist are all rivals. A Coherentist that accepts Intuitionism (and so **AP** as well as **COH**) is also a rival. So too is the Pure Coherentist. Any non-Intuitionist view is, by definition, a rival; Cartesians, Reliabilists, and Pragmatists are *ipso facto* rivals, even if they are sympathetic to, or even embrace, **TEST**. Any Non-Fundamentalist view is, by definition, a rival; if you don't believe epistemic principles are a priori knowable conceptual truths, then *a fortiori* you don't believe **TEST** is a priori necessary. If you are a Coherentist (Adler), a Reactionary (Fumerton), a Conservative (BonJour, Feldman), a Moderate (Pollock, Huemer), a Cartesian (Fumerton), a Reliabilist (Goldman), or a Pragmatist (Foley, Kusch), the Liberal Fundamentalist is one of your rivals.[7]

An interesting rival is the Moderate Fundamentalist. This is for three reasons. Firstly, there are many Moderate Fundamentalists; it is a live position. Secondly, the "testimony debate" (described at the opening) receives a sharp formulation when characterized as the debate between the Moderate and the Liberal Fundamentalist; the Liberal thinks (many) testimony-based beliefs are direct, the Moderate thinks they are all (necessarily) inferential. Lastly, the Moderate is a close rival to the Liberal. If there is a deep and convincing reason to think the Liberal cannot be right, it is a reason the Moderate should be able to articulate consistent with her position. Moderate Fundamentalism is thus a live position that is a clear occupant of one side of the testimony debate, and if there is a reason not to be a Liberal, the Moderate should be able to advance it.

In the rest of this section I say more about the Moderate-Liberal debate. In the next I explain why the Moderate is not entitled to make four particular arguments against the Liberal. This shows that whether something is a good reason for (or against) an epistemic principle is largely a function of which theoretical perspective is true. If Intuitionism is true, some considerations are relevant, others are not.

To better understand the Moderate-Liberal debate, consider first the parallel disagreement between the Conservative and the Moderate. The Conservative rejects **PER**; the Moderate embraces it. The Conservative thinks perception is *epistemically neutral*: a perceptual representation is, *in itself*, no reason or ground to believe anything at all about the external environment. For the Conservative, a perceptual belief is justified only if it can be inferentially supported by other, non-perceptual beliefs. Traditionally this means the subject must be able to infer that the way things seem to her in perceptual consciousness is best explained by the real world hypothesis. She cannot essentially rely upon any perceptual beliefs as premises. She needs to be able to infer that how things introspectively seem to her corresponds to the way they are in the world. If she can, she will have epistemically "reduced" perceptual beliefs to beliefs based on introspection and reason. Perceptual beliefs are, for the Conservative, epistemically inferential. The Moderate, on the other hand, is not so demanding. Perceptual beliefs are, for the Moderate, epistemically direct. The Conservative is a "reductionist" about perceptual beliefs; the Moderate is an "anti-reductionist".

The Moderate-Liberal disagreement is analogous. The Moderate holds that testimony-based beliefs, if justified, are justified inferentially on the basis of non-testimony-based beliefs; comprehending the presentation-as-true of another is, in itself, *epistemically neutral*. It is, *as such*, no reason or ground to believe that what the speaker said is true (Pritchard 2004: 328–30). The subject must be able to infer from non-testimony-based beliefs that testimony-based beliefs are, for the most part, reliable or justified in order for her testimony-based beliefs to be justified. The qualification "non-testimonial" is essential. The hearer cannot appeal to testimony-based beliefs about the reliability of testimony in an ineliminable way for that would presuppose that (at least some) testimony-based beliefs are justified without inferential support. If A's say-so that P is, in itself, no reason to believe P, then B's say-so that A is trustworthy is, in itself, no reason to believe A.

The natural way to "reduce" (inferentially support in the required way) testimony would be for the hearer to appeal to his own first-hand experience of the reliability of the particular speaker, or speakers of that kind, or of testimony in general.[8] The hearer would have to (be able to) "reduce" his testimony-based beliefs to beliefs purged of testimonial reliance, using either enumerative induction or inference to the best explanation. If she could do it, her testimony-based beliefs would thereby epistemically "reduce" to inductively based (reasoned) beliefs, beliefs inferred from or based on a non-testimonial induction base; justified testimonial beliefs *just are* beliefs "reductively" justifiable.

The Moderate is more demanding than the Liberal, just as the Conservative is more demanding than the Moderate. The Liberal does not require the subject to "reduce" testimony-based beliefs to non-testimony-based beliefs; the Liberal is an "anti-reductionist" about testimony while the Moderate is a "reductionist."

There are two standard objections to reductionism about testimony. They parallel two standard objections to reductionism about perception. The first is the "paucity of evidence argument". The argument is that the reduction is not possible, for actual agents do not possess enough first-hand evidence to carry it out. Hence if ordinary testimony-based beliefs are, by and large, justified, then "reductionism" (Moderate foundationalism, Fundamentalist or not) is false (Coady 1992; cp. Fricker 1994, 1995; Lipton 1998; Lyons 1997). The second is that even if the reduction is possible, requiring it is overly demanding; the requirement to reduce hyper-intellectualizes testimonial justification (Burge 1993; Strawson 1994; cp. Adler 2002). These two objections parallel objections to reductionism about perception. The first is that the "reduction" cannot succeed; subjects cannot derive the justification for perceptual beliefs from non-perceptual beliefs. The second is that the "reduction", even if it is possible, is too demanding on ordinary subjects.

So far I have introduced two new ideas: the four versions of foundationalism defined in terms of the epistemic principles, and the four theories of the nature of epistemic justification. I used those new ideas to describe the Liberal Fundamentalist and her rivals: Cartesians, Reliabilists, Pragmatists, coherentists and other foundationalist Intuitionists. I then compared the Liberal to a close rival, the Moderate Fundamentalist. In the next section I show why four possible arguments against the Liberal are ineffective on the assumption that at least the first six principles (the ones the Moderate embraces) are a priori necessary truths; i.e. on the assumption that Intutionism is correct. This will show that what one thinks about which principles are true is largely a function of which of the four theoretical perspectives one employs. The next section concludes the first main part of the paper.

Four Arguments Against Liberal Fundamentalism

Let us assume that Intuitionism is correct, and also that at least the first six epistemic principles are all a priori necessary truths, but that it is still an open question whether **TEST** is also a priori necessary. In this section I explain why four arguments against **TEST** are ineffective on that assumption.

The first argument goes like this. Testimony is not a necessarily reliable process; error and deceit might outnumber truth and sincerity (Graham 2000*a*). Hence it cannot be a priori necessary that comprehending the presentation-as-true of another confers justification on belief in what the speaker presented-as-true (cp. Adler 2002; BonJour 2002; Fricker 1994; Faulkner 2000). This argument is ineffective on the assumption that Intuitionism is correct, for necessary reliability is not a necessary condition upon justification (either direct or inferential justification). The Cartesian places this condition upon justification; the Intuitionist (and so the Moderate Fundamentalist) does not. If Intuitionism is true (and so Cartesianism is false), the *mere* fact that testimony is not *necessarily* reliable is neither here nor there.

The second argument has two versions. The first goes as follows. Perceptual beliefs are *de facto* more reliable than testimony-based beliefs, hence perceptual justification is direct and testimonial justification is inferential. The second goes like this. Testimony-based beliefs inferentially backed by non-testimony-based beliefs are more reliable than testimony-based beliefs without such backing. Hence testimony-based beliefs without inferential backing from non-testimony-based beliefs are not justified but beliefs with such backing are. Hence testimonial justification is inferential and not direct. Both versions rely upon the principle that differences in *degree* of reliability determine differences in epistemic *kind* (inferential vs. direct) (cf. Goldman 1979, 1992; Pritchard 2004: 343–4). But if the Moderate is right this principle is false. This is because introspection may be more reliable than perception, and perception may be more reliable than memory (with or without backing), but introspection, perception, and memory are all, according to the Moderate, epistemically *direct*. The Moderate does not reason from differences in *degree* of reliability to differences in epistemic *kind*. A *fortiori*, if perception supported by other beliefs is more reliable than perception without such support, it does *not* follow that perceptual-beliefs without such support enjoy *no* justification (that they are epistemically *neutral*). And so, if testimony-based beliefs epistemically supported by other beliefs are more reliable than beliefs without such support, it again does not follow that beliefs without such support enjoy no justification as such, that they are epistemically neutral.

The third argument goes like this. TEST is true only if testimony without inferential backing is a *de facto* reliable belief-forming process. However, it is not. Hence TEST is false. But the Moderate Fundamentalist cannot argue this way, for the Moderate is not a Reliabilist. At best he can offer defeaters by appeal to *de facto* reliability considerations. If Intuitionism is correct and Reliabilism is not, considerations of *de facto* reliability do not in themselves determine what necessary *a priori* epistemic principles are true. Reliability considerations must play a part in a *complete* treatment of testimony (especially for testimonial *knowledge*), but if Intuitionism is correct, *de facto* reliability (itself) does not enter into whether a source does or does not confer *justification*.[9]

The fourth argument goes as follows. Justified perceptual beliefs sometimes defeat testimony-based beliefs. Hence perceptual beliefs are "epistemically prior" to testimony-based beliefs. Hence testimony-based beliefs depend upon positive epistemic support from perceptual beliefs for justification; testimony is inferential and not direct. The principle this argument relies upon is that if a belief from source N sometimes defeats a belief from source M, source M cannot be direct but must be inferential. The Moderate Fundamentalist, however, must reject this principle. That is because the Moderate accepts that perception, memory, and introspection are all sources of direct justification, but also must accept that perceptual beliefs sometimes defeat memory beliefs, that memory beliefs sometimes defeat perceptual beliefs, that introspective beliefs sometimes defeat perceptual beliefs, that perceptual beliefs sometimes defeat introspective beliefs, that introspective beliefs sometimes defeat memory beliefs, and that memory beliefs sometimes defeat introspective beliefs. The Moderate accepts **INT**, **MEM**, and **PER**, and so holds that these sources produce justified beliefs. If they do, they also produce defeaters for other beliefs, sometimes beliefs from those very sources. That a source is a source of defeaters for beliefs from another source, or even from itself, does not show that the other source depends for justification on inferential support from another source, or even from itself. Applied to testimony, this means that the argument does not show that testimony depends upon non-testimonial sources for justification. The fact that my perception defeats your testimony does not show testimony is inferential and not direct. Indeed, the fact that testimony-based beliefs sometimes defeat perceptual beliefs does not show that testimony is prior to perception. For example, you say you see a VW coming over the horizon and I correct you. Then my testimony would defeat your perceptual belief. But that possibility, though familiar, clearly does not show that you must inferentially support (derive) all of your perceptual beliefs from testimony-based beliefs.

These four arguments all fall short if we assume that the first six epistemic principles are a priori necessary, that at least Moderate Fundamentalism is correct. They all also fall short even if we assume Conservative Fundamentalism, for the Conservative does not rely upon necessary reliability, differences in degree of reliability, *de facto* reliability, or relations of defeat to determine epistemic kinds.

What if we were to assume Cartesianism (and so assume Reactionary Fundamentalism, for instance) instead of Intuitionism? That *would* show that **TEST** is false, for testimony is not necessarily reliable (BonJour 2002). But it would also show that **PER** and other sources of direct and inferential justification are false. It would not give us a reason to think that **TEST** *itself* is suspect.

What if we were to assume Reliabilism or Pragmatism? Then, possibly, some of the arguments just listed would show that there are (contingent) differences in epistemic kind; they could show that while perception, memory, and introspection (or certain kinds of perceptual belief forming processes and methods, and so on for memory and introspection) are direct, testimony is inferential. If testimony is not de facto reliable but perception is, or perception is considerably more reliable than testimony, then perception confers justification without inferential backing (according to the Reliabilist) but testimony does not. Or if testimony-based beliefs without inferential backing are held by the relevant community to fall short of justification but beliefs with such backing are held to pass the test, then (according to the Pragmatist), perception is direct but testimony is inferential (Goldman 1979, 1992).

What one thinks about the epistemic status of testimony is thus largely a function of what theoretical perspective one holds about the nature of epistemic justification generally and further what one thinks about the relevant facts. If you *are* an Intuitionist, certain familiar considerations, I have just argued, do not undermine Liberal Fundamentalism. But if you are *not* an Intuitionist, then you think Liberal Fundamentalism is *ipso facto* false and **TEST** is not a priori necessary. **TEST** may still be an empirical contingent truth, but that depends upon which rival perspective is correct and how the facts turn out. What you think about testimony is driven in large part by what theoretical perspective on epistemic justification you think is correct. It will largely determine what considerations lead you to embrace or reject **TEST**. If you are *not* an Intuitionist, certain considerations are *relevant*. But if you *are*, those very considerations may be neither here nor there.

I have discussed only four arguments against the Liberal here. There are a number of other possible arguments. I shall discuss one such argument in the next section. I have discussed some other arguments elsewhere.[10]

I have now concluded the first main part of this essay. I have described Liberal Fundamentalism and (some of) its rivals and shown that certain arguments against it are ineffective on the assumption that Intuitionism is correct. I have not, however, argued that Intuitionism *is* correct. That is a very large topic best treated at length on another occasion. Nor have I argued that the Liberal is correct. That too is a large topic for another time. However, I do say a few things in defense of the Liberal in the next part of the paper.

WEAK LIBERAL FUNDAMENTALISM

In this part I make use of the third new idea, the distinction between *pro tanto* and on balance justification. I use it to distinguish Strong and Weak readings of the epistemic principles, and then two versions each (Strong and Weak) of both Moderate and Liberal Fundamentalism. I compare Weak Liberal Fundamentalism with its Strong Liberal and Moderate rivals. I then respond to an objection against the Liberal. The objection does not require the falsity of Intuitionism for its force; it is an objection the Moderate is free to lodge against her Liberal rival. The Weak version *prima facie* avoids the objection while the Strong version does not. Weak Liberal Fundamentalism thus emerges as the more plausible variant.

Pro Tanto vs. On Balance

In this section I distinguish between *pro tanto* and on balance justification. I should first say a few words about *prima facie* justification.

It is customary to qualify principles governing justification with the phrase "prima facie". Each principle given above thus should include "prima facie" in between the words "confers" and "justification". *Prima facie* justification is *defeasible* justification. Further information may undermine or override the justification one holds for a belief. So if I seem to see a red apple on the picnic table, then the experience, many would hold, confers perceptual justification on the belief that there is a red apple before me. But if I am told or have reason to believe that it is a fake, or if I remember taking mind-altering drugs just before coming to the picnic, then my justification has been defeated. In order to regain the justification from the perceptual experience I would need to defeat the defeaters with even further information. I would have to have a reason to believe that you are fooling, or that it is probably is not a fake, or a reason to believe that the mind-altering drugs have no effect on how well I see things. If there are no defeaters in the first place, or if the defeaters present have been defeated in turn by further information, then the prima facie justification I enjoy is not defeated (defeat is absent).

Is lack of defeat sufficient to convert *prima facie* justification into *on balance* justification? The standard view is that it is. Witness Alston and Huemer:

I have proposed an account of the *prima facie* epistemic justification of beliefs. . . . The justification will be *ultima facie* provided there are not sufficient overriders from within the subject's knowledge and justified beliefs. (Alston 1988: 227)

When a belief is said to be *prima facie* justified . . . the belief's justification can be defeated by countervailing evidence. . . . The appearances are presumed true, unless proven false. This means that when it seems as if P and no evidence emerges contravening P, it is reasonable to accept P. (Huemer 2001: 100)

Though commonplace, I believe this is incorrect, at least for both perceptual and testimonial justification. Undefeated *prima facie* justification is not *a priori* equivalent to *on balance* justification. I distinguish *pro tanto* from *prima facie* justification. I then distinguish Strong from Weak versions of both Moderate and Liberal Fundamentalism. The Strong view holds that undefeated *prima facie* justification necessarily converts to on balance justification. The Weak view does not. In the rest of this section I shall focus on perception, turning to testimony in the sections following. The Weak view for perceptual justification is supported by the examples that mark the distinction.

"Pro tanto", as I understand it, means "as far as it goes" or "to that extent". I contrast it with "on balance". A *pro tanto* justification is a consideration in favor of a certain belief. If a certain belief is *pro tanto* justified by a perceptual experience it does not follow that the belief is justified *on balance*. A *pro tanto* justification may only justify the belief to a certain *degree*. Epistemologists have shown sensitivity to this distinction (e.g. Audi 2001; Pritchard 2004). Those sensitive to the distinction, however, have not marked it. Its significance should not be overlooked.[11]

The distinction between *some* evidence and *enough* is obvious in the case of inductive reasoning. The distinction between *some* and *enough* also applies to cases of psychologically non-inferential, *prima facie* justified, perceptual beliefs. I will here show by a series of steps that the justification one has for an empirical perceptual belief comes in degrees. This is, of course, widely believed. But it implies that there is a point at which the justification converts from *pro tanto* to *on balance* justification, for it is also widely believed that many perceptual beliefs—beliefs held roughly as strongly as each other—are on balance justified, but not that *all* of them are (Goldman 1979).

Imagine looking through a narrow steel pipe and seeming to see only the outlines of a red apple. Here your visual experience is focused in on a single object and you have no other information about any other objects and relations before you. The rest is, as it were, all dark; you can't see anything else because the pipe is too narrow. Here it seems all you have justification for is that there is probably a red apple out there, and little justification for beliefs about its particular size or distance, whether it is sitting on something or being held up, and so forth, *from the experience itself*. You normally use other information that is presently lacking to help figure those things out. Suppose the experience causes you to believe (automatically and non-inferentially in the normal way) that there is a red apple of ordinary size a certain distance away. The experience confers *prima facie pro tanto* justification on the belief, but surely not *on balance* justification.

Now imagine removing the pipe and picking up more information. You can now see much more of the scene; your experience represents a good deal more than before. The visual experience of the red apple continues to confer some justification on the belief. The other parts of the enlarged experience confer more justification, and do so in two ways. First, they confer justification on related *beliefs*, such as that there is a table below the apple, a tree to the left, and so forth. All of these beliefs in turn confer some justification on the belief that there is an apple on the table by *integration*. And second, other parts of your visual field indirectly confer justification on the belief. The more the rest of the visual field makes intelligible the existence of a red apple before you, the more justified your belief is. All of your visual (and other sensory) experiences and beliefs *fit together*.

Consider third moving around the table. Then you will have a number of additional and distinct experiences of, and beliefs about, the apple. These will confer additional justification. Consider fourth the experiences retained in memory. They will also contribute. Consider also possible interactions with other people who also seem to see the apple. If they act as if all is normal, or talk about the apple, or pick it up and eat it, all of this confers additional justification on your belief.

All of this "evidence" is evidence "in the foreground". But consider also all of your background knowledge about apples, picnic tables, medium sized-dry goods, the nature of vision and light, and so forth. These beliefs also contribute to the justification of your belief. These beliefs make up your evidence "in the background" (Adler 2002).

Your first visual experience through the pipe confers some justification on your belief that an apple is there. It looks like an apple. Additional experiences and beliefs then confer additional justification. Moving around the apple furthers this process. Touching it, eating it, talking about it, and so forth, makes a difference. It feels like an apple, tastes like an apple, and everyone agrees that it is an apple. At some point your *pro tanto* justification converts to *on balance* justification. Indeed, you go from *some* (less than enough) to *more than* enough.

Although the example involves an apple, the example is a standard one of perceptual belief. However, being an apple might not be a perceptible property. If not, the example can be substituted with a red solid sphere at a certain distance. A first quick glance from one eye with few surrounding distance cues of a partially occluded sphere may automatically and normally cause a belief that there is a red sphere at a certain distance. Binocular vision would confer more information and justification. Walking up to the sphere, walking around it (seeing all sides), touching it, and so on, all contribute justification. The first quick glance, though sufficient for belief, is not on its own sufficient for on balance justification.

It is clear that "coherence" (very broadly understood) plays an important role in converting *pro tanto* to *on balance* justification. Integration is essential. Many of the various visual and other perceptual experiences and perceptual beliefs present the same "content": that there is an apple. It is conceivable that on balance justification for a belief is only conferred on a belief that comes in a "cluster" of other beliefs, or comes along with a cluster of sensory or other relevant experiences (cf. Sosa 2002). A belief not inferentially based on another may receive epistemic support from other beliefs, or from other "experiences", from one or more sources, where the beliefs and experiences are all appropriate to the content of the target belief. Perhaps no on balance justified belief is an island.

This view of perceptual justification, though perhaps not entirely novel (cf. Haack 1993), is motivated by what moves both the foundationalist and, I think, the coherentist, without embracing the idea that justification somehow emerges from relations of mutual inferential support (where P justifies Q and Q justifies P), or that only a belief can confer justification on another belief. True, justification starts with experiences as the foundationalist supposes. True, such justification is often not enough as the coherentist supposes. False, I claim, that experience alone or inferential support from other beliefs *alone* is typically sufficient for on balance perceptual justification. Clusters of experience and belief convert *pro tanto* to on balance justification, at least for many ordinary perceptual beliefs.

Psychologically non-inferential beliefs are (or at least can be), from the epistemic point of view, both direct and indirect. They do not depend upon other beliefs for *prima facie pro tanto* justification, and so in that sense are immediately justified: direct. But they positively, and not just negatively, depend upon other beliefs for *on balance* or *sufficient* justification, and so in *that* sense are mediately justified: indirect. Thus the Moderate Fundamentalist should be an epistemic *inferentialist* about *on balance* justification, while remaining a *non*-inferentialist about *prima facie pro tanto* justification.

One might deny, or at least try to deflate the significance of, the distinction between *pro tanto* and on balance justification by distinguishing between either all-out-belief from degrees of belief, or belief that definitely P from belief that probably P, and then claiming that all *pro tanto* justification for a belief amounts to is just on balance justification for a belief that P held to a certain degree, or for a belief that P is likely to a certain degree. But this move would confuse the psychological with the epistemic. A wise man may proportion his belief to the evidence, but a tentative endorsement that P may still be strongly justified, and a resounding endorsement of P may only be weakly justified. We need terms to mark these facts.

The logical distinction between *prima facie* justification and *pro tanto* justification is this. *Prima facie* justification is necessarily defeasible. *Pro tanto* justification is not; indefeasible *pro tanto* justification is a conceptual possibility. There is a further contrast. Undefeated *prima facie* justification does not necessarily *imply* a possible falling short of on balance justification. Undefeated *prima facie* justification *could*, for some source of justification, *ipso facto* count as *on balance* justification. *Pro tanto* justification, however, just means justification that *may* fall short. '*Prima facie*' means *defeasible* justification, '*pro tanto*' means *some* justification.

I will not here try to say what exactly converts *some* justification into *enough*, or when some *is* enough. This is a complicated issue. I hope to discuss it elsewhere.

We can now state Strong and Weak readings of **PER**.

(**PER$_s$**) If S's perceptual system represents x as F (where F is a perceptible property), and this causes or sustains in the normal way S's belief of x that it is F, then that confers *prima facie* justification on S's belief.

(**PER$_w$**) If S's perceptual system represents x as F (where F is a perceptible property), and this causes or sustains in the normal way S's belief of x that it is F, then that confers *prima facie pro tanto* justification on S's belief.

The Weak Moderate foundationalist embraces **PER$_w$** without commenting on its modal status, and the Intuitionist version, the Weak Moderate Fundamentalist, embraces **PER$_w$** as a priori necessary. With the distinction between *pro tanto* and on balance justification in hand, and the corresponding distinction between

Strong and Weak readings of the epistemic principles, I am now in a position to state and defend Weak Liberal Fundamentalism in the next section.

Weak Liberal Fundamentalism

Just as there are two possible versions of **PER**, so too there are two possible versions of **TEST**:

(TEST$_s$)   If a subject S (seemingly) comprehends a (seeming) presentation-as-true by a (seeming) speaker that P, and if that causes or sustains in the normal way S's belief that P, then that confers *prima facie* justification on S's belief that P.

(TEST$_w$)   If a subject S (seemingly) comprehends a (seeming) presentation-as-true by a (seeming) speaker that P, and if that causes or sustains in the normal way S's belief that P, then that confers *prima facie pro tanto* justification on S's belief that P.

I favor the weaker version. I say why below. Weak Liberal Fundamentalism, however, is not the standard version of Liberal Fundamentalism. The distinction between Weak and Strong versions has not been marked (Burge 1993: 467–8, 1997: 21, 22, 45 n. 4; Dummett 1993: 423; McDowell 1998: 435; Weiner 2003: 257; cp. Fricker 2002: 379; Lackey 1999: 474).[12]

Weak Liberal Fundamentalism is a position intermediate between Strong Liberal Fundamentalism and Moderate Fundamentalism (either Weak or Strong). The Strong Liberal Fundamentalist holds that a hearer's belief that P based on comprehending a presenter's presentation-as-true that P enjoys on balance justification absent defeat. The Strong position holds that *on balance* justification is (absent defeat) *direct*. The Moderate Fundamentalist, on the other hand, denies that testimony *as such* confers *any* justification on belief. Testimony is, according to the Moderate Fundamentalist, evidentially neutral. If any testimony-based belief enjoys any justification, its epistemic status is entirely inferential. Not only that, the inferential support must be of a certain sort; the reasons supporting the belief must not be ineliminably and wholly testimonial; the reasons must be *genuinely* "reductive" reasons. The Strong Liberal Fundamentalist denies that testimony-based beliefs must be supported by reasons, *a fortiori* by reductive reasons. And the Moderate Fundamentalist denies that *any* justification, *pro tanto* or on balance, for testimony-based beliefs is direct; *a fortiori* it denies that testimony enjoys direct *pro tanto* justification.

The Weak Liberal stands in between these two positions. She agrees with the Strong Liberal that reductive reasons are not necessary for on balance justification. She agrees with the Moderate that testimony-based beliefs do not *as such* enjoy on balance justification (absent defeat). But she disagrees with the Strong Liberal that additional epistemic support is not often needed for on balance justification for testimonial beliefs, and it disagrees with the Moderate that genuinely reductive reasons are always required for any justification for testimony-based beliefs. The Weak Liberal holds that no additional support of any kind (reductive or non-reductive) is required for *prima facie pro tanto* justification, but also that additional support (whether reductive or non-reductive) is often required for on balance justification. When it comes to *pro tanto* justification, the Weak Liberal holds that testimony is epistemically *direct*. But when it comes to *on balance* justification, it holds that testimony is epistemically *inferential*. Weak Liberal Fundamentalism is weaker (it claims less about on balance justification) than Strong Liberal Fundamentalism but stronger than Moderate Fundamentalism.

An analogy may be helpful. Suppose an on balance justified belief that P costs a dollar. The Strong view holds that comprehending a presentation-as-true that P provides the hearer with an entire dollar. Absent other fees (defeaters), the hearer can buy the on balance justified belief. The Weak view holds that comprehending a presentation-as-true that P often fails to provide the hearer with an entire dollar, but for all that it provides the hearer with some money. With a little more money to spend, the hearer can buy the on balance justified belief. The Moderate Fundamentalist, on the other hand, thinks comprehending a presentation-as-true that P is like a check. In itself it is worthless. Unless there is money in the bank backing up the check, you can't buy anything with it. And the money in the bank, according to the Moderate Fundamentalist, can't come from testimony either (just as you can't pay your credit card bill with that very same credit card). The Strong Liberal view holds that comprehending the presentation-as-true of another that P *as such* provides *enough* justification (absent defeaters). The Weak Liberal view holds that it provides *some*. The Moderate view holds that it provides *none*.

Is Liberal Fundamentalism Too Permissive?

I now discuss an objection to Liberal Fundamentalism. It is an objection the Moderate Fundamentalist (among others) is entitled to make, unlike the four objections discussed above. The objection is that Liberal Fundamentalism is too strong or too permissive, that it would entail that many testimony-based beliefs without inferential support would be justified where, intuitively, they are not. Merely comprehending another's presentation-as-true is not, the objection goes, sufficient for justified belief in the content of what was presented, at least in very many cases, even absent defeat. Additional support is necessary for on balance justification.[13]

This objection clearly targets Strong Liberal Fundamentalism. Strong Liberal Fundamentalism is also the standard version of the view in print, as noted above. But it is not clear that this complaint applies to Weak Liberal Fundamentalism. The complaint is that acceptance without additional support is too permissive. The Strong view disagrees: undefeated acceptance without support is fine. The Weak view leaves that question open. It is entirely consistent with Weak Liberal Fundamentalism that additional support is necessary for on balance justification. Hence the objection seems to have no, or at least considerably less, force against the Weak position. Since I think (though have not argued here) that there are good prima facie reasons in favor of the Liberal view generally, and since the Weak view is more defensible than the Strong, I prefer Weak Liberal Fundamentalism. It seems defensible against a standard complaint.

Perception and Testimony Compared

I now want to make a point about the comparison between perception and testimony. I believe the right account for both is the Weak account, PER_w and $TEST_w$. Both principles are supported by the data. Just as the justification from testimony as such often fails to confer on balance justification for a testimony-based belief, so too (I argued above) that justification from perception as such often fails to confer on balance justification for a perceptual belief. The right accounts of perception and testimony, I believe, parallel one another.

There is, however, a tendency in the literature to compare perception and testimony unfavorably. Just having a perceptual experience of something being so and so is supposed to be *enough* for on balance justification in the perceptual case, but *not* enough in the testimonial case. Hence it is inferred that there must be a fundamental difference in kind between perception and testimony (e.g. Pritchard 2004: 343–5).

This inference, I believe, is based on a mistake. I think some are led into thinking there is such a contrast because they fail to see that in the perception case there are a large number of interlocking experiences and beliefs that individually confer *pro tanto* justification and collectively confer on balance justification, but in the testimony case only one piece of *pro tanto* justification is in focus, the one presentation-as-true whether P. For instance, compare looking at an apple on a table and being told that there is an apple on a table in the park over yonder hill. In the visual case, over a relatively small portion of time, one will have a number of distinct but interlocking experiences of, and beliefs about, the apple. One's belief that there is an apple will enjoy plenty of justification; its justification on balance will, most likely, be over-determined (Conee and Feldman 1985: 29–30). Now compare the hearer who is told by a speaker (a speaker that the hearer doesn't know first-hand and knows very little about otherwise) that there is an apple on the table yonder. Here all the hearer may have in favor of the belief is this one presentation-as-true. There may be no, or only a very little, additional support. There is thus a difference between the perceptual case and the testimony case. The *perceiver* (with many experiences and other related beliefs to go on) will enjoy on balance justification for that same belief, but the *hearer* (with only one presentation-as-true to go on) will only enjoy *pro tanto* justification for the belief that there is an apple on the table. I grant this (de facto) difference. But it is no reason to compare perception and testimony unfavorably. All this difference shows is that typically in the perceptual case enough justification is present for on balance justification, but that in many testimonial cases only *pro tanto* justification is present.[14] If we were to compare just one perceptual experience with one presentation-as-true that might help bring the analogy between the epistemologies of perception and testimony into sharp relief. One report may really be like just one perceptual experience.[15] Both are some, but often not enough, for justification on balance. Comparing memory with testimony reinforces this point. Remembering something may be just as good, all else being equal, as being told.

Additional Supporting Reasons

If the Weak Liberal is right, on balance justification for testimony-based beliefs will often require additional support. No on balance justified testimony-based belief, the slogan would go, is an island. Additional support, obviously, can come from a number of sources. You tell me it is an apple, and I take a look myself. But additional support can also come from other testimony-based beliefs. There are four ways this might happen.

First, additional presentations-as-true may fit together with the original presentation, though they are about different things. Suppose you meet someone on a plane and you start a conversation. She tells you that she is a highly trained mathematician working for Xerox in Palo Alto engaged in pure research. You may find this an unlikely occupation, but you do not disbelieve her. During the conversation she starts talking about Palo Alto, about other researchers at Xerox, and where she studied mathematics, and engages you in a discussion about the nature of numbers and sets. You may only have been *pro tanto* justified in believing that she is a mathematician doing pure research at Xerox at the start of the conversation. Indeed, if that was all she said and then she turned away, you might only have been justified on balance in believing that she said she was a mathematician. But at the end of the actual conversation it seems that you are on balance justified in believing that she is a Xerox employed mathematician.[16]

The second, and perhaps more obvious way additional presentations may help, is by going directly to the fact that the original presentation-as-true is about. A witness may tell you that he saw the killer drive away in a red van. Another, independent witness, may tell you the same thing. And so on. The more independent witnesses, the Liberal holds, the better. At some point, presumably, the justification the hearer's belief enjoys converts from *pro tanto* to on balance justification.

The third and certainly very common way additional presentations often help is by going to the trustworthiness of the target interlocutor. That is, if you are talking to A, being told by B that A is trustworthy will confer some additional warrant on trusting A.

A fourth way is by answering defeaters. Suppose I have reason to think C is not trustworthy. D can tell me that she is generally trustworthy, or that she has an adequate reason in this case to be sincere. Or suppose I have reason to think E, though obviously sincere, does not know what he is talking about. F can tell me that, appearances notwithstanding, E really does know what he is talking about.

Justified beliefs are often supported by experiences and beliefs from a number of different sources. They all work together. Testimony-based beliefs support perceptual beliefs; perceptual beliefs support memory beliefs; memory beliefs support testimony-based beliefs, and so on. According to the Liberal, perception, memory, introspection, testimony, and reason all as such confer justification on the beliefs they normally cause and sustain.

My overall goal in this essay is to bring more clarity to the testimony debate. Although I favor the Liberal position, I have not argued for it directly here. Hopefully the clarity speaks in its favor, or at least removes some sources of opposition. Given one's overall point of view in epistemology, the Liberal position may be a non-starter, or it may be a rather plausible extension of what one already believes. Making explicit one's overall point of view should reveal why one might reject it off the bat, or reveal why one might find it a plausible accounting for our justified reliance upon the word of others.

REFERENCES

Adler, Jonathan (2002), *Belief's Own Ethics* (Cambridge, Mass.: MIT Press).

Alston, William (1988), 'An Internalist Externalism', *Synthese*, 74: 265–83; repr. in his *Epistemic Justification: Essays in the Theory of Knowledge* (Ithaca, NY: Cornell University Press, 1989).

Audi, Robert (1988), 'Justification, Truth, and Reliability', *Philosophy and Phenomenological Research*, 49: 1–29.

―――(1997), 'The Place of Testimony in the Fabric of Knowledge and Justification', *American Philosophical Quarterly*, 34: 405–22.

―――(2001), *The Architecture of Reason* (Oxford: Oxford University Press).

―――(2002), 'The Sources of Belief', in Paul Moser (ed.), *Oxford Handbook of Epistemology* (Oxford: Oxford University Press).

―――(2004), 'The *A Priori* Authority of Testimony', *Philosophical Issues*, 14.

BonJour, Laurence (1999), *In Defense of Pure Reason* (Cambridge: Cambridge University Press).

―――(2002), *Epistemology: Classic Problems and Contemporary Responses* (Lanham, Md: Rowman and Littlefield).

Burge, Tyler (1993), 'Content Preservation', *Philosophical Review*, 102: 457–88.

―――(1997), 'Interlocution, Perception, Memory', *Philosophical Studies*, 86: 21–47.

―――(1999), 'Comprehension and Interpretation', in L. Hahn (ed.), *The Philosophy of Donald Davidson* (La Salle, IU.: Open Court).

―――(2003), 'Psychology and the Environment: Reply to Chomsky', in M. Hahn and B. Ramberg (eds.), *Reflections and Replies* (Cambridge, Mass.: MIT Press).

―――(2004), 'Perceptual Entitlement', *Philosophy and Phenomenological Research*, 67: 503–548.

Coady, C. A. J. (1973), 'Testimony and Observation', *American Philosophical Quarterly*, 10: 149–55.

—— (1992), *Testimony: A Philosophical Study* (Oxford: Clarendon Press).

Conee, Earl, and Feldman, Richard (1985) 'Evidentialism', *Philosophical Studies*, 48: 15–34.

Dummett, Michael (1993), 'Testimony and Memory', in his *The Seas of Language* (Oxford: Oxford University Press).

Faulkner, Paul (2000), 'The Social Character of Testimonial Knowledge', *Journal of Philosophy*, 97: 581–601.

Fricker, Elizabeth (1987), 'The Epistemology of Testimony', *Proceedings of the Aristotelian Society*.

—— (1994), 'Against Gullibility', in B. K. Matilal and A. Chakrabarti (eds.), *Knowing from Words*, (Dordrecht: Kluwer Academic Press).

—— (1995), 'Telling and Trusting: Reductionism and Anti-Reductionism in the Epistemology of Testimony, A Critical Notice of Coady 1992', *Mind*.

—— (2002), 'Trusting Others in the Sciences: *a priori* or Empirical Warrant?', *Studies in History and Philosophy of Science*, 33: 373–83.

Goldman, Alvin (1979), 'What Is Justified Belief?', in G. Pappas and M. Swain (eds.), *Knowledge and Justification* (Dordrecht: Reidel).

—— (1992), 'Epistemic Folkways and Scientific Epistemology', in his *Liaisons: Philosophy Meets the Cognitive and Social Sciences* (Cambridge, Mass.: MIT Press).

Graham, Peter J. (1997), 'What is Testimony?', *Philosophical Quarterly*, 47: 227–32.

—— (2000*a*), 'The Reliability of Testimony', *Philosophy and Phenomenological Research*, 61: 695–708.

—— (2000*b*), 'Conveying Information', *Synthese*, 123: 365–92.

—— (2000*c*), 'Transferring Knowledge', *Noûs*, 34: 131–52.

—— (2004), 'Metaphysical Libertarianism and the Epistemology of Testimony', *American Philosophical Quarterly*, 41: 37–50.

—— (forthcoming), 'Theorizing Justification', in M. O'Rourke and J. Campbell (eds.), *Knowledge and Skepticism: Contemporary Topics in Philosophy*, vol. v (Cambridge, Mass.: MIT Press).

Haack, Susan (1993), *Evidence and Inquiry* (Oxford: Blackwell).

Huemer, Michael (2001), *Skepticism and the Veil of Perception* (Lanham, Md.: Rowman and Littlefield Publishers).

Kusch, Martin (2002), *Knowledge by Agreement* (Oxford: Oxford University Press).

Lackey, Jennifer (1999), 'Testimonial Knowledge and Transmission', *Philosophical Quarterly*, 49: 471–90.

—— (2003), 'A Minimal Expression of Non-Reductionism in the Epistemology of Testimony', *Noûs* 37: 706–23.

Lehrer, Keith (1994), 'Testimony and Coherence', in B. K. Matilal and A. Chakrabarti (eds.), *Knowing from Words* (Dordrecht: Kluwer Academic Publishers).

Lipton, Peter (1998), 'The Epistemology of Testimony', *British Journal for the History and Philosophy of Science*, 29: 1–31.

Lyons, Jack (1997), 'Testimony, Induction, and Folk Psychology', *Australasian Journal of Philosophy*, 75: 163–78.

McDowell, John (1998), 'Knowledge by Hearsay', in his *Meaning, Knowledge, and Reality* (Cambridge, Mass.: Harvard University Press).

Pritchard, Duncan (2004), 'The Epistemology of Testimony', *Philosophical Issues*, 14: 326–48.

Quinton, Anthony (1973), 'Autonomy and Authority in Knowledge', in his *Thoughts and Thinkers* (London: Duckworth).

Root, Michael (1998), 'How to Teach a Wise Man', in Kenneth Westphal (ed.), *Pragmatism, Reason, and Norms* (New York: Fordham University Press).

—— (2001), 'Hume on the Virtues of Testimony', *American Philosophical Quarterly*, 38: 19–35.

Ross, Angus (1986), 'Why do We Believe what We are Told?', *Ratio*, 28: 69–88.

Rysiew, Patrick (2000), 'Testimony, Simulation, and the Limits of Inductivism', *Australasian Journal of Philosophy*, 78: 269–74.

Sosa, Ernest (2002), *Epistemic Justification*, with Laurence BonJour (Oxford: Blackwell Publishers).

Stevenson, Leslie (1993), 'Why Believe What People Say?', *Synthese*, 94: 429–51.

Strawson, P. F. (1994), 'Knowing from Words', in B. K. Matilal and A. Chakrabarti (eds.), *Knowing from Words* (Dordrecht: Kluwer Academic Publishers).

Weiner, Matthew (2003), 'Accepting Testimony', *Philosophical Quarterly*, 53: 256–64.

NOTES

1. Robert Audi distinguishes between (a) basic or direct belief (belief not inferentially based upon another belief), (b) sources of basic belief, and (c) basic sources, sources of belief that do not operationally depend upon other sources of belief. He holds that testimony-based beliefs are direct, that testimony is a source of basic beliefs, but denies that it is a basic source, for it operationally depends upon perception. See Audi (1997, 2002, 2004, and Chapter 1 in this volume). As I am using the terms "direct" and "basic", I mean to imply epistemic independence, that a belief does not depend upon another for prima facie pro tanto justification. I mean what he means by the "a priori authority" of a source.

2. I have characterized testimony-based beliefs elsewhere (Graham 2000*a*).

3. The disjunctive phrase "either sincere or reliable or both" is meant to accommodate "hybrid" views like Faulkner's (2000) that require only positive inferential support for sincerity, but not for reliability. Fricker sometimes suggests she is OK with sincerity, but not with reliability (1994).

4. Though it is consistent with the requirement that the way held is *per se* reliable: reliable in normal conditions when functioning normally (cf. Burge 2004 on "reliably veridical").

5. I hope to discuss the Intuitionist on **PER** on another occasion.

6. The principles the Reliabilist or the Pragmatist accepts may be (some of) the principles listed above, close analogues, distant cousins, or wholly new. It is unlikely, however, that some of the principles, or close analogues, would not show up on either the Reliabilist's or the Pragmatist's list at all.

7. Elizabeth Fricker's position, elaborated in a number of papers (1994, 1995, 2002), is complex; it defies easy categorization. I hope to discuss it at some length on another occasion. For some discussion, see Weiner (2003).

8. Another way one might "reduce" testimony is to demand that the hearer be able to show *a priori* that the speaker is trustworthy. I will not discuss this route in what follows.

9. *De facto* reliability surely matters for knowledge (as opposed to justification). And, again, as above, *per se* reliability *may* be required for justification (I remain neutral here), and this is *consistent* with Intuitionism.

10. One commonly made argument against the Liberal is that there is a fundamental epistemic difference in kind between perception and testimony because perception is a natural process operating according to natural laws but testimony goes through the will of the speaker, i.e. the speaker may always choose to lie or mislead. This fact in turn generates a number of different arguments against the Liberal when combined with other premises. I have discussed one of these arguments in Graham (2004).

11. Burge uses the phrase 'prima facie pro tanto' as well (1993: 467–8; 2003: 463). However, he seems to use 'prima facie' and 'pro tanto' interchangeably. I do not.

12. Pritchard (2004) may be an exception. He distinguishes a "modest" version of "credulism" (the Liberal view) from a "bare" version. From what he says, the modest version may parallel the Weak Liberal view as here defined. He does not defend such a view. In fact, he argues against it. See n. 15.

13. I have heard this objection many times. Something like it seems to drive Fricker's rejection to the Liberal view in her "Against Gullibility" (1994) and elsewhere. Pritchard states it explicitly (2004: 328–30). It seems to be widely shared.

14. However, if one were to look to the background for support in the testimonial case, there would be a good deal there as well (Adler 2002; Fricker 2002). The difference seems to be that in the perceptual case in the foreground lots of additional support is obvious, but that is not as clearly so in the testimonial case.

15. Pritchard disagrees. He says if A sees his car in the driveway, but had no reason to believe it would or would not be there, then A's belief is (on balance) justified. But if A is told that his car is there, and has nothing else to go on, then his belief is not (on balance) justified. "In the perceptual case, it does seem entirely plausible to suppose the agent is justified in forming this belief. ... The situation is very different, however, when it comes to the [testimony-based belief that the car is in the driveway]. ... Intuitively, without independent ... grounds this ... belief is not justified" (2004: 342–3). Pritchard does not consider the additional support the perceptual belief enjoys from the entire visual field over time, as I do in my case of the apple, and he does not consider comparing the two cases for equivalence in pro tanto justification. Perhaps he might change his mind after taking these facts into consideration. He appeals to differences in the extent and nature of the *reliability* of perception versus testimony to support his conclusion that perception and testimony differ (2004: 343–4). I have replied to this kind of argument above. It does not, I think, support his conclusion.

16. This example is due to Audi (1997).

5

Knowledge: Instrumental and Testimonial

Ernest Sosa

If a belief held on authority turns out to be correct, what most saliently explains this fact must surely involve the discovery and transmission of the relevant information. Relatively little of the credit belongs to the ultimate believer, by comparison, if all he did was to trust the authoritative source without question.

In order to constitute knowledge, a testimony-derived belief must be accurate because competent, which should not be thought to require that the most *salient* explanation of its being right must involve the individual competence manifest by the subject in holding that belief. The explanatorily salient factors will probably lie elsewhere; what *mainly* accounts for the belief's correctness will likely involve others and their cognitive accomplishments.

That insightful point must be properly appreciated and accommodated.[1] Testimonial knowledge is a collaborative accomplishment involving one's informational sources across time. Consider what is required: the gathering, retaining, transmitting, and receiving of information, with pertinent controls applied each step of the way. Consider the aptitude, competence, or intellectual virtue required for any full account of how the ultimate belief outcome amounts to knowledge when true because competent. Many people might be involved, acting mostly individually, while unaware of the others. Think of the documents consulted by a historian, of those responsible for their production, for their preservation and transmission unaltered, and so on; think of those who help with the production of a text, and of those who collaborate to produce a book; think of the copies of the book preserved, relevantly unaltered, by librarians and others; all of which eventuates in one's reading of the text and acquiring certain information about something far away and long ago.

Accordingly, there is a large external element in the knowledge of the members of a civilization advanced enough to exploit testimony as extensively as we do. Our knowledge will depend deeply and extensively on factors beyond the scope of anyone's reflective perspective. That is not, however, distinctive of knowledge through testimony, as may be seen if we compare a closely related "instrumental" sort of knowledge.

A deliverance of a proposition by an instrument is epistemically reliable only if that proposition belongs to a field, and that instrument is so constituted and situated, that not easily would it then deliver any falsehood in that field.

The deliverances of an instrument are answers to questions. By punching certain keys we pose to a calculator questions of the form 'What is the sum of x and y?' By placing a thermometer at a certain location and time, we can ask it a question of the form 'What is the ambient temperature there and then?' The deliverances of an instrument are its answers to such questions that might be posed to it. An instrument is reliable insofar as it would tend to answer them correctly.

The reliability of an instrument varies with its situation. What makes it reliable for a given situation is that so situated it would not easily answer relevant questions incorrectly.

It is the thermometer that is a reliable instrument, not just its screen. What is the difference that makes this difference? True, the screen needs the aid of the attached thermometer. But so does the thermometer need to be properly situated. It cannot be insulated, for example, nor can the temperature in the relevant space be too heterogeneous. If the thermometer is to tell the ambient temperature reliably, it must be appropriately situated in certain contingent ways, ways in which it might *not* have been situated, perhaps *very easily* might not have been situated.

Whether physically unified or dispersed, however, it is the larger instrumental system that is deeply operative. The guidance device in your car, for example, is not just a screen for the broader GPS system. It is more interestingly a seat of its relevant functions than is the thermometer screen. The thermometer screen is not a similarly important seat of its temperature-indicating functions. Nevertheless, the device in your car is not like the whole thermometer either.

When we trust the instrument readings on which we increasingly rely, such as displays on screens, we presuppose a field of propositions, and a situation, such that we take an instrument so situated to be reliable for that field: not easily would it then deliver a proposition in that field unless that proposition were true.

The man in the street needs no deep understanding of the instruments on which he relies.[2] He relies on his GPS devices, cellular telephones, atomic watches, and computer terminals with little or no awareness of how they depend on relations to other devices that more importantly seat the relevant functions. Let us use the term 'quasi-instruments' for devices that come more fully within our purview than do the fuller instruments involved.

Take the gauges that we face as driver of a late-model car. Most of us have a paltry conception of them as little more than screens, displays, that keep us informed about the amount of fuel in our tank, our speed, the rpm of our motor, etc. We take the display to be part of a fuller instrument that reliably delivers its deliverances. But who knows how the display on our dashboard reliably connects with its relevant subject matter? Our conception hardly extends beyond the distinctive screen or display.

When we thus rely epistemically on a quasi-instrument, then, even in the near-limiting case of the screen, we presuppose reliability. In thus *relying* we make manifest our assumption of *reliability*. We take the deliverance, even when understood as just the display on the screen, as more than accidentally connected with its truth. We take it to be at least safe, in that not easily would that screen display a false deliverance. This trust could be properly acquired in any of several ways. I might have it simply because I then think as I am told. I might acquire it, alternatively, through inductive generalization, even through trial and error. Some such trust is required, but it is worthless if just arbitrary.

What, more explicitly, might be the content of the required trust, however acquired? Whether our trust derives from testimony or from our own inductive generalization, we trust that a proposition in the relevant field would be true, or would tend to be true, if delivered by this instrument.

That is only a first approximation, however, since we still need to distinguish between outright and dependent safety, which yields the following improved condition:

> S knows that p on the basis of an indication I(p) only if either (a) I(p) indicates the truth outright and S accepts that indication at face value, or (b) for some condition C, I(p) indicates the truth dependently on C and either (i) S accepts that indication as such guided by C (so that S accepts the indication as such on the basis of C), or else (ii) C is constitutive of the normal conditions for the operation of that source.

Such reliability is required in the instruments and quasi-instruments on which we rely, if our reliance upon them is to be epistemically effective. It might be thought that instrumental knowledge can be reduced to non-instrumental knowledge, including testimonial knowledge, but this is dubious. Our access to the minds of others is after all *mediated* by various instruments, and we must trust such media at least implicitly in accessing the testimony all around us. So there is a kind of instrumental knowledge prior to and essentially involved in testimonial knowledge.

Many of our epistemic instruments are reliable because they are responsive to their environment. This seems true of thermometers, speedometers, fuel gauges, and many other instruments, whose deliverances are safe because they are thus responsive. A thermometer is reliable, for example, because its deliverances are safe; not easily would they be false. This is because it *senses* the ambient temperature, being so constituted and so related to its surroundings that the ambient temperature will cause it to read accordingly. Given such responsiveness, no wonder the thermometer's deliverances are systematically safe: not easily would it issue an *incorrect* deliverance. (That is, it might easily issue deliverances, if it is consulted, but not easily false ones.)

Not all reliable instruments are reliable through a systematic safety of their deliverances that derives from responsiveness to their proper field, not if this requires efficient causal input. Consider, for example, a calculator, about as reliable an instrument as any. If you give it a question, your calculator returns a correct answer with extremely high safety and reliability. But the reliability of a calculator, and the associated systematic safety of its deliverances, do not derive from responsiveness to its field through efficient causation. The facts of arithmetic do not efficiently cause the calculator to display the right answer on its screen when you consult it.

Yet in some sense the calculator gives its answer *because* it is the true answer. Indeed, we can predict its answers with extreme power and reliability if we predict that it will answer with truth. But in what sense does it answer as it does *because* it is the true answer? What sort of causation could be at work if not *efficient* causation? Here the explanation will presumably run via the fact that the artefact is designed to be accurate by an efficient and intelligent designer. But this shifts the question to that of how that designer gets to be himself so reliable a calculator, given the lack of efficient causation from the facts of arithmetic to the contents of his mind.

We have no need of efficient causation to explain the reliability and systematic safety of *cogito* beliefs such as the belief that one thinks and the belief that one exists. Consider, indeed, any propositional content whose conditions of understanding or truth preclude its being entertained while untrue. No such content could possibly gain our assent without being true, which makes our competence in such assents infallibly reliable.

One might even extend the scope of *cogito* assent far beyond the *cogito* itself, to demonstrative introspective thought. One is bound to be right in assenting to <This is thus>, if the conditions of reference for the relevant uses of 'this' and 'thus' are constituted essentially through the episode attended to and its content. If it succeeds at all in attributing something to anything, <This is thus> is bound to be true if the property attributed by "is thus" is selected by the attribution from among phenomenal properties of the item picked out as 'this'.

Cogito propositional contents hence extend beyond *cogito* claims in a strict sense restricted just to *cogito* itself and perhaps *sum*. Take any propositional content whose truth is introspectively accessible, and whose conditions of understanding and truth guarantee that it must be true if entertained with understanding. Any such propositional content can now count as a *cogito* content in a broader sense. Assenting to *cogito* contents thus broadly conceived manifests an epistemic competence, one highly reliable in its safe deliverances. But its reliability and safety are not to be explained through any efficient responsiveness to its field.

The same goes for the reliability of calculators and the systematic safety of their deliverances. Indeed, no more than that of a mechanical calculator is our own calculating competence to be explained through our efficient responsiveness to the facts of arithmetic, these being incapable of causal efficacy.

A wide variety of competencies are reliable, therefore, and their deliverances systematically safe, independently of any responsiveness to causal efficacy. Yet such deliverances are still somehow delivered "because" they are true. What sort of "because" might this be, if not that of efficient causation?

Is it a "because" of teleology or function, involving either a calculator consciously designed to give *true* answers, or the design of a Creator, or of fitness-selecting Mother Nature? No, epistemically efficient competence *need* not derive from *any* design, whether intentional or unintentional, divine or evolutionary. Swampman cases show this clearly enough. Lightning in a swamp might serendipitously cause molecules to come together into the form and substance of an intelligent Swampman. It may be doubted that Swampfolk are really physically possible; but this does not show them to be metaphysically impossible a priori. Insofar as we aim to understand what it would be to enjoy epistemically worthy beliefs, ones that are epistemically justified or even amount to knowledge, insofar as we are trying to understand what is involved with a priori necessity in such justification and knowledge, to that extent will Swampfolk be relevant *even if* they are physically impossible. For all we know, BIVs, Rings of Gyges, Twin Earth, and transplanted split brain hemispheres may all be physically impossible, but that would not make them irrelevant to philosophical inquiry aimed at understanding the fundamental nature of morality, personal identity, or reference and mental content.

Our stance is quite compatible with the relevance of theology or evolution to whether we know and how we know. After all, the better we know about our competencies and how they yield our beliefs, the better we understand their sources. The more *justifiedly* we can attribute our beliefs to them, moreover, the better also is the epistemic quality of these beliefs. Some limit is hence built into the epistemic prospects of Swampfolk. For, at an important juncture they are denied any further possibility of explanation and deeper assurance about their epistemic competencies.

Some of our justification for trusting the instruments that we rely on does plausibly have an inductive basis. Once we trust a particular device repeatedly with good results, we gain inductive support for its reliability. Justification for trusting our instruments derives also, of course, from testimony. But our awareness of testimony as testimony itself relies on instrumental knowledge. We must interpret our interlocutors, so as to discern the thoughts or statements behind their linguistic displays. From oral or written displays we can tell what someone is saying, and thinking.

Interpretative knowledge, I am suggesting, is a kind of instrumental knowledge. You ask a question of someone. Assuming sincerity and linguistic competence, what they utter reveals what they think (and on similar assumptions reveals
also what they say). This means that we can tell what they think (or say) based
on a deliverance conveyed by their utterance. Interpretative knowledge of what a
speaker thinks (says) is thus instrumental knowledge that uses the instrument of
language. Language is a double-sided instrument serving both speaker and audience. Hearers rely on the systematic safety of the relevant deliverances. Not easily
would the speaker's utterance deliver that the speaker thinks (says) that such and
such without the speaker's indeed thinking (saying) that such and such.

Speakers do not speak just about what they think. On the default assumption,
however, which must be that of sincerity, as is known to both speaker and audience, the speaker's utterance does give to understand what the speaker thinks.
So, the utterance carries a deliverance as to the speaker's mind, as well as any
deliverance it may deliver as to its more direct subject matter.

If we are to know a speaker's mind through his utterances, the speaker must
have a reliable competence to state his mind. He must be able through his utterances to deliver safe deliverances about what he thinks on the topic at hand.
These must be deliverances that would not be delivered unless their content (concerning what the speaker thinks) were true.

If any of this is put in serious enough doubt, the supposed instance of testimony will be disqualified as a source of knowledge about its direct content, for
that audience at that time. Testimonial knowledge thus presupposes instrumental knowledge, and it is out of the question to reduce *all* instrumental knowledge
to testimonial knowledge.

It might be countered that the linguistic instrumental knowledge highlighted
here itself counts as a kind of testimonial knowledge, for it is the testifier who
through his utterance gives to understand that he believes such and such. Since
"giving to understand" is a kind of communication, we might well consider it
a kind of testimony. This terminological option would distinguish two kinds
of testimony: the assertive and the non-assertive. Orthodox terminology would
restrict testimony to assertive testimony, however, so that non-assertive testimony might properly be grouped with deliverances of instruments more generally. Labels matter less, in any case, than a proper delineation of the phenomena,
with appreciation of what they interestingly share.

One way in which we could *not* hope to attain adequate justification for believing
an instrument to be reliable is through simple bootstrapping, whereby we accept
its deliverances on the sole basis of their being so delivered, and base a belief that
its deliverances *would* tend to be correct, and safe, simply on the inductive base
thus formed. That could not be how you gain all your justification for thinking

an instrument reliable; indeed, it could not be how you gain any, if you previously had none.

Just as one is a calculator, though not as accurate or powerful as an artefactual calculator, so one is a thermometer, though not as good as artefactual thermometers. What applies to us as temperature-sensors, moreover, applies to us as sensors more generally, as perceivers. Indeed, the instruments on which we depend most extensively and fundamentally are the perceptual modules included in our native endowment.

Much perceptual knowledge can thus be seen as instrumental. If our modules are reliable, we gain knowledge and epistemic justification by accepting their safe deliverances at face value.

We could hardly gain a justified belief by accepting a deliverance of an instrument trusted arbitrarily. Our trust in the instruments that we use to pry information off our environment cannot be just arbitrary. If we assume them to be reliable, and assume their deliverances to be systematically safe, these assumptions cannot be just intellectual whims. But nor can they all be justified exclusively on the basis of testimony. Nor can they possibly *just* lean on each other, with no support under them. How then can we ever be justified in thinking an instrument reliable, and its deliverances systematically safe?

That seems especially troubling when we see that among such instruments are to be found our perceptual modules. How could we come to know the reliability of *these* instruments? We could not do so through testimony in general, nor of course through direct bootstrapping. Could we perhaps manage it through some more indirect form of coherence-involving bootstrapping, where we do rely on perceptual input at some fundamental level without doing so in the ludicrous way of direct bootstrapping?

Epistemically justified trust in our sensory sources is a gift of natural evolution, which provides us with perceptual modules that encapsulate sensory content and reliability in a single package. We accept their deliverances at face value as a default stance, properly so. This is because the content delivered requires the reliability of the delivery in normal circumstances. What gives these introspectable sensory states the content that they have is substantially the fact that they normally respond to the truth of their content. They are thus apt for normally mediating between the relevant environmental facts suitable for such sensory uptake and the beliefs they tend to prompt.

Our senses are thus distinguished epistemically from ordinary instruments. We *can* have reasons for trusting our senses as we do, a trust justifiably based on these reasons. What is distinctive of our senses as epistemic instruments is that we do not need, and cannot have, sufficient reason for trusting each, with absolutely no reliance, either now or earlier, on any of the others.

Compare an ordinary instrument: a fuel gauge, thermometer, or speedometer, etc. As we go through an ordinary day, we find ourselves trusting such devices implicitly at many turns. We accept their deliverances at face value. What justifies such implicit trust? It could not possibly be direct bootstrapping. That would involve a vicious circle. The data required for our simple bootstrapping cannot be acquired with justification unless our implicit trust in the instrument is *already* justified.

Direct bootstrapping is of course as powerless to explain our justification for trusting our senses as it is to explain our justification for trusting our ordinary instruments. So, this is not what distinguishes our senses on one side from the instruments on the other. The difference is rather that our senses enjoy a kind of default rational justification denied to (ordinary) instruments. That is to say, we are default-justified in accepting the deliverances of our senses, but we need a rational basis for accepting the deliverances of our instruments.

We no longer need a *current* rational basis once enculturated as a competent instrument user in a technological society. The difference between instruments on one hand, and senses on the other, emerges only through memory. At some point we need a rational basis for trusting our instruments (unlike our senses), though epistemic justification can then be preserved through sheer memory even if we are later unable to recall the rational basis. But this is the way of epistemic justification generally and nothing peculiar to instrumental knowledge in particular.

Human testimony stands with the senses in providing default rational justification. And the same goes for the instrumental knowledge that gives us access to testimony through the instrument of language. The instrument of one's language is among those that we master through sub-personal means involving animal processes below the level of any kind of reasoning. And yet the instrumental knowledge that it enables is an essential link in the chain whereby we come to know much of what we know, whereby we attain our knowledge at its best, and at its most rational.

NOTES

1. The point is made by Jennifer Lackey in her review of Michael DePaul and Linda Zagzebski (eds.), *Intellectual Virtue: Perspectives from Ethics and Epistemology*, in *Notre Dame Philosophical Reviews* (Aug. 2004).

2. Nor does the woman; but I trust that context will continue to make it clear enough when my terms are gender-free.

PART III

REDUCTIONISM AND NON-REDUCTIONISM IN THE EPISTEMOLOGY OF TESTIMONY

6

Reductionism and the Distinctiveness of Testimonial Knowledge

Sanford C. Goldberg

ABSTRACT This paper aims to correct what I will argue are two common and related misconceptions in discussions of the epistemology of testimony. The first misconception is that testimonial knowledge is an epistemically distinct kind of knowledge *only if* there are testimony-specific epistemic principles implicated in the justification of beliefs formed through testimony. The second misconception is that anyone who endorses a reductionist position regarding the epistemic status of testimony, and so who denies the existence of testimony-specific epistemic principles, *ipso facto* ought to be hostile to the hypothesis that testimonial knowledge is epistemically distinctive. In this paper I argue against both misconceptions; I will do so by arguing for the distinctiveness hypothesis in a way that involves no premise any reductionist should want to deny.

1 THE CATEGORY OF TESTIMONIAL KNOWLEDGE

The core thesis of this paper is that even those who *deny* a certain uniqueness claim regarding the epistemic principles involved in testimonial justification, to the effect that

(1) The justification of beliefs through testimony implicates epistemic principles unique to testimony cases

should *acknowledge* a certain uniqueness claim regarding the distinctiveness of testimonial knowledge, to the effect that

(2) Testimonial knowledge is an epistemically unique kind of knowledge.

The significance of my core thesis lies in the fact that, to the extent that the matter of (2) is taken up, those who deny (2) typically do so on the basis of their rejection of (1); if my core thesis is correct, then such an argument is misguided in principle and even those who deny (1) should endorse (2).

I would like to thank Lizzie Fricker, Jennifer Lackey, and Ted Poston for very helpful comments on earlier versions of this paper.

Given my core thesis, it is very important to begin with a clear characterization of the subject-matter, which I am designating as 'testimonial knowledge'. Intuitively, testimonial knowledge is knowledge acquired *on the (epistemic) authority of another speaker*. Since we will want to focus on cases that bring out what, if anything, is distinctive of testimonial knowledge, we will restrict our attention to cases answering to the schema that is characteristic of such cases. Fricker (1994: 136–7) aptly characterizes this schema as "coming to know that something is so, through knowing that a certain speaker has asserted it to be so."[1]

But we can move beyond this intuitive characterization to a more explicit one, as follows. *A* has testimonial knowledge that *p* if and only if

(A) *A* knows that *p*;

(B) There is a speaker *S* whom *A* observed to offer testimony on occasion *O*, such that the proposition that *p* was understood by *A* to be presented-as-true in *S*'s testimony on *O*; and

(C) *A*'s knowledge that *p* depends for its status as knowledge on both (i) the reliability of *S*'s testimony on *O*,[2] as well as (ii) *A*'s epistemic right to rely on that testimony.

Condition (A) is straightforward: having testimonial knowledge that *p* entails knowing that *p*. Condition (B) is perhaps slightly less straightforward, but the basic idea is clear enough: having testimonial knowledge that *p* presupposes observing and understanding testimony in which that *p* is presented-as-true.[3] The need for the roundabout formulation on which the proposition that *p* is described as "presented-as-true" in the testimony, as opposed to a formulation which would describe the testimony simply as "testimony that *p*", is needed if we are to acknowledge that what the hearer can know on the basis of the testimony need not correspond exactly to what was asserted in the testimony itself. (That we should acknowledge this possibility is explicitly argued in (Goldberg 2001) and is implicit in a remark in (Burge 1993: 482 n. 20).) I should add that if the proposition that *p* is not presented-as-true in the testimony *A* observed, then *A*'s acquisition of the belief that *p* from the testimony, even if it does attain the status of knowledge, would not be knowledge acquired *on the epistemic authority of the speaker*. This brings me to condition (C), which expresses the epistemic dimension characteristic of testimony cases: *qua* knowledge, one's testimonial knowledge that *p* implicates a testifier's reliability regarding the truth of *p* (on the occasion of testimony to that effect), as well as one's own epistemic right to rely on that testimony. As we might put it: (C)(i) ensures that one's knowledge is acquired from what in fact was reliable testimony, and (C)(ii) ensures that one was epistemically entitled to accept that testimony. Although it is controversial to say what is involved with being epistemically entitled in this way—as we will see, this is an issue that separates reductionists from anti-reductionists regarding testimony—the need for the addition of (ii) is indicated once we recognize that it is one thing to be confronted with what in fact is reliable testimony, and quite another to be epistemically entitled to believe that the testimony was reliable. (I will return to this below.)

I submit that conditions (A)–(C) state individually necessary and jointly sufficient conditions on a subject *A*'s having testimonial knowledge that *p*. I also believe that conditions (A)–(C) are neutral with respect to (1) and (2). However, before I can confirm this, I want to identify the two main positions within the epistemology of testimony, reductionism and anti-reductionism, since it is in terms of a theorist's commitment to one of these positions that she typically will reason to her verdict regarding (1) and (2). After briefly presenting the reductionist and anti-reductionist positions, I will argue that it begs no question against either side to regard (A)–(C) as stating individually necessary and jointly sufficient conditions on *A*'s having testimonial knowledge that *p*. Simply put, accepting this characterization of testimonial knowledge is consistent with any position one takes regarding (1) and (2) respectively.

2 REDUCTIONISM AND ANTI-REDUCTIONISM

There are two traditional positions that have been formulated in connection with the epistemology of testimony. In characterizing these positions I am going to be following Fricker (1994). My reasons for doing so are strategic. First, Fricker's characterization of these positions links them directly to their respective views regarding (1), the thesis regarding epistemic principles unique to testimony. For this reason her characterization of these positions enables a quick summary of how one might think to argue *from* a denial of (1) *to* a denial of (2)—precisely the sort of argument I aim to be criticizing. Second and relatedly, Fricker herself appears to endorse the sort of argument I aim to be criticizing. Consequently, my use of her characterization of the positions will inoculate my argument against the charge that I have somehow begged the question e.g. by accepting a loaded characterization of the debate in the epistemology of testimony. Finally I might add, as a third reason to follow Fricker's characterization, that I find it to be a good characterization anyway.

According to Fricker, the core question confronting the epistemologist in connection with testimony pertains to the *justification* of beliefs through testimony. She characterizes the "problem of justifying belief through testimony" as "the problem of showing how it can be the case that a hearer on a particular occasion has the epistemic right to believe what she is told—to believe a particular speaker's assertion" (1994: 128). She then identifies two possible 'solutions' to this problem:

The solution can take either of two routes. It may be shown that the required step—from 'S asserted that P' to 'P'—can be made as a piece of inference involving only familiar deductive and inductive principles, applied to empirically established premises. Alternatively, it may be argued that the step is legitimised as the exercise of a special presumptive epistemic right to trust, not dependent on evidence. (1994: 128)

The first route is the *reductionist* route, the latter is the *anti-reductionist* route. From this it is clear that anti-reductionists accept, while reductionists deny, (1) (the thesis of epistemic principles unique to testimony cases).

Return now to the contention that the characterization of testimonial knowledge in Section 1 is neutral, both on the issue between the reductionist and the anti-reductionist, and on the truth-value of both (1) and (2).

Regarding the issue between the reductionist and the anti-reductionist, I submit that this matter is aptly cast as a debate over what it takes to satisfy (C)(ii).[4] Regarding (C)(ii), the reductionist will think that a hearer A has an epistemic right to rely on the say-so of a speaker S on a given occasion only if A has reasons (including those of a standard inductive sort) to think that S's assertion that p is a reliable indication of the truth of p. Such reasons will presumably involve A's beliefs regarding S's credibility in general, S's position *vis-à-vis* the subject-matter of her testimony, the *prima facie* plausibility of what S said (as determined by A's background beliefs), the absence of the trappings of guile or insincerity, and so on. (Of course, A's reasons for accepting the testimony need not involve all of these, though they may.) The important point for the reductionist is simply that the justification of A's belief in what another speaker S says does not appeal to any epistemic principle unique to testimony cases. Contrast the anti-reductionist position. For her part, the anti-reductionist will think that A has an epistemic right to rely on S's say-so as long as A has no (doxastic, normative, or factual) defeaters for the claim that S's say-so was reliable.[5] This sort of position goes hand-in-hand with another characteristic thesis endorsed by anti-reductionists, to the effect that there is a defeasible but presumptive right to trust other speakers. (This is the sort of testimony-specific epistemic principle whose existence the reductionist is anxious to deny.) It should be clear that (C)(ii) does not settle this matter, but instead only indicates that it is a matter to be settled (as part of a complete account of testimonial knowledge).

Regarding the truth-value of (1) and (2), I submit that the above characterization of testimonial knowledge entails nothing in this regard. Given the point of the previous paragraph, we have already seen this in connection with (1): the truth or falsity of (1) does not affect the adequacy of (A)–(C) as a characterization of testimonial knowledge, but rather affects how we should conceive of the satisfaction of condition (C)(ii). To see that the truth-value of (2) is independent of the adequacy of that characterization, it suffices to show that the supposition of either truth-value is consistent with that characterization. Suppose that (2) is true, that testimonial knowledge is a distinctive sort of knowledge. Then presumably something will make it distinctive, epistemologically speaking. What makes it distinctive may be that it is knowledge whose status as knowledge depends on epistemic principles unique to testimony; but perhaps what makes it distinctive is something else. (Indeed, I will be arguing for the latter case.) The point is simply that the supposition that testimonial knowledge is distinctive is consistent with treating (A)–(C) as individually necessary and jointly sufficient conditions on the possession of the sort of knowledge we are presently supposing is distinctive. Suppose then that (2) is false, that testimonial knowledge is *not* a distinctive sort of knowledge. Then presumably (1) is false; but nothing regarding our characterization of testimonial knowledge would follow. What would follow, rather, is that the sort of knowledge picked out by (A)–(C) is not an interesting epistemic kind. Under such circumstances, we might still want to retain the category of 'testimonial knowledge' so understood; but if we did we should be aware that it would have the same status as the category of, for example, 'microscope knowledge', where this is knowledge acquired by reliance on microscopes.[6] The point would then simply be that though we might have pragmatic reasons to continue to use the category, it is a bit of a grab-bag category that should not be taken to mark off a distinctive epistemic kind.

3 REDUCTIONIST ANTIPATHY FOR THE DISTINCTIVE-KIND HYPOTHESIS

My aim in this paper is to argue for (2), the epistemic distinctiveness of testimonial knowledge, in a way that does not depend on (1), the hypothesis of epistemic principles unique to testimony cases. To be sure, theorists who accept (1) have a reason to accept (2): if there are epistemic principles unique to testimony cases, then there is some reason to think that the sort of knowledge acquired through testimony is unique, insofar as a complete account of that knowledge will presumably invoke those principles unique to testimony (the uniqueness of those principles carrying over to render the knowledge unique as well). What I deny is the converse, that (2) is true *only if* (1) is. On the contrary, I want to argue that testimonial knowledge is epistemologically distinctive whether or not there are epistemic principles unique to testimony cases.

Before presenting the case for such a claim, I want to point out why I think it is worthwhile making this claim. To do so I want to cite reasoning from the literature in which (by all appearances) the issue of (2), the distinctness of testimonial knowledge, is taken up from the perspective of the assumption that (2) is true only if (1) (the claim asserting testimony-specific epistemic principles) is. The passage I cite is from Fricker; though I suspect that she is not the only philosopher to approach (2) from the perspective of the offending assumption.

Starting off a section of her 1994 paper with the question, "Is knowledge through testimony a distinctive category of knowledge at all?" (1994: 136), Fricker goes on to defend a qualified negative answer to this question. An examination of her reasoning suggests that the offending assumption, that an affirmative answer to her question turns on the existence of a testimony-specific principle of justification, may be playing a significant role in her reflections on the distinctiveness (or not) of testimonial knowledge. I quote her at length:

Testimony ... does indeed constitute a distinctive kind of *epistemic link*. There is a distinctive type of connection, characteristic of testimony, between a state of affairs, and a hearer's coming to believe in its obtaining. This connection runs through another *person*, a speaker—her own original acquisition of the same belief, her other mental states, her subsequent linguistic act, which transmits that belief to the hearer. There being this distinctive type of link between a hearer, and what she comes to believe, in testimony, means that there is a distinctive type of justification associated with testimony ...: we can identify a characteristic justificatory schema *S* [involving the move from 'Speaker *S* asserted that *p*' to '*p*']. A hearer has knowledge through testimony just when she has knowledge whose content is given by appropriate instances of the elements of *S*, and can cite such knowledge, or evidence for it, in defense of her belief. But what there is not ... is any new *principle of inference* or other normative epistemic principle involved, which is special to testimony. ... This makes the 'problem of justifying testimony' unlike the 'problem of induction'. In the latter, the task is to show the legitimacy of a general principle of inference, one which is broadly comparable to the principles of deductive inference in the way in which it validates particular inferences of the form in question. It is therefore appropriate to approach the 'problem of induction' at a completely general level. The task is to show that an arbitrary inductive inference is valid, by showing that the principle of inference involved in any such inference is a valid one. ... Now the anti-reductionist may mistakenly suppose that the task of justifying testimony must be approached by looking for some highly general premise or principle which would serve to justify an arbitrary testimony belief. ... My local-reductionist approach avoids the initial mistake. ... If what were in question were a special normative epistemic principle, concerning testimony as a *distinctive and unitary category of knowledge*, then it would indeed apply indifferently to an arbitrary piece of testimony, and the task of justifying it would need to be conducted at an abstract general level. ... But if there is no special epistemic principle in question, and what is common to all and only instances of knowledge through testimony is just a characteristic kind of belief-producing causal process, then there is no reason why what justifies belief in particular instances of testimony must be some proposition or principle applying to testimony in general. Instead, what justifies a hearer's belief in a particular assertion may be her knowledge of relevant facts about that assertion and speaker, which warrant her in trusting him. (Fricker 1994: 136–7; some italics added)

Fricker goes on to write that

Looking for generalizations about the reliability or otherwise of testimony, in the inclusive sense of serious assertions aimed at communication of belief, as a homogenous whole, will not be an enlightening project. Illuminating generalizations, if there are any, will be about particular types of testimony, differentiated according to subject matter, or type of speaker, or both. True, there is a belief-producing process characteristic of testimony, and consequently a generic type of justification, as captured in *S*. But when it comes to the probability of accuracy of speakers' assertions, and what sorts of factors warrant a hearer in trusting a speaker, *testimony is not a unitary category*. ... One aspect of this disunity is ... that while there are certain limited epistemic rights to trust involved in particular types of testimony, there is no blanket [presumption that one is entitled] to believe what is asserted without needing evidence of trustworthiness, applicable to serious assertions aimed at communication as a whole, regardless of subject matter and circumstance. (Fricker 1994: 137–8; italics mine)

Now it is not entirely clear that Fricker here is assuming that (2) only if (1), that is, that testimonial knowledge is a distinctive epistemic kind only if there are testimony-specific epistemic principles. But various things about these passages suggest that Fricker is making this assumption. First, having started off the section with the unqualified question whether "knowledge through testimony" is a "distinctive category of knowledge", Fricker moves without comment to the question whether there are any epistemic principles unique to testimony. (The lack of comments regarding such a transition would be explained if she is making the offending assumption.) Second, by the end of the section the only manner in which she addresses the unqualified question is by noting that testimony is not a "unitary category" insofar as "the probability of accuracy of speakers' assertions, and what sorts of factors warrant a hearer in trusting a speaker" are concerned. Admittedly, this leaves open the issue whether testimonial knowledge *is* a unitary category in ways that go beyond the fact (noted by Fricker) that there is "a belief-producing process characteristic of testimony". But nowhere does Fricker herself note this possibility, let alone endorse it. This silence is curious if she really does allow for the possibility envisaged: one would be forgiven for thinking that if Fricker does want to allow for the possibility that testimony *is* a distinctive category of knowledge, in ways that go beyond the fact that such knowledge involves a characteristic belief-producing process, she would have said so.[7]

These considerations do not vindicate the charge that Fricker is making the offending assumption that (2) is true only if (1) is. But they do suggest that something like this assumption may be playing a guiding, if implicit and perhaps unacknowledged, role in her thinking about the distinctiveness of testimonial knowledge.[8] In what follows I argue that such an assumption ought not to figure into our thinking about the distinctiveness of testimonial knowledge—whether we are reductionists (like Fricker) or not.

4 IN SUPPORT OF THE DISTINCTIVE-KIND HYPOTHESIS

In Section 2 I defended the contention that nothing in the category of testimonial knowledge, understood in terms of (A)–(C), begs any relevant questions. I now want to draw on that characterization to argue that testimonial knowledge so understood *is* a distinctive epistemic kind. The main interest of the argument to follow is that it assumes nothing that a reductionist should want to deny. If successful, it shows that a case can be made for (2), the epistemic distinctiveness of testimonial knowledge, even if we do not assume (1), the hypothesis of epistemic principles unique to testimony cases.

I want to begin with a programmatic statement of the position I will defend. My main contention is that testimonial knowledge is a distinctive kind of knowledge in that this sort of knowledge, but no other, is associated with *a characteristic expansion in the sorts of epistemically relevant moves that can be made by the subject in her attempt to identify the direct epistemic support enjoyed by her belief.* As I will try to bring out, this feature of testimonial knowledge reflects the fact that there is something epistemologically distinctive about relying on the epistemic authority of another rational being: it is because of what is distinctive in relying on the epistemic authority of another rational being, that there is a characteristic expansion in the sort of moves that can be made in defense of a belief acquired on such authority. The characteristic expansion, I suggest, is that testimonial knowledge gives rise to the hearer's right to *pass the epistemic buck* (in a sense to be characterized below) after her own justificatory resources have been exhausted. After arguing for this, I will argue further that the phenomenon of epistemic buck-passing should be recognized as a core part of the phenomenon that is testimonial knowledge, no matter one's attitude towards the claim that there are testimony-specific epistemic principles. This is because what generates the hearer's right to pass the epistemic buck is not any testimony-specific epistemic principle. That right is generated rather by the key features at play in cases in which one rational being relies on the authority of another rational being, in the course of shaping its beliefs.[9]

I want to begin with a simple case. Smith wants to know the temperature. She consults a thermometer visible from her kitchen window. The thermometer reads 44°F. Smith has strong inductive reasons to believe that the thermometer is reliable. So she forms the belief that it is 44°F. If challenged to defend her belief that it is 44°F, she will cite her reading of the thermometer, together with all of her evidence for thinking that the thermometer was reliable. (Some of this evidence will involve her inductive reasons for thinking that the thermometer is reliable; but presumably other evidence will come in the form of the coherence of the *present deliverance* of the thermometer with Smith's background beliefs regarding such matters as average temperatures for this time of year, what she can deduce regarding the range of possible temperatures from the day's visual appearances, etc.) Once she has cited all of this, she has *exhausted* the responses available to her in the face of a challenge to defend (or to identify the epistemic support enjoyed by) her belief that it is 44°F.

Now contrast this case with the following. Smith, wanting to know the temperature, asks Jones, who replies by telling her that it is 44°F. Smith knows Jones to be a most reliable source—someone who never asserts something for which he lacks substantial evidence. Consequently, on the strength of Jones's word, Smith forms the belief that it is 44°F. If challenged to defend her belief that it is 44°F, Smith will cite her observation of Jones's testimony, together with all of her (Smith's) evidence for thinking that Jones is a reliable interlocutor. (Again, some of this evidence will involve Smith's inductive reasons for thinking Jones to be a reliable interlocutor; but presumably other evidence will come in the form of the coherence of *Jones's present testimony* with Smith's background beliefs about average temperatures for this time of year etc.) But—and this is the key—even after Smith cites all of this, there remains a *further* response available to her in the face of a challenge to defend (or to identify the epistemic support enjoyed by) her belief that it is 44°F. She can simply *pass the buck to Jones*, as follows:

I've told you all the reasons I have for trusting Jones's testimony; so if what you want is more in the way of a defense of the claim that it is 44°F (as opposed to more in the way of a defense of the claim that Jones's say-so to that effect was trustworthy), you can simply *ask Jones himself*. He'll be able to provide considerations that more directly support the claim that it is 44°F (or else, failing that, will be able to direct you to the person from whom *he* acquired the belief).

Several points are worth noting about this sort of response.

First, the sort of challenge that might prompt this reply is a sort of challenge that can, and often does, arise in connection with beliefs formed through testimony. It is very important to Dien to know who won last night's baseball game. (No media sources are presently accessible to him.) Anita tells him that the Yankees won. Dien asks Anita how she knows this (this was not the reply Dien wanted!), and she tells him that Brad told her so. Because the outcome of the game is extraordinarily important to Dien, he wants more in the way of a defense of the claim that the Yankees won, than Anita's reasons for thinking Brad's say-so to that effect was reliable. (As is common in connection with testimony cases, Anita's reasons for trusting Brad's testimony fall short of establishing the truth of what Brad said.) Seeing this, Anita replies with a move of last resort: "OK, then, go ask Brad. Since he's the one who told me so, he'll be in a better position to address directly your concern regarding whether the Yankees won last night." There can be little doubt that these sorts of situations arise with some regularity.

Second, this "move of last resort" is an epistemically appropriate move for Anita to make at this point in the dialectic. Having exhausted her own justificatory resources in giving Dien her reasons for trusting Brad's testimony, and seeing that more epistemic support for what was attested is wanted, Anita points Dien in the direction where further epistemic support can be found: to Brad, the source himself. And it is clear that Anita is justified in believing that it is to Brad that Dien ought to be looking, if further epistemic support (for the claim that the Yankees won last night) is what Dien wants. Indeed, Anita's reasons for thinking Brad trustworthy on the present occasion are *ipso facto* reasons for thinking that further support for the claim at issue can be found in connection with him—either in the form of reasons Brad himself would be able to offer in support of the claim that the Yankees won last night, or else in the form of warrants generated by the process through which Brad formed the belief that the Yankees won last night (warrants that we might be able to discern, even if Brad himself cannot, by reflecting on those processes[10]).

Third, and relatedly, nothing in the story told so far should offend any reductionist sensibilities. This is for the simple reason that the move of last resort is a move that is epistemically appropriate only given that the recipient of the testimony (in this case, Anita) has *already* justified her reliance on that testimony. The reductionist may place as stringent conditions as she likes on the justified acceptance of testimony. The point remains that, even by the lights of a substantive reductionist requirement on testimonial justification, not all testimony a hearer is (by the lights of the reductionist conception) justified in accepting is true.[11] For this reason the question can still be raised whether the testimony, which the hearer justifiably accepted, was true. To address *this* question, the hearer's appeal to the source interlocutor is perfectly epistemically appropriate; indeed, it is unclear whether anything *other than* such an appeal can address this question at all.[12]

Fourth, the take-home point here concerns the epistemic significance of relying on the presentation-as-true of another rational source. Return to the case above in which we contrasted a subject's reliance on a thermometer's 'testimony' with reliance on another rational source's testimony to the effect that the temperature is 44°F. The point I wish to make is that reliance on the deliverances of another rational being has an epistemological significance absent from the case of reliance on mere instruments (e.g. thermometers); and that this difference reflects the different metaphysical status that rational beings have (relative to mere instruments). The difference in metaphysical status is reflected in the fact that rational beings themselves *rely on* (and *shape and express their views in accordance with*) evidence of the sort that reliable instruments *merely offer*. A rational being engages in the project of shaping its beliefs to fit the evidence it has. Because this project is to some degree under the being's own rational control, this shaping process can be done in better and worse ways (epistemologically speaking), in ways that are epistemically sanctioned, and in ways that are not. Consequently, the notion of epistemic responsibility finds a home here. The result is that, in relying on a rational being's testimony, one is relying on that being to have lived up to her relevant epistemic responsibilities.[13] A merely reliable instrument, by contrast, operates according to the laws of nature.[14] Because there is no 'rational control' to speak of, the notion of epistemic responsibility has no home here. In relying on the 'testimony' of a merely reliable instrument, one is relying on the laws of nature and the systematic and predictable effects these have in connection with the instrument's construction (when no noise-introducing factors intervene). It makes no sense to say that one is relying on the instrument to have lived up to its relevant epistemic responsibilities; the instrument has none.

The upshot of these reflections is that the reliance on the authority of another rational being is itself epistemologically significant—something that should be accommodated by any adequate epistemological account of testimony-invoking belief and knowledge. The proposal on offer is that the epistemological significance of such reliance is seen in the characteristic expansion of epistemically appropriate moves that can be made in response to challenges to defend (or to identify the epistemic support enjoyed by) one's belief. To a first approximation—though a slight modification will be introduced below, in

Section 5[15]—the point is this: in cases in which the knowledge was not acquired on the basis of testimony, the only epistemically appropriate moves that can be made in response to a "How do you know?" question are those in which one produces one's justifications for the belief in question—roughly, the reasons one has for believing it.[16] If the belief was acquired on the basis of another's testimony, however, a subject has *not* exhausted the epistemically appropriate moves available to her, once she has exhausted her justification for the belief. On the contrary, when the knowledge is testimonial knowledge, even after the subject has exhausted her justification for the belief, there remains the 'move of last resort', whereby she passes the epistemic buck onto her interlocutor. Since this move is epistemically appropriate—the subject is epistemically entitled to make this move—only if she has already vindicated her epistemic right to rely on the testimony in question, the hypothesis of epistemic buck-passing begs no question against even the most rabid reductionist regarding testimony.

5 ON THE DISTINCTIVE NATURE OF TESTIMONIAL SUPPORT

My claim so far has been that testimonial knowledge is a distinctive epistemic kind, not for implicating some testimony-specific rule of inference, but rather for being associated with the phenomenon of epistemic buck-passing. But it might be wondered whether this case for the distinctiveness of testimonial knowledge succeeds. One worry on this score concerns whether what I have been calling the phenomenon of epistemic buck-passing is involved in cases of *non*-testimonial knowledge.[17] If it is, then this feature of testimonial knowledge does not demarcate it as a *distinctive* epistemic kind. Another issue concerns whether the phenomenon of 'epistemic buck-passing' should be understood as an epistemic phenomenon in the first place. Perhaps this phenomenon merely registers an interesting *psychological* fact about testimonial knowledge, that when speakers have such knowledge, they are disposed to pass the buck in the manner described above. If so, then this feature of testimonial knowledge does not demarcate it as a distinctive *epistemic* kind. The comments that follow attempt to address both of these worries; I address the latter worry first.

Various things can be said in defense of the contention that the sort of buck-passing described above is to be understood in the first instance in epistemological terms.

The first point to be made builds on something implicit in the discussion in Section 4. Implicit in the discussion of the phenomenon of buck-passing is that we should distinguish between (a) the *justifications* that a hearer has to accept for what was attested, on the one hand, and (b) the *total epistemic support* that a hearer has for her belief that *p*, when this belief is a belief in what was attested. Take a case in which hearer *A* is justified in taking *S*'s testimony to be a reliable indication of the truth of what is being attested. Since *A* is justified in taking *S*'s testimony to be a reliable indication of the truth of what is being attested, *A* is justified in thinking that the testimony is properly based to count as knowledge. As a result, *A* is *prima facie* justified in thinking that whatever it is that provides the proper base for *S*'s testimony also provides a base, albeit inaccessible to *A* herself, for *A*'s own belief in what was attested.[18] This reflects the difference between (a) and (b): *A* is at least *prima facie* justified in believing that the epistemic support that her testimony-based belief enjoys outstrips what she herself can provide by way of a justification for that belief.

It is worth characterizing the nature of the sort of support at issue in (b). Our question is this: what sort of support, *beyond* the support provided by *A*'s justification for accepting *S*'s testimony, is provided by that testimony itself? I will call this sort of support *distinctly testimonial (epistemic) support*. Two immediate things should be noted about distinctly testimonial support: first, it is a sort of support that will typically be *inaccessible to the hearer A herself*; and second, nevertheless it is a sort of support that bears *more directly on A's testimony-based belief than A's own justification does*.

First, distinctly testimonial support is a sort of support that will typically be inaccessible to the hearer herself. This merely reiterates the point that speaker *S*'s basis for believing what she expresses in her testimony is itself not typically accessible, and certainly not accessible 'from the armchair', to hearer *A*. But at the same time, distinctly testimonial support bears more directly on *A*'s belief than *A*'s own justification does. As we noted above, *A*'s justification for believing that *p* is grounded in *A*'s belief that *S*'s testimony was reliable (or at least that it was not unreliable), which in turn is supported e.g. by *A*'s beliefs that *S* is generally trustworthy, that *S* is competent with respect to the subject matter of her present testimony, that what *S* said coheres with *A*'s relevant background beliefs, etc. We might say: these beliefs of *A*'s provide *direct* epistemic support for *A*'s belief that *S*'s testimony was reliable, and hence (given that *S*'s testimony was to the effect that *p*) provide *indirect* epistemic support to *A*'s belief that *p*.[19] This distinction between direct and indirect support is a key to understanding the possibility (noted above) of someone challenging *A*'s belief that *p*, even after recognizing that belief as justified. Confronted with such a challenge, nothing that *A* says to establish her right to accept the testimony will have a direct bearing; what *will* have such a bearing is the basis *A*'s *source* (= *S*) had for the belief she (*S*) expressed in the testimony *A* accepted.[20]

This distinction between direct and indirect epistemic support enables us to respond to the first worry mentioned at the outset of this section, to the effect that testimonial knowledge is not the only sort of knowledge associated with the phenomenon of epistemic buck-passing. Consider the following case. McSorley reports that there was a red car in Richardson's driveway a half-hour ago. Richardson (who was not home at the time) asks him how he knows that. McSorley responds that he distinctly remembers having seen a red car there. A lay epistemologist by nature, McSorley adds that memory and perception are reliable belief-forming processes. But when Richardson presses McSorley regarding how he knows *that*, McSorley simply shrugs: "I don't know; go ask the experts working on perception and memory." If this is a case of epistemic buck-passing, it challenges the idea that the phenomenon of epistemic buck-passing is what singles testimonial knowledge out as a *distinctive* epistemic kind.

Two things can be said in response. First, it is not clear that the foregoing *is* a case of epistemically acceptable buck-passing; some epistemic internalists will want to deny this. But even if we waive this first point, the challenge posed by this case can be met by appeal to the distinction between direct and indirect epistemic support. Testimonial knowledge is unique in that the epistemic buck-passing appropriate to it is an epistemically appropriate move whose point is to identify a *direct* source of epistemic support for the content believed. When Anita passes the buck to Brad, she does so in a context in which it is already settled that she has an epistemic *right* to rely on his testimony; what is at issue concerns the direct epistemic support for the content at issue (namely, that the Yankees won last night). Her passing the buck to Brad speaks precisely to this issue of direct epistemic support for the content believed. The contrast with the case above is clear. McSorley passes the buck to the relevant experts on perception, not to identify a source of further direct epistemic support for his claim *that there was a red car in Richardson's driveway a half-hour ago*, but rather to identify a source of direct epistemic support for the claim that perception and memory are reliable belief-forming processes. The result is that, even if he is entitled to pass the buck in this way, his doing so is a move that is epistemically distinct from the buck-passing move appropriate to testimony.

The contrast, then, is this. Testimony cases are those in which the subject's own justification for her belief provides only indirect support for what she believes—the point of buck-passing in such cases being to manifest the subject's awareness of further, direct epistemic support (albeit introspectively inaccessible to her) for what she believes. The case of McSorley's report of a red car in Richardson's driveway is one in which the subject's own justification for his belief already provides direct support for what he believes—the point of buck-passing in such cases being to provide further direct support for a hypothesis (the reliability of perception and memory) that itself provides further *indirect* support for what he believes. Distinctly testimonial support for a hearer's belief that *p*, then, is epistemic support that (in virtue of the hearer's reliance on her interlocutor's authority) both directly bears on the truth of *p*, and is introspectively inaccessible to the hearer herself.

It is worth noting that other authors have appreciated something very much in the spirit of my characterization of distinctly testimonial support. Thus Burge (1993: 485–6) distinguishes between a speaker's 'proprietary justification' and her 'extended body of justification', in a way that corresponds to my talk above of (a) the *justifications* that a hearer has to accept what was attested, on the one hand, and (b) the *total epistemic support* that a hearer has for her belief that *p*. And similarly, Faulkner's (2000) 'hybrid' theory of testimony distinguishes between the matter of being justified in accepting testimony, and the epistemic support a recipient would have once she has accepted a piece of testimony. Faulkner designates the former sort of support as falling under the 'principle of assent' and the latter as falling under the 'principle of warrant'; and he goes on to note that the 'extended warrant' of a proposition presented by testimony is

the conjunction of the warrant possessed by the original speaker for believing this proposition together with any further warrant provided by the chain(s) of communication. (2000: 591)[21]

My present point is a version of the same claim. Only the significance that I am attaching to this claim is not restricted to the nature of testimonial support, but rather is being used to suggest the sense in which testimonial knowledge is a distinctive epistemic kind. My claim has been that this distinctiveness is seen in what we all should recognize as the familiar 'move of last resort' appropriate to testimony cases; and that even reductionists about testimony ought to accept the hypothesis of distinctly testimonial knowledge, so defended.

6 CONCLUSION

The main ambitions of this paper have been (first) to defend the hypothesis that testimonial knowledge is a distinctive epistemic kind, and (second) to offer a defense that should not offend any party to the debate regarding the proper account of testimonial justification. If successful, my argument should put to rest any thought of denying the distinctiveness of testimonial knowledge on the grounds that there are no testimony-specific epistemic principles. More positively, it should convince all parties that (and in what sense) testimonial knowledge is an epistemically distinctive kind after all.

REFERENCES

Audi, R. (1997), 'The Place of Testimony in the Fabric of Knowledge and Justification', *American Philosophical Quarterly*, 34/4: 405–22.

Burge, T. (1993), 'Content Preservation', *Philosophical Review*, 102/4: 457–88.

Faulkner, P. (2000), 'The Social Character of Testimonial Knowledge', *Journal of Philosophy*, 97/11: 581–601.

Fricker, E. (1987), 'The Epistemology of Testimony', *Proceedings of the Aristotelian Society*, suppl. vol. 61: 57–83.

——— (1994), 'Against Gullibility', in B. K. Matilal and A. Chakrabarti (eds.), *Knowing from Words* (Amsterdam: Kluwer Academic Publishers), 125–61.

Goldberg, S. (2001), 'Testimonially Based Knowledge from False Testimony', *Philosophical Quarterly*, 51/205: 512–26.

Graham, P. (2000), 'Transferring Knowledge', *Noûs*, 34/1: 131–52.

Grice, H. P. (1989), *Studies in the Way of Words* (Cambridge, Mass.: Harvard University Press).

Jack, J. (1994), 'The Role of Comprehension', in B. K. Matilal and A. Chakrabarti (eds.), *Knowing from Words* (Amsterdam: Kluwer Academic Publishers), 163–93.

Lackey, J. (1999), 'Testimonial Knowledge and Transmission', *Philosophical Quarterly*, 49/197: 471–90.

——(2003), 'A Minimal Expression of Non-Reductionism in the Epistemology of Testimony', *Noûs*, 37/4: 706–23.

NOTES

1. As Fricker herself remarks (1994: 130), it is appropriate to restrict one's attention to these cases, since it is in these cases that one can get the clearest handle on what, if anything, is distinctive of the sort of epistemic support testimony provides. See also Jack (1994: 163), who speaks of such cases as 'radical communication', where "a hearer comes to believe what another says and there is no basis for his belief which is independent of the testimony itself."

2. See Fricker (1994: 147) and Graham (2000: 142) for a characterization of the relevant notion of reliability. (Here I aim to be neutral on how best to understand this notion.) And see also Lackey (2003) for a defense of the claim that among the necessary conditions on testimonial knowledge will be a condition on the environment in which testimony is received. (If Lackey is correct, this will affect the relevant notion of reliability.)

3. I borrow the notion of a presentation-as-true, as applied to testimony, from Burge (1993).

4. It might be thought that the issues between the reductionist and the anti-reductionist carry over to (C)(i) as well. That is, it might be thought that reductionists and anti-reductionists will disagree over the sort of epistemic support provided by the *de facto* reliability of a piece of testimony: the reductionist will maintain, while the anti-reductionist will deny, that the epistemic support provided by a piece of reliable testimony can be subsumed by the factors that entitle the hearer to accept that testimony. (Call this the 'Factors Generating Entitlement Exhaust Epistemic Support' thesis, or FGEEES for short.) However, one of the conclusions of this paper will be that the reductionist should *not* endorse the FGEEES thesis. On the contrary, reductionism is best construed (*à la* Fricker) as a position regarding the conditions on a hearer's having the *epistemic right* to accept what she is told. Construed in this way, reductionism is consistent with denying the FGEEES thesis; and in Sections 4 and 5 I present arguments to the effect that the reductionist *ought* to reject FGEEES. See also Lackey (Chapter 8 in this volume) for an argument against FGEEES. Although Lackey (who appears to assume that reductionism is committed to FGEEES) takes her argument against FGEEES to be an argument against reductionism itself, I note that reductionists have the option of taking her argument to be a reason not to be committed to FGEEES.

5. I borrow the notion of doxastic, normative, and factual defeaters from Lackey (1999: 474–6).

6. This way of putting the point was suggested to me by an anonymous referee for another paper of mine.
7. One final consideration might be worth noting. Fricker's point about 'no illuminating generalizations', which is meant to support the verdict that testimonial knowledge is not a 'unitary category', settles that matter *only if* the assumption of illuminating generalizations is *required* by the hypothesis that testimonial knowledge is a unitary category. So far as I can tell, the only reason for thinking that the assumption of illuminating generalizations *is* required by the hypothesis that testimonial knowledge is a unitary category, is if one thinks that the unitary category claim rests on the existence of testimony-specific epistemic principles (which the illuminating generalizations might then provide, or at least justify).
8. Although I should say that Fricker herself has told me (in private correspondence) that she did not intend to be making the offending assumption.
9. Some readers may recognize the appeal to the distinctiveness of relying on a rational being from Burge (1993). Unlike the argument from Burge (1993), however, here I aim to appeal to what is distinctively involved in relying on a rational being, not to warrant an anti-reductionist thesis, but rather to warrant a claim regarding the distinctiveness of testimonial knowledge. I share a premise with Burge, but I want to establish a different conclusion.
10. It might be thought: insofar as we are relying on the warrants (as opposed to the justifications) Brad had for claiming that the Yankees won last night, we are treating him as a (merely) reliable mechanism—thereby undermining the 'contrast' I am trying to make between, for example, the case of relying on *a thermometer* and the case of relying on *a person's testimony* regarding the temperature. But the contrast is not undermined even in this sort of scenario. First, the manner in which 'testimony' is 'produced' differs according to whether the source is a thermometer or a person. To wit: if a person asserts something for which she lacks adequate grounds, we blame her for not living up to her epistemic responsibilities. There is no analogue of this in the case of a thermometer: even if the thermometer is not functioning properly, and so in this sense 'provides' a false temperature reading, we would not blame the thermometer as failing to live up to its epistemic responsibilities—for it has none. And second and relatedly, unlike a thermometer, a person is, or at least is regarded as having the epistemic responsibility to be, rationally sensitive to conditions that would *defeat* her warrant for a given claim. So even if we are relying on Brad's warrant for the claim that the Yankees won last night, still, the fact that we are relying on Brad *qua* rational agent has epistemic significance. The proof of this is that, had something gone wrong in the process by which Brad arrived at his baseball belief—what he was watching on TV was not the Yankees game itself but rather a bunch of actors pretending (lamely!) to be playing a baseball game—we might well have blamed Brad for not having been alive to that. (He should have known as much: although the game was supposed to be Yankees vs. Red Sox, neither of the two teams wore the Yankees' tell-tale pinstripes.) No such blame has any place in connection with our reliance on a merely reliable instrument. I should say that, in appealing to a notion of epistemic responsibility and epistemic blame, I am *not* assuming that these notions exhaust the notion of epistemic justification; I regard that as an open question.

11. There may be epistemic externalists who would deny that there are justified but false beliefs (whether testimonial or otherwise). To those, the claim I am making could be reformulated by replacing 'justified' with one of the internalist or subjective justification notions they recognize. (If they recognize none, then the point could be case in terms of 'seeming subjective justification' or some such.)

12. It should be clear from this that, in passing the epistemic buck in the way appropriate to testimonial knowledge, the subject is *not* shirking her epistemic responsibilities. Rather she is pointing to a source of further (and, I will argue below, *direct*) epistemic support for the content believed—support which the recipient of testimony herself is not typically in a position to provide herself (at least not on the basis of what she can introspect).

13. It is worth noting in this connection that the relevant epistemic responsibilities include those attending the performance of the speech act of *assertion* (and any other speech acts, if any, apt for the transmission of knowledge). Consider for example Grice's norm of Quality, which he took to include the maxim, "Do not say that for which you lack adequate evidence" (Grice 1989: 27).

14. It might be thought that this contrast between merely reliable instruments and rational agents is weakened if the behaviour of the latter is governed by psychological laws. There may be something to this point. At the same time, and without putting too fine a point on it, we can say that even if rational agents are governed by psychological laws, it would seem that our knowledge of these laws, and our ability to apply these to particular cases to predict what a speaker will say, is (and, as a matter of practical fact, is likely to remain) deeply impoverished. This being so, there will remain an epistemic asymmetry between our reliance on merely reliable instruments and our reliance on rational agents. When the workings of the former are sufficiently well understood (take the case of the thermometer), we can vindicate our belief in their reliability by appeal to laws whose predictions in the present case we can discern; not so in the case of rational agents. I would hope that more can be said in defense of this asymmetry than the present epistemological point; but doing so will have to be the aim of another paper. (I thank Jennifer Lackey for indicating the need to address this matter.)

15. The modification will involve distinguishing between direct and indirect types of epistemic support. In Section 5 I discuss the need for this distinction.

16. I am *not* supposing, however, that what a subject does in response to a "How do you know?" question—namely, offering one's justification—is producing the sort of thing that renders one's true belief *knowledge*. Some writers (e.g. Plantinga) have argued that knowledge does not require justification at all; still others (e.g. Goldman), that the sort of justification required by knowledge is not the sort of justification that needs to be accessible to the subject herself. My present point does not require entering into these controversies.

17. I thank Ted Poston and Jennifer Lackey, both of whom (independently) made this suggestion to me. (The illustration to follow is Poston's.)

18. *A*'s justification, for thinking that whatever it is that provides the proper base for *S*'s testimony also provides a base for *A*'s own belief in what was attested, is *prima facie*: perhaps *A* has other beliefs which would defeat the epistemic support that *S*'s

testimony (and the evidence and warrants S herself had for what she asserted) would otherwise provide to A.

19. I admit that I am not entirely certain how best to explicate this distinction between direct and indirect epistemic support; but it has sufficient intuitive appeal, and it is sufficiently clear at least in outline, that it can be appealed to prior to having a complete analysis in hand.

20. Of course S's own ground for her testimony that p may not settle *all* questions regarding the truth of p. But my present point is only that S's ground can settle some questions which A's justification leaves open—there is an epistemic asymmetry here. It goes without saying that complications arise when S, in turn, is merely a link in a still-further chain originating prior to her. But then S will be in a position to pass the buck to her interlocutor, and so on, until such time as the original interlocutor is reached.

21. I note that a view such as Faulkner's, which allows for the transmission of warrants through chains of testimony, need not be seen as committed to the transmission view of testimonial *knowledge*, according to which in order for A to know or be justified in believing that p on the basis of S's testimony, S (or someone else in the chain preceding S) must know or be justified in believing that p.

7

Testimony and Trustworthiness

Keith Lehrer

This paper is concerned with the relationship between testimony, trustworthiness, and knowledge. Testimony leads to the acquisition of knowledge under some circumstances but not all circumstances. The problem is to analyze when testimony suffices for the acquisition of knowledge. A solution to the problem depends on the analysis of knowledge and testimony. I shall argue that when the knowledge acquired is discursive knowledge (Lehrer 1997, 2000), which is knowledge that involves justification and defensibility, the trustworthiness of self and others is a condition of knowledge. The condition of trustworthiness of others appears to pose a problem, however. I must evaluate the trustworthiness of others to evaluate their testimony. This leads to the question of whether I am trustworthy in my evaluation of their trustworthiness. That leads to the further question of how I am to evaluate my own trustworthiness without appeal to the intersubjective constraint based on the testimony of others. If, however, I must evaluate the trustworthiness of others before accepting their testimony, and I must evaluate my own trustworthiness by appeal to the testimony of others, then I am involved in a circle of evaluation from which there is no exit. The solution to the paradox is to be found in a virtuous explanatory loop of trustworthiness.

There is a simple theory about the role of testimony in knowledge that might be called a causal theory of knowledge or a transmission theory of knowledge. Such theories bypass the issue of evaluation as unnecessary. The model is bottom up and escapes from the circle of evaluation by ignoring it or adding it as a refinement. So the idea is that some fact causes a first person to form a belief. Then, as the result of communication, the first person causes a belief in another, and the causal sequence effected by communication continues from person to person. Assuming that the form of causation suffices for knowledge in the original belief and in the transmission of belief from person to person, causation suffices for the acquisition of knowledge from testimony.

The simple theory has a certain plausibility without any question. Reid (Lehrer and Beanblossom 1975; Smith and Lehrer 1985) noticed that a young child seems to be gullible by nature beyond the restraint of reason, partly because it does not understand the distinction between veracity and deception. Moreover, all of us retain this initial inclination to believe what we are told, according to

Reid, though we become constrained by our experience of error and deception. The causal theory has a plausibility derived from the causal influence of the speech acts of others. The acknowledged problem is that there are causal relationships between facts and beliefs and between the beliefs of one person and those of another that do not suffice to yield knowledge in the first instance or in the transmission. For example, suppose the subject of the belief is totally ignorant of the causal relation and has no idea why he or she believes what she does. This problem is met by complicating the simple theory, arriving at the modified simple theory. The modified simple theory says only that there is *some kind* of causal relationship that suffices to yield knowledge in the original belief, and *some kind* of causal transmission of the belief by testimony that suffices to transfer knowledge. Philosophers defending the modified simple theory have undertaken to explain what kind of causal relationship is required in both cases.

There is, however, a basic objection to such theories for obtaining discursive knowledge, namely, that the subject of the belief, whether of the original belief or the transmitted belief, might have no idea whether the belief is worthy of their trust. I have called this (Lehrer 2000) the opacity objection. The merits of the belief may be opaque to the subject. Therefore, the subject may not be in a position to justify or defend the belief. There is a reply to this objection that will take us to the heart of the issue. It is that some kinds of causal relations may have the result that the belief is formed in a special way, a reliable way, for example, or in conformity to some norm or rule that insures that the belief is justified. The reason that this takes us to the fundamental issue in the epistemology of testimony is that it assumes that there is some way that a belief is formed that is necessary and sufficient for knowledge. There are reasons to doubt that it is necessary and ones to doubt that it is sufficient. Let us consider them briefly.

A belief may be formed in some way that is evidentially defective. I may believe what someone tells me when I have reason to distrust their testimony. As I evaluate the belief, however, perhaps as the result of obtaining other evidence for the belief after forming it, I may decide that the person was trustworthy in this instance in spite of my original reasons for mistrusting the person. I acquire knowledge as the result of my subsequent evaluation. Does that mean that I had knowledge when I formed the original belief based on testimony that I had reason to distrust? I do not think I knew at the time that I formed the original belief. There was at that stage an objection I was in no position to meet, namely, that I had reasons to distrust the testimony on which I based my belief. It was not the formation of the belief but the subsequent evaluation of the belief on the basis of evidence obtained later that resulted in knowledge. If the later evaluation of the belief in terms of evidence was necessary, then the earlier formation of the belief on the basis of testimony was not sufficient. Moreover, if the evidence for the belief was sufficient for obtaining knowledge later, then the testimony might not have been necessary either.

There have been enough examples offered in support of the claim that causal theories about the formation and transmission of belief are neither necessary nor sufficient for knowledge so that the addition of further examples is not likely to influence conviction any more than the reiteration of such examples. Why would someone refuse to acknowledge the relevance of examples of people forming beliefs on the basis of epistemologically defective evidence of testimony and later acquiring knowledge on the basis of evidence obtained in the interval? One reason is that the simple theory can be modified in an *ad hoc* manner to require that the person have no reasons to distrust the testimony. It is natural to proceed in this way to refine a causal or reliablist theory of knowledge, but the refinement expands the account to include background considerations of the subject, namely, what reasons the person has for not accepting the testimony.

Once reasons for not accepting testimony are acknowledged to be necessary for the acquisition of knowledge, however, why should we deny that the reasons that we have for accepting testimony are relevant to the acquisition of knowledge? The negative route of requiring that we not have reasons for not accepting testimony is an attempt to conceal the importance of the positive route of acknowledging that we have reasons for accepting some testimony as being worthy of our trust and other testimony as unworthy of our trust. These reasons are relevant determinants of knowledge. When one seeks to justify or defend a claim to knowledge on the basis of testimony, the reasons one has for trusting or distrusting testimony become salient. Discursive knowledge of testimony depends upon such reasons.

So let us consider the role of testimony in the acquisition of discursive knowledge. Suppose someone tells me that p, and I accept what the person tells me, that p, as a result. Under what conditions do I know that p? Suppose that I ask myself whether I know that p and consider objections that might be raised against the claim that I know that p as the result of accepting that p on testimony. It might be objected that the person who has told me that p, let us call her the informant, does not know that p. Should we conclude that if the informant does not know that p, then we cannot know that p as a result of accepting that p because the informant tells us that p? Is it necessary for us to know that p that the informant knows that p?

It is surely an objection to the claim to know on the basis of testimony that the informant whose testimony one accepts does not know whereof she speaks, that is, does not know that p. The question is whether it is decisive, and the answer is negative. The reason is that the informant might have come to believe that p as a result of being told that p by another, a man she has reasons to think might deceive her. She does not know that p because there is an objection to accepting that p on the testimony of the man, namely, that he is not worthy of her trust, and she cannot meet the objection because of her reasons for thinking the man is untrustworthy.

However, suppose I know that the man knows whereof he speaks, contrary to reasons the informant has for thinking he is untrustworthy. I know that she is misled about his being untrustworthy because, whatever he tells her about the truth of p, he has obtained and conveyed the truth when he tells her what he does. So, when she tells me that p, having herself come to believe that p on the basis of the testimony of the man, despite her reasons for thinking that man is untrustworthy, I might be in a better position on the basis of my background system, my evaluation system, for evaluating the claim of the informant than she was in evaluating what the man told her. I am in a position to evaluate the testimony of the informant as having originated with a trustworthy source while she is not in a position to make that evaluation.

The foregoing example of the informant who herself believes and conveys something when she has reasons to consider her source untrustworthy is interesting in that she is herself untrustworthy both in believing what she is told and in the way she conveys what she is told to another. I acquire knowledge from what she has told me, not because she is trustworthy, but because I know that she is an accurate conduit of truth from a source who has knowledge. She has successfully obtained and transmitted truth, however untrustworthy she has been in forming and conveying her beliefs. There is a remaining question about the case, however. It is whether it is her testimony that justifies me in what I accept and converts to knowledge. The issue is subtle, but the answer is negative. She is a conduit of truth, and I may know that, but her testimony is not the evidence or justification that converts to knowledge, for she is untrustworthy. The justification that converts to knowledge is that she is conveying what the man said, and he is trustworthy. It is his trustworthiness, not her testimony, that is the evidence for the truth of what she says.

This reflection enables us to make the question concerning the evidence or justification of testimony more precise. Sometimes the testimony of a person that p is evidence that p, and sometimes not. It depends, though not only, on whether the person is herself a trustworthy informant in the sense that she has acquired and conveyed the information in a trustworthy way. Whether the informant's testimony is a source of evidence and justification also depends on the evaluation of the informant by the person who receives the information. The informant may be trustworthy when the person receiving the testimony thinks the informant is not trustworthy. Or, on the contrary, the person receiving the testimony, and even believing it, may think, with justification, that the informant is trustworthy, when he is not trustworthy. In the first case, the person receiving the information is not justified in accepting that the testimony is trustworthy. In the second case, the person is justified in accepting that the testimony is trustworthy, but the justification is defeated or refuted by some mistake the person has made, however unavoidable it may have been, in justifying acceptance of the testimony of the informant.

The testimony is in itself a source of evidence when the informant is trustworthy in the testimony. The testimony in itself does not constitute evidence otherwise. A person may have evidence, as in an example considered, that what the informant says is true which is based on knowledge about the etiology of the testimony when the informant is herself untrustworthy. That does not mean that the testimony in itself is a source of evidence. Knowledge of the etiology reveals that what the informant says is true in spite of the fact that the informant is herself untrustworthy. She is not worthy of trust even though we have evidence that what she says is true.

The preceding will not convince everyone that the testimony of the person is not a source of evidence by itself for the truth of what she says when she is untrustworthy. It may be modified to strengthen the conviction that the testimony is not by itself a source of evidence by supposing that the informant intends to lie by saying the opposite of what someone tells her. Suppose we add that the person who tells her what he does knows she will lie to us. As a result, he tells her the opposite of what he knows to be the case. If we know this as well, we will accept what she says. We will reason that the person who told her what he did told her the opposite of what he accepted and knew to be true. She then told us the opposite of what he said. So, we conclude what she says is true, since it corresponds to what the person knew who told her the opposite.

Her testimony, that is, her testifying to the truth of what she says, is no evidence by itself of the truth of what she says, for we know she is lying. However, given our knowledge of the history of it all, we conclude that what she said is true because it corresponds to what the man knew who told her the opposite of what she told us. We may know that what she says is true even though her testifying to the truth of what she says is no evidence by itself of the truth of her testimony. Suppose we only knew about her and her intentions. We would conclude that what she says is probably false because of her intention to lie.

This line of thought tests two divergent theories about testimony discussed by Coady (1992, 2002). One is reductive and says that the evidence of testimony is derived from induction and attempts to reduce the evidence of testimony to other evidence that the person is telling the truth (Hume 1978). On this account, when, and only when, we have inductive reasons, whether direct or indirect, for supposing that what a person says is true, does what the person says constitute evidence for the truth of what the person says. The other is nonreductive and foundational and supposes that testimony is an original source of evidence that cannot be reduced to another. On the reductive account, both examples involve an informant whose testimony is evidence. On the foundational account, the testimony of the informant is also evidence, though it may be defeated. The correct view, it seems to me, is neither of these. The informant in the two examples tells us something, and we have evidence for the truth of what we are told in both cases. However, the informant testifying to the truth of what she says, contrary to both accounts, is no evidence by itself, defeated or not, for the truth of what she says. The evidence for the truth of what she says lies in our knowledge of the history and etiology of what she says rather than in her testifying to the truth of it. The latter, considered in terms of our knowledge of her alone, would lead us to doubt what she says.

So when and how does testimony yield evidence? Part of the answer is that the person testifying to the truth of what she says must be trustworthy in what she accepts and what she conveys. Of course, the person does not need to be infallible to be trustworthy. A person can be fallible and worthy of trust. We may long for perfection, but we recognize the trustworthiness of those who sometimes err including ourselves. You do not have to be perfect to be trustworthy. Notice, however, that to be in a position to meet objections to accepting something on the basis of testimony, we must be in a position to meet the objection that the person is not trustworthy in testifying to the truth of her testimony. Moreover, since she may fail to be trustworthy either because of the way in which she accepts what she does, or in the way in which she conveys what she does, we must be able to meet the objection that she is not trustworthy in either of these ways. Furthermore, a person can be trustworthy in what she accepts but fail to be successful in obtaining truth. Since we are fallible and capable in principle of being invincibly deceived, trustworthiness is only contingently connected with success in obtaining truth. Thus, reliability considered as a high frequency of success in obtaining truth in what one accepts is not entailed by trustworthiness. This is contrary to Schmitt (1994, 2002).

It is clear that the trustworthiness of the informant is not sufficient for the conversion of our accepting what she tells us to knowledge. That she is untrustworthy is an objection that is met by her being trustworthy. But, as we have noted, trustworthiness is only fallibly connected with truth. So another objection is that her trustworthiness is not successfully truth-connected. To meet the objection we must accept that her trustworthiness is successfully truth-connected. We must accept not only that her trustworthiness is in general reliably truth-connected but, also, that in her current situation the trustworthiness of her testimony is successfully truth-connected. Thus, evidence and justification that converts testimony to knowledge assumes acceptance of her trustworthiness and the successful truth-connection of it. Is that sufficient? It is not.

What else is required for the evidence and justification of testimony to convert to knowledge other than our acceptance of her trustworthiness in her testimony and our acceptance of the successful truth-connectedness of her trustworthiness? The conversion requires that we be correct and not in error in our acceptance of the trustworthiness of her testimony and the successful truth-connectedness of it. There is a kind of subjective or, as I prefer to say, personal evidence and justification (Lehrer 2000) resulting from our background system of evaluation, of acceptance, preference over acceptance and reasoning about acceptance. The conversion to knowledge, however, requires that such personal justification not be refuted or defeated by errors in the background system.

We noted that the justification of testimony is neither reductive nor foundational. So what is the source of the justification? It is the background system to which we have referred and which we use to meet objections to the testimony we accept. Why are the reductive and foundational explanations of justification unsatisfactory? The answer becomes apparent when we press further to answer objections to accepting testimony. No sooner do we evaluate the trustworthiness of our informant, thus meeting the objection that the informant is not trustworthy, than a deeper question arises. Are we trustworthy in the way in which we evaluate the trustworthiness of the informant? We are trustworthy in the way in which we evaluate the trustworthiness of others, in part, as the result of experience. When we evaluate others as trustworthy on occasions when they are not, we learn of our mistake. However, one primary way in which we learn of this is through the testimony of others. False or deceptive testimony is sometimes revealed directly through experience, but it is very frequently revealed through the testimony of others. Moreover, intersubjective agreement with others, with their testimony, is a primary test of our own trustworthiness. When we are untrustworthy in what we accept or how we evaluate claims, including the testimony of others, this is often revealed to us by the testimony of others.

The foregoing reflections contain the explanation for why no foundational theory, whether reductive or nonreductive, of the evidence of testimony will prove adequate. There is an interactive loop between the trustworthiness of self and others in the evaluation and justification of testimony. To see this, consider the sort of justification that is necessary for discursive knowledge, namely, justification involving the defensibility of what is accepted in terms of a background evaluation system. One objection to the acceptance of testimony of another is that the other is not trustworthy in what he testifies to as the truth. The defense of accepting his testimony depends on evaluating his trustworthiness and on the reasonableness of the defense that he is trustworthy. But then one faces the objection that one is oneself not trustworthy in the evaluation of others. How is one to defend accepting that one is trustworthy in the evaluation of others?

There are two routes of defense. One is that one is in general trustworthy in what one accepts. That reply has the advantage, an important advantage, that it ends the regress of defense with a loop. Suppose one considers the objection that one is not trustworthy in accepting that one is trustworthy. One has an answer, for one accepts, contrary to the objection, that one is trustworthy in what one accepts. So it follows from what one accepts that one is trustworthy in accepting that one is trustworthy in what one accepts. The circularity of the defense is obvious and Schmitt (2002) has objected to my account on this ground.

An advantage of the circle is that it is explanatory. One's trustworthiness in what one accepts explains why one is trustworthy in accepting that one is trustworthy. So, one committed to maximizing explanation may justify accepting that one is trustworthy by the explanatory advantage of so doing. However, it is clear one's justification for accepting one's trustworthiness in evaluating the trustworthiness of oneself and others depends on other information about one's successes and failures in evaluating the trustworthiness of oneself and others. It also depends on information about how one corrects one's errors. Finally, then, this information about successes and failures in evaluating such trustworthiness is obtained, in part, from the testimony of others and from the constraint of intersubjective agreement.

My conclusion is that the foundational account of the evidence and justification of testimony fails because there is an essential loop in the justification for accepting the testimony of others. The briefest account of the loop is that the justification for accepting the testimony of others depends on evaluation of the trustworthiness of oneself and others and the consequences thereof. Let me put the matter in the first person. My justification for accepting my evaluations of others depends on my trustworthiness in evaluating others. My justification for accepting my trustworthiness in evaluating others depends on my accepting the testimony of others concerning my trustworthiness in evaluating myself and others. And there is the loop. My justification for accepting the testimony of myself and others depends on the trustworthiness of my evaluation of the testimony of others. This, in turn, depends on my accepting the testimony of others in a trustworthy way concerning my evaluations of the trustworthiness of myself and others.

The argument might be viewed as paradoxical because the circle might be viewed as vicious as Schmitt (2002) suggests. I shall argue, as I have before, that we are involved in a virtuous loop rather than a vicious circle. The reason is that foundationalism and externalism fail to provide a maximally explanatory account. Foundations and externalities leave us with the unexplained justification of first premises resulting from their foundational character or the unexplained justification of premises resulting from the opacity of the external conditions. By contrast, an account of the justification of testimony based on the evaluations of the trustworthiness of others constrained by intersubjective agreement in testimony does not leave us with unexplained justification. We accept that we are trustworthy in testimony with some qualifications. Either we are trustworthy or we are not. If we are trustworthy, our agreement about our trustworthiness explains why we are trustworthy in accepting our trustworthiness. If we are not trustworthy, our lack of trustworthiness should reveal itself in our experience and our lack of agreement with others about our trustworthiness.

Whatever trustworthiness we possess must be qualified to reflect the cognitive defects and duplicities we share. On some occasions, the testimony of others will not be worthy of our trust, and, if the truth were told, on some occasions our testimony will not be worthy of the trust of others. Often the proper response to the testimony of others is doubt and refusal to accept what they tell us. Moreover, there will also be disagreement about trustworthiness of various individuals as individuals decide how much weight to give to the testimony of others. With all the cognitive defects, duplicities, and disagreements, how can we make sense of the idea that our evaluations of the trustworthiness of ourselves and others are or should be constrained by intersubjective agreement?

First of all, it is important to remember the frequent robust agreement, in perceptual cases, for example. Of course, even in some simple perceptual cases our fallibility will dominate and lead us to be untrustworthy. In other cases, agreement will be conspiratorial and prove untrustworthy as well. However, our fallibility is compatible with our trustworthiness. We do not have to be infallible to be trustworthy. Moreover, the disagreement in evaluations of the trustworthiness of an individual may conceal a fixed point of convergence. I have argued (Lehrer 1997 and elsewhere) that the weights that individuals assign to others, and this applies to the weights assigned to the trustworthiness of others as well, may be aggregated to find convergence. Convergence results if the individuals giving some positive weight to others are connected by a vector in which each individual assigns positive weight to the next member of a full sequence of members as well as to himself or herself. This is a mathematical idealization. Short of a mathematical representation of evaluations and the aggregation thereof, there is sometimes qualitative convergence concerning when the testimony of others is trustworthy and when one is in a position to be trustworthy in evaluating their trustworthiness. That is something I assume, and I admit it cannot be proven to the satisfaction of a sceptic, but our acquisition of knowledge from testimony depends, in part, on the trustworthiness of others and of ourselves in evaluating their trustworthiness and our own.

Let me turn again to the virtues of the loop in the justification of accepting testimony and the role of evaluating the trustworthiness of testimony. The basic argument for the virtue of the loop is that the trustworthy evaluation of others depends on the assumption that I am trustworthy in the evaluation of myself as an evaluator of others. Let me put this in terms of meeting objections. Suppose

1. I accept that p on the testimony of T.

If I can meet all objections, then I can meet the objection

1OT. The testimony of T is not trustworthy.

Now suppose that I hold that it is more reasonable for me to accept that the testimony of T is trustworthy than to accept that it is not, that is, it is more reasonable for me to accept the denial of 1OT than to accept 1OT. That is a reply to the objection, at least from my own point of view. However, that reply depends on my trustworthiness in evaluating the trustworthiness of people because I must also meet the objection

2OT. You are not trustworthy in evaluating the trustworthiness of people, in particular, T.

Suppose that I hold (which means it is a consequences of my evaluation system) that it is more reasonable for me to accept that I am trustworthy in evaluating the trustworthiness of people, and, in particular, T, than to accept that I am not. Thus, it is more reasonable for me to accept the denial of 2OT than to accept 2OT.

So far so good. But now consider the objection:

> 3OT. You are not trustworthy in evaluating the trustworthiness of people, yourself included, because you do not accept the corrections of others concerning your evaluations of the trustworthiness of people, again, yourself included.

In reply, I must claim that it is more reasonable for me to accept the denial of 3OT than 3OT, where the denial is the reply

> 3OTR. I am trustworthy in evaluating the trustworthiness of people, myself included, because I do accept the corrections of others concerning my evaluations of the trustworthiness of people, myself included.

This reply will lead us into a loop of justification, for it is clear that corrections of others I accept are based in part on their testimony. To answer objections to my accepting the testimony of others, I should accept that I am trustworthy in evaluating the trustworthiness of others. However, I am trustworthy in accepting this claim about my trustworthiness only if I am trustworthy in accepting the corrections of others concerning my evaluations, that is, if I am trustworthy in accepting their testimony about the trustworthiness of my evaluations. So, I need to be trustworthy in accepting the testimony of others to be justified in accepting what they claim in testimony. I am trustworthy in accepting the testimony of others only if I am trustworthy in evaluating others. I am trustworthy in evaluating others, however, only if I am trustworthy in evaluating the testimony of others concerning the correctness of my evaluations. The solution to the problem this raises depends on recognizing that I must accept that I am trustworthy in my evaluations of people, myself included. Finally, my trustworthiness in accepting that I am trustworthy in accepting that I am trustworthy in this way depends on my accepting I am trustworthy in accepting the testimony of others. And that closes the loop. But, it is a virtuous loop.

To understand the virtue of the loop, consider two possibilities. The first is that I accept the testimony of others concerning my trustworthiness in evaluating people, myself included, at least when I evaluate them as worthy of my trust. The second is that I do not accept the testimony of others concerning my trustworthiness in evaluating people, myself included. In the first case, my view that I am trustworthy in evaluating people is confirmed and corrected by the testimony of others. In the second case, it is not. Though others might mislead me, their confirmation and correction, especially when I evaluate them as trustworthy, is a source of improvement of my own trustworthiness. So I should accept the testimony of others concerning my trustworthiness in evaluating people, at least when I evaluate them as trustworthy.

Now, suppose someone objects as follows. (This has similarity to an argument of Schmitt (2002) though I do not impute it to him.) I evaluate the trustworthiness of others when I accept the testimony that corrects and confirms my trustworthiness in evaluating people. Now, if I am not trustworthy in evaluating them, then my acceptance of their testimony, which corrects and confirms my trustworthiness, is useless. I cannot tell whether their corrections and confirmations are trustworthy because I cannot tell whether they are trustworthy in providing them. On the other hand, if I am trustworthy in evaluating them, then their corrections and confirmations are otiose. So my accepting their corrections and confirmations is either useless or otiose.

Notice, in reply, that there is some defect in this argument because my trustworthiness in evaluating others surely does depend in an important and useful way on the corrections and confirmations of others. Without the benefit of the corrections and confirmations of others, my judgements of the trustworthiness of people, myself included, would be egocentric and idiosyncratic, rather than socially and intersubjectively corrected and constrained. Extreme individualists may, of course, applaud independence from social and intersubjective constraint. But that position, though it may lead to truth on some occasions, is equivalent to a preference for ignoring information rather than evaluating it.

The circularity revolves around the following principle of trustworthiness of evaluation:

> TE. I am trustworthy in evaluating the trustworthiness of people, myself included, in what they accept and testify.

Notice that I might reason to this as a conclusion by the following path:

> T. I am trustworthy in what I accept.

Therefore,

> TT. I am trustworthy in what I accept about the trustworthiness of people.
>
> ATE. I accept that I am trustworthy in evaluating the trustworthiness of people, myself included, in what they accept and testify.

Therefore,

> TE. I am trustworthy in evaluating the trustworthiness of people, myself included, in what they accept and testify.

In this argument, T is the key premise, TT is inferred, though not deduced, from T, and ATE is a premise. TE is inferred, though not deduced, from TT and ATE. The reason that the inferences are not deductive is that trustworthiness is a general capacity to be trustworthy in more specific cases, and the inferences from a general capacity to trustworthiness in more specific cases are not deductive. Schmitt (2002) attributes to me the view that T is a universal statement, but that is contrary to the interpretation I proposed in Lehrer (1997) which he cites. The general capacity to be trustworthy is fallible in application to particular cases as are all general capacities. It is like the capacity to lift one hundred pounds that must allow for failure to succeed in lifting that weight in all cases even though the inference from the general capacity to success in particular cases is warranted inductively. In short, such inferences, though warranted, are defeasible under some conditions.

The argument begins with T, I am trustworthy in what I accept. Suppose one raises the question of whether I am reasonable to accept that premise. As I have argued elsewhere, I am reasonable to accept it if I am trustworthy in accepting it. But am I trustworthy in accepting T? Principle T has the important explanatory feature that if it is true, then it explains why I am trustworthy in accepting T by an inference of the sort that we have considered. My trustworthiness in accepting T is explained by my general trustworthiness in what I accept. Notice, however, that a further and more illuminating explanation of the reasonableness and trustworthiness of accepting T is explained by other things that I accept about my trustworthiness in the past and my success in obtaining truth and avoiding error thereby. Of course, part of what I accept about my past success will be based on the confirmations of others, that is, on testimony of others that I accept.

So there are two explanation of my trustworthiness in what I accept. There is a narrow explanation of why I am trustworthy in accepting T, and by inference, TE, based on the inference from my general trustworthiness. I am trustworthy in what I accept about my trustworthiness and the trustworthiness of others. This is a small but virtuous loop of explanation. It depends on the *truth* of T, however, not just the *acceptance* of it, even though I reason from my acceptance of it to the reasonableness of accepting it.

There is also a broader explanation based on inference from what I accept about my past successes in being trustworthy and succeeding in obtaining truth. Such explanation is more illuminating, but the loop in such explanation is equally apparent. What I accept about the past can only explain my general trustworthiness in what I accept if I am trustworthy in accepting those claims about the past. Thus, my general trustworthiness, which narrowly explains why I am trustworthy in accepting what I do, is broadly explained by what I accept about past successes in being trustworthy. The latter succeeds as a result of my being trustworthy in accepting what I do about my past successes, however. The broader explanation presupposes the narrower explanation as my trustworthiness and my acceptance of it loops back onto itself.

We have now reached the final question. Why is the loop virtuous rather than vicious in explanation? There are two answers. First, any complete theory of justification or trustworthiness will have to explain why we are justified or trustworthy in accepting the theory itself. So the theory must apply to itself to explain why we are justified or trustworthy in accepting it. Secondly, and equally important, our trustworthiness at any given time must result from what we have accepted in the past, including what we have accepted from the testimony of others. The result is that there is a kind of mutual support between the particular things we have accepted and our general trustworthiness in what we accept, including, of course, the particular things we have accepted. It is the mutual support among the things that we accept that results in the trustworthiness of what we accept.

The foregoing is an oft-told story of mine. What I add here is the extension of the argument to testimony. My trustworthiness in evaluating the trustworthiness of others depends on their trustworthiness. Their trustworthiness depends on both their honesty, on whether they accept what they say, and on whether they proceed in the right way for the purposes of obtaining truth and avoiding error. However, as examples of invincible deception reveal our fallibility, we note that the trustworthiness of ourselves and others may fail to be successfully truth-connected. We may, after all, proceed in the right way to accept what is true and fail because we are invincibly deceived.

Suppose, however, that our evaluation of the trustworthiness of others is optimal. We are trustworthy in accepting that they are trustworthy in their testimony. They are trustworthy in their testimony. Moreover, suppose their trustworthiness is successfully truth-connected. Then our acceptance of their testimony will be successfully truth-connected because they are trustworthy, as we accept them to be, and their trustworthiness is successfully truth-connected. Suppose we accept their testimony about our trustworthiness in evaluating the trustworthiness of people. We do so because we evaluate their testimony as trustworthy. They are trustworthy, and their trustworthiness is successfully truth-connected. Therefore, our acceptance of their testimony about our trustworthiness in evaluating the trustworthiness of ourselves and others is successfully truth-connected because their trustworthiness, which we accept, is successfully truth-connected. The truth-connectedness of their trustworthiness explains why we are trustworthy in accepting their testimony about our trustworthiness in evaluating their trustworthiness. They are trustworthy in telling us what they do about our trustworthiness. Their trustworthiness explains our trustworthiness when we accept their testimony.

Am I assuming a principle of parity that Schmitt (2002) suggests I have in common with Foley (1993, 1994) and Gibbard (1990)? The principle of parity says, in effect, that we are all trustworthy or none of us are. Each person might be inclined to accept that he or she is trustworthy. But we are not committed to assuming that others are trustworthy as a result. The reason is simple. If I assume that I am trustworthy in the evaluation of others, I might evaluate some as trustworthy and others as untrustworthy for good reasons contained in my background evaluation system. They might, of course, return the insult. However, there is a truth of the matter about trustworthiness. Whether I am justified in accepting that others are trustworthy or not in a way that converts to knowledge will depend both on my evaluations of trustworthiness and the truth of the matter about these evaluations.

Nevertheless, each person will begin by accepting that they are trustworthy in what they accept. As I run the argument concerning trustworthiness, I express my trustworthiness in the first person, recognizing, of course, that the reader may run the same argument. Each of us, I propose, may employ the trustworthiness argument beginning with the premise—I am trustworthy in what I accept. As I allow my readers that premise of their own trustworthiness, am I not committed, as Schmitt assumes I am, to the premise that all of us are trustworthy in what we accept? My readers may, with my blessings, trust themselves and accept that they are worthy of their trust in what they accept. However, not all will be as worthy of their trust as they accept themselves to be. I concede a need of initially accepting that one is trustworthy in what one accepts, but to accept something is not the same as to obtain truth in what one accepts, even concerning one's own trustworthiness. Some will accept that they are trustworthy when they are not, the demented and incompetent, for example. Though they accept that they are trustworthy in what they accept, and I may commiserate with their situation, I need not agree that they are trustworthy in what they accept. They are in error in accepting that they are trustworthy in what they accept.

The final question that arises concerning our acceptance of testimony is this. What converts our acceptance of the testimony of others into knowledge? The first part of the answer is that we must be trustworthy in our evaluations of the trustworthiness of others, and we must accept that this is so. Moreover, our trustworthiness must be successfully truth-connected, that is, the others must, in fact, be trustworthy and their trustworthiness must itself be successfully truth-connected. We must also accept that this is so. In short, our acceptance of their testimony must be justified in a way that is not refuted or defeated by any errors that we make in evaluating them and their testimony. Undefeated or irrefutable justified acceptance of the testimony of others is knowledge.

REFERENCES

Coady, C. A. J. (1992), *Testimony: A Philosophical Study* (Oxford: Oxford University Press).

——— (2002), 'Testimony and Intellectual Autonomy', *Studies in the History and Philosophy of Science*, 33/2: 355–72.

Foley, R. (1993), *Working without a Net: A Study of Egocentric Epistemology* (Oxford: Oxford University Press).

——— (1994), 'Egoism in epistemology', in F. Schmitt (ed.), *Socializing Epistemology: The Social Dimensions of Knowledge*, (Lanham, Md.: Rowman & Littlefield), 53–73.

Gibbard, A. (1990), *Wise Choice, Apt Feeling: A Theory of Normative Judgment* (Cambridge, Mass.: Harvard University Press).

Hume, D. (1978), *A Treatise of Human Nature* (2nd edn.), ed. L. A. Selby-Bigge, rev. P. H. Nidditch (Oxford: Oxford University Press) (first published 1739).

Lehrer, K. (1997), *Self-Trust: A Study of Reason, Knowledge, and Autonomy* (Oxford: Oxford University Press).

___ (2000), *Theory of Knowledge* (2nd edn., Boulder, Colo: Westview Press).

___ and Beanblossom, R. (1975), *Reid's Inquiry and Essays* (Indianapolis: Bobbs Merrill, Indianapolis) (new edn., Indianapolis Hackett Publishing Co.: 1984).

Schmitt, F. (1994), 'Socializing Epistemology: An Introduction through Two Sample Issues', in F. Schmitt (ed.), *Socializing Epistemology: The Social Dimensions of Knowledge* (Lanham, Md.: Rowman & Littlefield), 1–27.

___ 'Social Epistemology', in J. Greco and E. Sosa (eds.), *Blackwell Guide to Epistemology* (Oxford: Basil Blackwell), 354–82.

___ 'Testimonial Justification: The Parity Argument', *Studies in the History and Philosophy of Science*, 33/2: 385–406.

Smith, J. C., and Lehrer, K. (1985), 'Reid on Testimony and Perception', *Canadian Journal of Philosophy*, suppl. vol. 11: 21–38.

8

It Takes Two to Tango: Beyond Reductionism and Non-Reductionism in the Epistemology of Testimony

Jennifer Lackey

How precisely do we successfully acquire justified belief from either the spoken or written word of others?[1] This question is at the center of the epistemology of testimony, and the current philosophical literature contains only two general options for answering it: *reductionism* and *non-reductionism*. While reductionists argue that testimonial justification is *reducible to* sense perception, memory, and inductive inference, non-reductionists maintain that testimony is *just as basic* epistemically as these other sources. The aim of this paper is to challenge the current terms of the debate by, first, showing that there are serious problems afflicting both reductionism and non-reductionism and by, second, suggesting an alternate view of testimonial justification that goes beyond the reductionist/non-reductionist dichotomy.

1. REDUCTIONISM

There are two central components to reductionism. The first is what we may call the *Positive-Reasons Component*: justification is conferred on testimonial beliefs by the presence of appropriate *positive reasons* on the part of hearers. Since these reasons cannot themselves be ultimately testimonially grounded,[2] they must depend on resources provided by other epistemic sources—typically, sense perception, memory, and inductive inference. This gives rise to the second component—what we may call the *Reduction Component*. Because the justification of testimonial beliefs is provided by these non-testimonially

For very helpful comments on earlier versions of this paper, I am grateful to Robert Audi, Marian David, Sandy Goldberg, Peter Graham, Jason Kawall, Matt McGrath, Joe Shieber, Ernie Sosa, and audience members at the 2004 Pacific Division of the APA in Pasadena, CA. Most of all, I am, as always, indebted to Baron Reed in ways too numerous to list. With respect to this paper alone, if I inserted an endnote at every place in which his comments substantially altered my thinking, the pages of notes would outnumber those of the paper itself.

grounded positive reasons, testimonial justification is said to *reduce* to the justification of sense perception, memory, and inductive inference.[3]

But *what*, one might ask, is being reduced to *what*? Otherwise put, what are the *relata* of testimonial reduction? Two different answers are given to this question. The first answer—a view sometimes called *global reductionism*—is that the justification of *testimony as a source of belief* reduces to the justification of sense perception, memory, and inductive inference. In particular, global reductionists maintain that in order to justifiedly accept a speaker's report, a hearer must have non-testimonially based positive reasons for believing that *testimony is generally reliable*.[4]

There are, however, at least three problems with global reductionism that render it ultimately an untenable view of testimonial justification. The first is that, before accepting any testimony at all, including that of their parents and teachers, very young children would have to wait until they have checked the accuracy of enough different kinds of reports from enough different speakers to conclude that testimony is generally reliable. Not only is it wildly implausible to suppose that most young children—or even adults—are capable of engaging in such a process, it also becomes mysterious how they would be able to acquire the conceptual and linguistic tools needed for an induction to the general reliability of testimony *without accepting some testimony in the first place*.[5] Thus, if global reductionism is true, the very cognitive tools needed to acquire testimonial justification would be inaccessible to epistemic agents, thereby leading ultimately to skepticism about testimonial knowledge.

The second problem is that in order to have non-testimonially based positive reasons that testimony is generally reliable, one would have to be exposed not only to a non-random, wide-ranging sample of reports, but also to a non-random, wide-ranging sample of the corresponding facts. Both are problematic. With respect to the reports, most of us have been exposed only to a very limited range of reports from speakers in our native language in a handful of communities in our native country. This limited sample of reports provides only a fraction of what would be required to legitimately conclude that testimony is *generally* reliable. With respect to the corresponding facts, a similar problem arises: the observational base of ordinary epistemic agents is simply far too small to allow the requisite induction about the reliability of testimony. As C. A. J. Coady says:

it seems absurd to suggest that, individually, we have done anything like the amount of field-work that [reductionism] requires ... many of us have never seen a baby born, nor have most of us examined the circulation of the blood nor the actual geography of the world nor any fair sample of the laws of the land, nor have we made the observations that lie behind our knowledge that the lights in the sky are heavenly bodies immensely distant nor a vast number of other observations that [reductionism] would seem to require. (Coady 1992: 82)

Moreover, with many reports, such as those involving complex scientific, economic, or mathematical theories, most of us simply lack the conceptual machinery needed to properly check the reports against the facts. Once again, then, global reductionism leads to skepticism about testimonial knowledge, at least for most epistemic agents.

The previous two points focused on our ability to *know* or *determine* whether testimony is a generally reliable epistemic source. A third problem with global reductionism—one that has not been properly appreciated but is, to my mind, the most debilitating objection—is that it is questionable whether there even is an epistemically significant *fact of the matter* here.[6] To see this, consider, for instance, the following epistemically heterogeneous list of types of reports, all of which are subsumed under 'testimony in general': reports about the time of day, what one had for breakfast, the achievements of one's children, whether one's loved one looks attractive in a certain outfit, the character of one's political opponents, one's age and weight, one's criminal record, and so on. Some of these types of reports may be generally highly reliable (e.g., about the time of day and what one had for breakfast), generally highly unreliable (e.g., about the achievements of one's children, the looks of one's loved ones, and the character of one's political opponents), and generally very epistemically mixed, depending on the speaker (e.g., about one's age, weight, and criminal record). Because of this epistemic heterogeneity, it is doubtful, not only whether "testimony" picks out an epistemically interesting or unified *kind*, but also whether it even makes sense to talk about testimony being a *generally reliable source*.

Otherwise put, even if it turned out that the majority of testimonial reports are, as a matter of fact, both true and properly formed, this information would *not have much epistemic significance*. For concealed in this percentage are all sorts of epistemically salient facts: some people offer mostly false reports, some kinds of reports are mostly false, many true reports are about very mundane facts, and so on. Because of this, the mere fact that testimony is *generally* reliable has very little epistemic bearing on any *particular* instance of testimony. For instance, suppose that I came to learn that 70 per cent of all reports are both true and properly formed. What relevance would this information have to whether a particular instance of testimony is epistemically acceptable? Very little. For this information is so broad and conceals so many epistemically important differences that it would have virtually no straightforward epistemic application. Thus, even if global reductionism were entirely successful and it *could* be shown that testimony *is* generally reliable, this conclusion would have very little epistemic significance in itself.

The second version of reductionism—often called *local reductionism*—is that the justification of *each particular report or instance of testimony* reduces to the justification of instances of sense perception, memory, and inductive inference. Specifically, local reductionists claim that in order to justifiedly accept a speaker's testimony, a hearer must have non-testimonially based positive reasons for accepting *the particular report in question*.[7]

There are, however, two importantly different ways of understanding the local reductionist's Positive-Reasons Component. The first is:

PR-N: Appropriate positive reasons are *necessary* for testimonial justification.

The second, stronger, interpretation is:

PR-N&S: Appropriate positive reasons are *necessary and sufficient* for testimonial justification.

But notice: in order for testimonial justification to be *reducible* to sense perception, memory, and inductive inference, the positive reasons in question must be fully sufficient for justifying the relevant testimonial belief. Otherwise, there would be an asymmetry between the justificatory status of the *testimonial belief being reduced* and the *positive reasons doing the reducing*, thereby preventing the possibility of just such a reduction. Because of this, the Reduction Component of the local reductionist's view depends on reading the Positive-Reasons Component as the stronger PR-N&S. In what follows, however, I shall argue that such a requirement is false. This conclusion has particular significance. For, since local reductionism represents the *weakest* version of reductionism, an argument against it will thereby show that reductionism in the epistemology of testimony, *in general*, is false.[8]

To begin, consider the following:

> NESTED SPEAKER: Fred has known Helen for five years and, during this time, he has acquired excellent epistemic reasons for believing her to be a highly reliable source of information on a wide range of topics. For instance, each time she has made a personal or professional recommendation to Fred, her assessment has proven to be accurate; each time she has reported an incident to Fred, her version of the story has been independently confirmed; each time she has recounted historical information, all of the major historical texts and figures have fully supported her account, and so on. Yesterday, Helen told Fred that Pauline, a close friend of hers, is a highly trustworthy person, especially when it comes to information regarding wild birds. Because of this, Fred unhesitatingly believed Pauline earlier today when she told him that albatrosses, not the widely believed condors, have the largest wingspan among wild birds. It turns out that while Helen is an epistemically excellent source of information, she was incorrect on this particular occasion: Pauline is, in fact, a highly incompetent and insincere speaker, especially on the topic of wild birds. Moreover, though Pauline is correct in her report about albatrosses, she came to hold this belief merely on the basis of wishful thinking (in order to make her reading of *The Rime of the Ancient Mariner* more compelling).[9]

Now, does Fred justifiedly believe that albatrosses have the largest wingspan among wild birds on the basis of Pauline's report? Intuitively, no. For even though Helen's testimony provides Fred with excellent positive reasons for accepting the report in question, Pauline is not only a generally unreliable speaker, she is also reporting a belief which, though true, fails to be reliably produced or appropriately truth-conducive. Because of this, the testimony that Pauline offers to Fred also fails to be reliably produced or appropriately truth-conducive, thereby preventing it from leading to justified belief for Fred.[10]

What NESTED SPEAKER reveals is that the possession of good positive reasons by a hearer is not sufficient for justifiedly accepting a speaker's testimony. Why? Because the possession of positive reasons on behalf of a speaker's report, even objectively excellent ones, *does not necessarily put one in contact with testimony that is reliable.* There is, then, a further necessary condition for testimonial justification, one that requires that a speaker's testimony be reliable or otherwise truth-conducive. This additional 'speaker condition' can be fleshed out in different ways. For instance, most non-reductionists require that a speaker herself *competently believe* the proposition to which she is *sincerely testifying* in order for it to qualify as justified belief for her hearers.[11] Alternatively, it may be required only that the speaker's *statement* be reliably produced or truth tracking.[12] But however the speaker condition is fleshed out, the point that is of import here is that it is a condition that cannot be subsumed merely by requiring the possession of appropriate positive reasons on the part of the hearer. The presence of such reasons is, therefore, not sufficient for testimonial justification; accordingly, the stronger reading of the Positive-Reasons Component—i.e., PR-N&S—is false.[13]

What, then, are the consequences of this for the Reduction Component of reductionism? If the Reduction Component is correct, then there cannot be any difference between the justificatory status of the *testimonial belief being reduced* and the *positive reasons doing the reducing.* That is, to the extent that the positive reasons are justified, so, too, should the testimony in question be justified. This is just what it means for testimonial justification to be *reduced* to the justification of sense perception, memory, and inductive inference. But notice: in NESTED SPEAKER, we have an example in which there is precisely such a justificatory difference. In particular, Fred's positive reasons are fully epistemically justified and yet the testimonial belief in question is not. This shows that the Reduction Component of reductionism is false.

There are, however, at least two central objections that a reductionist may raise to this conclusion. First, it may be argued that NESTED SPEAKER simply describes a testimonial Gettier-type case, in which a hearer's belief is justified but true merely by accident. In particular, one may claim that, because of the excellent reasons he has for trusting Pauline, the true belief that Fred acquires from her testimony is *justified.* Our intuition that something is epistemically defective in such a case, however, can be explained by the fact that Fred's belief nevertheless falls short of *knowledge.*

By way of response to this objection, it will be helpful to compare NESTED SPEAKER with the following:

> UNNESTED SPEAKER: Max has known Holly for ten years and, over the course of these years, he has acquired excellent epistemic reasons for believing her to be a highly reliable source of information on a wide range of

topics. Indeed, during this time, she has never offered, to Max or anyone else, a report that has been either insincere or improperly formed. Currently, however, Holly is in the midst of a personal crisis, which she effectively conceals from those around her, and her emotional state of mind leads her to report to Max that her purse has been stolen, despite having absolutely no evidence for thinking this to be the case. Max, detecting nothing amiss, readily accepts Holly's testimony. Now, it turns out that Holly's purse was in fact stolen: while she was at Caribou Coffee earlier today, a young man slipped it off her chair and into his backpack.

Notice first that in UNNESTED SPEAKER, Max not only has excellent epistemic reasons for accepting Holly's testimony, *Holly is also a generally reliable testifier*. The problem is simply that, on this particular occasion, Holly acts completely out of epistemic character and offers a report for which she lacks adequate evidence. What's more, she gets veritically (though not financially!) lucky: her report turns out to be true. Because of this, one may plausibly regard UNNESTED SPEAKER as a Gettier-type case, i.e., as a case of justified true belief that falls short of knowledge. In particular, one may argue that Max's excellent positive reasons for Holly's testimony combined with her general reliability as a testifier render his true belief about the stolen purse *justified*, though not an instance of knowledge.[14] Accordingly, UNNESTED SPEAKER would fail to show that there can be a difference between the justificatory status of the testimonial belief being reduced and the positive reasons doing the reducing.

In NESTED SPEAKER, however, while Fred has excellent positive reasons to accept Pauline's testimony, *she is not a reliable testifier in any sense of the word*. For not only does Pauline hold her belief about the wingspan of albatrosses on the basis of wishful thinking, she is also in general a highly incompetent and insincere testifier. In other words, with respect to most topics most of the time, Pauline believes to be true what is in fact false, reports what she herself does not believe, or both. Thus, positive reasons can come apart from even *general* reliability.[15] Moreover, given the degree and depth of Pauline's unreliability, there is simply no plausible sense in which the belief that Fred forms on the basis of her testimony could be justified. Unlike UNNESTED SPEAKER, then, NESTED SPEAKER simply cannot be plausibly regarded as a Gettier-type case.[16]

One may pursue a second line of resistance to NESTED SPEAKER, however, by arguing that Fred's 'excellent epistemic reasons' on behalf of Pauline's testimony are not 'appropriate' in the relevant sense. For, one may say that the only positive reasons that are appropriate are ones that render it likely in an objective sense that the testimony in question is true. Since Helen is incorrect in her assessment of Pauline, it may be thought that such an assessment fails to provide Fred with positive reasons that satisfy this criterion.

But as NESTED SPEAKER is described, Fred *does* have reasons that, by one measure, render it objectively likely that Pauline's testimony is true. In particular,

Fred's positive reasons place those beliefs from Pauline's testimony in a category that contains beliefs that are or would be mostly true; namely, *those beliefs that are supported by Helen's testimony*. For instance, were Fred to decide between accepting the reports of two different speakers, one of whom has the support of Helen's testimony and another who lacks this support, most of the time Fred would do well to accept the reports of the former. That is, most of the time, forming beliefs from sources supported by Helen's testimony would lead to the truth. In this sense, then, the positive reasons that Fred possesses for Pauline's testimony *do* render it likely in an objective sense that her testimony is true. The problem is that, by other measures of objective likelihood, Fred's positive reasons *do not* render it likely that Pauline's testimony is true. Fred's belief about the wingspan of albatrosses also belongs to a category that contains beliefs that are or would be mostly false; namely, *those beliefs that are supported by Pauline's testimony*. Moreover, because Pauline is the direct source of the belief, it is clear that her unreliability is not offset by the excellence of Fred's reasons for believing her. So, although Fred does have excellent positive reasons for believing Pauline's testimony, the belief in question is not justified.[17]

It is, therefore, not enough for testimonial justification that a hearer have even epistemically excellent positive reasons for accepting a speaker's testimony — the speaker must also do her part in the testimonial exchange by offering testimony that is reliable or otherwise truth-conducive. Thus, PR-N&S is false and, accordingly, reductionism in the epistemology of testimony is false.

2. NON-REDUCTIONISM

In contrast to reductionists, non-reductionists altogether reject both versions of the Positive-Reasons Component and the Reduction Component as well, that is, they maintain that positive reasons are neither necessary nor sufficient for testimonial justification and, accordingly, that testimonial justification is an irreducible epistemic source. What non-reductionists hold is that hearers are justified in accepting the testimony of speakers so long as two conditions are satisfied: (i) the report in question has to be reliably produced, typically through the speaker being both a competent believer and a sincere testifier, and, (ii) the hearer in question cannot have any relevant defeaters — that is, any counterbeliefs or counterevidence — for such a report.[18] In this way, so long as there is no evidence against accepting a speaker's report, the hearer has no positive epistemic work to do in order to justifiedly accept the testimony in question.[19] In what follows, however, I argue that this is false — hearers *do* have some positive work to do for testimonial justification. Specifically, I show that although PR-N&S is false, PR-N is nevertheless true. Thus, I show that non-reductionism is false.

To begin, notice that in denying even the weaker reading of the Positive-Reasons Component of reductionism — i.e., PR-N — non-reductionists commit themselves to saying that testimonial justification can be acquired in the complete absence of *any* positive reasons on the part of the hearer. Let us, therefore, consider such a case.

ALIEN: Sam, an average human being, is taking a walk through the forest one sunny morning and, in the distance, he sees someone drop a book. Although the individual's physical appearance enables Sam to identify her as an alien from another planet, he does not know anything either about this kind of alien or the planet from which she comes. Now, Sam eventually loses sight of the alien, but he is able to recover the book that she dropped. Upon opening it, he immediately notices that it appears to be written in English and looks like what we on Earth would call a diary. Moreover, after reading the first sentence of the book, Sam forms the corresponding belief that tigers have eaten some of the inhabitants of the author's planet. It turns out that the book is a diary, the alien does communicate in English, and it is both true and reliably written in the diary that tigers have eaten some of the inhabitants of the planet in question.

Now since the book in question is written by an alien, Sam truly has no epistemically relevant positive reasons: he has no commonsense psychological alien theory, he has no beliefs about the general reliability of aliens as testifiers, he has no beliefs about the reliability of the author of this book, he has no beliefs about how 'diaries' function in this alien society, and so on. Moreover, if Sam attends to the narrative voice of the author in the hope of trying to assess her competence and sincerity, he would be engaged in a fruitless activity since there is no reason to believe that signs of competence and sincerity on the planet in question correspond to these signs on Earth. Sam cannot even compare the content of the reports in this diary to his background beliefs since he does not know that the words in this book are used in the same way that we on Earth use them. So, here is a case in which a hearer truly fails to have any positive reasons on behalf of a speaker's testimony. Let us suppose, further, that there is nothing about the diary that provides Sam with relevant counterbeliefs or counterevidence. The crucial question we now need to ask is whether Sam is justified in believing that tigers have eaten some of the inhabitants of the planet in question on the basis of the alien's diary.

Here the answer should clearly be no. Despite the fact that the alien's report is both true and reliable, it seems plainly irrational epistemically for Sam to form the belief in question on the basis of the alien's testimony. For, it may very well be accepted practice in alien society to be insincere and deceptive when testifying to others. Or, normal alien psychology may be what we Earthlings would consider psychosis. Or, the language that the aliens use, though superficially indistinguishable from English, may really be Twenglish, where Twenglish uses the 'negation' sign for affirming a proposition. Or, 'diaries' in the alien society may be what we on Earth regard as science fiction, and so on. For all Sam knows when he reads the book, each of these scenarios is just as likely as the possibility that these aliens are reliable testifiers who speak English. But, in the absence of any way to discriminate among these possibilities, it seems clear that the appropriate epistemic response is to withhold belief.[20]

It is of further interest to note that the general diagnosis offered of ALIEN appeals only to features to which non-reductionists are already committed. To see this, recall that the second condition of non-reductionism requires that the hearer in question not possess any relevant defeaters for accepting a speaker's report. For instance, if I believe that you frequently lie but nevertheless come to believe that owls are raptors on the basis of your testimony, then, according to non-reductionism, my testimonial belief fails to qualify as justified or known even if it is in fact true and reliably formed. Why? Because even non-reductionists agree that testimonial justification is incompatible with at least certain kinds of epistemic *irrationality*.[21] What ALIEN reveals, however, is that accepting a speaker's report in the complete absence of positive reasons can be just as epistemically irrational as accepting such a report in the presence of a defeater—indeed, perhaps even more so. If I, for example, have a defeater by virtue of believing that you *only occasionally* lie, would it be more epistemically irrational for me to trust your testimony than it would be for Sam to trust the alien's in the absence of positive reasons? Not at all. For while Sam knows *absolutely nothing* about the alien in question, I have all sorts of beliefs, both about humans in general and about you in particular, that are relevant to my acceptance of your testimony—for instance, I believe that humans often speak sincerely, that reports on Earth are usually offered to communicate information, that you do not exhibit any clear signs of being deceptive, and so on. Against the background of all of this incredibly rich positive information, my belief that you merely occasionally lie seems rather epistemically insignificant when compared with the fact that Sam doesn't even know whether aliens actually speak English. Accepting testimony in the absence of positive reasons can, then, be even more irrational than accepting testimony in the presence of defeaters. Thus, by showing that epistemic irrationality is involved in accepting a speaker's report in the complete absence of positive reasons—even more than in some cases in which defeaters are present—ALIEN poses a challenge to non-reductionists on their own terms.[22]

Now, one way the non-reductionist may respond to ALIEN is to deny that Sam satisfies the relevant conditions in his acceptance of the contents of the 'diary.' Specifically, it may be argued that Sam fails the no-defeater condition because a context like that envisaged above, in which there is absolutely no epistemically relevant information about the speaker, report, or context, provides the hearer in question with evidence against the testimony in question.

However, this response is unacceptable since, *ex hypothesi*, there is nothing about the diary that suggests that its contents are false or that its author is unreliable. Hence, Sam has no relevant defeaters. Any residual discomfort that one may have about granting justified belief in this sort of case simply reveals one's intuitions that positive reasons are necessary for testimonial justification. For the only negative reason it is appropriate to say that Sam has with respect to the alien's 'diary' is *the absence of positive reasons*. Since the fundamental difference between non-reductionism and reductionism is precisely over the need for positive reasons, this reply is simply not available to the non-reductionist.

A second strategy for denying the force of ALIEN is to argue that the non-reductionist's principle applies only to humans because only those who are members of *our* institution of testimony fall under it. The aliens may very well have their own institution of testimony on their planet, and their practices and epistemic principles may be quite similar to ours. But we cannot assume this similarity. Non-reductionism would thus be limited in its applicability to members of our species only and, accordingly, Sam would fail to be justified in accepting the alien's testimony.

An obvious response to this objection is simply to modify the counterexample so that the testifier in question is in fact a member of our institution of testimony. For instance, suppose that Sally has been in a coma for the past two months and, upon waking, discovers that she has lost all of her previous knowledge except for her competence with the English language. Upon leaving the hospital, she stumbles upon a diary of an unknown author and begins reading it. Now, *ex hypothesi*, Sally no longer has commonsense beliefs about human psychology, she no longer has beliefs about the general reliability of humans as testifiers, she no longer has beliefs about how diaries function in our society, and so on. Is Sally justified in accepting the contents of the diary? Since this case is similar to the alien example in all *epistemically relevant* respects, the answer must be no. So, restricting the scope of non-reductionism to humans will not avoid this objection.

Furthermore, it seems that the primary explanation for why different epistemic standards would be invoked, depending on whether the speaker in question is a human or an alien, is precisely that we have all sorts *of epistemically relevant beliefs about our institution of testimony, and fail to have them in the case of the aliens*. For consider: why aren't we entitled to assume that the aliens are like us in all relevant respects? The natural answer seems to be that we do not have any *reason* to believe that this is the case. Thus, the very criterion for saying who is or is not a member of our institution of testimony is simply whether we have positive reasons for their testimony—which begs the question.

We have seen, then, that the hearer must also do her part in a testimonial exchange by having at least some epistemically relevant positive reasons for accepting the report in question. Thus, PR-N is true and, accordingly, non-reductionism with respect to testimonial justification is false.

3. DUALISM

In a testimonial exchange, information is typically transmitted between two central participants: the speaker and the hearer. My diagnosis of what has gone wrong in the epistemology of testimony is this: reductionists and non-reductionists alike have attempted to place all of the epistemic work on only one or the other of these participants and, in so doing, have ignored the positive justificatory contribution that needs to be made by the other.

Reductionists, on the one hand, focus entirely on the hearer in a testimonial exchange. For in order for testimonial justification to be reduced to the justification of perception, memory, and inference, all of the justificatory work needs to be shouldered by the hearer since it is precisely her positive reasons that are supposed to provide the reductive base. Reductionists, then, are committed to saying, first, that the reasons possessed by a hearer wholly determine the justificatory status of a given testimonial belief, and, second, that nothing about the speaker (apart from what may already be captured by the hearer's positive reasons) has epistemic relevance to the justification of a hearer's testimonial belief. But, as we have seen, both of these theses are false. For, as NESTED SPEAKER showed, no matter how excellent a hearer's positive reasons are on behalf of an instance of testimony, a speaker may still offer a report that is thoroughly unreliable. Because of this, an adequate account of testimonial justification must include a condition requiring that the testimony in question be reliable or otherwise truth-conducive.

Non-reductionists, on the other hand, capture the work that needs to be done by the speaker in a testimonial exchange, but neglect the positive contribution that a hearer needs to make. Specifically, they correctly require the reliability of the speaker's testimony, but then mistakenly assume that the hearer merely has to satisfy the no-defeater condition.[23] However, as ALIEN showed, no matter how reliable a speaker's testimony is, this cannot by itself make it rationally acceptable for a hearer to accept her report. For this, the hearer needs to have some epistemically relevant positive reasons on behalf of the testimony in question.

The upshot of these considerations is that it takes two to tango: the justificatory work of testimonial beliefs can be shouldered exclusively neither by the hearer nor by the speaker.[24] To put it somewhat crudely, the speaker condition ensures reliability while the hearer condition ensures rationality for testimonial justification.[25] Thus, we need to look toward a view of testimonial justification that gives proper credence to its *dual* nature, one that includes the need for the reliability of the speaker (from non-reductionism) and the necessity of positive reasons (PR-N from reductionism). Accordingly, an adequate view of testimonial justification needs to recognize that the justification of a hearer's belief has dual sources, being grounded in both the reliability of the speaker and the rationality of the hearer's reasons for belief. More precisely, we should accept what I shall call *dualism* in the epistemology of testimony, which includes at least the following:

> *Dualism:*[26] For every speaker A and hearer B, B justifiedly believes that *p* on the basis of A's testimony that *p* only if: (1) B believes that *p* on the basis of the content of A's testimony that *p*, (2) A's testimony that *p* is reliable or otherwise truth conducive, and (3) B has appropriate positive reasons for accepting A's testimony that *p*.

Because dualism specifies only necessary conditions, there may be other conditions that need to be added for a complete account of testimonial justification.[27] What is of import, here, however, is that testimonial justification requires positive epistemic contributions from *both* the speaker *and* the hearer. Though this point is not acknowledged by any of the standard views in the current literature, it should be obvious: acquiring testimonial justification involves an exchange between *two* parties. And in order for such an exchange to properly result in justification, both parties need to do their epistemic work.[28]

Let us now take a closer look at the specific conditions expressed in dualism. Regarding (1), since we are here interested in *testimonial* justification, this condition specifies that the hearer must form the belief in question on the basis of the *content* of the speaker's testimony. This is to preclude cases where a belief is formed, either entirely or primarily, on the basis of features *about* the speaker's testimony. For instance, if you say, in a soprano voice, that you have a soprano voice and I come to believe this either entirely or primarily on the basis of hearing your soprano voice, then my resulting justification is either or partially perceptual in nature.[29] Condition (1), therefore, is included to prevent cases of this sort from qualifying as instances of *testimonial* justification.[30]

With respect to (2), the details of the reliability of the speaker's testimony can be fleshed out in several different ways. The most common strategy is to require that the speaker in question be both a competent believer and a sincere testifier—the speaker must form her own belief in an epistemically acceptable fashion, and then report to others what she herself believes.[31] Alternatively, it may be required that the speaker's *statement*, rather than her belief, be somehow reliable, perhaps by being either *sensitive* (*à la* Nozick)[32]—the speaker would not state that *p* if *p* were false—or *safe* (*à la* Sosa)[33]—the speaker would not state that *p* without it being so that *p*. Either way, while more could certainly be said about the details of (2), there is no reason to question the general tenability of such a condition.

In contrast, serious doubts over the plausibility of a condition such as (3) have been expressed repeatedly in the literature. Indeed, all of the standard arguments against reductionism focus specifically on the Positive-Reasons Component. For instance, Mark Owen Webb claims that, '[t]he cause of the trouble [with reductionism] seems to be the requirement that our beliefs based on the testimony of others be based on beliefs in us about the reliability of testimony. This higher-level requirement ... places too great a burden on the believing subject, since it requires of him all kinds of knowledge about people, their areas of expertise, and their psychological propensities, which knowledge most subjects simply lack' (Webb 1993: 263). Following this, Richard Foley maintains that the problem with reductionism 'is that it threatens to cut us off from expertise and information that others have and we lack ... After all, many people with expertise and information that we lack are people about whom we know little. Hence, there may be little or no basis for us to grant them derivative authority' (Foley

1994: 57–8).[34] Moreover, even when we do have adequate positive reasons for accepting a speaker's testimony, it is often argued, as P. F. Strawson does, that 'the checking process ... consists in nothing other than seeking confirmation from other sources of testimony' (Strawson 1994: 25).[35]

These quotations express two slightly different concerns: (a) ordinary epistemic agents simply do not have enough information to acquire positive reasons strong enough to justify accepting most of the testimony that is intuitively justified, and (b) even when agents do have enough information to justify accepting particular instances of testimony, the positive reasons themselves often are indebted to testimony. Now, since the Reduction Component was the focus of my arguments in Section 1, my reasons for rejecting reductionism obviously differ in significant ways from those expressed in (a) and (b). But, more importantly, by arguing on behalf of the Positive-Reasons Component (i.e., PR-N), my view is also targeted by these very objections. My purpose in what follows, then, is to defend condition (3) of dualism from (a) and (b). To this end, I shall make three central points.

First, one of the primary reasons that (a) is frequently raised as a problem for reductionism is that reductionists are committed to PR-N&S rather than to PR-N. In particular, they must maintain that positive reasons are both necessary and sufficient for testimonial justification and, therefore, that positive reasons must carry *all* of the justificatory burden for testimonial beliefs. This, in turn, lends itself to the concern expressed in (a): how can we possess enough information to adequately justify all of our testimonial beliefs? While traveling to London for the first time, do I, for instance, have enough information about a random local British newspaper to adequately justify the beliefs that I acquire while reading it?

In contrast to reductionism, dualism has the justificatory work being *shared* between the speaker and the hearer, leaving the work for the positive-reasons condition far less burdensome. Specifically, since condition (2) of dualism takes care of the reliability of the testimony in question, (3) merely has to ensure that the hearer's acceptance of the testimony is rationally acceptable. More precisely, on my view, the positive reasons possessed by a hearer need to be such that they render it, at the very least, *not irrational* for her to accept the testimony in question. This is a substantially weaker condition than that required by reductionists. To see this, consider, again, my accepting the reports of a random British newspaper. Even if I do not have specific beliefs about British newspapers, I have all sorts of beliefs about England, the people who live there, their government, their social and political values, and so on. Surely, this information is enough to make it *not irrational* to form beliefs on the basis of British newspapers, even if it is not itself fully sufficient for *justifying* such beliefs.

Second, and also in response to (a), it is important to notice that there are all sorts of positive reasons that can have epistemic significance and, therefore, be relevant to the satisfaction of condition (3) of dualism.[36] For instance, suppose that I know nothing personal about Harold or his testifying habits—I met him for the first time on the subway today. I ask him for directions and, while making direct eye contact with me, he responds in an able and confident manner that my destination is four blocks to the south. Now, despite the fact that I have no background with Harold, I may have a substantial amount of inductive evidence for believing that people are generally both sincere and competent when providing directions in normal contexts, that reports made with sustained eye contact are typically sincere ones, or that reports made ably and confidently are typically competent ones.

More precisely, even if a hearer, B, has not observed the general conformity of prior reports of a speaker, A, and the corresponding facts, B may *have observed a general conformity of other relevant reports and facts*. In particular, there seem to be at least three classes of inductively based positive reasons that are available to epistemic agents for distinguishing between reliable and unreliable testimony.

The first class includes criteria for individuating epistemically reliable *contexts* and *contextual features*.[37] For instance, one may take a less critical attitude in the context of an astronomy lecture or a *National Geographic* report than one does in the context of an astrology lecture or a *National Enquirer* report. The explanation for this disparity may appeal not only to the *negative* evidence that has been inductively acquired for reports received in the latter contexts, but also to the *positive* evidence that has been accumulated for believing that reports received in the former contexts tend to be reliable. Or consider the different attitudes that may be taken toward a calm and coherent stranger reporting a robbery a few blocks away versus an apparently confused person who is smelling of alcohol reporting the same information. Again, the difference in responses may be explained by both positive reasons and defeaters: previous inductive evidence indicates that the contextual features in the first scenario suggest a reliable testifier while the contextual features in the second scenario suggest an unreliable testifier. Similar remarks can be made about countless other contextual factors, such as facial expressions, eye contact, mannerisms, narrative voice, and so on.

The second broad class of positive reasons includes criteria for distinguishing between different kinds of *reports*.[38] So, for example, a hearer may quite reasonably take an uncritical stance when a speaker is reporting the time of day, her name, what she had for dinner, and so on. On the other hand, one may take a more critical stance when receiving a speaker's testimony about political matters, the achievements of her children, alien encounters, UFO sightings, and the like. Here, prior evidence acquired about subject matters or types of reports provides recipients of testimony with epistemically relevant positive reasons.

The third class includes criteria for individuating epistemically reliable *speakers*.[39] For instance, one may have accumulated inductive evidence for believing that accountants tend to be reliable sources of information about taxes, while politicians in the middle of their campaigns tend to be unreliable sources of information about the characters of their political opponents. In such cases, a pattern of interaction with speakers who fall under various relevant types enables hearers to acquire positive reasons for accepting some of the reports that they are offered.[40]

What these considerations suggest is that ordinary hearers are confronted with a plethora of epistemically relevant positive reasons that come in a variety of forms. Such reasons are often not explicitly brought to mind but they nonetheless play a crucial role in our epistemic lives, as we tacitly discriminate among and evaluate pieces of incoming information and compare such input with our background beliefs.[41] This point is borne out by noticing just how difficult it is to construct a case in which a speaker truly fails to have *any* relevant positive reasons for accepting a given report. Indeed, even in ALIEN, the fact that the book in question is written in what looks like English and appears to be what we would call a diary may provide Sam with positive reasons for thinking the alien's society is similar in some crucial respects to Earth.

The third point I should like to make is in response to (b), the objection that even when ordinary epistemic agents have enough information to justify particular reports, the positive reasons themselves are often indebted to testimony. Here, it is crucial to notice that the positive reasons for accepting a speaker's testimony can themselves depend on testimony, so long as they are not *ultimately and entirely* testimonially grounded. In particular, in order to avoid circular appeals to testimony, one can reject

> (i) For each report, R, the positive reasons justifying R cannot themselves be acquired from the testimony of others.

and still accept

> (ii) For each report, R, the positive reasons justifying R cannot ultimately be testimonially grounded, where this means that the justificatory or epistemic chain leading up to R does not 'bottom out' in testimony.

To see this, recall the case of NESTED SPEAKER: through the course of their friendship, Fred acquired excellent inductively based positive reasons for believing that Helen is a highly reliable source of information on a wide range of topics. Because of this, he readily accepts Helen's testimony that Pauline, a close friend of hers, is a highly trustworthy person, especially when it comes to information regarding wild birds. This, in turn, leads him to accept Pauline's testimony that albatrosses have the largest wingspan among wild birds. To link this up with the above distinction, Fred's positive reasons for Helen's testimony satisfy both (i) and (ii), whereas Fred's positive reasons for Pauline's testimony satisfy only (ii). In particular, Fred's positive reasons for accepting Helen's reports have been acquired via sense perception, memory, and inductive inference, and so they are not based on further testimony in the most direct sort of way. Regarding Pauline's testimony, however, Fred's positive reasons for accepting her report are based on further testimony in this direct sense; but the epistemic chain ultimately 'bottoms out' in a non-testimonial source, namely, Fred's inductive evidence for Helen's reliability. It is this weaker sense of being non-testimonially grounded—expressed in (ii)—that is crucial for avoiding circularity. According to dualism, the reasons invoked for accepting a speaker's testimony can, and often are, themselves acquired from the testimony of others. Indeed, there can be epistemic chains involving many more speakers than two. For instance, A's reason for accepting B's testimony may be the testimony of C which, in turn, may be based on the testimony of D, and so on. What is crucial for satisfaction of (2) is *that the final link in the epistemic chain in question is non-testimonially justified.*

Perhaps an analogy will help here: in order to avoid both a vicious regress and the problem of circularity, traditional foundationalism requires that a justificatory chain ultimately bottom out in foundational, or basic, beliefs. But it does not require that each justified belief be, in turn, directly justified by a basic belief. Similarly, in order to avoid both a vicious regress and circular appeals to testimony, the positive-reasons condition requires that the justificatory chain ultimately bottom out in a non-testimonial source. But, it does not require direct non-testimonial grounding for each testimonial belief.

Moreover, even the final link in the chain can be partially indebted to testimony, so long as there is enough non-testimonial support to render it not irrational to accept the report in question. For instance, suppose I form beliefs on the basis of reading an internet site about Howard Dean because Jack, an acquaintance of mine from the Political Science Department, told me that it is a reliable source of information. Why do I trust Jack? In part, because my colleague, Jill, told me that he is an honest, competent, Democrat. However, I have also had enough personal interaction with Jack to acquire a partial non-testimonial basis for relying on his testimony. So long as this partial non-testimonial basis is sufficient to render it not irrational to trust the Howard Dean website, Jack can be the non-testimonial source in which this chain bottoms out.

Once it is clear, therefore, first, that the positive reasons required in (3) of dualism only need to render it *not irrational* for the hearer to accept the testimony in question, second, that there are a *multitude of kinds of reasons* that have epistemic significance, and, third, that *the positive reasons in question can themselves rely on testimony*, so long as they do not do so entirely and ultimately, (a) and (b) simply lose their force.

There is, however, a further concern that may be expressed about condition (3) of dualism. To see this, recall that the argument motivating the inclusion of this condition was ALIEN. But now, one might ask, couldn't a parallel argument be constructed regarding other, purportedly more basic, epistemic sources, such as sense perception, memory, and inference? For instance, suppose that after her involvement in a car accident, Olivia has complete amnesia with respect to her perceptual faculties, that is, she remembers nothing about either the workings or the deliverances of such faculties. Upon waking from the car accident and seeing the face of her sister, Olivia forms the corresponding perceptual belief. Intuitively, is such a belief justified? Since this case is similar in all of the relevant respects to ALIEN, shouldn't we conclude here, as we did there, that it would be irrational for Olivia to hold such a belief in the absence of epistemically relevant positive reasons on behalf of her perceptual faculties? If so, there seems to be a problem of overgeneralization here. For now it looks as though positive reasons are needed to justifiedly hold, not just testimonial beliefs, but *any* beliefs. And this, in turn, leads us into all of the problems facing traditional internalist theories of epistemic justification, such as infinite regresses, circularity, foundations, and so on.

Although a complete response to this concern lies outside the scope of this paper, I shall here highlight three salient ways in which testimony differs epistemically from other sources of belief. These differences allow us to conclude that, although ALIEN shows that positive reasons are needed for testimony, no similar case can be constructed for our other cognitive faculties; the need for positive reasons thus does not generalize.

First, testimonial beliefs are acquired from *persons*.[42] Persons, unlike other sources of belief, have all sorts of different intentions, desires, goals, motives, and so on. Some of these desires and goals make it very advantageous to lie, to exaggerate, to mislead, and to otherwise deceive. Indeed, recall that in the discussion following ALIEN, some of the considerations motivating the need for a condition like (3) of dualism were that 'it may very well be accepted practice in alien society to be insincere and deceptive when testifying to others. Or, normal alien psychology may be what we Earthlings would consider psychosis'. Since both of these possibilities appeal to features distinctive of persons, they are relevant only in the case of testimony.

Of course, it may be argued that other sources of belief can lead us just as far astray epistemically as testimony. For instance, aren't the paradoxes just as misleading as incompetent testifiers, and aren't perceptual hallucinations and illusions just as deceptive as compulsive liars? Given these parallels, it looks like the mere fact that testimonial beliefs are acquired from persons fails to distinguish it epistemically from other sources of belief.

By way of response to this point, notice that there are two aspects that are often involved in rendering a speaker a reliable source of belief: her competence as a believer and her sincerity as a testifier.[43] Accordingly, when a hearer acquires a false belief from a speaker, one (or both) of these aspects is typically responsible: either A reports that p when p is false because A herself erroneously believes that p (i.e., A is an incompetent believer), or A reports that p when p is false because A intends to deceive her hearer (i.e., A is an insincere testifier). But now notice: the paradoxes, perceptual illusions, hallucinations, and so on all parallel only the testimonial case of incompetent believing—there simply is no analogue of insincere testifying with non-testimonial sources of belief.[44] For insincerity involves the *intention* to deceive or mislead, and intentions of this sort are distinctive of persons. When my rational and perceptual faculties lead me astray epistemically, they do not *intend* to do so.[45] Because of this, failures in the case of testimony are much more *unpredictable* than failures in non-testimonial cases.

A second and somewhat related difference between testimony and other epistemic sources concerns the varying degrees of likelihood that such sources are unreliable. For instance, the possible worlds in which most of my perceptual beliefs are indistinguishably false—for instance, worlds in which I am unknowingly a brain-in-a-vat or the victim of an evil demon—are quite distant from the actual world. Indeed, even possible worlds in which *many* of my perceptual beliefs are indistinguishably false are rather far away—worlds, for instance, where my perceptual faculties frequently malfunction and yet I do not suspect that they do. In contrast, the possible worlds in which most of my testimonial beliefs are indistinguishably false—for instance, worlds in which I was raised by parents who belong to a cult, or worlds in which my government is highly corrupt, or worlds in which my society is highly superstitious—are much closer. Indeed, for many people, this is true in the *actual* world. Given this much greater chance for error in the case of testimony, the rational acceptance of the reports of others requires positive reasons in a way that is not paralleled with other cognitive faculties.

This brings us to the third and, to my mind, most important epistemic difference between testimony and other sources of belief. To fully appreciate this point, let us return to our perceptual amnesiac, Olivia, and imagine an average day for her after leaving the hospital: she stops at the store to buy some groceries, bumps into some acquaintances on her way home, watches an episode of *Seinfeld* on TV while eating dinner, and spends some time on the internet before going to bed. Along the way, Olivia forms perceptual beliefs about all sorts of things, including beliefs about the vegetarian items that Trader Joe's carries, the kinds of trees losing their leaves, the number of children her acquaintance now has, which *Seinfeld* episode is on, and the color of the background of the MSN website. Now, because of her perceptual amnesia, Olivia's acquisition of these perceptual beliefs is not governed by any acquired principles of perceptual belief formation. But even in the absence of such principles, it seems reasonable to conclude that the overall status of Olivia's daily perceptual beliefs would be very high epistemically. For Olivia's beliefs are most likely quite similar to those that would have been acquired by a subject in the same circumstances who does have acquired principles of perceptual belief formation governing her acceptance. Why? Because sense perception, like other non-testimonial sources, is fairly *homogeneous*—there is, for instance, simply not much of a difference epistemically between Olivia seeing groceries at Trader Joe's and Olivia seeing trees without their leaves. Accordingly, when forming non-testimonial beliefs, subjects do not need to be very discriminating in order to be reliably in touch with the truth.[46]

Now compare Olivia's day with Edna's. Edna, Olivia's best friend, was in the same car accident that caused Olivia's perceptual amnesia. In Edna, however, the accident caused *testimonial* amnesia: she remembers nothing about either the workings or the deliverances of testimony. After leaving the hospital, Edna's day was nearly identical to Olivia's. For instance, she stopped at the same grocery store, bumped into the same acquaintances on the way home, watched the same episode of *Seinfeld*, and visited the same internet sites before going to bed. Now, because of her testimonial amnesia, Edna's acquisition of testimonial beliefs along the way was not governed by any principles of testimonial belief formation. As a result, Edna trusted to the same extent all of the testimonial sources she encountered throughout the day—which included a copy of the *National Enquirer* that she read at the grocery store, her acquaintance's 3-year-old daughter, the characters of Jerry and George on *Seinfeld*, and an extremist, evangelical Christian internet site she stumbled upon while surfing the web—and she believed everything that she was either told or read along the way—which included testimony that a woman from Georgia was abducted by aliens, that there are *real* princes and princesses at Disneyland, that licking the envelopes of cheap wedding invitations can lead to one's death, and that those who are gay will be sent to eternal damnation.

Did Edna fare as well epistemically as Olivia? Not at all. In the absence of acquired principles governing the acceptance of testimony, Edna was led very far astray epistemically. She trusted the *National Enquirer* as much as she would have trusted the *New York Times*, she trusted a 3-year-old's depiction of Disneyland as much as she would have trusted an adult's, she trusted the characters on a sitcom as much as she would have trusted those interviewed in a *National Geographic* documentary, and she trusted the rantings of an extremist, evangelical Christian internet site as much as she would have trusted news found on the MSN website. Because of this, Edna's beliefs are very different from those that would have been acquired by a subject in the same circumstances who does have her testimonial practices governed by such epistemic principles.

Thus, testimony is quite unlike other sources of belief precisely because it is so wildly *heterogeneous* epistemically—there is, for instance, all the difference in the world between reading the *National Enquirer* and reading the *New York Times*. Moreover, this heterogeneity requires subjects to be much more discriminating when accepting testimony than when trusting, say, sense perception. Non-testimonial analogues of ALIEN, therefore, simply fail to motivate a positive-reasons condition similar to (3) of dualism.

4. BEYOND REDUCTIONISM AND NON-REDUCTIONISM

In closing, I shall discuss two of the central and most important consequences that dualism has for the epistemology of testimony.

First, dualism provides easy resolutions to many of the central and most divisive disagreements between reductionists and non-reductionists. For instance, because reductionism holds that testimony is reducible to other epistemic sources, such a view is often attacked for underestimating or devaluing the importance of testimony. On the other hand, because non-reductionism endorses the complete independence of testimony from those sources that could non-circularly provide positive reasons, such a view is often criticized for sanctioning gullibility and intellectual irresponsibility. Dualism, however, avoids both of these objections: testimony is an irreducible epistemic source, thereby avoiding the charge of underestimating or devaluing the importance of testimony, and hearers need positive reasons in order to acquire testimonial justification, thereby avoiding the charge of sanctioning gullibility and intellectual irresponsibility.

Second, dualism correctly moves the focus of the current debate *beyond* reductionism and non-reductionism. As we have seen, a central component of reductionism—indeed, the one for which the view derived its name—is that the justification of testimony *reduces* to the justification of sense perception, memory, and inductive inference. Testimony does not, therefore, make any justificatory contributions of its own—whatever appearances there are to the contrary can ultimately be reduced to the epistemic contributions of these other sources. Otherwise put, if reductionism is true, there is *no* specifically testimonial justification. There is only justification for beliefs acquired *through* testimony. But this view gives testimony far too little epistemic credit. For, as we saw in NESTED SPEAKER, the reliability of the report in question is not something that can be reduced to perceptual, memorial, and inferential justification. Since the reliability of the report in a testimonial exchange is a necessary condition of the justification of beliefs acquired via testimony, testimonial justification itself is not reducible. Thus, contrary to reductionism, there *is* justification that is distinctly testimonial in nature.

Non-reductionists, on the other hand, claim that since testimony is just as basic a source of justification as sense perception, memory, and inductive inference, hearers may be justified in accepting the reports of speakers, albeit defeasibly, *merely* on the basis of a speaker's testimony. In this way, testimony is construed as a completely independent and autonomous source of justification, needing neither the direct input nor the assistance of any other sources.[47] But this view gives testimony far too much credit. As we saw in ALIEN, to accept a speaker's testimony *in the complete absence* of positive reasons on behalf of the testimony in question is to exhibit an epistemically unacceptable kind of irrationality, one that is incompatible with testimonial justification. Moreover, since there would be vicious circularity if the positive reasons were themselves entirely and ultimately acquired via testimony, direct input and assistance are needed from sense perception, memory, and inductive inference. Thus, contrary to non-reductionism, testimonial justification *depends on* the justificatory resources of other epistemic sources.

In showing the need for positive epistemic work from both the speaker and hearer, we have seen that testimonial justification is neither reducible to nor completely independent from sense perception, memory, and inductive inference.

Thus, insofar as we wish to make genuine progress in the epistemology of testimony, we need to move beyond the debate between reductionism and nonreductionism.

REFERENCES

Adler, Jonathan E. (1994), 'Testimony, Trust, Knowing', *Journal of Philosophy*, 91: 264–75.
____ (2002), *Belief's Own Ethics* (Cambridge, Mass.: MIT Press).
Alston, William P. (1989), *Epistemic Justification: Essays in the Theory of Knowledge* (Ithaca, NY: Cornell University Press).
Audi, Robert (1997), 'The Place of Testimony in the Fabric of Knowledge and Justification', *American Philosophical Quarterly*, 34: 405–22.
____ (1998), *Epistemology: A Contemporary Introduction to the Theory of Knowledge* (London and New York: Routledge).
Bergmann, Michael (1997), 'Internalism, Externalism and the No-Defeater Condition', *Synthese*, 110: 399–417.
____ (2004), 'Epistemic Circularity: Malignant and Benign', *Philosophy and Phenomenological Research*, 69: 709–27.
Austin, J. L. (1979), 'Other Minds', in his *Philosophical Papers*, 3rd edn. (Oxford: Oxford University Press).
BonJour, Laurence (1980), 'Externalist Theories of Epistemic Justification', *Midwest Studies in Philosophy*, 5: 53–73.
____ (1985), *The Structure of Empirical Knowledge* (Cambridge, Mass.: Harvard University Press).
____ and Sosa, Ernest (2003), *Epistemic Justification: Internalism vs. Externalism, Foundations vs. Virtues* (Oxford: Blackwell Publishing).
Burge, Tyler (1993), 'Content Preservation', *Philosophical Review*, 102: 457–88.
____ (1997), 'Interlocution, Perception, and Memory', *Philosophical Studies*, 86: 21–47.
Chisholm, Roderick M. (1989), *Theory of Knowledge*, 3rd edn. (Englewood Cliffs, NJ: Prentice-Hall).
Coady, C. A. J. (1992), *Testimony: A Philosophical Study* (Oxford: Clarendon Press).
____ (1994), 'Testimony, Observation and "Autonomous Knowledge" ', in Matilal and Chakrabarti (1994: 225–50).
Dummett, Michael (1994), 'Testimony and Memory', in Matilal and Chakrabarti (1994: 251–72).
Evans, Gareth (1982), *The Varieties of Reference* (Oxford: Clarendon Press).
Faulkner, Paul (2000), 'The Social Character of Testimonial Knowledge', *Journal of Philosophy*, 97: 581–601.
____ (2002), 'On the Rationality of our Response to Testimony', *Synthese*, 131: 353–70.
Foley, Richard (1994), 'Egoism in Epistemology', in Schmitt (1994: 53–73).
Fricker, Elizabeth (1987), 'The Epistemology of Testimony', *Proceedings of the Aristotelian Society,* suppl. vol. 61: 57–83.
____ (1994), 'Against Gullibility', in Matilal and Chakrabarti (1994: 125–61).
____ (1995), 'Telling and Trusting: Reductionism and Anti-Reductionism in the Epistemology of Testimony', *Mind*, 104: 393–411.

—— (2002), 'Trusting Others in the Sciences: A Priori or Empirical Warrant?', *Studies in History and Philosophy of Science*, 33: 373–83.

—— (forthcoming), 'Knowledge from Trust in Testimony is Second-Hand Knowledge', *Philosophy and Phenomenological Research*.

Goldman, Alvin I. (1986), *Epistemology and Cognition*, (Cambridge, Mass.: Harvard University Press).

—— (1992), *Liaisons: Philosophy Meets the Cognitive and Social Sciences* (Cambridge, Mass.: MIT Press).

—— (1999), *Knowledge in a Social World* (Oxford: Clarendon Press).

Greco, John and Sosa, Ernest (eds.) (1999), *The Blackwell Guide to Epistemology* (Oxford: Blackwell Publishers).

Hardwig, John (1985), 'Epistemic Dependence', *Journal of Philosophy*, 82: 335–49.

—— (1991), 'The Role of Trust in Knowledge', *Journal of Philosophy*, 88: 693–708.

Hawthorne, John (2004), *Knowledge and Lotteries* (Oxford: Oxford University Press).

Hume, David (1967), *An Enquiry Concerning Human Understanding*, in L. A. Selby-Bigge (ed.), *Hume's Enquiries* (Oxford: Oxford University Press).

Insole, Christopher J. (2000), 'Seeing Off the Local Threat to Irreducible Knowledge by Testimony', *Philosophical Quarterly*, 50: 44–56.

Lackey, Jennifer (1999), 'Testimonial Knowledge and Transmission', *Philosophical Quarterly*, 49: 471–90.

—— (2003), 'A Minimal Expression of Non-Reductionism in the Epistemology of Testimony', *Noûs* 37: 706–23.

—— (2005), 'Testimony and the Infant/Child Objection', *Philosophical Studies*, 126: 163–90.

—— (forthcoming *a*), 'Learning from Words', *Philosophy and Phenomenological Research*.

Lipton, Peter (1998), 'The Epistemology of Testimony', *Studies in History and Philosophy of Science*, 29: 1–31.

Lyons, Jack (1997), 'Testimony, Induction and Folk Psychology', *Australasian Journal of Philosophy*, 75: 163–78.

McDowell, John (1994), 'Knowledge By Hearsay', in Matilal and Chakrabarti (1994: 195–224).

Matilal, Bimal Krishna, and Chakrabarti, Arindam (eds.), (1994), *Knowing From Words* (Dordrecht: Kluwer Academic Publishers).

Millgram, Elijah (1997), *Practical Induction* (Cambridge, Mass.: Harvard University Press).

Nozick, Robert (1981), *Philosophical Explanations* (Cambridge, Mass.: Belknap Press).

Owens, David (2000), *Reason without Freedom: The Problem of Epistemic Normativity* (London and New York: Routledge).

Plantinga, Alvin (1993), *Warrant and Proper Function* (Oxford: Oxford University Press).

Pollock, John (1986), *Contemporary Theories of Knowledge* (Totowa, NJ: Rowman and Littlefield).

Reed, Baron (forthcoming), 'Epistemic Circularity Squared? Skepticism about Common Sense', *Philosophy and Phenomenological Research*.

Reid, Thomas (1993), *The Works of Thomas Reid*, ed. Sir William Hamilton (Charlottesville, Va.: Lincoln-Rembrandt Publishing).

Reynolds, Steven L. (2002), 'Testimony, Knowledge, and Epistemic Goals', *Philosophical Studies*, 110: 139–61.

Root, Michael (2001), 'Hume on the Virtues of Testimony', *American Philosophical Quarterly*, 38: 19–35.

Ross, Angus (1986), 'Why Do We Believe What We Are Told?', *Ratio*, 28: 69–88.

Rysiew, Patrick (2002), 'Testimony, Simulation, and the Limits of Inductivism', *Australasian Journal of Philosophy*, 78: 269–74.

Schmitt, Frederick F. (ed.) (1994), *Socializing Epistemology: The Social Dimensions of Knowledge* (Lanham, Md.: Rowman and Littlefield).

——— (1999), 'Social Epistemology', in Greco and Sosa (1999: 354–82).

Sosa, Ernest (1996), 'Postscript to "Proper Functionalism and Virtue Epistemology"', in J. L. Kvanvig (ed.), *Warrant in Contemporary Epistemology* (Lanham, Md.: Rowman & Littlefield: 271–81.

——— (1999), 'How Must Knowledge Be Modally Related to What Is Known?', *Philosophical Topics*, 26: 373–84.

——— (2000), 'Contextualism and Skepticism', in J. Tomberlin (ed.), *Philosophical Issues*, suppl. to *Noûs* 34: 94–107.

——— (2002), 'Tracking, Competence, and Knowledge', in P. Moser (ed.), *The Oxford Handbook of Epistemology* (Oxford: Oxford University Press).

Stevenson, Leslie (1993), 'Why Believe What People Say?', *Synthese*, 94: 429–51.

Strawson, P. F. (1994), 'Knowing From Words', in Matilal and Chakrabarti (1994: 23–7).

Webb, Mark Owen (1993), 'Why I Know About As Much As You: A Reply to Hardwig', *Journal of Philosophy*, 90: 260–70.

Weiner, Matthew (2003), 'Accepting Testimony', *Philosophical Quarterly*, 53: 256–64.

Welbourne, Michael (1979), 'The Transmission of Knowledge', *Philosophical Quarterly*, 29: 1–9.

——— (1981), 'The Community of Knowledge', *Philosophical Quarterly*, 31: 302–14.

——— (1986), *The Community of Knowledge* (Aberdeen: Aberdeen University Press).

——— (1994), 'Testimony, Knowledge and Belief', in Matilal and Chakrabarti (1994: 297–313).

Williams, Michael (1999), *Groundless Belief: An Essay on the Possibility of Epistemology*, 2nd edn. (Princeton: Princeton University Press).

Williamson, Timothy (1996), 'Knowing and Asserting', *Philosophical Review*, 105: 489–523.

——— (2000), *Knowledge and Its Limits* (Oxford: Oxford University Press).

NOTES

1. I am here assuming that justification is necessary, and, when added to true belief, close to being sufficient for knowledge. There are some other kinds of justification (e.g., justification grounded entirely in one's subjective perspective) that may escape some of the arguments I give in this paper. In these cases, my arguments can be read as targeting reductionism about testimonial *warrant* or *knowledge*.

2. This condition is included to avoid circularity, i.e., testimonial beliefs ultimately justifying other testimonial beliefs.

3. Proponents of different versions of reductionism include Hume (1967), Fricker (1987, 1994, 1995, and Chapter 10 in this volume), Adler (1994 and 2002), Lyons (1997), Lipton (1998), and Van Cleve (Chapter 2 in this volume). For a nice discussion of Hume's version of reductionism, see Root (2001). Lehrer (Chapter 7 in this volume) develops a qualified reductionist/non-reductionist view of testimonial justification and knowledge.

4. More precisely, this is *one* version of global reductionism. The other version requires that 'a hearer have evidence that *most of what she has ever learned through testimony is true*, where this evidence does not in any way rest on knowledge acquired by her through testimony' (Fricker 1994: 134). Though this weaker version of global reductionism avoids some of the objections raised to the stronger one, it faces problems of its own. Most notably, in the absence of a good reason to believe that *most of what one has ever learned through testimony* adequately and non-randomly represents either *testimony in general* or *testimony that one will encounter in the future*, it is unclear why this reason would justify future acceptances of testimony.

5. For a detailed discussion of some of the specific justificatory issues that arise regarding young children's acceptance of testimony, see Lackey (2005).

6. A notable exception is Fricker (1994). As she says, 'looking for generalisations about the reliability or otherwise of testimony . . . as a homogenous whole, will not be an enlightening project. Illuminating generalisations, if there are any, will be about particular types of testimony, differentiated according to subject matter, or type of speaker, or both. . . . [W]hen it comes to the probability of accuracy of speakers' assertions, and what sorts of factors warrant a hearer in trusting a speaker, *testimony is not a unitary category*' (Fricker 1994: 139; emphasis added).

7. 'My reliance on a particular piece of testimony *reduces locally* just if I have adequate grounds to take my informant to be trustworthy on this occasion independently of accepting as true her very utterance' (Fricker 1995: 404).

8. Strictly speaking, I shall argue that even the weakest version of only the *Reduction Component* of reductionism is false, leaving the Positive-Reasons Component of reductionism untouched. (Indeed, I shall argue in the next section that the Positive-Reasons Component is correct.) However, since I am taking the Reduction Component to be an essential part of reductionism (what, after all, is reductionism with no reduction?), a view that merely includes the Positive-Reasons Component does not qualify as a reductionist view.

9. A point of clarification: I refer to this case as NESTED SPEAKER because the justification for accepting one speaker's report is *nested within* the positive reasons for accepting another speaker's report. More precisely, the justification for accepting Pauline's testimony is nested within the positive reasons for accepting Helen's testimony.

10. This is not to say that a belief that fails to be reliably produced or appropriately connected with the truth will *necessarily* render a report based on such a belief unreliable. Indeed, I have elsewhere argued that the epistemic status of beliefs and reports can come apart so that an unreliable believer can nonetheless be a reliable testifier. (See Lackey 1999, 2003, and forthcoming *a*.) Rather, the problem with Pauline's testimony in NESTED SPEAKER is that her unreliability as a believer leads her to also be an *unreliable testifier*.

11. For discussions specifically about the role of competence and sincerity in testimony, see, for instance, Welbourne (1979, 1981, 1986, and 1994), Hardwig (1985 and 1991), Ross (1986), Fricker (1987, 1994, 1995, forthcoming, and Chapter 10 in this volume), Plantinga (1993), McDowell (1994), Audi (1997, 1998, and Chapter 1 in this volume), Root (2001), Owens (2000), and Adler (2002). For indirect endorsements of competence and sincerity as necessary conditions for testimonial knowledge (justification), e.g., via the stronger requirement that the speaker have the knowledge (justified belief) to which she is testifying, see Burge (1993 and 1997), Williamson (1996), Dummett (1994), Reynolds (2002), and Schmitt (Chapter 9 in this volume).

12. See Lackey (1999, 2003, and forthcoming *a*).

13. A proponent of reductionism may object to the conclusion of NESTED SPEAKER by arguing that justification—unlike, for instance, warrant and knowledge—is primarily an *internalist* notion. For instance, if I were a brain-in-a-vat and had no idea that I was, one might argue that I would still be *justified* in believing that I am here typing at this computer, even if I do not *know* that I am. Similarly, one might claim that in NESTED SPEAKER, the belief that Fred forms on the basis of Pauline's radically unreliable testimony is *justified*, even if it does not qualify as *knowledge*. (I am grateful to Peter Graham for pressing this point.)

By way of response to this objection, I shall make four points. First, it is not at all uncommon in the literature to find justification being discussed, either entirely or partially, in externalist terms. To name just a few, see Alston (1989), Goldman (1992), and BonJour and Sosa (2003).

Second, many reductionists are equally reductionistic about warrant and knowledge (though, of course, a truth condition is added when testimonial knowledge is at issue). Hence, for those who hold that justification is a purely internalist notion, my arguments in this section can simply be recast as arguments against reductionism about testimonial *warrant* or *knowledge*.

Third, in Section 3, I shall argue that justification has two central components: (i) a reliability component and (ii) a rationality component. Thus, if I were a brain-in-a-vat and had no idea that I was, my belief that I am here typing at this computer would still satisfy the *rationality* constraint of justification. More precisely, even though my beliefs in a skeptical scenario would fail the reliability constraint and, hence, would not be justified, they would nevertheless be *rational* (indeed, such beliefs would possess many other positive epistemic properties, such as being held in an epistemically responsible way, being epistemically virtuous, and so on). So, given the distinction between (i) and (ii), my view of justification is able to explain the intuition that skeptical scenario victims both *possess* and *lack* something epistemically important: they possess rationality, but lack reliability and hence justification.

Fourth, if justification is understood as a purely internalist notion, then it is not entirely clear what connection, if any, it has to knowledge. Traditionally, justification has been understood as necessary and, when added to true belief, close to sufficient for knowledge. On this reading of justification—the one that I am here assuming—internalists and externalists are engaged in a *genuine* debate about the *same* condition for knowledge. Moreover, on this traditional reading, it is clear why justification has epistemic value: it converts, with some help from a

Gettier-condition, true belief into knowledge. In contrast, on the purely internalist conception of justification assumed by this objection, not only does the internalism/ externalism debate turn out to be quibbling over entirely different concepts, it also becomes unclear what the precise epistemic value of justification is.

14. Let me emphasize that this is how one might plausibly construe the case; it is not, however, how I would characterize it. Despite the fact that Holly is a generally reliable testifier, I would hold that Max's belief on the basis of her testimony fails to be justified because the report itself is not reliably produced. (For more on this condition of testimonial justification, see Lackey (1999, 2003, and forthcoming *a*).) On my view, the virtue of NESTED SPEAKER, in comparison with UNNESTED SPEAKER, is that it entirely precludes this sort of plausible reading.

15. It is also worth noting that analogues of NESTED SPEAKER cannot be constructed for other epistemic sources since it exploits features unique to the case of testimony, i.e., the ability to have one's justification for accepting a speaker's report nested within the positive reasons for accepting another speaker's report.

16. I am grateful for an exchange with Sandy Goldberg that prompted the addition of both UNNESTED SPEAKER and the discussion contrasting it with NESTED SPEAKER.

17. A further reductionist strategy for resisting the conclusion of NESTED SPEAKER is to make it part of the definition of 'appropriate' that the reasons in question lead hearers to reports that bear a reliable connection with the truth. This would make it impossible for a subject to have appropriate positive reasons for believing a report that wasn't reliably connected with the truth. This strategy, however, has at least one of two unattractive consequences. It either (i) makes the requirement for positive reasons so externalistic that it undermines the central motivation for endorsing the Positive-Reasons Component in the first place; namely, to preserve a link between epistemic justification and subjective rationality, or (ii) it makes the requirements for testimonial justification so stringent that there would be far less testimonial justification than is intuitively acceptable.

18. More precisely, there are two different kinds of defeaters that are standardly taken to be incompatible with justification (and knowledge). First, there are what we might call *psychological defeaters*. A psychological defeater is an experience, doubt, or belief that is had by S, yet indicates that S's belief that *p* is either false or unreliably formed or sustained. Defeaters in this sense function by virtue of being *had* by S, regardless of their truth value or justificatory status. Second, there are what we might call *normative defeaters*. A normative defeater is a doubt or belief that S ought to have, yet indicates that S's belief that *p* is either false or unreliably formed or sustained. Defeaters in this sense function by virtue of being doubts or beliefs that S *should have* (whether or not S does have them) given the presence of available evidence. For various discussions of what I call psychological defeaters see, for example, BonJour (1980 and 1985), Nozick (1981), Pollock (1986), Goldman (1986), Plantinga (1993), Lackey (1999, 2003, and 2005), Bergmann (1997 and 2004), and Reed (forthcoming). For discussions involving what I call normative defeaters, approached in a number of different ways, see BonJour (1980 and 1985), Goldman (1986), Fricker (1987 and 1994), Chisholm (1989), Burge (1993 and 1997), McDowell (1994), Audi (1997 and 1998), Williams (1999), Lackey (1999,

2003, and 2005), BonJour and Sosa (2003), Hawthorne (2004), and Reed (forth-coming). What all of these discussions have in common is simply the idea that evidence can defeat justification (and knowledge) even when the subject does not form any corresponding beliefs from the evidence in question.

19. For various versions of non-reductionism, see Austin (1979), Welbourne (1979, 1981, 1986, and 1994), Evans (1982), Ross (1986), Hardwig (1985 and 1991), Coady (1992 and 1994), Reid (1993), Burge (1993 and 1997), Plantinga (1993), Webb (1993), Dummett (1994), Foley (1994), McDowell (1994), Strawson (1994), Williamson (1996 and 2000), Goldman (1999), Schmitt (1999), Insole (2000), Owens (2000), Rysiew (2002), Weiner (2003), and Goldberg (Chapter 6 in this volume). Some phrase their view in terms of knowledge, others in terms of justification or entitlement, still others in terms of warrant. Audi (1997, 1998, and Chapter 1 in this volume) embraces a non-reductionist view of testimonial knowledge, but not of testimonial justification. Stevenson (1993), Millgram (1997), and Graham (Chapter 4 in this volume) defend restricted versions of non-reductionism. Faulkner (2000) develops a 'hybrid' reductionist/non-reductionist view of testimonial justification and knowledge, though it differs in some crucial respects from the dualist theory I suggest later in this paper.

20. It was suggested to me by Lizzie Fricker that another type of example that may make the same general point would be a person receiving testimony over the internet, with absolutely no epistemically relevant information about the source of the testimony. (Fricker also mentions this sort of case in her (2002).)

21. Even outside the epistemology of testimony, this is a very widely accepted view. For instance, adding a no-defeater condition to theories of epistemic justification that are otherwise externalist has become the standard response given to the counterexamples found in BonJour's (1980 and 1985). See, for instance, Nozick (1981), Goldman (1986), and Plantinga (1993).

22. I am grateful to comments from Joe Shieber that prompted the addition of this point.

23. For additional arguments showing the inadequacy of standard versions of non-reductionism, see Lackey (2003).

24. A non-reductionist who appreciates the need for justificatory contributions from both the hearer and the speaker is Goldberg (Chapter 6 in this volume), who characterizes the hearer's epistemic contribution in terms of the *right* she has to rely on the testimony that is offered. It is precisely the possession of positive reasons, however, that I argue constitutes this right.

25. I say 'crudely' because I do not want to suggest either that the speaker condition is entirely divorced from questions of rationality or that the hearer condition is entirely divorced from questions of reliability.

26. Of course, my use of this term has no direct bearing on its use in other contexts, such as in the philosophy of mind.

27. In Lackey (2003), I argue that there are at least two additional conditions needed for testimonial justification, one requiring that the hearer is a properly functioning recipient of testimony and another requiring that the environment is suitable for the reception of reliable testimony.

28. A rough taxonomy of the three competing positions, then, is as follows:

    Reductionism: Reduction Component and Positive-Reasons Component (PR-N&S)
    Non-Reductionism: No-Reduction Component and No-Positive-Reasons Component. Dualism: Positive-Reasons Component (PR-N) and No-Reduction Component

29. This example is a slight variation of one found in Audi (1997). For further discussion of the distinction inspired by these sorts of cases, see Lackey (1999).

30. It should be noted that there is a weaker version of (1) (henceforth, (1*)) that requires only that B believe that *p* on the basis of the content of A's *testimony*, not that such a belief be based on the content of A's testimony *that p*. There are at least two different kinds of cases that might support including (1*) rather than (1). For instance, suppose that Ben asks me whether it is snowing outside and I respond by saying, 'There is a shovel in the closet'. Here, one might say that Ben is justified in believing that it is snowing outside on the basis of my testimony that there is a shovel in the closet. Thus, one might claim that (1) of dualism is, in fact, too strong since one can be testimonially justified in believing that *p* on the basis of the content of a speaker's testimony that *q*. The second type of case that may pose a problem for (1) can be seen by considering the following: suppose that Ruth asks me whether I bought flowers at the farmer's market and I respond with a nod. Here, it might be argued that Ruth is justified in believing that I bought flowers at the farmer's market on the basis of the non-verbal testimony provided by my nod. In this way, one might claim that while testimonial justification for believing that *p* is acquired on the basis of the content of my testimony, it is not based on the content of my testimony *that p*.

    Although I think both types of examples may provide convincing evidence for including the weaker (1*), there are also compelling reasons to prefer the stronger (1). With respect to the first type of case, for instance, one might argue that Ben's justification for believing that it is snowing outside relies too heavily on memory and inference to qualify as *testimonial*. In particular, one might claim that Ben must rely on background information stored in memory about the relationship between shovels and snow and explicitly infer that it is snowing outside from my testimony that there is a shovel in the closet. And even though memory and inference arguably play a role in the acquisition of all instances of testimonial justification, one might claim that here the role of memory and inference is simply too significant for the resulting justification to properly be regarded as testimonial. Regarding the second type of case, it may be argued that though I do not explicitly state that I bought flowers at the farmer's market, there is a clear sense in which the non-verbal testimony provided by my nod has this as its content. For just as my responding 'Yes' in this context amounts to 'I bought flowers at the farmer's market', so too does my nodding in this context amount to testifying to this proposition.

    I do not wish to here choose between (1) and (1*). Though I am leaving the stronger (1) in my characterization of dualism, this condition can easily be substituted with the weaker (1*) for those convinced by the cases discussed above.

31. For arguments showing that neither competent believing nor sincere testifying is necessary for being a reliable testifier, see Lackey (forthcoming *a*).

32. See Nozick (1981).
33. See Sosa (1996, 1999, 2000, and 2002). See also Williamson (2000).
34. In a similar spirit, Frederick Schmitt says that '[t]he objection [to reductionism] . . . I regard as most persuasive [is] that we have too little first-hand experience to provide a nontestimonial basis for induction to the reliability of testimony in all instances in which testimonial belief is intuitively justified' (Schmitt 1999: 359).
35. Similarly, Frederick Schmitt claims that '[m]y belief in the reliability of . . . testimony sometimes has what passes for a first-hand inductive base, but this passing first-hand basis is itself indebted to testimony for its justification' (Schmitt 1999: 360).
36. This point has been suggested by other proponents of a positive-reasons require-ment—most notably, by Fricker (1987, 1994, 1995, and 2002) and Faulkner (2002).
37. Specifically, even if B has not observed a general conformity between A's reports and the truth, B may have observed the general conformity of reports delivered in contexts of kind C and the truth. So, if B believes that A's report is delivered in a C-context, then this, combined with B's inductive evidence regarding contexts of kind C, may give B an epistemically relevant positive reason for A's testimony.
38. In particular, even if B has not observed a general conformity between A's reports and the truth, B may have observed the general conformity of reports of kind R and the truth. Thus, if B believes that A's report is an instance of kind R, this, com-bined with B's inductive evidence regarding R-reports, may give B an epistemically relevant positive reason for A's testimony.
39. Specifically, even if B has not observed the general conformity between A's reports and the truth, B may have observed the general conformity of speakers of kind S and the truth. Thus, if B believes that A is an S-speaker, then this, combined with B's inductive evidence regarding S-speakers, may give B an epistemically relevant positive reason for A's testimony.
40. The reasons from each of the three classes discussed may be either at the level of tokens or types.
41. This point is frequently noticed in the case of negative evidence, that is, it is readily acknowledged that average epistemic agents have acquired ample inductive evidence for believing that certain conversational features, such as nervousness, lack of eye contact, and confused behavior, suggest *incompetence, insincerity, and unreliability.* But positive reasons are just the flip side of defeaters. For just as we have accumu-lated this type of negative inductive evidence, we have also accumulated positive inductive evidence for believing that certain contextual features are indicators of competence, sincerity, and reliability.
42. I am using the term 'person' broadly so that non-human animals from whom we are able to acquire testimonial beliefs qualify as persons in this sense.
43. As mentioned in n. 31, I argue in Lackey (forthcoming *a*) that neither of these aspects is *necessary* for a speaker to be a reliable testifier, though they are often con-stitutive of being a reliable testifier.
44. For a very nice discussion of this point, see Faulkner (2000).
45. A possible non-testimonial exception to this claim is the relationship between self-deception and certain memories. (I am grateful to Baron Reed for pointing this out.) A subject may, for instance, deceive herself by calling into question memories

that are too painful to remember. While this is true, it is quite doubtful whether self-deception can be overtly conscious and therefore intentional in the way that insincere testimony is. What is more plausible is that self-deception takes place at the unconscious level, and indirectly induces false belief. Thus, failures in memory deriving from self-deception are more analogous to failures in perception regarding some sub-personal glitch in how the faculty works.

46. My point here is not that all non-testimonial sources are homogeneous *to the same extent*—there may, for instance, be more variation between memories from different stages in one's life than there is among different kinds of perceptual experiences. My point is, rather, that there is a striking difference between the amount of variation found within non-testimonial sources as compared with testimony as an epistemic source. Moreover, if there are some non-testimonial sources—perhaps, for instance, inductive inference—that are as epistemically heterogeneous as testimony, then a positive-reasons condition may be needed to justifiedly accept the deliverances of these sources as well. What I wish to establish here, however, is that the conclusion of ALIEN does not generalize to *all* epistemic sources.

47. There are two qualifications to this thesis: first, though other epistemic sources are not necessary for justification and knowledge, according to non-reductionism, they are of course needed for accessing the testimony of others, e.g., sense perception is required to hear the spoken testimony of others. Second, even if these other epistemic sources do not provide justification for accepting the testimony of speakers, they can inhibit justification and knowledge by generating defeaters.

PART IV

TESTIMONY AND THE EXTENT OF OUR DEPENDENCE ON OTHERS

9

Testimonial Justification and Transindividual Reasons

Frederick F. Schmitt

This paper explores one aspect of the general question in what sense knowledge on the basis of testimony, and more exactly belief justified on the basis of testimony, is social. I take it to be uncontroversial that testimonial *knowledge* is social in a fairly strong sense. One might initially express the social claim this way: testimonial knowledge of a proposition depends on the knowledge of the testifier. That is,

I know that *p* on *T*'s testimony that *p* only if *T* knows that *p*.[1]

According to this condition, testimonial knowledge is social in the sense that my having testimonial knowledge entails that there is knowledge belonging (in the normal case) to an individual other than myself.[2] This precise condition of testimonial knowledge has in fact been forcefully challenged (Lackey 1999; Graham 2000), but I take it to be uncontroversial that something in the vicinity of this condition is correct, and a strong social claim for testimonial knowledge is beyond question.[3]

By contrast, *testimonially justified belief* is clearly not social in a way closely analogous to this social condition on testimonial knowledge.[4] It is *not* true that

My belief *p* is justified on the basis of *T*'s testimony only if *T* has a good reason to believe *p*.

To be sure, testimonially justified belief is uncontroversially social in a weaker sense. If my belief *p* is justified on testimony, it does follow by the meaning of "on testimony" that there is testimony, hence a testifier, hence (in the normal case) an individual distinct from me. My belief cannot be justified on testimony that does not exist. So there being testimonially justified belief entails that there is a testifier. Nevertheless, my having a testimonially justified belief that *p* does not entail that my testifier herself is in any positive epistemic position. I can have a justified belief that there are strawberries in the refrigerator on Tina's testimony even if Tina has no good reason to believe this, if I justifiedly though mistakenly

I would like to thank Jennifer Lackey for help in revising the paper.

believe that Tina has a good reason to believe this. So my belief p's being justified on the basis of T's testimony does not entail that T has a good reason to believe p. Testimonially justified belief is not social in this strong sense.[5]

Despite this, I think that a qualified social claim about testimonially justified belief is defensible. In particular, there are instances of testimonially justified belief p for which I lack a justified belief that the testifier has a good reason to believe p, and I lack any other good reason to believe p. In such cases, if there is to be a relevant good reason for me to believe p, it must be possessed by my *testifier* rather than by me. What I wish to defend, then, is the following initially implausible two-part thesis:

> If my belief p is justified on testimony, then my testifier T possesses a good reason to believe p, unless I possess such a reason.
> I can have a belief p justified on testimony even though I possess no good reason to believe p.[6]

Indeed, I wish to defend a stronger and even less intuitive social thesis, which I will call the Transindividual Basing Thesis, or the *Transindividual Thesis* for short:

> (T1) If my belief p is justified on testimony, then it is justified on the basis of the testifier's good reason to believe p, unless on the basis of a good reason to believe p I myself possess.
>
> (T2) My belief p can be justified on testimony even though my belief is not justified on the basis of a good reason to believe p I possess.[7]

If I fail to base my belief that there are strawberries in the refrigerator on a good reason I possess, my belief can still be justified on Tina's testimony, but not if it fails to be justified on the basis of Tina's good reason—e.g., because she lacks a good reason: she did not look carefully enough in the refrigerator this morning. My testimonial justification for believing p is in this sense hostage to whether my testifier possesses a good reason to believe p. One might be inclined to dismiss the Transindividual Thesis on the conceptual ground that, by the very notions of "basing," "reason," and "reasoning," basing a belief on a reason entails reasoning to the belief from the reason; yet, by the very notion of "testimony," the chain from the testifier's reason, through testimony and testimonial uptake, to my belief does not count as reasoning. But I find "basing" too vague a term to carry the weight of this short objection.

The case for the Transindividual Thesis, in a nutshell, is this. The first component, (T1), follows from the plausible assumption

> (G) Any justified belief p of mine is justified on the basis of a good reason to believe p suitably related to me.

For suppose (G) and suppose my belief p is justified on testimony. If I do not possess a good reason to believe p, then the only remaining candidate for a reason on the basis of which my belief is justified is a reason possessed by the testifier.

Hence, my belief p must be justified either on the basis of a reason I possess or one possessed by the testifier. This conclusion is just (T1). Once (G) is granted, the case for (T1) is convincing. I will simply assume (G) without argument for the time being. In Section 2, however, I will argue for (G) restricted to testimonially justified beliefs. I will do so on the ground that in the case of a testimonially justified belief, we have no plausible alternative to basing on a good reason as that in virtue of which the belief is justified.

The second component of the Transindividual Thesis, (T2), is supported in this way. My testimonially justified belief p cannot always be justified on the basis of a justified belief that the testifier has a good reason to believe p (alternatively, that the testifier is reliable on the topic of p). For my belief that the testifier has a good reason to believe p is itself ultimately justified on the basis of testimony—on the basis, say, of my testimonially justified belief q. As it turns out, this testimonially justified belief q is not in turn nontestimonially justified on the basis of any good reason I possess—obviously not on the basis of the reason that the testifier has a good reason to believe p, on pain of circularity, but also on the basis of no other good reason I possess. Hence, I can be justified in my testimonial belief even though I do not possess a good reason to believe p. This is (T2).

While I regard this case for (T2) and thus the overall case for the Transindividual Thesis as promising, I do not claim to be able to develop the case for (T2) in full. Instead, I will offer a *conditional* case for the Transindividual Thesis, and even that only tempered and in outline. The Thesis is analogous to an intra-individual basing thesis for memorially justified belief, which I will call the *Transtemporal Thesis*:

(M1) If my belief p is justified on (the basis of) memory, then it is justified on the basis of my original good reasons to believe p, unless on the basis of a good reason I currently possess to believe p.[8]

(M2) I can be justified in believing p on memory, even though I am not justified in believing it on the basis of a good reason I currently possess to believe p.

For example, if my original reason to believe that there are strawberries in the refrigerator was no good—the product of a hasty look in the refrigerator this morning—then, assuming I base my belief on no current good reason, my belief is not now justified. The Transtemporal Thesis is, I take it, intuitively very plausible and widely accepted, even if not wholly uncontroversial.[9] My aim in this paper is to show, albeit in outline, that there is a case for the Transindividual Thesis for testimonial justification (in particular (T2)) analogous to the obvious and, I assume, widely accepted case for the Transtemporal Thesis for memorial justification (M2). I will not attempt to argue here that the case for the Transtemporal Thesis really supports that thesis. My claim is merely conditional and tempered: the case for the Transindividual Thesis about testimonially justified belief is nearly as strong as that for the Transtemporal Thesis about memorially justified belief. In other words, if you accept the intuitively plausible Transtemporal Thesis on the basis of the obvious case for it, then you ought to find probative the analogous case for the intuitively implausible Transindividual Thesis. (I note at the outset that what I say defends a fortiori the intuitively more plausible weaker social claim with which we started, that my belief p is justified on testimony only if either I or the testifier possesses a good reason to believe p, and I can have a belief p justified on testimony even though I possess no good reason to believe p. So if you, quite forgiveably, have a special grudge against the stronger and more counterintuitive Transindividual Thesis about basing, remember that the discussion can easily be translated into a defense of the weaker, somewhat more palatable claim about possessing reasons.)

1 THE CONDITIONAL CASE FOR THE TRANSINDIVIDUAL THESIS

The case for the Transtemporal Thesis is analogous to the nutshell case I mentioned for the Transindividual Thesis. We assume (G), that my justified belief p must be based on a good reason. The case for component (M1) of the Transtemporal Thesis exactly parallels the case already made for (T1) of the Transindividual Thesis. I take the case for component (M1) to be convincing, once (G) is granted.

The case for component (M2), that my belief can be memorially justified even though not justified on the basis of a current reason, is this. It is claimed that there are beliefs intuitively justified on memory for which there is no available candidate for a good current reason on which the beliefs are based. There are two sorts of candidates for a good current reason that need to be ruled out here: a current reductive reason and a current nonreductive reason.[10] The ground for (M2), then, is that there are instances of memorially justified belief for which there are no good current reductive and no good current nonreductive reasons. Although many of the points to be made in favor of (M2) will be familiar from the literature on memorial justification, the reader must indulge my going through them to bring out a favorable comparison with the case for the testimonial analogue (T2).

Reductive Reasons. Any memorially justified belief p is justified on the basis of a good current *reductive* reason only in virtue of being justified on the basis of a deductive, inductive, or other justifying inference from that reason. Such a reason is a belief and must itself be justified in order to provide justification for my memorially justified belief p. The relevant feature of any such current reductive reason, the feature that prevents my memorially justified belief from being based solely on a current reductive reason, is that such a current reductive reason depends on memory. If my belief is justified on memory in virtue of being based on a current reductive reason r, it is so justified by inference from r, and r

must therefore itself be a justified belief. But as it happens, any current reductive reason that could support my memorially justified belief is itself justified on memory.[11] So (assuming that memorial justification depends only on current reasons) memorial justification on the basis of a current reductive reason depends ultimately on a current reductive reason memorially justified on the basis of a current *nonreductive* reason, on pain of a regress of memorial justification on the basis of reductive reasons. My current reductive reason *r* must ultimately be justified on memory on the basis of a current nonreductive reason (if on any current reason at all) in order to stem the regress. In this sense, reductive reasons are parasitic on nonreductive reasons. This means that a current nonreductive reason is the ultimate basis of memorial justification on the basis of a current reductive reason, and hence the ultimate basis of any memorial justification on the basis of current reasons. Thus, assuming that my memorially justified belief can be based on a current reductive reason only if that reason is itself justified on memory, the case for the Transtemporal Thesis need only show that there are instances of memorially justified beliefs for which there is no basis in good current nonreductive reasons. The question arises whether being ultimately justified on the basis of a current nonreductive reason does not touch off a further regress of reasons (whether current reductive or current nonreductive reasons); but current nonreductive reasons, unlike current reductive reasons, need not themselves be justified on memory. The answer is that no such regress need arise. For current nonreductive reasons need not be beliefs that must themselves be justified in order to provide justification for my memorially justified belief *p*. Indeed, it is natural to think of current nonreductive reasons as states other than beliefs, hence not even susceptible of justification at all.

But why say that my belief *p* is memorially justified on the basis of a current reductive reason only if the reason is itself justified on memory? In lieu of answering the question for each of the various candidates for current reductive reasons, I will answer it for one paradigmatic candidate, which I believe to be the most promising candidate for a current reductive reason—a statistical (or track-record) reason:

> My belief *p* is justified on memory on the basis of a statistical syllogism from an inductively justified generalization that memorial beliefs of a certain type *X* (where, e.g., type *X* is recollection of a vivid experience) tend to be true, together with an introspectively justified belief that my belief *p* is a memorial belief of type *X*.

No doubt in instances in which I have a memorially justified belief, my belief often can come to be justified on the basis of a current reductive reason of the specified sort. But the question is whether, if my belief came to be justified on this basis, the reason would escape being ultimately justified on memory. The answer to this question is No. For the premise that memorial beliefs of type *X* tend to be true is inductively justified. But my belief in this premise is inductively justified on the basis of justified beliefs that given memory beliefs of type X are true, for sufficiently many and varied memorial beliefs. Yet in general, my belief that a particular memorial belief of type X is true is justified on the basis of that and other memorial beliefs, hence on the basis of memory. So any memorial belief justified on the basis of the statistical reason must ultimately be justified on the basis of memorial beliefs. Hence, my belief p is memorially justified on the basis of a current reductive reason of the statistical sort only if the reason is itself justified on memory. This means that current reductive statistical reasons do not terminate a regress of memorial justification. Thus, to avoid a regress of statistical reasons, current reductive statistical reasons must be justified on the basis ultimately of current nonstatistical reasons. Indeed, these current nonstatistical reasons must be current nonreductive reasons if other current reductive reasons suffer the same problem as current statistical reductive reasons. And though I cannot make the case here, I believe that similar arguments apply to other candidates for current reductive reasons. If so, a memorial belief justified on the basis of a current reductive reason is ultimately justified on memory. Hence, a current reductive reason does not terminate a regress of memorial justification. A belief memorially justified on the basis of a current reductive reason must therefore be justified ultimately on the basis of a current nonreductive reason, if it is to be justified solely on the basis of current reasons. Hence, the question whether (M2) holds comes to whether some memorially justified beliefs lack an ultimate basis in good current nonreductive reasons. We will address that question momentarily.

In the meantime, let us turn to testimonially justified belief and ask whether a reductive reason I possess for such a belief must also ultimately be justified on the basis of testimony, hence ultimately justified on nonreductive reasons I possess if justified solely on the basis of reasons I possess. Let us consider a statistical basis for testimonially justified belief parallel to the statistical basis for memorially justified belief we just considered. In the case of a statistical basis,

> my belief p is justified on testimony on the basis of a statistical syllogism from an inductively justified generalization that testimonial beliefs of a certain type X (where, e.g., type X is belief on the testimony of a socially recognized expert in the field to which p belongs) tend to be true, and an introspectively or perceptually justified belief that my belief p is of type X.[12]

I am inductively justified in believing this generalization on the basis of justified beliefs that given testimonial beliefs of type X are true, for sufficiently many and varied testimonial beliefs.

Here a problem analogous to the problem for memorially justified belief arises. In general, I am justified in believing that a particular testimonial belief of type X is true only on the basis (in part) of that or other testimonial beliefs. There are two grounds for saying that in general I am justified in believing that a particular testimonial belief is true only on the basis of that testimonial belief or some others. One ground is that although I may be able to verify firsthand some of the relevant testimonial beliefs, I am not able to do so for sufficiently many and varied testimonial beliefs to afford a basis for induction.[13] A different ground for the claim is that in general perceptual beliefs on the basis of which I verify my testimonial beliefs are themselves justified in part on the basis of prior testimonially justified beliefs. Although no one has decisively established these points (nor is it even clear how the issue could be decisively settled), most of those writing recently on the viability of a statistical reduction for testimonial justification have endorsed one or both of these points.

If either point is accepted, then a statistical reason for my testimonially justified belief is itself ultimately justified on testimony. Hence, my belief p is testimonially justified on the basis of a reductive reason of the statistical sort that I possess only if the reason is itself justified on testimony. Thus, to avoid a regress of statistical reasons I possess, reductive statistical reasons I possess must be justified on the basis of nonstatistical reasons I possess. As in the case of memorial justification, these nonstatistical reasons must be nonreductive reasons I possess. For there is a parallel regress for all the candidates for reductive reasons.[14] We thus reach the conclusion that a testimonial belief justified on the basis of a reductive reason I possess is ultimately justified on the basis of a nonreductive reason I possess. Admittedly, the case here that a testimonially justified belief is ultimately justified on the basis of a nonreductive reason I possess (if solely on the basis of reasons I possess) is not as strong as the parallel case that a memorially justified belief is ultimately justified on the basis of a current nonreductive reason (if solely on the basis of current reasons), but it does seem presumptive at the present time.

Nonreductive Reasons. We have seen that testimony and memory are in a similar boat regarding reductive reasons: for each of them there is a case that justification on the basis of reductive reasons is parasitic on justification on the basis of nonreductive reasons. There is a case that current reductive reasons are justified on the basis of memory and hence on current nonreductive reasons, and there is a parallel case for testimony. We may now proceed to the question whether there are memorially justified beliefs not justified ultimately on the basis of good current nonreductive reasons. There is a case in favor of an affirmative answer. If the answer is affirmative, then there are memorially justified beliefs not justified ultimately on the basis of any current reasons at all—thus, (M2).

There are two sorts of candidates for current nonreductive reasons (or justification) that might be taken to justify a belief memorially in a manner that does not reduce to perceptual, inductive, or other inferential justification—coherentist justifications and foundationalist reasons.[15] The case for (M2) must show that there are memorially justified beliefs for which both coherentist and foundationalist ultimate justifications are missing.

Regarding a *coherentist* ultimate justification, plausibly there are many instances of memorially justified beliefs that are not ultimately justified by coherence with other current beliefs. I will assume here that justification by coherence requires that the belief p bears a relation of coherence to some set of relevant beliefs or to each member of some set of relevant beliefs. Similar remarks apply, I think, on the view that justification by coherence requires membership in a set of beliefs each of which coheres with other members of the set.

I remember isolated incidents—e.g., that I sampled octopus at age five. I may be justified in this belief even though it coheres only very weakly with any set of current beliefs of mine that are relevant to it. I may be justified in this belief even though I believe only such things as that I heard the word "octopus" around this time, that I ate seafood in my youth, that my memory is generally reliable, and that my memory tells me that I sampled octopus at age five. The relation of coherence my belief that I sampled octopus at age five bears to any set of such relevant beliefs is far too weak to make my belief justified. This is an intuitive point, but it may be reinforced with this argument. The following principle would seem to govern the relation between coherence and justification if coherence is ever a sufficient condition of justification:

> If my belief p coheres sufficiently with a set of relevant beliefs to be justi-
> fied in virtue of this coherence, then in a case in which I believe not-p but
> maintain the beliefs in this set altered only to accommodate differences in
> beliefs as to what my memory tells me and beliefs that follow from such
> beliefs, and I hold no beliefs outside the set that would undermine justific-
> ation for believing p, my belief not-p would not sufficiently cohere with the
> altered set of beliefs to be justified in virtue of its coherence with the set.

This principle of coherence bears on examples of the present sort. Instead of a case in which I remember that I sampled octopus at age five, imagine a case as similar to this with respect to my beliefs as possible, but in which what I remember is the negation of the proposition I remember in the original case. In this altered case, I remember that I did not sample octopus at age five. I have the beliefs in the specified set for the belief p, corrected for what memory tells me. I also have no beliefs outside this set that would undermine my justification for believing p. It seems that my belief not-p coheres about as well with the altered set of relevant beliefs as my belief p coheres with the original set of relevant beliefs. So the coherence of my belief not-p should be sufficient for the justification of that belief, on a coherence theory of justification, if the coherence of my belief p is sufficient for the justification of that belief. Thus, the principle of coherence entails that the coherence of my belief p is not sufficient for the justification of that belief. A coherence theory is inconsistent with the justification of my belief p, contrary to intuition. This conclusion reinforces the point that there are memori-ally justified beliefs that, if based on current reasons at all, are not ultimately justified on the basis of current reasons in virtue of coherence with those reasons.

There is a parallel case, about as strong as the memorial case, that some testi-monially justified beliefs, if justified on the basis of reasons I possess, are not ultimately justified in virtue of coherence with those reasons. For I may be justified in believing that there are mussels in New Zealand on someone's say-so, even though my belief coheres only very weakly with any set of relevant beliefs of mine. I may be justified in my testimonial belief even though I know nothing that is relevant to this belief, other than such uninformative generalities as that the testifier is an adult human being, that adult human beings generally speak the truth, that New Zealand has a seashore, that people who may have communicated with my testifier have visited New Zealand, and that mussels live in the sea. The relation of coherence that my belief that there are mussels in New Zealand bears to these relevant other beliefs is far too weak to make my testimonial belief justified. The plausible coherence principle of justification mentioned above entails this same conclusion. These points are enough to cast doubt on a coherentist ultimate justification of testimonial beliefs.

Turning now to a *foundationalist* ultimate justification of memory beliefs, the question is whether all my memory beliefs not ultimately justified by coherence are ultimately justified on the basis of these current states, or features of states:

> my seeming to remember that p
> my feeling that I remember that p
> my believing that I originally had a good reason to believe p
> the strength of my memory belief p.

(My believing that I originally had a good reason to believe p is understood here as supplying a noninferential basis for my memorial belief in the way that the states of seeming and feeling that I remember are supposed to provide such a basis.) There is a case for a negative answer to our question: a memorially justified belief need not be ultimately justified by coherence or on the basis of any of these reasons.[16] This is enough to support (M2).

To see why a negative answer is in order, observe, with regard to the first three candidates on this list, that these states are implausible candidates for a basis on which all my memorially justified beliefs are justified. Suppose someone asks me, "How many bedrooms does your house have?" I reply without hesitation, "Five." I remember, and am justified on the basis of memory in believing, that my house has five bedrooms. In the typical case, I do not experience a state of seeming to remember or feeling that I remember, nor do I form a belief, memorial or otherwise, that I had good reason to believe p. Certainly, in some cases, I am aware that I remember p. But there is no mental state of awareness on which I could base my belief p. To say that I am aware that I remember p is just to say that I know that I remember p, and I can readily access this knowledge if prompted to do so.

Now, in some such cases, I would develop a feeling that I remember p if asked the question, "Are you sure you have remembered p?" But such a feeling is subsequent to my memorially justified belief, and thus my belief cannot be initially justified on the basis of the feeling. Moreover, the states of seeming to remember and of feeling that I remember and the second-order belief typically do not arise unless I consider whether I remember. If I do not consider whether I remember, then typically I will have no such states. These states seem to serve a function when a doubt arises as to whether p, and they help to settle that doubt in favor of p by confirming p in virtue of justifying a belief that I remember p. Note too that there seem to be cases in which I do remember p, but when I consider whether I remember p, I do not seem to remember p, and so I doubt that I do remember. In these cases, initially at least, I am justified in believing p in virtue of remembering, even though I never seem to remember p. I never develop a state of seeming to remember p, or a feeling that I remember p, or a second-order belief that I originally had a good reason to believe p. Colin Radford's example of my correctly answering a quiz show question about the year of Queen Elizabeth I's death is plausibly a case of this sort. Of course, the points so far show only that there are memorially justified beliefs that lack a foundationalist ultimate justification of one of the first three kinds. What we seek is a memorially justified belief that lacks both a coherentist and a foundationalist ultimate justification. Plausibly, my memorially justified belief that I sampled octopus at age five lacks a coherentist ultimate justification, and it may lack a foundationalist ultimate justification of the first three kinds.

The fourth candidate for a current nonreductive reason, the *strength* of my memorial belief, avoids the charge that it does not usually accompany the memorial belief. Plausibly, all memorial beliefs have at least a vague degree of strength. Moreover, the strength of a memorial belief is simultaneous with the belief, so that, as far as timing goes, a memorial belief could be based on its strength after its inception, though not at the moment of its inception, since basing is plausibly a causal relation that takes time and thus requires that the state on which the belief is based obtains before the first moment of basing. Even so, there is something peculiar about saying that a memorial belief is justified only *after* the moment of its inception, not at that moment. More importantly, it is implausible, if it is even intelligible, that my belief is justified on the basis of its own strength, even if we refer here to its strength immediately prior to the time of justification. Presumably, in the simplest case, barring overdetermination, my belief is justified on the basis of something, x, only if, were x not to obtain, my belief would not obtain. This means that if my belief is justified on the basis of its own strength, it follows that were my belief not to have its actual strength prior to a time t, it would no longer obtain at t. But there is no plausibility in the idea that my belief would cease after inception if its strength at inception were different from what it actually is (were less than required for justification). So there is no plausibility in the proposal that my memorially justified belief is justified on the basis of its own strength. Thus, there do seem to be cases of memorially justified beliefs that lack both a coherence ultimate justification and any foundationalist ultimate justification. These memorially justified beliefs are not justified on the basis of any current reasons. This makes a case for (M2).

Turning now to a foundationalist ultimate justification of testimonial belief, there are several candidates for nonreductive reasons I possess on which testimonially justified beliefs might be based:

my seeming to believe *p* on testimony
my believing that the testifier has good reason to believe *p*
the strength of my testimonial belief *p*
my seeming to understand the testimony that *p*.

The question of course is whether all testimonial beliefs not ultimately justified by coherence are justified ultimately on the basis of one or another of these states. The case for a negative answer seems nearly as good as the case for a negative answer to the analogous question for memory. I will treat the first three candidates in this section and the fourth candidate in the next section.

Regarding the first two candidates, they do not always or even usually accompany testimonially justified beliefs. We may restrict our attention to the presence of these states at the moment I form my belief on testimony, since, on the view we are challenging here, testimonial justification for my belief later on may be assumed to depend only on my having had one of these states at some time (at the moment of forming my belief on testimony) and not on my having one of them at each moment my belief is testimonially justified. In many cases of testimonially justified belief, I do know that I believe on testimony at the moment I form my belief. But my testimonially justified belief *p* is not always accompanied by my seeming to believe on testimony or by my believing that the testifier has good reason to believe *p*. I pick up things that people say without attending to who is saying them and even without realizing that anyone has said anything or that I have picked something up by testimony. If, as a result of being asked whether I believe *p* on testimony, I consider the matter shortly after I have formed the belief, in many cases I will seem to believe *p* on testimony, and I will believe that the testifier has good reason to believe *p*. But this is not necessary for my belief to be testimonially justified. It is enough if I have picked up the belief in the sorts of circumstances I often do, however unreflective I may be about the uptake. A view worthy of serious consideration is that my uptake must be sensitive to certain considerations: my belief *p* is not testimonially justified unless I would not have formed the belief *p* were I to have reason to believe the testifier is untrustworthy on the topic of *p*. But even if this is so, I need not actually have the thought that the testifier is trustworthy on *p*.

In addition to this point, there are other points against the first two candidates. Regarding the first candidate, it is not entirely clear that there is any state of my seeming to believe on testimony, and so not clear that there is any candidate state of this sort on the basis of which I might believe *p*. There is no doubt that it can seem to me that I believe on testimony, but it does not follow from this that there is any phenomenal or other mental state of my seeming to believe on testimony. Again, there are phenomenal states that indicate that I believe on testimony, such as a sense that I would answer "Yes" if asked whether I believe that *p* on testimony. But these phenomenal states need not be present when my belief *p* is justified on testimony. Regarding the second candidate, it seems doubtful that my mere belief that my testifier has a good reason to believe *p* would be enough to make my belief *p* justified (in the absence of a coherence justification for my belief *p*). To be sure, my belief *p* might be justified on the basis of a justified belief that my testifier has a good reason to believe *p*. But that is not the proposal in question here. The proposal is that my mere belief that my testifier has a good reason to believe *p* is enough to make my belief *p* justified, whether or not I am justified in believing that my testifier has a good reason to believe *p*. This seems doubtful.

The third candidate, the strength of my testimonial belief, falls to a criticism exactly like the one we have already brought against the analogous candidate for memorially justified belief.

These reflections lead to the conclusion that testimonially justified belief need not be based on any of these candidate states. The same points apply to a case like my testimonial belief that there are mussels in New Zealand. This, then, is a testimonially justified belief lacking both a coherentist and a foundationalist ultimate justification. Such an example is enough to support (T2). The case for (T2) seems nearly as strong as that for (M2).

2 BURGE ON TESTIMONIAL ENTITLEMENT

In making the case for (T1), I assumed what I take to be a plausible condition on justified belief, (G):

> Any justified belief *p* of mine is justified on the basis of a good reason to believe *p* suitably related to me.

To be more exact, the case for (T1) depends on (G) restricted to testimonially justified belief. I will not offer a defense of an unrestricted (G) in this paper. But I do need to defend (G) restricted to testimonially justified belief, since the case for the Transindividual Thesis depends on it. A conditional defense would be enough for my purposes: (G) restricted to testimonially justified belief is as well supported as (G) restricted to memorially justified belief. There is work on testimonial justification that might be taken to call this into question. In particular, Burge (1993, 1997) has proposed a view incompatible with (G) restricted to testimonial justification and with (T1) as well. (Burge at one point endorses something like (G) restricted to memorial justification, but he also endorses the contradictory view, as Edwards (2000) notes. I will say only a word about Burge's view of memorial justification below and focus rather on his view of testimonial justification.[17])

(T1), recall, says:

> If my belief *p* is justified on testimony, then it is justified on the basis of the testifier's good reason to believe *p*, unless on the basis of a good reason to believe *p* I myself possess.

By contrast, Burge holds the view that my belief can be testimonially justified though not based on any good reason. This view is incompatible with (T1).[18] The defense of the restricted (G) and of (T1) thus requires undermining Burge's view. This defense is relevant not only to the restricted (G) and (T1) but also to (T2). For undermining Burge's view also undermines the fourth candidate above for an ultimate basis of testimonial justification, my seeming to understand the testimony that *p*.

Burge expresses his view in this sentence:

in interlocution ... we have a general a priori prima facie (pro tanto) entitlement to believe putative assertions that we seem to understand. (1997: 21)

I note before proceeding that Burge distinguishes entitlement from justification: justification for a belief must be grasped by the subject, while an entitlement need not be. For present purposes, I assimilate entitlement to justification. I will not directly address Burge's claim that my entitlement to believe on testimony is a priori. (On the Transindividual Thesis this claim is in one straightforward sense mistaken: our testimonial justification has whatever status—a priori or a posteriori—is possessed by the testifier's justification for believing *p*.)

I will focus on this principle, to which I take Burge to be committed:

> (U) If *p* is putatively asserted and I seem to understand the putative assertion that *p*, then I am prima facie entitled to believe *p*.

Principle (U) ascribes my testimonial entitlement to believe *p* to *p*'s being putatively asserted and my seeming to understand this putative assertion. Principle (U) does not assume that *p*'s being putatively asserted or my seeming to understand the assertion is a state on the basis of which I might be entitled to my testimonial belief.

I observe that we cannot clearly object to principle (U) in a way parallel to the way we objected earlier to the view that testimonially justified beliefs are always justified on the basis of my seeming to believe on testimony, by pointing out that my belief *p* can be justified on testimony even though I do not realize that I believe *p* on testimony. If what entitles me to believe *p* is my seeming to understand a putative assertion that *p*, this apparently does not require that I realize that I understand *p* as a result of uptake from testimony or from putative assertion. So the fact that my belief can be entitled on testimony without my realizing that I understand *p* as a result of uptake from testimony does not preclude satisfying the antecedent of principle (U).

The objection to principle (U) must rather be that *p*'s being putatively asserted and my seeming to understand the assertion is too slim a basis for testimonial entitlement. This objection seems to me intuitive and compelling. It is very implausible to suppose that the mere fact that p is putatively asserted and I seem to understand the assertion, is enough to make me entitled to believe p (on the basis of testimony). The implausibility is great enough that I feel no need to press a case against principle (U). We may instead ask why Burge would think that the mere fact that I understand what someone has said entitles me to believe it. It will suffice to criticize Burge's argument for principle (U).[19]

I take memorial and testimonial entitlement to be in the same boat here. The memorial analogue of (U) has no intuitive plausibility, and so the question is whether Burge can make a case for this analogue. As it happens, Burge's argument for the memorial analogue of (U) fares better on principle (b1) discussed below than his argument for (U) does. This means that my defense of (T1) against Burge's account of testimonial entitlement is stronger than the analogous defense of (M1) from Burge's account of memorial entitlement. This difference favors a conditional defense of the Transindividual Thesis. So I need only treat the testimonial case here.

Burge's exposition of his argument for principle (U) (1993: 469) requires some interpretation. Lacking room for exegesis, I offer the following reading without further apology:

(a) If a presentation that p is a seemingly intelligible presentation as true, then it is prima facie a presentation of a rational source;

(b) If a presentation that p is prima facie a presentation of a rational source, then it is prima facie a presentation of a source of truth (i.e., a source that tends to present truths);

(c) If a presentation that p is prima facie a presentation of a source of truth, then I am prima facie entitled to believe p.

Conclusion: If a presentation that p is a seemingly intelligible presentation as true, then I am prima facie entitled to believe p.

The Conclusion of this argument is equivalent to principle (U) on the assumption that a presentation that p is a seemingly intelligible presentation as true if and only if p is putatively asserted and I seem to understand the assertion.

The weakest premise in the argument is premise (b).[20] I propose to evaluate Burge's support for (b) and consider the plausibility of (b) in the course of doing so.

Burge supports premise (b) on the ground that a rational source has a veritistic function—it functions to produce true presentations.[21] Evidently Burge infers from this ground that

(b1) If a presentation that p is prima facie a presentation of a rational source, it is prima facie a presentation of a source having a veritistic function (i.e., the function of producing true presentations).

He then assumes:

(b2) If a presentation that *p* is prima facie a presentation of a source having a veritistic function, it is prima facie a presentation of a source of truth.

These two assumptions, (b1) and (b2), together yield (b). This, on my reading, is Burge's support for (b). There are, however, two difficulties with this appeal to the function of producing true presentations.

First, (b1) is implausible. We can grant that rational sources can and sometimes do have the function of producing true presentations. But rational sources do not necessarily have the function of producing true presentations. It is plausible that rational *belief-formation* (or other cognition) has the function of producing true *beliefs*. Thus, (b1) is plausible for memory conceived as a rational source of memorial beliefs. But what Burge needs to support (b) for testimonial entitlement in such a way that it can be combined with a plausible (c) to yield the desired conclusion, is not this innocuous claim, but rather the tendentious claim that rational *interlocution* has the function of producing true *presentations* of the source. It is far from obvious that rational interlocution has the function of producing true presentations. What is plausible is that rational interlocution has the function of furthering the welfare and the goals of the interlocutors (as Faulkner (2000) has emphasized against Burge). Sometimes truth in presentation is a means to this end. But it does not follow that rational interlocution always or ever has the function of producing true presentations. It merely follows that truth in presentation is sometimes a means to fulfilling the function of rational interlocution. This undermines Burge's support for (b). It also reveals that (b) itself is questionable.

A second difficulty with Burge's support for (b) is that (b2) is dubious. Even if a rational source has a veritistic function (has the function of producing true presentations), it clearly does not follow that it is a source of truth—that it really does tend to present truths. The source might have this function but perform it poorly. So why should it follow from the fact that a presentation is prima facie a presentation of a rational source having a veritistic function, that it is prima facie a presentation of a source of truth? Apparently Burge assumes that if one has a prima facie reason to think that a source has a veritistic function, this gives one prima facie reason to think that the source fulfills its function.

I concede that if one had a prima facie reason to think that generally things that have a function fulfill the function, and one had no reason to think that a prima facie presentation of a rational source having a veritistic function fails to fulfill its function, then Burge's assumption would hold. But first, we have no a priori prima facie reason to think that generally things having a function fulfill them. It seems conceivable that things do not generally fulfill the functions they have. This seems conceivable for artifacts that have assigned functions. We could assign functions to clocks and other devices we design, but many or most of these devices could fail to fulfill the functions we assign them either through malfunction that results from unexpected interference from the environment or through inept design. (Admittedly our tools for building the devices would have to function well enough and often enough to enable us to build the devices, but this does not entail that generally artifacts fulfill the functions they have.) But it also seems conceivable that biological organisms, organelles, and organs could fail generally to fulfill the biological functions they have. This is clearly conceivable on an etiological account of biological function, on which something x has the function of doing A when x exists only because ancestors of x did A. Such an etiological account requires that at one time ancestors of x did A, but it does not entail that x does A or even that in doing A ancestors of x were fulfilling the function of doing A. So it does not entail that generally biological entities fulfill the functions they have. It is also clearly conceivable that natural things could fail generally to fulfill the functions they have on the analogical account according to which something x has the function of doing A when it is as if x were designed to do A. For it may be as if x is designed to do A even though it is also as if x is ineptly designed to do A, or even though it is also as if x fails to do A as a result of environmental interference. In short, it seems conceivable that things do not generally fulfill functions they have. If so, I see no a priori prima facie reason to think that generally things that have a function fulfill the function. So a prima facie reason to think that generally things that have a function fulfill the function cannot give Burge the a priori entitlement for testimonial belief he seeks.

A second point is that it is doubtful that there is even an a posteriori prima facie reason to think that generally things that have a function fulfill them. The biological domain is full of examples of organisms and organs that have functions they generally fail to perform. Antibodies have the function of killing viruses, but most never get the chance. Sperm have the function of fertilizing eggs, but most don't. It is difficult or impossible to figure whether in the majority of cases, organisms, organs, and organelles fulfill the functions they have. This is difficult if only because we have no ready way to individuate organisms and functions. Without such an individuation, or perhaps even with one, there is no good reason to expect that generally biological entities fulfill the functions they have. Burge would have to claim that we have a prima facie reason to believe that cognitive functions are superior to biological ones in how generally they fulfill the functions they have, but I can see no warrant for such a claim. We are left with no secure a priori or a posteriori prima facie reason to think that a source having a veritistic function fulfills its function. So we have no reason to think (b2) holds. And without support for either (b1) or (b2), Burge has no support for premise (b), hence none for principle (U).

The upshot is that we have no support for Burge's view that I am prima facie entitled to believe p if p is putatively asserted and I seem to understand the assertion. So we have no support for the view that I can be justified in a belief on testimony without being justified on the basis of a good reason to believe p. Nor do we have support for the view that my seeming to understand the testimony that *p* can supply a good reason in virtue of which I am justified in believing *p* on testimony.

As we saw in Section 1, we also have no support for an account of testimonial justification that appeals only to reasons possessed by me on the basis of which my testimonial belief is justified—indeed, we have reason to reject such an account. The case against reasons of mine, both reductive and nonreductive, as a basis for testimonially justified belief seems nearly as strong as the case against current reasons, both reductive and nonreductive, as a basis for memorially justified belief. And there is no case for the intuitively unappealing claim that seeming understanding makes me prima facie justified in my testimonial beliefs. In the case of memory, we are led back to the thought that in some instances of memorially justified belief, I am justified in believing *p* on the basis of my original good reason to believe *p*. I am so justified whenever I am not justified on the basis of a current good reason to believe *p*, as often happens. The analogous thought for testimony is nearly as well supported: in some instances of testimonially justified belief, I am justified on the basis of the testifier's good reason to believe *p*. I am so justified whenever I am not justified on the basis of my own good reason to believe *p*. This is the Transindividual Thesis.

3 ARE THERE ASYMMETRIES BETWEEN TESTIMONIAL AND MEMORIAL JUSTIFICATION THAT DISFAVOR TRANSINDIVIDUAL BASING?

Are there any differences between testimonial justification and memorial justification that undermine the conditional case for the Transindividual Thesis given the Transtemporal Thesis, or that make the Transindividual Thesis less plausible than the Transtemporal Thesis? In this last section of the paper, I examine three suggestions of such differences and find them wanting.

(1) *Sensitivity to Reasons in the Basing Relation.* There is some plausibility to the suggestion that basing requires a *sensitivity* to reasons for belief. One such sensitivity requirement defines sensitivity as *counterfactual dependency*. In the case of intra-individual basing, the counterfactual dependency sensitivity requirement is this:

> My belief *p* is based on reason *r* only if it is sensitive in the sense that I would not believe *p* if I did not possess reason *r*.

One might generalize this sensitivity requirement to cover not only intra-individual basing but also transindividual basing:

> My belief *p* is based on reason *r* only if I would not believe *p* if reason *r* did not obtain (or exist).

One might worry that this generalized counterfactual dependency sensitivity requirement poses a problem for the Transindividual Thesis. Perhaps it does, but it poses no problem for the Transindividual Thesis that it does not also pose for the Transtemporal Thesis.

To begin, note that, for purposes of defending the Transindividual Thesis, I need claim only that testimonially *justified* beliefs are based on the testifier's reason for believing p, and only that they are so based when the subject possesses no good reason to believe p. I need not claim that unjustified testimonial beliefs can be based on the testifier's reason to believe p, or that testimonially justified beliefs for which the subject possesses good reason to believe p can be based on the testifier's reason. Note next that in the typical case, testimonially justified beliefs are counterfactually sensitive to reasons possessed by the testifier. I am testimonially justified in believing that Napoleon was exiled to St Helena. And I would not believe that Napoleon was exiled to St Helena if my sixth grade teacher had not had her reason to believe the proposition. In the nearest world in which my teacher lacks her reason, she also fails to testify that Napoleon was exiled to St Helena—in which case I fail to believe the proposition. The sensitivity of the testimony to the testifier's reason ensures that I am sensitive to the testifier's reason.

Admittedly, there are also many cases of testimonially justified belief in which the counterfactual sensitivity fails—I would believe p on a certain testimony even if the testifier lacked her reason to believe p, because the testifier would testify that p even if she lacked this reason. She might do so because she has practical motives for testimony that would cause her to testify that p even if she lacked reason r, or she might do so because she would believe p for reasons other than reason r if she lacked that reason. Now, not all of these cases of testimonially justified beliefs are inconsistent with the counterfactual dependency sensitivity requirement. For some of them are cases in which I possess a good reason to believe p, and the Transindividual Thesis is not committed to my testimonial beliefs being based on the testifier's reason in these cases. On the Transindividual Thesis, all cases in which my testimonial belief is justified but the testifier lacks a good reason to believe p would fall into this irrelevant category. Nevertheless, there are bound to be some cases that force the proponent of the Transindividual Thesis to reject a strict version of the generalized counterfactual dependency sensitivity requirement, in favor of some subtly qualified version that will no doubt be difficult to formulate.[22]

But memory is in nearly the same boat. In some instances in which I am justified in believing p on memory, I would still believe p even if I had lacked my original reason. There are many ways this can happen. Imagine that I believe that I sampled octopus at age five on the basis of an original sensory experience. But even if I had lacked my original reason, I would still have believed the proposition because I would have done so on the basis of a different experience of sampling octopus at age five. Or imagine that I would still have believed the proposition if I had lacked my experience because I would have seemed to remember the experience when in fact my belief was really conjecture. These are common enough cases. Some of these cases are bound to run afoul of the counterfactual dependency sensitivity requirement. These instances show that the counterfactual dependency sensitivity requirement will need qualification for memorial beliefs if it is be consistent with the Transtemporal Thesis. It remains to be seen whether the qualification needed to reconcile the sensitivity requirement with the Transtemporal Thesis can motivate whatever qualification is needed to reconcile the requirement with the Transindividual Thesis. But for now the need for a qualification prevents the counterfactual dependency sensitivity requirement from posing a clear threat to the Transindividual Thesis.

Despite this, one might hold that a different, probabilistic sensitivity requirement poses a greater threat to the Transindividual Thesis:

> My belief p is based on reason r only if it is probabilistically sensitive to r, in the sense that the conditional probability that I do not believe p, given that r does not obtain, is sufficiently high.

For one might propose that even in cases of testimonially justified belief where the testifier has a reason r to believe p, and the counterfactual dependency sensitivity requirement is satisfied, the conditional probability that I do not believe p, given that r does not obtain, is fairly low. One might propose that for any testimonial belief for which the testifier has a reason r, the conditional probability that I do not believe p, given that r does not obtain, is the frequency with which I do not believe q given that the testimonial reason s fails to obtain, over all cases of testimonial belief q for which the testifier has reason s. But it happens often enough in cases of testimonial belief that the testifier has motives against speaking the truth and testifies that p even when he lacks a reason to believe p. Testifiers often enough have motives for lying and act on them, testifying to propositions for which they have no reason. In most of these cases, I believe p even though the testifier lacks a reason to believe p. If these cases figure in the frequency with which the conditional probability for any given belief is identified, then this frequency is fairly low. So for any given case of testimonially justified belief p, the conditional probability that I do not believe p given that the testifier's reason fails to obtain is fairly low. Thus, on the probabilistic sensitivity requirement for basing, my testimonially justified belief cannot be based on the testifier's reason. All testimonially justified beliefs fail the probabilistic sensitivity requirement. Thus, testimonially justified beliefs for which I lack a reason fail to be based on the testifier's reason, contrary to the Transindividual Thesis.

There is nothing in the case of memorial belief comparable to nonveritistically motivated testimony. So there is nothing about memorial belief that would comparably reduce the probabilistic sensitivity of memorially justified beliefs to reasons. This suggests that, if conditional probability is defined as the frequency specified above, the degree of sensitivity of my testimonially justified belief is significantly lower than the degree of sensitivity of my memorially justified belief.[23] If the conditional probability for my testimonial belief is enough lower than the conditional probability for my memorial belief, then the Transindividual Thesis will find no protection against the problem posed by the probabilistic sensitivity requirement by comparing the case of testimony with that of memory.

In defense of the Transindividual Thesis, I grant that there may be a difference in the specified frequencies for testimonial beliefs and for memorial beliefs. But I would respond that this fact tells against the Transindividual Thesis only if the conditional probability for a given testimonial belief required for probabilistic sensitivity to reasons is identified with the specified frequency. On this identity, the beliefs on testimony that are nonveritistically motivated reduce the degree of sensitivity for every testimonial belief, including those that are testimonially justified on veritistically motivated testimony. But why should the degree of sensitivity for each testimonial belief be defined as the frequency over all my testimonial beliefs? Why should instances of nonveritistically motivated testimony be relevant to instances in which testimony is veritistically motivated? On a more discriminating account of the degree of sensitivity, my testimonial beliefs in cases of veritistically motivated testimony would exhibit a high degree of sensitivity. I see no reason to prefer the less discriminating account to the more discriminating one, and so I see no ground for thinking that testimonially justified beliefs must fail the probabilistic sensitivity requirement for basing on the testifier's reasons. There is no clear case against the Transindividual Thesis by appeal to the probabilitistic sensitivity requirement.

To make an additional point in defense of the Transindividual Thesis, there is a factor favoring the probabilistic sensitivity of testimonial beliefs that may countervail any reduction in probabilistic sensitivity from instances of nonveritistically motivated testimony, even if conditional probability is defined as the specified frequency. Testifiers generally have strong social incentives to present only truths, and they consequently have a motive for testifying to p only when they possess a reason to believe p. There is no comparable social incentive for remembering only when one has a reason. The social incentives to present truths may compensate for nonveritistic motivations. So even if we identify the conditional probability with the frequency over all testimonial beliefs, the conditional probability for a testimonially justified belief may not be substantially lower than the conditional probability for a memorially justified belief. The upshot is that there is no clear warrant for saying that testimonially justified beliefs fail the probabilistic sensitivity requirement while memorially justified beliefs satisfy the requirement. This point is enough for a conditional defense of the Transindividual Thesis.

(2) *The Role of Reasons in Reasoning.* One might object to the Transindividual Thesis on a second ground. This ground appeals to a principle of basing: when I base my belief p on a reason, my doing so entails a normative constraint on my reasoning. The constraint is that I ought to reason in light of this reason when I engage in further reasoning. According to this constraint, I ought to take the reason into account in an appropriate way where it is relevant. In the case of a reason to believe having a propositional content, reasoning in light of my reason means reasoning from the assumption that its content is true. Since I am not typically

aware of the content of reasons on which, according to the Transindividual Thesis, my belief p is based, I cannot conform to this normative constraint. But if I cannot conform to the constraint, for a given reason r, then, since "ought" implies "can," it is not the case that I ought to reason in light of r. But then, by the principle that basing on r imposes the normative constraint, my belief p is not based on r. The Transindividual Thesis thus runs afoul of this constraint on reasons.

Testimony and memory differ here. In many instances of memorial belief, I can and do recover the original reason on which I based my belief (or a reason with the same content), and I can and do reason in light of the reason. But in testimonial belief, it would defeat the economy that motivates reliance on testimony if I were often to acquire the reason on which my testimonial belief is based. Moreover, I am often unable to acquire the testifier's reason, either because I am unable to interrogate the testifier, or because I am unable to understand the testifier's reason or its bearing on p.[24] Thus, in many instances of memorial belief, I can and do conform to the normative constraint that I ought to reason in light of my original reason, whereas in most cases of testimonial belief, I do not do so, and should not do so (on pain of defeating the motivation for testimonial belief), and in many cases I cannot do so. The principle of basing does not hold for most cases of testimonially justified belief.

The proponent of the Transindividual Thesis may reply to this objection simply by observing that, while in many instances of memorial belief, I can and do recover my original reason, I cannot do so in many other instances. These instances plausibly include instances of memorially justified belief in which I lack current reasons for belief. I cannot reason in light of my original reason to believe that I sampled octopus at age five. So the principle of basing does not hold in many instances of memorial beliefs, including many intuitively justified instances. Thus, the principle is at odds with the Transtemporal Thesis as well as the Transindividual Thesis. Moreover, the economy of reliance on memory is also compromised if we require reasoning in light of original reasons for memory beliefs. The principle of basing must therefore be rejected if we accept the Transtemporal Thesis. Rejecting the principle on this ground is, however, compatible with accepting certain weaker principles of basing. These weaker principles include the following:

> When I base my belief on a reason, then I ought to reason in light of that reason if:
> I am currently in possession of the reason; or
> I ought to be aware of having the reason.

A weaker principle specific to testimonial belief is this:

> When I base my belief on a testifier T's reason, then I ought to reason in light of that reason if I am aware that my belief is based on T's reason, and I am aware of what T's reason is.

If I base my belief that Napoleon was exiled to St Helena on T's testimony, and I am aware that I base my belief on T's reason, as well as aware what T's reason is, then I ought to reason in light of T's reason. The Transindividual and Transtemporal Theses are clearly compatible with these weaker constraints, even though not with the stronger constraint. This is enough for a conditional defense of the Transindividual Thesis.

(3) *Responsible Belief.* The Transindividual Thesis is in fact inconsistent with a responsibilist conception of justified belief. According to *individualistic responsibilism,*

> I am justified in believing p just in case I act in an epistemically responsible manner in believing p.

For present purposes, we may say that my acting in an *epistemically responsible manner* in believing p is a matter of making my best effort to believe what is true in believing p, in the specific sense that in believing p I act in a manner that would reflect my best effort were I concerned solely to believe what is true. (I leave "epistemically" tacit from here on in.)

Individualistic responsibilism is inconsistent with the Transindividual Thesis for the following reason. In some instances of belief on testimony, making my best effort to believe what is true leads me to believe p, even though both the testifier and I lack a good reason to believe p. I rely on T's testimony but despite appearances T has no good reason to believe p. On individualistic responsibilism, I am justified in believing p. But on the Transindividual Thesis, I am not so justified, since both the testifier and I lack a good reason to believe p. Thus, the Transindividual Thesis is inconsistent with individualistic responsibilism. Individualistic responsibilists will regard this as an adequate reason to reject the Transindividual Thesis.

One might think that testimony and memory differ here. For in the case of memorial belief, unlike testimonial belief, I am the subject of the original belief p. This, one might think, means that the Transtemporal Thesis can be reconciled with a *longitudinal* version of individualistic responsibilism. It is true that I can make my best effort to believe p on memory—my best *current* effort—even though I had no good original reason to believe p. And this does show that making my best current effort does not entail that I have a good original reason. So the Transtemporal Thesis is inconsistent with *current individualistic responsibilism*:

> I am justified in believing p on memory just in case I currently make my best effort to believe p on memory.

But, one might think, there is no inconsistency between the Transtemporal Thesis and *longitudinal individualist responsibilism*:

> I am justified in believing p on memory just in case I currently make my best effort to believe p on memory, and I also made my best effort to believe p in the original episode of belief-formation.

For, one might think, if I made such an effort in the original episode, and not just currently, I must have had a good reason to believe *p*. My being justified in believing *p* on memory entails that I had a good reason to believe *p*—enough for justified belief on memory according to the Transtemporal Thesis. So the Transtemporal Thesis is, and the Transindividual Thesis is not, consistent with a suitably formulated individualistic responsibilism.

I think the proponent of the Transindividual Thesis should reply to the objection by maintaining that even longitudinal individualistic responsibilism is really inconsistent with the Transtemporal Thesis. So individualistic responsibilism has no more force against the Transindividual Thesis than against the Transtemporal Thesis. The point against the consistency of longitudinal individualistic responsibilism and the Transtemporal Thesis is the familiar one that making my best effort in originally believing *p* does not entail that I had a good reason to believe *p*. I will not make the case here, since it is well enough established elsewhere (Alston 1989; Schmitt 1993).

To see the parallel point regarding testimony, let us consider an attempt by Owens (2000: chs. 9, 11) to reconcile the Transindividual Thesis with a *social* responsibilism for testimonial belief that parallels longitudinal individualistic responsibilism for memory. On Owens's proposal, as I read him, a subject's acting responsibly in believing *p* on testimony is not, contrary to individualistic responsibilism, sufficient for being justified in believing *p*. But responsibility still accounts for the epistemic value involved in justified belief. More exactly, Owens proposes that, although I fail to be justified in a testimonial belief *p* when the testifier lacks a good reason to believe *p*, and although this may be so even when I act responsibly in believing *p*, my lack of justification for my belief in such cases is attributable to a failure of responsibility—not on my part, but on the part of the testifier. A testimonially justified belief *p* does not require merely that I act responsibly in believing *p*. It requires in addition that the testifier acts responsibly in testifying to *p*. Not only must I act responsibly in believing *p*, but also a rational source to whom I can transfer responsibility for the truth of my belief *p* must act responsibly in testifying to *p*.[25] It can happen that I act responsibly in believing *p*, but my belief is unjustified because the testifier, to whom I transfer responsibility in believing *p*, does not act responsibly in testifying to *p*.[26]

Owens, then, proposes a socialized version of responsibilism for testimony parallel to longitudinal responsibilism for memory. We may call it *social responsibilism*:

> A belief is justified if every rational agent to whom responsibility for the belief applies or can pass acts responsibly with regard to the belief.

Acting responsibly with regard to the belief in the case of the *subject* means acting responsibly in believing *p*, while acting responsibly with regard to the belief in the case of the *testifier* means acting responsibly in testifying. Owens takes social responsibilism to be compatible with the Transindividual Thesis, just as longitudinal individualistic responsibilism is said to be compatible with the Transtemporal Thesis.

The difficulty for Owens's position is that social responsibilism is not in fact consistent with the Transindividual Thesis.[27] Here too we may note that my testifier's belief may be responsible even though she lacks a good reason to believe *p*. It is possible to make a forceful case for the inconsistency between the Transindividual Thesis and social responsibilism by considering features of testimony. Begin by noting that on the Transindividual Thesis, my testimonially justified belief is ultimately justified on the basis of some ultimate testifier's nontestimonially justified beliefs. For example, the justification of my testimonial belief that Napoleon was exiled to St Helena ultimately traces to the perceptually justified beliefs of eyewitnesses. This seems inherent in the idea of the Transindividual Thesis. The Thesis, worked out in full, would allow a testimonially justified belief to be justified on the basis of a chain of testimonially justified beliefs of testifiers, a chain initiated by the testimony of an ultimate member possessing a good reason to believe *p*. The initial good reason must itself be nontestimonial, on pain of a regress of testimonial justification.

Now, even the perceptually justified beliefs of eyewitnesses on which my belief is based are themselves based partly on testimony. An eyewitness knows that these are British troops in part on their say-so. And a witness's belief is based on prior testimony about such matters as what a uniform is, what the color red is, etc. This shows that, on the Transindividual Thesis, each testimonial belief justified on the basis of the testifier's reasons is ultimately based on nontestimonial reasons distributed across an entire earlier population of testifiers. In many cases, a subject's believing only a proposition for which there are good distributed reasons is certainly not under the subject's control (or even sensitive to the testifier's reasons for belief) in the manner that would seem to be required for blaming a subject for believing a proposition for which distributed reasons are lacking. Often enough, subjects cannot avoid picking up testimonial beliefs when good distributed reasons are lacking. In these cases, they cannot be blamed for believing as they do despite there not being distributed good reasons for belief. Let us also note that often enough, testifiers cannot refrain from contributing their share of the distributed basis for testimony, short of standing permanently mute. They have no choice but to add their small contribution to the distributed reasons; they must do so whether or not their contribution contributes to the goodness of the distributed reasons. Thus, they cannot be blamed for testifying to propositions as they do, any more than they can be blamed for the reasons they have. So it often enough happens that I inherit a belief ultimately based on bad distributed nontestimonial reasons, but neither I nor my sources engage in any blameworthy acts. People inherit bad systems of classification and explanation for which no individual, or for that matter community, is blameworthy. Nothing guarantees that people have the resources to produce well-thought-out systems of these sorts. No individual or community can be blamed for belief in the demon theory of disease, though we do not think that there were ever good distributed reasons to believe the theory. So if a subject is a member of a community encumbered with belief in that theory and believes on testimony that her niece caught a fever from possession by demons, there is no one to whom she can transfer blame for her belief's being based on a bad reason. A social responsibilist will have to allow that her belief is justified, contradicting the Transindividual Thesis.

The upshot of these reflections is that we cannot reconcile social responsibilism with the Transindividual Thesis. Owens is mistaken in thinking there is any prospect of reconciliation. But this is not a genuine problem for the Transindividual Thesis. It introduces no asymmetry between testimony and memory. For considerations similar to those regarding testimony apply to memory. I can make my best effort in my original belief-formation and fail to come up with a good reason to believe *p*. So in the case of memorial justification, it does not help to move to longitudinal responsibilism, extending my responsibility to my original belief-forming episode. That will not ensure that I have a good reason. Longitudinal responsibilism is thus inconsistent with the Transtemporal Thesis. Testimony and memory are in the same boat once again.

The foregoing replies seem enough to fend off the threat of an asymmetry between testimonial and memorial justification and to leave intact my conditional claim that the case for the Transindividual Thesis is nearly as strong as that for the Transtemporal Thesis.

My conclusion in this paper is that there is a case for the Transindividual Thesis for testimonial justification nearly as strong as that for the Transtemporal Thesis for memorial justification. So if we accept the memorial Thesis on the basis of the latter case, we should also accept the testimonial Thesis with nearly as much enthusiasm, counterintuitive though it may be.

Two questions remain. One question is why, if there is a case for the Transindividual Thesis nearly as strong as that for the Transtemporal Thesis, we find it intuitive to say that my memorially justified belief is based on my original reason, but we find it counterintuitive to say that my testimonially justified belief is based on my testifier's reason. Perhaps the answer begins by saying that we tend to think of the basing relation as a psychological relation, and thus we find it more natural to ascribe the basing relation within a single subject than to ascribe it across interlocution, which involves a nonpsychological component. But of course this only trades one question for another: why do we think of the basing relation as psychological? Since the current state of our thinking about the basing relation leaves us with only a dim idea of what the basing relation is, we currently have little satisfactory theory to guide us in trying to answer this question.

The more important question is what implications my conclusion has for the basing relation. I must leave it at this: the inclining case for the Transindividual Thesis makes an equally inclining case to characterize the basing relation in such a way that it can hold between my belief and a reason possessed by my testifier. On such a characterization, the basing relation is not a pure psychological relation and in some cases involves transmission of information over a nonmental communicative channel, in particular an interlocutionary channel. This point fits with a characterization of the basing relation that tries to capture its value according to the view that the basing relation has value because it affords an alignment of one's belief *p* with the preponderance of existing reasons for and against *p*. To the extent that testifiers' reasons align with the preponderance of existing reasons, and testifiers testify to propositions that align with the reasons they possess, and recipients believe the propositions to which testifiers testify, testimonial beliefs will align with the preponderance of existing reasons. To this extent, then, the relation between testimonial beliefs and testifiers' reasons will function to do what the basing relation does in virtue of which it has value: afford the alignment of one's belief *p* with the preponderance of existing reasons. These remarks may be enough to vindicate applying the term "basing" to the relation between testimonial beliefs and testifier's reasons, allowing a nonpsychological component in some basing relations. I note, however, that these remarks suggest that the relation between testimonial beliefs and testifier's reasons functions to do what the basing relation does even when the subject possesses reason to believe *p*. So they vindicate applying the term "basing" to this relation even in cases where, on the Transindividual Thesis, testimonial justification does not require basing on the testifier's reason.

REFERENCES

Alston, William (1989), 'The Deontological Conception of Epistemic Justification', in William Alston, *Epistemic Justification* (Ithaca, NY: Cornell University Press), 115–52.

Audi, Robert (1996), 'Memorial Justification', *Philosophical Topics*, 23: 31–45.

＿＿ (1997), 'The Place of Testimony in the Fabric of Knowledge and Justification', *American Philosophical Quarterly*, 34: 405–22.

Burge, Tyler (1993), 'Content Preservation', *Philosophical Review*, 102: 457–88.

＿＿ (1997), 'Interlocution, Perception, and Memory', *Philosophical Studies*, 86: 21–47.

Coady, C. A. J. (1992), *Testimony: A Philosophical Study* (Oxford: Oxford University Press).

Conee, Earl, and Feldman, Richard (2001), 'Internalism Defended', in Hilary Kornblith (ed.), *Epistemology: Internalism and Externalism* (Oxford: Blackwell), 231–60.

Edwards, Jim (2000), 'Burge on Testimony and Memory', *Analysis*, 60: 124–31.

Faulkner, Paul (2000), 'The Social Character of Testimonial Knowledge', *Journal of Philosophy*, 97: 581–601.

Foley, Richard (1994), 'Egoism in Epistemology', in Frederick F. Schmitt (ed.), *Socializing Epistemology: The Social Dimensions of Knowledge* (Lanham, Md.: Rowman and Littlefield), 53–73.

Gibbard, Allan (1990), *Wise Choices, Apt Feelings: A Theory of Normative Judgment* (Cambridge, Mass.: Harvard University Press).

Goldberg, Sanford (2001), 'Testimonially Based Knowledge from False Testimony', *Philosophical Quarterly*, 51: 512–26.

Goldman, Alvin (1999), 'Internalism Exposed', *Journal of Philosophy*, 96: 271–93.

Graham, Peter (1997), 'What is Testimony?', *Philosophical Quarterly*, 47: 227–32.

——— (2000), 'Transferring Knowledge', *Noûs*, 34: 131–52.

Korcz, Keith Allen (1997), 'Recent Work on the Basing Relation', *American Philosophical Quarterly*, 34: 171–91.

Lackey, Jennifer (1999), 'Testimonial Knowledge and Transmission', *Philosophical Quarterly*, 49: 471–90.

——— (forthcoming), 'Memory as a Generative Epistemic Source', *Philosophy and Phenomenological Research*.

Lehrer, Keith (1997), *Self-Trust: A Study of Reason, Knowledge, and Autonomy* (Oxford: Oxford University Press).

Lyons, Jack (1997), 'Testimony, Induction and Folk Psychology', *Australasian Journal of Philosophy*, 75: 163–77.

Owens, David (2000), *Reason Without Freedom: The Problem of Epistemic Normativity* (London: Routledge).

Roth, Abraham (2003), 'Practical Intersubjectivity', in Frederick F. Schmitt (ed.) *Socializing Metaphysics: The Nature of Social Reality* (Lanham, Md.: Rowman and Littlefield), 65–91.

Schmitt, Frederick F. (1987), 'Justification, Sociality, and Autonomy', *Synthese*, 73: 43–85.

——— (1992), *Knowledge and Belief* (London: Routledge).

——— (1993), 'Epistemic Perspectivism', in John Heil (ed.), *Rationality, Morality, and Self-Interest: Essays Honoring Mark Carl Overvold* (Lanham, Md.: Rowman and Littlefield), 3–27; repr. in Hilary Kornblith (ed.), *Epistemology: Internalism and Externalism* (Oxford: Blackwell, 2001), 180–206.

——— (1999), 'Social Epistemology', in John Greco and Ernest Sosa (eds), *The Blackwell Guide to Epistemology* (Oxford: Blackwell), 354–82.

——— (2002), 'Testimonial Justification: The Parity Argument', *Studies in History and Philosophy of Science*, 33: 385–406.

Senor, Thomas (1993), 'Internalistic Foundationalism and the Justification of Memory Belief', *Synthese*, 94: 453–76.

NOTES

1. It follows from this condition that justified true belief is not sufficient for knowledge on testimony, since it does not entail that the testifier knows. A weaker condition requiring that the testifier be in some positive epistemic position with respect to *p* will have the same consequence.

2. I say belonging to another individual in the normal case because it would seem to be possible for my past self to testify to my current self—through a diary, for example. Indeed, I might not even realize that I am testifying to myself.

3. Neither Lackey nor Graham denies that testimonial knowledge is social in requiring that the testifier be in *some* positive epistemic position. Goldberg (2001) has given a Gettier-inspired counterexample purporting to show that I can know on the

basis of *false* testimony. Goldberg's counterexample does not in fact strike down the condition stated in the text, but only the condition: I know that *p* on the basis of *T*'s testimony that *q* only if *T* knows that *q*. Indeed, the counterexample has force against the latter condition only on the assumption that the testifier knows that *p*; so it actually *assumes* the condition stated in the text.

4. I use "testimonial belief," "testimonially justified belief," and "testimonial knowledge" to mean, respectively, belief entirely based on testimony, belief justified entirely on the basis of testimony, and knowledge on the basis entirely of testimony. (Similarly for "memorial belief" and "memorially justified belief.") I use "justified in believing *p*" in whatever sense being justified in believing *p* is required for knowing *p*. Knowing *p* requires being *doxastically* justified in believing *p*, which entails a belief *p* and the belief *p*'s being based on good reasons. Being doxastically justified in believing *p* in turn requires being *propositionally* justified in believing *p*, which entails neither a belief *p* nor a basing relation, but only possessing good reasons for believing *p*. I focus here on doxastic justification, rather than propositional justification, for two reasons. First, if doxastic justification is social in the sense we are considering, propositional justification will be as well. For essentially the same case can be made for the sociality of testimonial propositional justification as for testimonial doxastic justification. Second, doxastic justification is required for knowledge, and much of my knowledge depends on my testimonial knowledge. Similarly, any of my beliefs that are justified on the basis of testimonially justified beliefs must be justified on the basis of my doxastically and not merely propositionally justified testimonial beliefs. In these respects, doxastic justification is more important than propositional justification.

5. Two remarks on testimony and testimonial justification: (a) I assume that *T* testifies that *p* when *T* presents *p* as true. I do not think that the presentation required for testimony must be linguistic or even symbolic (it could be ostensive). Testifying does not entail that *T* presents *p* to an audience intentionally. Simon could speak to what he thinks is an empty desert, but if a hearer overheard his speech, the hearer could know things on testimony. I could write a diary without intending anyone to read it; but if someone did read it, they might believe propositions expressed in the diary on testimony. Moreover, I can pick up testimony without realizing that I am doing so. I suspect we pick up a fair bit of what we know in just this way. (b) I am focusing on this condition: My belief *p* is justified on the basis of *T*'s testimony. But the epistemology may be the same for my uptake from *T*'s mere belief, without testimony or a presentation as true. For further discussion of what is involved in testimony, see Coady (1992: ch. 2) and Graham (1997).

6. This condition involves a simplification. It seems possible for me to believe *p* on *T*'s testimony even though *T* testifies to some *q* from which I infer *p*, rather than to *p* itself. A fully general principle would have to allow for such a case, but I will not attempt to construct such a principle here. I will make the simplifying assumption that in all cases in which I believe *p* on testimony, I do so on the basis of *T*'s testifying that *p*.

7. I would expect the Transindividual Thesis to be denied by almost everyone. See, for example, Audi (1997). The Thesis is endorsed by Owens (2000: chs. 9, 11). And as Edwards (2000) argues, Burge (1993) ought for consistency to accept the Thesis.

For defense of a parallel thesis about reasons for action, that I can have practical reasons for action that belong to others, see Roth (2003).

8. Lackey (forthcoming) has argued that (M1) needs qualification. In particular, there are cases in which a subject comes to be justified in a belief on memory even though she lacks current and original justification. For, although her belief would otherwise originally be justified, its justification is defeated by a misleading belief she possesses; yet she has since lost this defeating belief. I am not entirely certain that there are such cases because I am not entirely certain that a belief that would otherwise be justified can be defeated merely by the possession of a misleading background belief. However, anyone persuaded by the example will need to qualify (M1) so that it requires only that, in instances in which current justification is lacking, the subject would otherwise have had original justification if she did not possess a misleading defeater. Lackey also presents an example that shows that original belief can be lacking in cases of memorial justification. This shows that the original justification, if it is required, may be merely propositional rather than doxastic justification.

9. The Transtemporal Thesis is not entirely uncontroversial because it is inconsistent with typical versions of accessibility internalism (see Schmitt 1992: ch. 4 for discussion of accessibility internalism). For a case against accessibility internalism, see Goldman (1999). For defense of internalism from Goldman's criticisms, see Conee and Feldman (2001).

10. One might claim that we can rule out all current reasons as the basis for a memorially justified belief quite easily, on the conceptual ground that, by the very notion of memory, no belief justified on the basis of *current* reasons can be a *memorially* justified belief. One might then appeal to this argument in support of (M2): we have memorially justified beliefs, but none can be based on current reasons. I find this conceptual case for (M2) too facile to carry conviction. I note, however, that if it is a good argument for (M2), there is equal plausibility in the analogous ground for (T2). Since this would make the conditional case for (T2), we may therefore ignore the argument here.

11. There are other arguments for the same conclusion. First, any current reductive reason that could support my memorially justified belief must itself be justified on memory, simply because, by the very notion of memory, my belief *p* would not count as justified on memory in virtue of being justified on the basis of a justifying inference from a current reason unless that reason is itself justified on the basis of memory. Second, one might ask just what is required for a reason *r* to be current when the belief *p* is justified on the basis of a justifying inference from *r*. Any inference takes time. Presumably the reason *r* must itself be preserved in memory if it is to count as current. So for purposes of the inferential justification, *r* must be justified partly on the basis of memory. I find these arguments too swift to carry weight, and I will not attempt to assess them but instead rely on the argument I give in the text.

12. It is worth noting that there is a special problem for the statistical reduction of memorial justification that does not apply to the statistical reduction of testimonial justification. For the degree of justification supplied by a statistical syllogism is indifferent to how well memory tracks what the subject has past reasons to believe, once the inductive premise that memorial beliefs of type *X* tend to be true is justified. But the degree of memorial justification does intuitively diminish with a reduction

in such tracking. There is no analogous problem for testimonial justification. In this regard, memorial justification on the basis of current reductive reasons is in worse shape than testimonial justification on the basis of possessed reductive reasons.

13. For criticism of the statistical basis along these lines, see Schmitt (1987, 1999) and Coady (1992). For a defense of the statistical basis, see Lyons (1997).

14. For reduction by appeal to charity, see Coady (1992: ch. 4). For criticism of reduction by appeal to charity, see Lyons (1997). For reduction by the argument from parity, see Gibbard (1990), Foley (1994), and Lehrer (1997). For criticism of that argument, see Schmitt (2002).

15. One might allow that a coherentist justification is a justification in virtue of which I have a reason for my belief, but deny that it is a justification in virtue of which my belief is based on any reasons. My attitude toward this, for present purposes, is that a coherentist account of the justification for my memorially or testimonially justified belief will not be very plausible unless we can treat coherence relations as entailing or otherwise conforming to a basing relation. If this is not so, then a coherentist justification is ruled out of court by (G) on the assumption that the suitable relation must be a basing relation.

16. For a defense of a nonreductive foundationalist account of memorial justification, see Audi (1996). For criticism of foundationalist accounts along lines similar to those scouted here, see Senor (1993).

17. Edwards points out that Burge contradicts himself. Burge's Acceptance Principle clearly entails that I am a priori entitled to my memory belief even if my belief originally lacked entitlement, but Burge explicitly says that my entitlement to my memory belief *presumes* an original entitlement (1997: 44 n. 2). The latter claim is most naturally interpreted as an endorsement of our Transtemporal Thesis for memorial justification. Burge also seems to contradict himself in the parallel way in the case of testimony (1997: 39–40). Edwards suggests, correctly in my opinion, that Burge should endorse what I am calling the Transindividual Thesis for testimonial justification.

18. I note, however, that Burge's view does entail (T2), that my belief can be justified on the basis of testimony even though not justified on the basis of any reason I possess.

19. More exactly, I will criticize one of Burge's two arguments. The argument I leave out is that "if *p* is the content of an intelligible message, it must bear a relation to a subject matter, and thus it is prima facie true" (1993: 476). The argument here, I surmise, assumes a principle of charity about content: an intelligible message gets its content from a relation to a subject matter and so belongs to a set of propositions about that subject matter most of which are true. I can see that one who is entitled to believe this principle of charity can be entitled to believe *p* by arguing that *p* from the principle as a premise. But most people do not believe the principle of charity, are not entitled to believe it, and do not argue from it. So appeal to the principle cannot explain their entitlement to testimonial beliefs. The mere availability of an argument from the principle is not enough to entitle me to believe *p*. Moreover, the degree of frequency of true testimonial belief entailed by charity (namely, a frequency of a mere fifty percent or better) is not sufficient to make the process of testimonial uptake reliable enough for entitled belief, on any plausible reliabilist account of entitled belief.

20. There is another difficulty with Burge's argument for the Conclusion, a serious one. "Prima facie" is always prima facie *to* a subject. Trouble reveals itself when we ask: to which subject is *p* prima facie a presentation of a rational source or source of truth in (a), (b), and (c)? Is the subject *me*, or is it a third party theorist? Arguably, *p* is not prima facie to *me* a presentation of a rational source or source of truth, at least not in a sense that entails that I am prima facie entitled to believe that it is a presentation of a rational source or source of truth. The mere fact that a source is seemingly intelligible to me can hardly make me entitled to believe that the source is rational. Surely it doesn't do so if I lack good reason to believe that there is a connection between intelligibility and rationality. At the very least, we would have to add that I have good reason to believe that there is such a connection. But then Burge's account of entitlement would apply only to subjects with enough sophistication to believe that there is a connection between intelligibility and rationality. His account would lose generality. If, by contrast, *p* is taken to be prima facie, to a third party theorist, a presentation of a rational source or source of truth, then (a), (b), and (c) have no plausibility. For although a third party theorist may have good reason to believe intelligibility and rationality are connected, and can therefore infer from *p*'s being a seemingly intelligible presentation to its being a presentation of a rational source, the availability of this inference to a third party theorist would hardly make *me* entitled to believe *p*. This is a difficulty even for a view that, like Burge's, allows for entitlement when the subject does not grasp the reason. There just isn't any plausibility to the idea that an argument from this kind of principle of charity could entitle me to a belief when I have no notion of charity. It isn't like the case in which I am entitled by the reliability of my perceptual process even though I am unaware of the process or its reliability.

21. Burge suggests supporting the claim that if a presentation *p* is prima facie a presentation of a rational source, then I am prima facie entitled to believe *p* (a consequence of (b) and (c)) by appeal to the function of reason: presentation *p* "is prima facie preserved (or received) from a rational source, or resource for reason; reliance on rational sources—or resources for reason—is, other things equal, necessary to the function of reason" (1993: 469). But then Burge appears to drop the idea of appealing to what is necessary to the function of reason. So I will not discuss it here.

22. Note that there is a similar difficulty for the Transindividual Thesis posed by the plausible weaker requirement of sensitivity to *good* reasons for testimonially justified belief: I am testimonially justified in believing *p* on the basis of reason *r* only if I would not believe *p* if the testifier lacked a good reason to believe *p*. The temporal analogue of this requirement poses an analogous problem for the Transtemporal Thesis.

23. I note that the fact that testimonial uptake occasionally involves misunderstanding does not further detract from the conditional probability for testimonial belief. True, there is no phenomenon of memory comparable to misunderstanding. But misunderstanding is not a case in which the testifier lacks a reason to believe *p*, testifies that *p*, and I believe *p*. So it does not lower the specified frequency. The same goes for misspeaking and mishearing in testimony.

24. This does show that on the Transindividual Thesis, I can base my belief on a reason I don't understand. A proponent of the Transindividual Thesis has to live with this consequence.

25. Acting responsibly in testifying to *p* is presumably the testifier's making her best effort in testifying in the sense of acting in a manner that reflects her best effort were she concerned solely to testify to the truth.

26. Owens speaks of transferring responsibility for the truth of *p*, but perhaps it is better to speak of transferring responsibility for there being good reasons for *p* available to appropriate subjects.

27. Owens in fact observes that social responsibilism as characterized here does not really supply a sufficient condition of testimonial justification compatible with the Transindividual Thesis. I cannot, merely by acting responsibly in believing *p*, and relying on a testifier who acts responsibly in testifying that *p*, ensure that the testimony and its uptake are free of all the defects that could prevent my belief from being justified (on the Transindividual Thesis). For neither the testifier nor I need be blameworthy for her misspeaking, my mishearing, or my misunderstanding the testimony—perhaps a loud noise startled one or the other of us, but having had no reason to expect it to cause any of these defects, we proceed with testimony and uptake. But these mishaps prevent my belief from being justified nonetheless. It is unjustified simply because I believe *p*, but the testimony is that *q*, and the testifier has no reason for *p*, so that my belief is baseless. Owens thus recognizes that acting responsibly is not the whole story of justification, once the Transindividual Thesis is accepted. However, Owens seems to regard this as a relatively minor qualification of social responsibilism. My point in the text is that social responsibilism is more deeply incompatible with the Transindividual Thesis than Owens recognizes.

10

Testimony and Epistemic Autonomy

Elizabeth Fricker

1. DIVISION OF EPISTEMIC LABOUR VERSUS THE IDEAL OF INDIVIDUAL EPISTEMIC AUTONOMY

A reference point in philosophical investigation of knowledge from testimony is the ideal of the 'autonomous knower'. This ideal type relies on no one else for any of her knowledge. Thus she takes no one else's word for anything, but accepts only what she has found out for herself, relying only on her own cognitive faculties and investigative and inferential powers. Descartes explicitly espoused this ideal, and method, in his *Meditations* (Descartes 1641). Locke equally rejected 'other men's opinions floating in one's brain' as not constituting knowledge (Locke 1690). The wholly autonomous knower will not accept any proposition, unless she herself possesses the evidence establishing it. Thus she will not accept anything on the basis of another's word for it, even when she has evidence of their trustworthiness on the topic in question.

Such extreme purism restricts how much one can come to know very severely. We humans are essentially social creatures, and it is not clear that we do or could possess any knowledge at all which is not in some way, perhaps obliquely, dependent on testimony. How exactly does the system of empirical belief— hopefully knowledge—of each of us depend on others' testimony? There is certainly massive causal reliance on testimony in the process by which each of us develops into a language-user and thinker, 'grows into possession of a world'.[1] The initial stages of language acquisition by a child inevitably occur through a

Earlier versions of this paper were given at a workshop on 'Testimony, Trust and Action' in King's College Cambridge in September 2003, at a conference on 'Moral Testimony' in the Philosophy Department at Birmingham University in March 2004, and at a conference at the Inter-University Centre in Dbrovnik, Croatia, in May 2005. I received very useful comments from audiences at these events, in light of which I corrected various errors. I am also very grateful to both John Hawthorne and Stephen Schiffer for valuable comments and discussion on an earlier draft. The research for this paper was done between January and June 2002, during a period of leave funded by my employers, Magdalen College and Oxford University, and by a Fellowship from the Mind Association. My thanks for their support.

process of simple trust[2] in its teachers—parents and other carers. In this cognitive developmental process learning meanings is not separable from coming to grasp and accept our shared basic world picture, the common-sense theory which structures and frames our empirical thought. There is, for instance, no distinction to be drawn between learning the meanings of 'chair', and 'horse', and 'jump', and 'cook', and learning about chairs, and horses, and jumping, and cooking.[3]

The fact that each of us is causally reliant on others' testimony in the historical process by which she acquires her system of concepts and beliefs does not entail that, once adult, each of us remains epistemically dependent on testimony for her empirical knowledge. Perhaps each of us can afterwards push away the ladder of trust in others, up which she has climbed into possession of a world. Beliefs which were first acquired through a process involving simple trust in testimony, and were initially epistemically based on testimony (as we may say once core normative epistemic concepts become applicable to the developing child, viz. when she becomes a thinker capable of epistemic self-criticism), may later acquire an alternative basis. It may be that beliefs from the epistemic source of perception, linked by memory and extended by inference, can take over, together with support from inference to the best explanation and broader coherence. Suppose one could, once epistemically matured, thus push away the ladder of testimony, retaining only the portion of one's beliefs which remain epistemically supported without reliance on it. In maintaining the ideal, one would then be restricted to what one learns from one's own senses and preserves in memory, plus whatever one can get to by use of one's own inferential powers from that base—with a ban on even reasoned, empirically backed trust in the word of others!

There is reason to doubt that one can in that way eliminate all epistemic dependence on testimony in one's mature system of empirical belief, even if prepared drastically to prune it. For one to do so, her original epistemic dependence on testimony would have, everywhere, to be replaced by adequate support from other epistemic sources, or the belief in question dropped. Now of course it often happens in particular cases that one first learns of something through another's testimony, and then is later able to confirm it for oneself through perception, perhaps combined with memory and inference. My daughter tells me her new teacher wears glasses; later I see the teacher for myself. The weather forecaster on Tuesday predicts that it will rain on Wednesday; Wednesday proves wet. Facts about a foreign country known to one at first only through travel literature and friends' reports are confirmed by perception, when one travels there oneself. In these and countless similar cases one later gets first-hand perceptual evidence of what one first believed on testimony. In such cases contrary perceptual evidence would decisively falsify the testimony.

There are other ways, less direct but no less powerful, in which alternative grounds for belief can grow strong enough to take over the support of a belief originally acquired from and based on testimony. Inference to the best explanation and explanatory coherence more broadly can take over the support of many beliefs originally based solely on others' testimony. It is plausible, for instance, that one's implicit beliefs about what the words of one's language mean no longer rest on the past trusted testimony through which they were learned. One's linguistic interactions with others would not run as smoothly as they do, if one's first teachers had deceived one! (See Adler 1994; Lyons 1997.)

Nonetheless the role of past trusted testimony in the system of empirical belief of each of us is fundamental, because it has shaped the conceptual frame within which current individual perceptions are made—how the sensory given is conceptualized to yield perceptual experience and belief.[4] Thus, in our three examples above, while it is true that subsequent contrary perception would refute the earlier testimony, these perceptions are themselves subtly dependent on a framework of concepts shaped in part by earlier trust in testimony. I see the teacher's reading glasses, but that she is my daughter's teacher I know only through a set of background beliefs in which testimony is inextricably involved. When it rains on Wednesday I see and hear the rain; but my knowledge that it is Wednesday is testimony-infected, and that very concept and its application is one constituted by human consensus involving testimony. Similarly, when I visit Australia for the first time, in one way I gain personal confirmation of what I had previously known of only through testimony; but my knowledge that I am in Australia at all depends on testimony in multifarious and hard to pin down ways: initially I knew where my flight landed only through trusting the testimony of travel agent and airline personnel, and though the evidence of roadsigns and so forth may take over, these are all put there by human agency, and constitute a kind of testimony. Moreover, the controlling idea in terms of which I conceptualize and slot in all my own personal experiences—of the spherical planet earth with its land masses and seas, its countries, nations, and other geopolitical institutions, its history and prehistory—was acquired from testimony.

This brief sketch has shown how the epistemic dependence on testimony in the beliefs of each of us socially embedded twenty-first-century individuals is subtle and widespread, if not all-pervading. A more sustained enquiry is needed to see whether it could in principle be eliminated by such an individual while leaving her any beliefs at all. Worse yet for the would-be epistemic autonome: it may not be sharply determinable at all, whether and when freedom from oblique epistemic dependence on testimony is achieved, since isolating the contribution of testimony from that of other sources of support, in a system of belief with rich explanatory coherence, is not a clear-cut matter. It is at any rate certain that, in order to live up to the ideal of individual epistemic autonomy, a very great deal of what is believed by a normal member of a modern society, with its extended division of epistemic labour, would have to be bracketed, given up—most of geography, history, the natural and social sciences including medicine, and so forth.

Giving all that up is no more a serious practical possibility than living out the life of a more thoroughgoing sceptic—one who doubts even the evidence of the senses as indicators of a perceptible external world. Who would really give up the fruits of the sciences including all technology, medicine, dentistry, foreign travel, as well as historical understanding and knowledge—and so on? The epistemically autonomous individual could not trust an electrician to wire her (self-built!) house for her, since she would not accept his testimony about what he was going to do, and that it would work safely; nor her doctor to prescribe medicines; nor would she try ski-ing because her friends (she could not have many!) told her it was fun.

We have found that testimony, for each of us in our modern social and epistemic predicament in which division of epistemic labour along with other sorts is the rule, is an essential source of empirical grounding for her beliefs about the world she finds herself in, and her own place in it. This system of empirically based belief is richly coherent, including its ability to explain its own sources.

Notice that the trust in testimony of which I am stressing the ubiquity need not however be given uncritically, without empirical grounds. I have argued elsewhere that a mature recipient of testimony need and should not trust another's word without adequate empirically based warrant to do so. We have seen that it is impractical to live up to the supposed ideal of individual epistemic autonomy. One cannot live in a modern scientifically and technologically sophisticated society, nor have any social life at all, without trusting others in almost one's every action. But this is not to say that one's trust in the vast heritage of knowledge and know-how built up from others' investigations, expertise, and experience must be blind—uncritical and undiscriminating. Good empirical grounds for taking a fresh instance of testimony to be sincere and reliable—or for being distrustful of it—are often to be had; and inference to the best explanation and rich coherence within one's accumulated system of belief can support, *ex post*, one's reliance on some earlier pieces of testimony, while equally discrediting others. (I here barely touch on issues which need much fuller discussion. See Adler 1994; Coady 1992; Fricker 1994, 2002, 2005.)

Still, one who trusts testimony discriminatingly, only when she has an adequate empirical basis to do so, and whose past trust is now vindicated through support from explanatory coherence, is yet dependent on testimony in her beliefs, and actions based on them. If I take others' word for things, I extend my knowledge far beyond the range I could achieve on my own, but by this very fact I am not epistemically autonomous. I believe many things for which I personally do not possess the evidence, and my believing is premised on the supposition that some other person or set of persons jointly has, or had, access to that evidence, and evaluated it correctly. (These points are expanded in Section 4, below.)

We have seen that even if one could, by a heroic effort of epistemic reconstruction, push the ladder of past trusted testimony away, the project of attaining and maintaining the ideal of complete individual epistemic autonomy is not an attractive or feasible one—one would forgo too much! Is there reason to regret this? In this paper I shall respond to this question by addressing a closely related one: In what way exactly is one's epistemic self-governance necessarily compromised, by one's practically inevitable dependence on others' testimony? Putting the question the other way about: In what way, and to what extent, can one maintain one's epistemic self-governance despite one's inevitable reliance on others' testimony, and the technological fruits of others' knowledge and expertise, in almost every area of one's life?[5] I will first prepare the ground to address this question by considering another: In what circumstances, and on what topics, may one properly accept and learn from another's testimony? In developing an answer to this question we will find material relevant to answering our first one.

2. THE CIRCUMSTANCES AND TOPICS OF PROPER ACCEPTANCE OF TESTIMONY

In what circumstances and on what topics may one person with epistemic propriety accept the testimony of another and by so doing learn, acquire knowledge, from her? Conversely: What are the circumstances in which, and topics on which, one person may tell something to an audience, thereby expressing her knowledge, and reasonably intend and expect to be believed, trusted—to have her word on the matter accepted? These are distinct questions, but the mutuality of the illocutionary act of telling means that their answers will coincide, where the expectation of being trusted is well founded.[6]

2.i A Precondition for Testimonial Spreading of Knowledge

As a preliminary I note a precondition for testimony to be given and received at all. For an act of telling to succeed there must be mutual understanding. A message must be got across and accepted. So there must be a proposition which the teller intends by her action to present as true, and this must be identical with the one grasped by her audience as so presented, and accepted by her.[7] This does not, in itself, entail a shared language. Nor does it entail that, when a shared language is employed, the message conveyed is what the speech act literally means—a proposition which the sentence used is conventionally apt to convey, and is plausibly interpreted as specifying on that occasion.[8] But communication of a message is most commonly effected by use of sentences of a shared language in accordance with the constraints of their literal meaning, to make explicit assertions. The occasions on which other media are feasible vehicles are relatively few and far between. This being so, the spreading of knowledge by means of testimony, or something like it, is possible to any significant extent only when there is a shared language, and mutual understanding of speech acts between speaker and audience.

Our common-sense view—which I shall not question here—is that we do indeed share a language, including its semantics, with our co-speakers to an extent sufficient for mutual understanding and successful communication. But one can learn from another's testimony only when one does not already know what she tells one. Hence, if difference of opinion regarding the truth value of some sentence S entailed difference of meaning attached to S, there would be no learning from others regarding the proposition expressed by S.[9] This observation is, I think, enough to discredit extreme 'holistic' theories about the fixation of meaning (already implausible). But there are certain areas of discourse where disagreement might be thought to undermine the supposition that meaning is shared. If this suspicion were confirmed, then learning from testimony in the strict sense (as opposed to changing one's language to conform more with others) would be shown to be impossible in these areas.

Difference of opinion due to ignorance, where one party simply lacks firm belief either way on the topic, is unproblematic. Equally, disagreement in the strong sense of conflict of opinion is unproblematic, when its origin is traceable to different access to evidence. (In such a case pooling of evidence will produce convergence of opinions.) It is when disagreement in judgement persists despite similar access to evidence that, in certain areas, the supposition of shared meaning may be threatened. If there are certain subject matters where disagreement of judgement in response to the same evidence entails difference of meaning, then there can be no learning from testimony in the strong sense of deferring to others' judgement, letting it override one's own, on those topics.

It is a point familiar from a certain style of philosophical account of how meanings and beliefs are simultaneously attributed to someone, that a tentative interpretation of an utterance which yields a difference of opinion between interpretee and interpreter not explained by differential access to evidence, is thereby thrown into doubt. Other aspects of the total interpretation being equal, it is more 'charitable' hence a priori better warranted, to interpret the other as meaning something else (see Davidson 1984). But other aspects may well not be equal, and so the defeat of the assumption of shared meaning is generally not instantaneous. We all have had futile arguments—"It's green"; "No it's not, it's yellow"—where the suspicion lurks that there is not really a substantial matter at issue, rather than a non-concordance of linguistic usage at its vague edges, compounded perhaps by a pig-headed refusal of the out-of-line debater to adjust her usage. Equally we all have had arguments where it seems certain that there is a substantial, not merely a semantic matter at stake—"It's unfair that you let Julian go in the front of the car, but you never let me", although progress towards agreement may seem no less hard to achieve.

Colour concepts, and other simple perceptually applied concepts; plus moral and also aesthetic concepts, are ones where sorting out substantive from merely linguistic disagreement on particular occasions is difficult; no less difficult than giving an account of how the precise content of those concepts is fixed. In these and some other cases, there really may be no way to distinguish between deferring to others' judgement about the application of an already shared concept, and adjusting one's concept. (We remarked earlier that, in one's initial acquisition of one's language, there is no sharp line between acquiring new information, beliefs, about things one already has a concept of; and acquiring those concepts.)

These considerations will be relevant in a full investigation of the possibilities for learning from testimony about these topics. It will be important to bear them in mind, when considering to what extent one can defer to others' judgement on moral and aesthetic matters. There may prove to be limitations on this grounded in considerations about meaning, for aesthetic judgement in particular, I suspect.[10] Having noted this, I will not explore it more fully here.

2.ii A Principle Concerning Deferential Acceptance

With these points about the need for shared meaning made, we can proceed with the main positive idea. We can formulate a general principle:

Testimony Deferential Acceptance Principle (TDAP 1): For one properly to accept that P on the basis of trust in another's testimony that P—her word that P[11]—requires that she be epistemically well enough placed with respect to P so that were she to have, or make a judgement to form a conscious belief regarding whether P, her belief would almost certainly be knowledge;[12] and that she be better epistemically placed with respect to P than oneself; and that one recognize these things to be so.

TDAP1 specifies a condition necessary for epistemically proper trusting acceptance of another's testimony on some topic. It is not sufficient, because while the hearer's cognizance of the testifier's strong epistemic position vis-à-vis the topic makes it rational for her, other things being equal, confidently to expect the testifier's judgement about the matter in question to be correct—to deem her competent about the matter in question—TDAP1 does not speak to the question of the testifier's sincerity. As I have argued elsewhere, the overall trustworthiness of a speaker's testimony breaks down into these two quite separate components. In this investigation I concentrate on the circumstances in which deferential acceptance of another's judgement, as expressed in her sincere testimony, is epistemically proper. Thus, having noted the need for adequate warrant to believe the speaker sincere, I put further consideration of sincerity aside, assuming in what follows that insincerity is not an issue in whether to trust the other's testimony.[13]

The matter of sincerity is one reason why TDAP1 specifies only a necessary, not a sufficient condition, for epistemically proper deference to another's testimony. The only other reason I can think of why other things would not be equal, regarding the hearer's expectation of correctness of the testifier's expressed judgement, is if she were also aware of significant contrary testimony. Contrary testimony will be epistemically significant if it either comes from another equally well-qualified expert; or, in some cases, if it is from many mutually independent sources, albeit not especially expert ones.[14] A more refined condition incorporating these two factors, which is normatively both necessary and sufficient for deferential acceptance is:

> **TDAP 2:** One properly accepts that P on the basis of trust in another's testimony that P—her word that P—just if she speaks sincerely, and she is epistemically well enough placed with respect to P so that were she to have, or make a judgement to form, a conscious belief regarding whether P, her belief would almost certainly be knowledge; and she is better epistemically placed with respect to P than oneself; and one recognizes all these things to be so; and one is not aware of significant contrary testimony regarding P.

TDAP 2 specifies when it is proper to accept another's testimony that P outright. There will also be situations where neither party is in a position to make a knowledgeable judgement as to whether P, but one is better epistemically placed than the other. In these cases it will be epistemically rational for the worse-placed person to defer to the other's opinion, while falling short of taking her utterance as an expression of knowledge; hence forming only a tentative belief regarding P. This is required when, for instance, an informed decision about how to act is urgently needed. There may be some topics for which this situation is the rule—that is, where knowledge as opposed to more or less well-grounded speculation is very hard to come by.[15] It remains true that one should not accept outright another's testimony that P, unless one reasonably believes her to be so placed as to (almost certainly) form knowledgeable belief regarding P. Hence TDAP2 is the correct general principle governing the outright acceptance of another's testimony.

An explanatory comment is needed on the role of the complementary 'internal' and 'external' components of epistemic propriety in TDAP1 and 2. I have formulated TDAP1 and 2 incorporating both internal and external components, because I am concerned to describe what happens when things go right, and thus how knowledge is spread by means of testimony. Externally, things are going right when the testifier speaks from her expertise-generated knowledge, and is sincere. But epistemic rationality has a key internal component: it is not rational to accept unquestioningly the testimony of an expert who, so far as one knows, is no such thing. And, though not all-in epistemically proper, it is subjectively rational and epistemically blame-free to accept another's testimony, when one falsely but justifiedly believes her to be an expert about the topic, being deceived about this through no fault of one's own. I am against purely exernalist accounts of when acceptance of testimony is epistemically proper. These fail to incorporate the requirement that the subject maintain epistemic responsibility for her own beliefs. In Section 3 I spell out the implications, and means of satisfying, this requirement.[16]

We may distinguish between a weak and a strong form of deference to another's testimony:

Weak Deferential Acceptance occurs when I form belief that P on the basis of trust in another's testimony that P, when I myself have no firm pre-existing belief regarding P; nor would I form any firm belief regarding P, were I to consider the question whether P using only my current epistemic resources, apart from the current testimony to P.

Strong Deferential Acceptance occurs when I let another's trusted testimony regarding P override my own previous firm belief, or disposition to form a firm belief, regarding P.

The distinction between strong and weak deferential acceptance may or may not turn out to be important. First off, it seems that there could be subject matters where strong deferential acceptance is never epistemically appropriate, although weak deference can be. This fact may illuminate the nature of that subject matter.

Whether for weak or strong deferential acceptance, it seems that TDAP2 is the correct normative principle: her sincerity not being in question, and my being aware of no significant contrary testimony, it is epistemically proper that I defer to another's testimony in forming belief regarding P, or in overriding my own previous belief regarding P, just if I recognize that she is better epistemically placed than I am to determine whether P; and it is epistemically proper that I accept her testimony outright just if I recognize this, and also that she is so placed as to form (almost certainly) knowledgeable belief regarding P. We may introduce a thin and inclusive sense of 'expert' capturing this core normative necessary condition for deferential acceptance expressed in TDAP1 (which is also normatively sufficient, apart from the matters of sincerity and absence of significant contrary testimony):

S is an expert about P relative to H at t just if at t, S is epistemically well enough placed with respect to P so that were she to have, or make a judgement to form a conscious belief regarding whether P, her belief would almost certainly be knowledge; and she is better epistemically placed than H to determine whether P.

2.iii Bases of Expertise

We can now explore the different possible bases of such relative epistemic expertness of S over H regarding some collection of propositions P comprising a subject matter W. In so doing we will be developing a description of the various circumstances in which it is epistemically proper, when she knows them to obtain, for one person deferentially to accept another's testimony regarding some subject matter. The idea of someone's being epistemically 'well placed' regarding P is used so far in a broad catch-all sense. We will now see how a variety of specific circumstances may contribute to this. One is literally the spatio-temporal location of the person; another is particular skills and perceptual and cognitive equipment she possesses.

There are various kinds of situation in which it is obvious and unproblematic that S will at that time be epistemically expert relative to H regarding some subject matter W.

Case One: W is an observable event or state of affairs, and S is or was at the time of its occurrence so positioned as to be able to observe it, whereas H was not.

Suppose, for instance, that Natalie went to the RadioHead concert in South Park, while I did not. Then—assuming she has normal observational and memory capacities—she knows quite a bit of what happened during it, and I can learn from her telling me about it. Without access to some such eyewitness account (written or spoken), I cannot know very much about what happened. Of course Natalie is not my only possible informant. And there may be a limited amount I can infer from other sources of evidence—walking there the next day I observe huge numbers of empty drinks cans scattered around, and see the stage being dismantled. But I cannot learn any detail except from testimony; and only hers is conveniently available.[17]

Natalie is an expert on what happened at the concert, relative to me. Hence—if she is truthful—I can learn from her. But her expert status on the topic relative to me is highly accidental. It is based in a mere happenstance about our locations on one particular day, not on any more stable and intrinsic epistemic talent, skill, or base of knowledge that she possesses whereas I lack. Had I possessed a ticket and gone to the concert, while Natalie stayed at home, I would instead have been the expert vis-à-vis her. Such merely accidental and extrinsic expert status is often brief and transient. Emily is momentarily an expert relative to me about what is in the fridge; but only until I take a look for myself.

Case Two: Superior perceptual skill of S over H.

Now suppose Natalie and I are both at the concert, and are trying to make out what is happening on the stage from some distance. I am shortsighted, whereas Natalie has excellent distance vision. She reports 'the supporting band is coming on' and I accept her report, not being able to see anything specific for myself. Or I may think I can see something different, but I allow my visually based judgement to be overruled by hers, in the knowledge that she has better distance vision than me.[18] This case is more interesting. Natalie is an expert relative to me about what is happening in the distance not because of an accidental difference in our locations, but due to a superior epistemic skill she has relative to me, which is (in a relaxed sense) intrinsic, and fairly stable. She is not just accidentally better placed, that is spatio-temporally located, than me, regarding the topic; she is better epistemically equipped than me to make judgements of a certain kind—namely, judgements about events occurring in the visual perceptual distance. Let us say that she is not only currently an expert relative to me about the happenings on the stage, in the thin sense defined above; but that this is due to an epistemic *expertise* she possesses relative to me, regarding a range of matters-in-circumstances. Specifically:

> *S has an expertise relative to H on some subject matter W at a time t* just if S has a superior ability at t to determine the truth of propositions in W which is based in superior perceptual and/or cognitive skills and knowledge, and is hence (in a relaxed sense) intrinsic, or has a crucial intrinsic component.

Exercise of an expertise will almost certainly require that the environment be normal in various respects—as with perceptual skills—and so is intrinsic only in a sense which is relaxed, though surely intuitive. Exercise of specialized cognitive skills may require access to equipment, even laboratories; but has a crucial intrinsic component. An expertise is, in this lenient sense, a superior epistemic power possessed by a person due to her specific differentiating characteristics, such as superior perceptual skills, or specialized field of training and knowledge. Her expertises are relatively stable properties of a person, since they are not owed to mere accidents of spatio-temporal location, but are more deep-seated properties of that person; some owed to genetic endowment, but many acquired through special training or education.[19]

S's possessing a superior perceptual ability to H is one kind of expertise which S may have relative to H. This may be due to native differences in perceptual equipment, as with acute versus poor distance vision. But differential perceptual ability may also be due to training and background knowledge. An expert at cricket can see and describe what is taking place during the game—"It was a fast ball that moved in from outside the off stump, and the batsman caught an edge on it, and was caught behind by the wicket-keeper"—when a novice will have discerned almost nothing specific at all. The same goes for aural perceptual abilities, for instance to discern and describe the harmonic progressions in a complex piece of music; or to catch and understand the words of speech in a particular language. Because background knowledge and skills inform and shape perception in this way, there is no sharp distinction between perceptual versus knowledge-based expertise. Many bases of expertise involve both in inextricable combination. The complex perceptual-cum-knowledge-based skill provides a superior ability to determine the truth of a range of propositions in certain circumstances. Other bases of expertise are more heavily grounded in specialized knowledge and training, with a lesser role for associated perceptual skills. This includes scientific knowledge and skills in experimental procedures and the evaluation of data; and technological knowledge and know-how, such as that of the garage mechanic, builder, or computer technician. Most purely cognitive is superior ability at reasoning in a particular abstract domain such as mathematics.

When another has expertise relative to me in a certain, perhaps esoteric, field of knowledge, it is clear that I can and should—assuming I trust in her sincerity—defer to her in forming beliefs about the domain in question. Where the field is sufficiently advanced and complex, I may not even be able to evaluate the arguments, nor the significance of the evidence, myself; and I may lack the native talents to acquire the skills to do so, even if I had both time and inclination (see Hardwig 1991). We will draw out the significance of these facts in the next section.

We can make some observations about the relations between weak and strong deference, and expertise. Deference to another is appropriate (assuming that she has, like me, a normal endowment of perceptual and cognitive skills) when she but not I has had access to the relevant evidence—for instance, when she but not I has had opportunity to exercise normal perceptual judgemental abilities, as in Case One. Since I have no basis for firm belief in such cases, this will be weak deference. I learn from the other about something of which I would otherwise be ignorant. Her report informs me, rather than overriding my own prior firm belief. Thus we can conclude that: **Weak deference is often appropriate, even when the other has no superior expertise to me regarding the topic, she is merely contingently more expert than me, at this moment.**

In contrast, when I and the other both have access to relevant evidence,[20] deference to her will be appropriate only if I accept that she has a relevant epistemic power, an expertise, which is superior to mine. Since *ex hypothesi* we each have access to relevant evidence, I also have a basis for firm belief myself; so this will generally be strong deference. In this type of situation a stronger kind of deferring to another's epistemic power, her superior authority, is involved. I accept the other's judgement as overruling my own, in light of my acknowledgement of her superior epistemic power regarding the matter in question. Our Case Two above instances such strong deference. Natalie has an expertise relative to me on events going on in the perceptible distance. Thus she is better epistemically equipped than me to make judgements about what is taking place on the stage in the park, even though we are standing next to each other, and each able to look towards the stage. If my vision is as good as Natalie's, then I will rationally defer to her testimony regarding what went on at the concert only if I was not there myself. But if I know her sight is better than mine, I may and should rationally allow her reports of her perceptual judgements to overrule my own perceptually based judgements, when we are similarly spatially located.

We may thus conjecture that: **Strong Deference is appropriate only when the other has a superior expertise—an intrinsic epistemic power—to me.**[21] This is largely true, although there are two counter-cases. First, it can be that I have a basis adequate for firm belief, but S, while having no relevant greater epistemic powers than me, has a stronger one which trumps it. For instance, I believe that Tom is away on holiday on the basis of my memory of his testimony of three weeks ago; but Chloe testifies to having seen Tom in town today. It is not determined whether I should accept Chloe's testimony in these circumstance, without further details. But there surely will be some cases of this kind, where it is right to accept another's testimony overriding one's own previous firm belief, because she has had access to fresh evidence, though her relevant epistemic powers are no greater than mine. One factor which would do the trick is if Chloe's testimony was independently corroborated by many others. This is our second type of counter-case: I should bow to others' testimony about some matter, even if their skills and evidential position severally are not superior to mine, if weight of numbers is massively on their side. Notwithstanding these counter-cases, our conjecture captures a general tendency.

3. DEFERENCE ON MORAL AND AESTHETIC MATTERS?

We started with the idea that it is rational to defer to another's apparently sincere testimony on some topic P just if I recognise that she is better placed than me to judge whether P (and I am aware of no significant contrary testimony regarding P). This being so, learning from testimony is possible only in domains where it makes sense to think that one person can be better placed than another to make judgements. This in turn requires some notion of objective standards of evidence and correct judgement for the domain in question. If any basis whatever on which a judgement is made is as good as any other, then the idea of another's being better placed than me does not apply. In fact this restriction imposes little more than the very idea of judgement imposes in the first place. There is a determinate content to judge only if there are standards for correct judgement, independent of what seems to any particular individual to be correct. However, it could perhaps be that this minimal notion of objectivity applies in some domain, but for some reason someone else can never be better placed than me to make judgements about it, or at least it could never be rational for me to believe this. Some accounts of self-ascriptions of certain conscious mental states would place them in this category. Exploring the possibility or otherwise of rational deference to testimony may give fresh insights onto this topic, as well as others, though I cannot pursue this thought further here.[22]

We are investigating the circumstances in which, and topics on which, it can be rationally permissible, indeed mandatory, deferentially to accept another's testimony. Whether and if so in what circumstances deference to others' testimony on moral and aesthetic matters is ever rational—epistemically and morally proper—is a large topic, an adequate discussion of which would require a separate paper. But I shall make a key preliminary point. The kind of objectivity in standards of judgement which we have just seen to be required—the idea that there are better and worse ways of arriving at judgements in the domain—is relatively unproblematic, and no more than common sense, for both moral and aesthetic judgements. Thus it is only a very moderate thesis to hold that there is such a thing as superior expertise on moral and aesthetic matters. This view can be held without commitment to any metaphysically outlandish and epistemically problematic form of moral or aesthetic realism. The notion of objectivity which must be invoked need not be understood in terms of correspondence with wholly mind-independent facts, and more or less accurate means of homing in on those. (There may or may not be any domains in which we wish so to understand it!) The required notion of objectivity of judgements in the moral and aesthetic domains can be explained in terms of better and worse ways of arriving at judgements of the class in question, with better and worse defined otherwise than in terms of homing in on mind-independent truth.[23] This being so, there is nothing immediately incoherent, or metaphysically neck-out-sticking, about the idea of moral and aesthetic experts. The idea accords with common sense, and normal practices of deference. Aesthetic experts are those who are specially trained, experienced, and knowledgeable in a certain area—say Baroque music, or Renaissance painting. One would defer to them about the qualities, including aesthetic ones, of items in their field of expertise. The idea of moral experts is equally valid. Some people are especially trained, experienced, and knowledgeable in the kinds of considerations involved in making moral judgements. Such expertise may be primarily in a specific field, involving a particular kind of empirical matter.[24] A quasi-realist about the moral, or aesthetic, can make perfect sense of expertise in these domains. I may defer to an expert in an aesthetic field because I know my own opinion-forming processes are crude and uninformed, untrained, in the relevant aesthetic—which amongst Caravaggio's paintings are the greatest masterpieces; or what is a specially good example of an early nineteenth-century English transfer-printed cup and saucer. (Learning through deference, I may come in time to be a bit of an expert myself!)

I might defer for similar reasons in a moral matter. Or I might defer, or seek advice here, not because of a general lack of expertise, but because my consultant is better placed than me—a relative expert—regarding the current matter. She may know more of the relevant background facts about a difficult case regarding custody of children in divorce proceedings, or she may unlike me be impartial, not being involved in the situation as I am. Or I may just want a second opinion, or to talk the matter over with someone else, as part of the process of forming my own judgement. Would it be just, or cruel, to carry out my threat and deprive my son of his *Beano*,[25] for getting into trouble at school for fooling about in class again? This is the kind of situation where one may want to confer, and maybe defer to another's judgement.

A full investigation of the possibilities for, and constraints on, rational deference on moral and aesthetic matters must canvas more considerations than those raised here. I suggested earlier that there may be constraints deriving from the meaning of aesthetic predicates—their tie to a specific non-judgemental cognitive-cum-affective response in the subject—on the extent to which deference on aesthetic matters is possible. (One possibility is that only weak, never strong deference, is rationally possible.) For deference on moral judgements, there are important ties with the idea of individual autonomy and responsibility which may place limits. In the present paper I merely wish to point out that the idea of expertise on these topics is an everyday and apparently sensible one, and thus that deferential acceptance of testimony on these matters is prima facie rationally possible, as well as being a common occurrence (see Jones 1999).

We have briefly reviewed the various bases on which another person may sometimes be far better placed than oneself to make judgements about a certain subject matter. We saw that such superior epistemic status is sometimes based in accidents of location, and may be short-lived; but is sometimes based in intrinsic and relatively stable differences in epistemic powers between two individuals. When I appreciate that another person is thus expert relative to me, it is not merely rationally permissible, but rationally mandatory, to defer to her judgement over my own conclusions, regarding the subject matter in question. This being so, one may question whether the supposed ideal figure of the autonomous knower, who refuses ever to trustingly accept another's testimony, a fortiori will never allow her own judgement to be corrected by another's, is really such an ideal after all. I will return to this question in my final section. First I address my earlier question: To what extent can one maintain one's epistemic self-governance despite one's inevitable reliance on others' testimony, and the technological fruits of others' knowledge and expertise, in almost every area of one's life?

4. RELIANCE ON OTHERS' WORD AND EPISTEMIC SELF-GOVERNANCE

We have seen, as encapsulated in TDAP2, how it is rational to accept another's word on a topic, and even to allow her expressed judgement to override one's own prior opinion, when one knows that she is strongly placed epistemically, and better placed than oneself, regarding the matter in question. For each of us, her appreciation of her own circumscribed and feeble epistemic powers and small position in the larger scheme of things, together with her grasp of folk psychology, including where applicable appreciation of others' superior expertise and epistemically more advantageous position, entails that deference to others' opinions is rational, in these circumstances. Lack of such appreciation of one's limited powers and others' superior ones, and an accompanying refusal to bow to others' judgement or advice even when they are clearly relatively expert, is pig-headed irrationality, not epistemic virtue or strength.

Does this mean, then, that there is after all no loss of epistemic autonomy incurred by the way in which, in our modern condition, we rely on others' knowledge and its technological fruits for whole swathes of our fabric of knowledge and in our daily lives (as sketched in my introduction)? It does not. It is crucial for the maintenance of epistemic self-governance that our trust in the word of others is given not blindly and universally, but discriminatingly. By trusting only cannily, and with good grounds, we can do much to retain epistemic self-governance. I shall return to this theme shortly. But there is still an important loss of autonomy, as I will now explain.

I mentioned our awareness of our own cognitive limitations, our feeble powers. We can only see what is here and now, and that only to a limited extent. Our memories even of this are less than total and often corrupt, and our inferential powers are feeble. A superior being, one who lacked our cognitive limitations, and could do all the work herself, in finding out about the universe, could be epistemically autonomous in a way that no one of us, with our limited research time and processing capacities, is able to be. She would not need to take anything on trust from another's word, because she would have the epistemic power to check up, to find out for herself about everything she wanted to know, without reliance on others. We are not such beings, and so we can extend our knowledge beyond a small base only through rational trust in the spoken or written word of others. My trust in another's word is rational when I have good grounds to believe her competent about her topic and sincere, and by this means I can know about all kinds of matters which I lack the time or talents to find out for myself. But this knowledge from trust in testimony is knowledge at second hand (or third, or fourth . . .), and as such my epistemic position vis-à-vis what I know is in at least one respect inferior to when I know at first hand.

When I form belief that P through my trust in a speaker's word given to me that P, her testimony that P, I take her to speak from knowledge. That is, this is a normative commitment of my accepting her utterance at face value, as an expression of knowledge. If I come to know she does not speak from knowledge, this is a normative defeater for my belief. Additionally, in my own view of knowledge as requiring adequate grounds, I must be disposed upon reflection to form the belief that she speaks from knowledge. This belief is an essential justifying ground for my belief in what I am told and trustingly accept, and so must itself be knowledge. In short: my reason for believing P true is because I believe, or am disposed to form belief upon reflection, that my informant is telling me what she knows. This being so, I know only because someone else's knowledge has been passed on, spread to me by the mechanism of telling, of testimony.[26]

Knowledge can be passed on in this manner through many links in a chain of trusted testimony. But the regress must stop eventually with someone who knows that P not from trust in testimony. The following axiom holds:

> T: If H knows that P through being told that P and trusting the teller, there is or was someone who knows that P in some other way—*not* in virtue of having been told that P and trusting the teller.

It is a consequence of T that if someone knows that P through trust in testimony, there must be some other way in which P is or once was known. Hence T has the corollary:

T corollary: For any proposition P that can be known, there must be some way other than trust in testimony through which P can or once could be known.[27]

Why cannot a chain of trusted testimony go in a circle, falsifying T? The regress must end with someone who knows that P in some other way, because knowledge requires evidence or grounds. When I know that P from someone's testimony, my personal ground for my belief that P, the warrant in virtue of which I am entitled to it, is my knowledge that my informant knows that P. But in taking P to be known I am rationally committed to an existential supposition: that there is, that it is to say that some individual or group of persons between them possesses, evidence or warrant for P, which is not just that someone they trust has told them that P. As T expresses, knowledgeable belief based on trusted testimony implicitly refers back to the existence of a non-testimonial ground or warrant for what is testified to: the ground or warrant in virtue of whose possession the original teller(s) spoke from knowledge.[28] Hence there cannot be a state of affairs that is known of only through trust in testimony. A chain of testimonially spread belief which went in a circle would lack any empirical grounding, and what is believed would not be true unless by luck.[29] Consonant with this fact, there is a sense of 'the evidence for P', used in scientific-style discourse, when it is asked: "What is the evidence for P?", in which someone's testimony that P is not evidence for P at all. For instance the question: "What is the evidence that smoking causes lung cancer?" is not answered by responding: a lot of distinguished scientists have asserted that it does. The question asks for an account of the *real* evidence, the evidence on which the experts' conclusion is based. The well-groundedness of belief spread about through testimony depends on the existence of such non-testimonial evidence for P—that is, on its possession, perhaps distributedly, upstream in the chain of informants.

Now we see the respect in which knowledge from trust in testimony is in one way inferior owing to its being at second hand. When I know that P solely from trust in testimony, I do not possess the evidence for P. Instead, my knowledge is premissed on the existential supposition that there is non-testimonial evidence for P, although I myself do not possess it. I am rationally committed to the proposition that a person or persons upstream in the chain of informants between them possess that evidence—the grounds for believing P true. Where the proposition is an empirical one that is part of a theory, I am also rationally committed to the proposition that these others have evaluated the evidence and drawn conclusions from it correctly (often, this ability is a large part of a special expertise the others possess vis-à-vis me).[30] Is it a weakness in my epistemic position regarding P that my ultimate ground for believing P is this derivative second-order one, the proposition—which I must be disposed to form belief in—that there is empirical warrant,[31] though unknown to me, for believing P? Where my informant's expert status vis-à-vis me is accidental, it does not seem a worry.—My son tells me there is still some milk left in the fridge, and I believe him. But if it mattered a lot I could easily check up for myself, and if what he told me were false I would quickly find out. I can get to the first-hand evidence, if need be, and I can evaluate it correctly. But where my reliance on others depends on an expertise they possess relative to me which is more deep-seated, and I lack the ability to check up for myself if it seems worth it, the existential supposition and dependence on others' epistemic skills and truthfulness is more troubling.[32]

Epistemic dependence on others is troubling first because it is risky—there are many motives for deceit, and causes of honest error, on the part of each of us; and while each can try to trust only where there is ground to expect sincerity and competence, as elaborated below, each link in a chain of testimonial transmission incurs its own risk of error. It is troubling second, because along with the epistemic dependence on others comes a no less risky practical dependence on them, in many areas—for instance, for maintenance of all the technological devices on which one depends every day, from electric lighting to computer to driving one's car, and so forth. Third, epistemic dependence on others, while it extends one's knowledge base so enormously, also lessens one's ability rationally to police one's belief system for falsity. There are many things a layperson believes for which she would not know how to assess the scientific evidence which supports them, even if presented with it. This being so, these beliefs of one will lack the characteristic sensitivity to defeating evidence, should it come along, which is usually taken to be a hallmark of belief which amounts to knowledge.[33]

I have spelled out the bad news for epistemic self-governance entailed by our dependence on the word of others. The good news is that—as I already emphasized—our trust in others need and should not be given blindly, but cannily, only where it is due. Although cognitively limited beings as we are, we must perforce rely on others if we want to enjoy the epistemic and technological riches of modern society, we can take care only to trust those we have good reason to hold worthy of our trust.[34] Fortunately we all have some basic cognitive equipment to help us assess both the sincerity and competence of others in many, though by no means all circumstances. This is because we are all experts (though of varying degrees of skill) in one special topic, namely that of folk psychology. Thus, where we do not have access to or cannot evaluate the evidence for propositions in some domain ourselves, we move one level up, and instead evaluate the experts, our human sources of knowledge about this domain.[35] But assessing an informant's trustworthiness is not always easy, and sometimes there are not sufficient epistemic resources available to the layperson to enable a firmly based evaluation to be made at all. The risks involved in trusting others are considerable, especially where there are motivations for deception at work. As I have been arguing, there is often good empirical ground for trusting others, and where so it is consistent with our maintenance of our epistemic self-governance, our responsibility for our own beliefs, that we believe on trust in the word of others, relying on their report for the truth of something where we do not possess for ourselves the evidence, and may not even be capable of appreciating its significance. Moreover, as we saw in Section 2, where I know another to be epistemically expert relative to me on a topic, it is not just rationally permissible, but rationally mandatory for me to accept her judgement in preference to my own, just so long as I have good ground to trust her sincerity. Where there is not good ground to believe an informant trustworthy, however, epistemic self-governance entails that we should not accept the reports of others. Caution and canniness should govern our response to others' testimony. Unless we exercise it, we fail to maintain responsibility for our own beliefs.

5. THE IDEAL REVISITED

I return now to the figure with which I began, the autonomous knower, who trusts no one else's word on any matter, hence believes only where she herself possesses sufficient evidence, non-testimonial grounds, for what is believed. In the light of the material of the last section we can clarify the autonomous knower in this way: she never believes on the basis of a second-order warrant for belief, the belief that someone else knows, someone else possesses evidence showing the truth of the proposition believed. Is this figure really an ideal? We observed that a superior being, with all the epistemic powers to find out everything she wanted to know for herself, could live up to this ideal of complete epistemic autonomy without thereby circumscribing the extent of her knowledge. Given the risks involved in epistemic dependence on others we saw in the last part of the previous section, this superior being is, I suppose, epistemically better placed than humans are. That is, if she knew at first hand just as much as I myself know in large part through trust in others' testimony, she would be epistemically more secure, hence both practically more independent, and—in some abstract sense—more autonomous than I am. In the same way that I might regret that I cannot fly, or live to be 300 years old, I might regret that I am not such a being.[36]

But what of a human, with no more than human perceptual, physical, and cognitive powers, who attempted to maintain a regime of complete epistemic autonomy—that is to say, who never took anyone's word for anything, and never deferred to another's judgement on any matter? We have seen that rational prudence dictates that one should bestow trust only where it is due; where one has good grounds to believe one's informant competent and sincere. But equally, as encapsulated in TDAP2, where there is good ground to believe another expert relative to oneself, it is not just rationally permissible, but mandatory, deferentially to accept the other's judgement. So what would this individual's beliefs about others have to be like, for her refusal ever to believe on anyone else's say-so to accord with maintenance of a rationally coherent system of beliefs? If rational at all, she would be not an ideal, but rather a paranoid sceptic about others' intentions and capacities. Or perhaps she would be severely cognitively lacking, simply lacking any adequate grasp of what other people are, their capacities and positions in the world—not a master of folk psychology, but an individual solipsist. She cannot ever admit that anyone else knows anything which she does not independently know herself since—as we saw—to admit this is to provide oneself with a second-order warrant to believe that thing oneself ('A knows that P' entails that P, and this entailment is a priori and obvious). One might wonder also whether she trusts the recorded beliefs of her own past self, as written down in her personal diaries and other records. The human would-be epistemic autonome on closer investigation is not an ideal, but either paranoid or severely cognitively lacking, or deeply rationally incoherent. We all can remember occasions on which someone we know has irrationally refused to change her opinion in response to testimony from someone evidently better placed to judge of the matter than she is. The individual autonome carries this irrational tendency to its irrational extreme.

For each one of us the extent and occasions on which she should accept and rely on others' testimony is a delicate matter, decisions about which require careful assessment on particular occasions. But that there are some occasions on which it is rational deferentially to accept another's testimony, and irrational to refuse to do so, is entailed by her background knowledge of her own cognitive and physical nature and limitations, together with her appreciation of how other people are both like and in other respects unlike herself, hence on some occasions better epistemically placed regarding some matter than she is herself. I may rationally regret that I cannot fly, or go for a week without sleep without any loss of performance, or find out for myself everything which I would like to know. But given my cognitive and physical limitations as parametric, there is no room for rational regret about my extended but canny trust in the word of others, and enormous epistemic and consequent other riches to be gained from it.

REFERENCES

Adler, Jonathan (1994), 'Testimony, Trust and Knowing', *Journal of Philosophy*, 91: 264–75.

Blackburn, Simon (1984), *Spreading the Word* (New York: Oxford University Press).

Burge, Tyler (1993), 'Content Preservation', *Philosophical Review*, 102: 457–88

Clement, Fabrice, Koenig, Melissa, and Harris, Paul (2004), 'The Ontogenesis of Trust', *Mind and Language*, 19/4: 360.

Coady, C. A. J. (1992), *Testimony: A Philosophical Study* (Oxford: Clarendon Press).

Davidson, Donald (1984), *Enquiries into Truth and Interpretation* (Oxford: Oxford University Press).

Descartes, René (1641), *Meditations on First Philosophy*, in *The Philosophical Works of Descartes*, ed. Haldane and Ross vol. i. (Cambridge: Cambridge University Press, 1967).

Fricker, Elizabeth (1994), 'Against Gullibility', in B. K. Matilal and A. Chakrabarti (eds.), *Knowing from Words*, (Amsterdam: Kluwer Academic Publishers), 125–61.

—— (1998) 'Self Knowledge: Special Access versus Artefact of Grammar—A Dichotomy Rejected', in C. Wright, B. Smith, and C. MacDonald (eds.), *Knowing Our Own Minds* (Oxford: Clarendon Press), 155–206.

—— (2002), 'Trusting Others in the Sciences: A Priori or Empirical Warrant?', *Studies in History and Philosophy of Science*, 33: 373–83.

—— (2005), 'Testimony: Knowing through being Told', in I. Niiniluoto, M. Sintonen, and J. Wolenski (eds.), *The Handbook of Epistemology* (Netherlands: Kluwer Academic Publishers).

—— (forthcoming), 'Second-Hand Knowledge', *Philosophy and Phenomenological Research*

Goldberg, Sanford (2001), 'Testimonially Based Knowledge from False Testimony', *Philosophical Quarterly*, 51: 512–26.

Goldman, Alvin (2002), 'Experts: Which Ones Should You Trust?', *Philosophy and Phenomenological Research*, 63/1: 85–110.

Grice, H. (1957), 'Meaning', *Philosophical Review*, 66: 377–88.

Hardwig, John (1985), 'Epistemic Dependence', *Journal of Philosophy*, 82: 335–49.

—— (1991), 'The Role of Trust in Knowledge', *Journal of Philosophy*, 88: 693–708.

Jones, Karen (1999), 'Second-Hand Moral Knowledge', *Journal of Philosophy*, 96: 55–78.

Locke, John (1690), *An Essay Concerning Human Understanding*, abridged and ed. John (London: Everyman, 1993).

Lyons, Jack (1997), 'Testimony, Induction and Folk Psychology', *Australasian Journal of Philosophy*, 75: 163–78.

McDowell, John (1994), *Mind and World* (Cambridge, Mass.: Harvard University Press).

Quine, W. V. O. (1953), 'Two Dogmas of Empiricism', in his *From a Logical Point of View* (Cambridge, Mass.: Harvard University Press).

Schiffer, Stephen (1972), *Meaning* (Oxford: Oxford University Press).

Welbourne, Michael (1994), 'Testimony, Knowledge and Belief', in B. K. Matilal and A. Chakrabarti (eds.) *Knowing from Words* (Amsterdam: Kluwer Academic Publishers), 297–313.

NOTES

1. See McDowell (1994). I am talking here about humans, and how they are psycho-developmentally able to acquire language-and-thought; not about other logically possible intelligences, nor the philosophical fiction who springs instantaneously into existence, a functional replica of a human. 'Testimony' here is to be taken broadly, to include verbal teaching and coaching by others. It would be a mistake to obscure our dependence on trust in others' sincerity and competence, in this developmental process, through a definitional stop.

2. By 'simple trust' I mean: trusting response to what others tell or teach us, by one who as yet lacks the conceptual resources to entertain doubts about the reliability of others' teaching. This is the inevitable initial condition of the infant learning its first words through interaction with its carers. (However many writers on testimony exaggerate how long this initial condition persists—don't underestimate children—they get wise pretty soon! See Clement, Koenig, and Harris (2004).)

3. A distinction cannot be drawn between analytic versus synthetic, amongst the familiar platitudes involving cluster concepts like these, and so many other of our concepts. See Quine (1953).

4. Mature visual experience is basically the result of the visual system's best guess as to what is out there, given the proximal stimulus to the retina. Some of this is hardwired and hence culturally invariant, notably the perception of 3-D shaped solid objects. But perception is also soaked by thicker, culture-specific concepts, so that its perceptual deliverances to consciousness are much richer: it's a mobile phone; a tomato; my daughter—these and their like are typical parts of the content of perceptual experience, not inferences from it.

5. Complete epistemic autonomy, as described here, by definition requires not relying on anyone else's testimony for any of one's knowledge. I shall explore whether a weaker, but crucial, notion of epistemic self-governance—epistemic responsibility for one's own beliefs—is consistent with accepting things on other people's word for them.

6. That is to say, there is—as will be developed below—a set of conditions regarding speaker's and hearer's circumstances such that both the offering, and the acceptance, of testimony on a topic is objectively epistemically appropriate just when they obtain; so that a speaker gives testimony epistemically properly, and a hearer epistemically properly accepts it, when each knows these to obtain. (Where the speaker or hearer believes justifiedly, but falsely, that they do so, her act or response is subjectively but not all-in epistemically proper.) See Fricker (forthcoming) for a supporting account of the speech act of telling. I there show how the nature of the communicative speech act of telling is crucial to the question when, and on what basis, the teller may properly be believed—to the epistemology of telling, and testimony more broadly. The qualification 'epistemic' to the type of propriety here is not idle—a telling could be epistemically appropriate, but grossly inappropriate in some other dimension, e.g. irrelevance, or rudeness.

7. When going for detail some qualifications are needed here. First, for statements made with sentences containing indexicals, understanding may require grasping an appropriately related content or proposition, rather than the very same one—same referent but different senses: "I'm hungry"; "It's hot here", uttered in a telephone conversation. Second, there can be cases where something is correctly conveyed by testimony, although the utterance is partly misunderstood; it may be that only the correctly understood part is believed. See Goldberg (2001).

8. There clearly can be Gricean (Grice 1957; Schiffer 1972) acts of communication which do not employ language as their medium. There are also non-literal message-conveying linguistic utterances such as ironic or sarcastic ones. And a speaker may succeed in getting her message across, be correctly interpreted and believed, despite using words wrongly in some respect—not in accordance with the constraints and permissions of the literal meaning of the sentence she mistakenly employs. Even where communication of what is literally asserted in the speech act occurs, presuppositions and conventional implicatures may be conveyed too. These acts all share with paradigm tellings the successful getting across of a message. I shall not investigate here the respects in which they differ; except to say that where what is conveyed

is not explicitly asserted there is, I believe, a diminution in the responsibility for the truth of what is got across incurred by the utterer. This is one reason to reserve the term 'telling' for acts of communication via explicit assertion exploiting literal meaning, as is done in ordinary parlance.

9. I am being careless here about distinguishing sentence types from particular utterances of them effecting speech acts, and the role of context in fixing what precise proposition a particular utterance of a sentence expresses. This matter, though crucial and pervasive in natural language, is tangential to the current point. The fastidious reader may imagine the necessary complicating adjustments.

10. "There are very beautiful pictures in the Uffizi in Florence, though I have never seen them."—this sounds deviant to my ear. As opposed to "There are said to be very beautiful pictures in the Uffizi, though I have never seen them". On the other hand "There are famous paintings by Botticelli in the Uffizi, though I have never seen them" sounds fine.

11. I form belief that P on the basis of trust in another's testimony that P, when I do so because I take her utterance at face value, as an expression of her knowledge that P. In so doing I take her word for it that P. There is a variety of other cases where a hearer forms belief that P in response to observing testimony that P, which are not cases of trust in that testimony. Fricker (forthcoming) contrasts these cases with the case of trust in the testimony, and argues that the latter relatively narrow category is the key epistemic kind to discern, in theorizing how knowledge can be spread by means of testimony. The condition proposed in TDAP for forming belief in what is stated would not be correct, for a broader category. Rather, it further characterizes the narrow category.

12. There is scope for further refinement here: it could be that an informant is very unlikely to form a belief that P which is not knowledge; but is more prone to error, or careless judgement, than not-P. This kind of one-sided reliability is quite plausible in some cases—e.g. someone who is slow to make a judgement of guilt of another—and a hearer could be aware of this epistemic disposition of an informant. But more usually, someone will be in this way reliable regarding P only if she is also similarly reliable regarding not-P. TDAP as formulated specifies this stronger condition. Perhaps someone could be self-deceived, so that she in some sense 'really knows' that P, while kidding herself, and telling others, that not-P. TDAP concerns knowledge expressed in conscious judgement, and so excludes repressed knowledge, if such is possible.

13. In contrast with her competence, or expertness as I am here calling it, I think that one is entitled to presume a speaker sincere, unless there are specific cues or other evidence calling this into question. This fact is not an epistemic principle special to testimony, but is fall-out from correct general principles governing the ascription of mental states to other persons. See Fricker (1994).

14. The issues here are delicate. Mere weight of numbers of concurring testifiers does not per se increase the probability of correctness; it depends on the details regarding the likely explanation of how they have come to hold their expressed beliefs. See Goldman (2002) for an excellent discussion of what epistemic resources a layperson may have, to decide which to trust out of two experts giving contrary testimony.

15. For instance regarding various future matters: the weather, currency and interest rate movements, etc. Here one should defer to and act on the basis of the best advice; while being aware that it is not knowledge—hence hedging one's bets accordingly.

16. An account such as Wellbourne (1994), which holds it sufficient for the recipient of testimony to come to know, that the hearer speaks from knowledge, is purely external and as such violates my requirement. However accounts like Burge (1993) or Coady (1992), which maintain an entitlement to trust testimony as such which is however defeasible, can be seen instead as proposing a specific thesis regarding how internal rationality is satisfied, in this case—albeit one with which I disagree. (In the case of perception, it is plausible that epistemic responsibility permits one to take one's senses on trust, unless aware of defeaters.)

17. This is why one knows so little about what goes on during one's children's days at school!

18. Can I know this, without begging the question—ungroundedly trusting her testimony over mine? Certainly: I have found on many previous occasions that what she has judged from a distance proves correct, as we get nearer. The fact that expertise is time and circumstance relative, often transient, means that another's epistemic expertise relative to oneself can often be conclusively established by oneself, despite one's own inferior epistemic power.

19. Expertise of S has been defined as relative to another person, H. But we can easily extract a more general concept of expertise, which is a superior epistemic power regarding some topic relative to all those without the specialist training or skills in question—the layperson or non-specialist.

20. The notion of 'access to relevant evidence', and certainly of two persons having equal access to relevant evidence, is fraught with difficulty, given the theory-dependence of one's observational powers—as my cricketing example above illustrates. It does not bear much theoretical weight in the present argument, and all I require is that there be some cases where it clearly applies, and others where it clearly does not. I intend that it holds of Case Two, and similar situations.

21. Is superior expertise also normatively sufficient for strong deference? No, since two people both with superior expertise to me may supply contrary testimony. Apart from this, I cannot think why else it should fail to be.

22. Fricker (1998) argues, on precisely this point, that accepting the possibility of correction of one's self-ascriptions of mental states made through avowal, by other evidence from one's behaviour, which might be pointed out to one by others, is a condition for one to be ascribing a genuine concept in these self-ascriptions.

23. I here make a large, but unoriginal claim, which requires at least a fat book for adequate defence. I have in mind positions like the 'quasi-realism' of Blackburn (1984).

24. The inextricable interweaving of fact and value in the considerations relevant to a final conclusion on a complex matter reinforce this point. Consider, for instance, the members of a panel appointed to draw up proposed legislation controlling research using human embryos. Both scientific and moral expertise are required, and intelligent conclusions rest on inextricable understanding of both. Another example of a specific partly moral expertise is making decisions about when children should be taken away from their parents and into care.

25. The *Beano* is a popular comic-strip magazine for children, in the UK.
26. Knowledge requires grounds, and if I trust a speaker who tells me something true but does not herself know it, my own belief will be based on a false premiss and so not be knowledge. This is the general conception of knowledge I favour, and my account of knowledge from testimony is shaped by it. Even if a different view of necessary conditions for knowledge is taken, that the speaker knows what she tells is clearly a rational commitment of a belief based on trust in testimony.
27. The 'other ways' may however include deduction, induction, or inference to the best explanation from premisses some of which were supplied by diverse bits of testimony. See Fricker (forthcoming). The tense qualification is important here—the original informant may have since died, or simply forgotten what she once knew and told to others.
28. T and its corollary do not imply the stronger claim: For any P which is known, there is someone who knows it in a way which has no epistemic dependence on testimony. This stronger claim is false, as is explored in Fricker (forthcoming). The source of testimonially spread knowledge that P may have learned some of the facts from which she inferred P from others' testimony. Thus the ultimate, non-testimonial evidence for any complex theoretical proposition may be possessed only distributedly, by the members of a group. See Hardwig (1991).
29. This remark remains true, but needs careful explanation, when we are dealing with facts constituted by human practices—the boundary between two countries, what something's name is, and so forth. The testimony itself would not make the belief true, but enough people acting on belief in it would do so.
30. My belief is premissed on these suppositions not in the strong sense that I must occurrently believe them; rather, they are normative commitments of my forming belief on trust in testimony. As such, I must come to acknowledge them if talked through it—and my trust is normatively defeated if I come to believe any of them false.
31. I say 'warrant' here rather than 'grounds', since there are some types of belief—e.g some beliefs regarding one's own mental states, and perhaps basic perceptual beliefs—which are empirically warranted, but not by *grounds* for belief.
32. Epistemic dependence of this sort is explored in a series of seminal articles by Hardwig (1985, 1991). Hardwig suggests the schema: 'H has reason to believe that S has reason to believe that P → H has reason to believe that P.' The schema only holds of prima facie reason, however—I could know that S has reason to believe that P, while myself being aware of defeaters for those reasons. Our present point is that *the reasons in question are different*. As I have been emphasizing, the ground for belief supplied by trust in testimony is a second-order one. My reason to believe is that I believe that my informant knows that P, hence that she or someone upstream of her has a non-testimonial warrant to believe that P. My original source's reason to believe is this non-testimonial warrant, the evidence for P.
33. A further point is that once the original source of a testimonially spread belief is no longer available, the original warrant for the belief is no longer retrievable. However this feature characterizes most of our beliefs. Cognitively limited beings that we are, we generally form a belief from the evidence, then store the fact in memory and

jettison the evidence. The lack of sensitivity to potentially refuting new evidence is, in contrast, a risk of testimonial belief only.

34. It should be abundantly clear by now that I am against all accounts of how knowledge may be gained through testimony which do not require that the recipient trusts only where she has good grounds to do so. They are inconsistent with the requirement of individual rationality, that epistemic self-governance in the sense of responsibility for policing one's beliefs for truth, is maintained by the individual, the thinking, believing, and acting subject. A rational individual cannot delegate this responsibility to others, although as I am elaborating here, the requirement can be discharged by moving up a level: evaluating the reporters, when we are unable to test their reports for truth directly.

35. In Fricker (1994, 2002) I discuss how non-question-begging evaluation of the dual components of a speaker's trustworthiness, her sincerity and competence, is often possible. See also the excellent discussion in Goldman (2002).

36. No heavy commitment to the coherence of the conception of this superior being is intended or incurred. I use her merely as a heuristic device in the development of my argument.

PART V

NEW AREAS AND NEW
DIRECTIONS IN THE
EPISTEMOLOGY OF TESTIMONY

11

Pathologies of Testimony

C. A. J. Coady

I am going to deal with some of the ways in which various forms of telling things to others come under moral or epistemic suspicion. Since I'm considering this against the background of what is (according to me) our very deep reliance upon testimony and the associated trust in others that accompanies it, then I am thinking of these ways as pathologies, in that they present as distortions of or diseases of the normal case of telling and relying on what is told. But, as we shall see, they have very different morphologies and there is a real question about how much of a distortion they might be. In particular, there is a question whether they deserve (all of) the moral and epistemic odium or suspicion that is their usual lot.

The phenomena I shall discuss are gossip, rumour, and urban myth. Another obvious candidate is lying but I shall not treat of it here. Lying is an interesting phenomenon with many different facets of philosophical interest, but since it arises from the deliberate intention to deceive an audience by saying what the speaker believes to be false it is too obvious a pathology of testimony to be treated in a paper concerned with more ambiguous candidates for that title. A more interesting candidate in the present context is the phenomenon of "spin" but reasons of space will prevent my treating of that; it must await another occasion. Gossip, rumour, and urban myth are different in many ways, most notably perhaps in their relation to the truth and the position of the speaker with regard to truth. As already noted, lies are distinguished at least by the intention to say what is believed by the speaker to be false. By contrast, it is plausible to think that gossip is standardly sincere, and may be true and known to be true. Rumour may be true and believed to be true but the justificatory base for speaking it is weak, and urban myth is more legend than rumour—it is more frozen and immune to refutation, but it can function in a similar way to more ephemeral rumours. Initially, I shall treat these phenomena as though they involved mere transmission of propositions, but of course this is a considerable simplification and even abstraction from the reality. Gossip, rumour, and especially urban myth are highly narrative in form; they are presented in a dramatic mode, sometimes even in song or poem, and they often contain, explicitly or implicitly, strong interpretive and evaluative elements. Here, as elsewhere, the picture of transmission as the passing on of a lump of information in a single line of transference from individual to individual is misleading. Nonetheless, the misleading picture reflects something right, namely, the fact that testimony begins with some form of witnessing. This need not be a perceptual encounter though that is a primary case of witnessing. It can also consist in a proof or an expert judgement, as I have previously argued (Coady 1992: 48, 51–62). Here I mention the point only to deal with one claim about gossip that seems wrong. It is made by Laurence Thomas who gives the following example as a clear case of gossip:

Austin: I can't believe that they are awarding her the Nobel prize in physics. Must be because she is a woman.
Lee: To tell you the truth I have been thinking the same thing myself.
(Thomas 1994: 47)

Thomas thinks this is "surely gossip" (Thomas 1994: 48), but I think it is better described as malicious speculation. I suspect Thomas treats this exchange as obvious gossip because he thinks that gossip, as in the example, must express negative feelings about the subject of the gossip. As we shall see, this negativity need not be a feature of gossip, but, in any case, I am interested in gossip as a possibly degenerate form of testimony, and the exchange between Austin and Lee makes no pretence of being a testimony transaction. Austin's "message" is a speculation; he has witnessed nothing relevant in even the most extended sense of "witnessing". These are points to return to.

   Thomas might reply that he doesn't think of gossip as a form of testimony, even a degenerate form. It is true that there are usages of "gossip" that are wider, and perhaps looser, than the use I am interested in, uses in which any casual exchange or conversation about anything whatever may count as gossip. Sometimes people think this way when they talk of a "gossip session" or "shooting the breeze".[1] Just chatting about one's own exploits or commenting, speculating, and guessing about aspects of the known exploits of others could then be gossip, but in the sense of the term that interests me you cannot gossip about yourself and conveying guesswork and so on doesn't count as gossip. There is then a degree of stipulation about my approach, but any initial characterization of the topic will involve some stipulation and will express particular theoretical interests. I claim on behalf of my account that it captures a great deal of what people normally mean by gossip (and of rumour and urban myth) and illuminates significant moral and epistemological scenery.

   Let us begin with gossip. There is quite an extensive literature on gossip, some of it philosophical, but a lot of it sociological. There are disputes about how to define the topic, as we have already seen, so I will not offer a tight definition, but rather give some necessary marks of the concept of gossip as I understand it. I shall take it that gossip has the following features: it is usually conveyed by those who believe it to be true, it can be the transmission of perfectly justified beliefs, it need not be malicious though it sometimes is. Its subject matter is invariably personal, though of course it can be about persons who represent or are thought to typify groups. It is also transgressive, in at least the sense that the transmission of the information can be presumed to be unwelcome to the subject of it. Some theorists claim that gossip is distinguished by the triviality of its subject matter. It is, they say, essentially "idle talk". It is understandable that this should be said, but it remains contentious. After all, gossip about someone's job prospects or manoeuvrings, about their adulterous conduct, about a political leader's financial dealings are all matters that may have momentous consequences for the individual concerned and for others affected by his or her actions. Acknowledging this, Rosnow has amended the claim to make it more plausible by concentrating on the style of communication rather than its content. It is the setting and context of the conversation that must have at least the appearance of the casual. As he puts it, the exchange should be "characterized by a kind of *belle indifference*". The talk should be "packaged" to appear as idle (Rosnow 2001: 210). This is indeed more plausible and seems to capture something typical of gossip. It is reflected in the casual, bantering tone adopted by many newspaper gossip columnists. One philosopher agrees that an idle tone is characteristic of gossip but takes this to be a moral defect of it. She says, "It is characteristic then of gossip to fail to give matters their due regard; gossip often involves a mismatch between the tone and substance of the discussion. Such a mismatch may simply reveal superficiality or it may constitute a failure of empathy and moral understanding" (Holland 1996: 203). I shall deal with this criticism later, but it is worth noting at this point that much of the literature on gossip is concerned with its moral status. Most of the criticism of gossip is moral rather than epistemic. This suggests that gossip exhibits no essential epistemic difference from ordinary testimony; there is no reason why gossip should be less reliable than ordinary testimony. In what follows, I shall try to assess the moral objections to gossip, but also raise some points about its possible epistemological deficiencies. There is one more mark of gossip that needs to be mentioned, namely, that there is something essentially restricted or intimate about at least the initial range of gossip. This point is hard to make clearly, but the basic idea is that the natural home in which gossip begins is that of a small group, though, of course, the information may spread from small group to small group until the news becomes widespread. Someone is not gossiping who shouts the information from the rooftops for all and sundry to hear.

The debate about the moral status of gossip (sometimes cast as a debate about its positive or negative social impacts) is basically between those who think that gossip violates some significant moral constraint, such as respect for persons, and those who think that gossip has an important social role. These latter sometimes ignore the supposed violation, but sometimes acknowledge it and think that it is outweighed by the good effects.[2]

First, the moral objections to gossip. Some of these proceed as though gossip must always be malicious. If this were true, then there would indeed be a black mark against it from the beginning. But it is clearly not true, at least if the malice in question is seen as stemming from a motivation to do harm. Many gossips have no interest in maligning the object of their talk, they are just interested in the buzz of the topic and the status their communication gives them. Indeed, gossip need not retail anything disreputable about its object. I may gossip about something you are doing that is either neutral or positive with respect to your reputation, as when I retail some confidential facts about your soon to be successful house sale or the secret that you are about to be elevated to the peerage. What seems true is that there must be something unwelcome to the gossipee about the revelation you are conveying. The subject of the gossip must at least be presumed not to want the information in question conveyed either generally or to that particular audience.[3]

I shall proceed as if this unwelcome aspect is essential to gossip, though there are in fact several counter-examples to an unqualified version of this claim. Some very trivial newspaper "gossip", about, for example, a society wedding may totally lack the unwelcome aspect, but for this very reason we may not want to treat it as gossip, or not as paradigmatic gossip. It is more like advertising or public relations offered under the pretence of news. More interestingly, there is a range of cases where the subject of the gossip may positively welcome the spreading of the information, and may indeed be the source of it, yet the information be both significant and somehow transgressive. Consider the case of academic gossip about who is to be offered a new position. If we think of the successful candidate as either the source, or as least the cheerful subject, then the unwelcome thesis seems imperilled.[4] There are two possible responses here. One is to shift focus on the subject of the gossip so that the gossip is about the actions of the appointments committee, and only secondarily about the status of the successful candidate. Members of the committee will find the gossip unwelcome—either in reality or by the conventions of confidentiality to which they are obliged to adhere. Another alternative is to say that the candidate may actually welcome the spreading of the news, but must take the stance of finding the transmission unwelcome. To adopt a useful test for gossip, we should ask: would the conversation stop or suffer embarrassment if the candidate suddenly entered the room? If the answer in the present case is, "Yes" then there seems a sense in which the candidate must be viewed as finding the transmission unwelcome whatever he privately thinks.

It is this unwelcome feature of gossip that provides one significant purchase for the moral critic. Granted that gossip need not be retailed with the aim of damaging the subject of it, might it nonetheless count against any proposed good in gossip that it must run counter to the subject's desire that the information remain confidential or at least restricted? One philosopher has argued that, because of this, gossip violates the Kantian injunction to treat others as ends in themselves and not merely as means. Prima facie, there is some plausibility in this. The gossiper need have no regard for the good of the person whose fortunes they report, the facts about them are recounted (at best) merely for the pleasure it gives the speaker and the audience, and possibly for the regard the gossiper achieves by reason of his/her knowledgability. Does this violate the Kantian injunction? This is one of the points at which the injunction is hard to interpret. Am I treating someone only as a means if I drive tourists by their handsome house to show them a fine example of the sort of Victorian architecture typical of the area? And suppose I know that they don't want their house to be the object of tourist gazing? What this suggests is that the test of "failing to treat someone as an end" cannot rule out all cases of acting against their wishes, even where these wishes are concerned with their privacy. But, perhaps we can only allow such disregarding where the disregard is aimed at achieving some good, and the fact is that gossip has no such purpose.

There are two problems with this. The first is that gossip arguably does have such a purpose, or purposes, and the second is that, even if it doesn't, the subject's desire for privacy, confidentiality, or secrecy may be unreasonable. The social psychologists that give a positive account of gossip often stress that it has a role in solidifying social norms. The idea seems to be that gossip about the behaviour of others takes place in an explicit or implicit context of norms and the evaluation commonly invoked (Oooh, she didn't! Gosh, fancy that! . . .) has the effect of reinforcing those norms. As Rosnow puts it: "the consequences of rumour and gossip also reflect the extent to which social norms can be enforced on individuals who ostensibly threaten or violate them. In small groups, for example, gossip may be a way of shepherding the herd by saying 'These are the boundaries, and you're crossing them'" (Rosnow 2001: 224). Rosnow here seems to be running two different things together. On the one hand, the effect of reinforcing the norms for the group involved in the retailing and hearing of the gossip, and on the other, the enforcing of the norms on the person gossiped about. The latter will not be the direct effect of the gossip since that person, in the first instance, at any rate, doesn't hear it. The former may well take place and lead to the latter.

The reinforcement thesis raises two further puzzles. The first concerns the generally favourable attitude of social scientists to this reinforcement (of either kind), and the second concerns the empirical claim itself that the attitude rests upon. On the first, it is strange (as Holland has pointed out) that the cementing of existing norms is simply taken for granted as a positive outcome. Perhaps this reflects the persistence of the simple-minded cultural relativisms that have been so influential, and so damaging in the history of anthropology and related studies. Whatever the explanation, it is obvious that existing social norms may be either good, bad, or indifferent from a moral perspective. The reinforcement provided by gossip may be to solidify widespread immoral prejudices against blacks, women, homosexuals, foreigners, immigrants, or whatever, and where this is so, it constitutes an objection to the role of gossip not an endorsement of it. As to the second, the role of gossip may just as easily be the breaking down of social norms as the protection of them. In societies with rigid public codes, gossip may serve to show the hypocrisy of those who proclaim and enforce them, thus leading to the destruction of respect for those elites and even of the codes themselves. So, gossip about the sexual behaviour of various influential leadership groups may lead to the erosion of strong sexual censorship regimes, and gossip about the perks and lifestyle of Communist leaders may have played a part in undermining public confidence in the professed values of fraternity and equality. It is also possible that both reinforcement and subversion can occur together (though directed towards different prevailing norms). Pre-Revolutionary France provides a case in point. In a society in which formal news outlets were stereotyped and tightly controlled by those in power, the primary source of information about the King and the ruling elites came from gossip and rumour. As Robert Darnton has argued in his fascinating book, *George Washington's False Teeth*, gossip and rumour about the French Court not only provided a rare source of personal and political information but thereby possibly played a part in preparing the ground for the Revolution (Darnton 2003: ch. 2). It did this by exposing the hypocrisy of the Court and the unworthiness of the King and his dependence on the intrigues of others. Some of the underground transmission was classical gossip retailed at selected sites such as the Tree of Cracow in the grounds of the Palais-Royal. Other was more rumour, though sometimes beginning as gossip, and other again was song and coded poetry circulated by paper notes or memorized word of mouth. Again, as with the reinforcement story, the question of whether the undermining is good or bad requires independent adjudication. More broadly, the question whether gossip has good or bad outcomes cannot be given a global answer. It all depends on the context and the actual outcomes. We cannot, however, rule out in advance the possibility that the outcomes will be good.

Another good outcome claimed on behalf of gossip is the way gossip can improve individuals' self-regard. By a process of what some have called "downward comparison" we may come to think better of ourselves by comparing our behaviour or character to that revealed of some other person by gossip (Suls and Goodkin 1994: 173; Ben-Ze'ev 1994: 19). The revelation that some famous person, for instance, has feet of clay may reassure us about the normalcy of our own feet. Again, the two questions posed earlier arise regarding this claim. First, it is not clear that bad information about others is a particularly sensible or healthy way of achieving a sound understanding of one's own worth. Self-congratulation can result in self-delusion. Second, the deflating information about the worth of others may equally well give rise to the sense that one should lower one's own standards rather than take pride in maintaining them. Either way of course there may be some solidifying effect of the gossip exchange; the deluded may be mutually bound by their delusions and a group may find some agreeable cohesion in mutually endorsed lowering of expectations of self and other. One possible connection of gossip with norms is that whereby the conveyors of gossip may be led to reassess their moral views by finding that their audience is not as shocked by the gossip as the speakers had expected. Gossip may therefore assist in what could be a useful form of self-criticism.[5]

A further potentially positive feature of gossip that is perhaps too obvious to be remarked upon by social psychologists is the fact that many people find the telling and receiving of gossip enjoyable. Most people are curious to know the truth not only about the physical world or mathematics but also about the deeds and misdeeds of other people. Sometimes this curiosity has a functional point in orienting us towards the people with whom we are going to interact: this is the idea that social psychologists are getting at with their somewhat simplified talk of norm reinforcement and the like. But sometimes the satisfaction of the curiosity is simply fascinating in itself, even if it can also be useful. We are interactive social beings who spend a great deal of our lives in conversation, much of it about other people. News about their journey through life with its pitfalls and triumphs is intrinsically interesting to most people, and it is often even more interesting when we know or believe that we are not going to hear it from them.

I have claimed that gossip is pleasurable for many of us, but there are those who find gossip of any sort uninteresting, even distasteful. They inject a chill of disapproval into the gossip room and often produce a cessation of the activity until they depart. Thereafter, the gossip resumes and often expands to include them as subjects! It would be interesting to explore this difference in attitude and some of its nuances, such as those who are happy to hear gossip but not to retail it, but I shall not pursue this matter here. Of course, it is necessary to stress that when I refer to the pleasure of gossip as good, I do not mean that it is an unqualified good. Pleasure is at best only one good among others; it can be outweighed by other goods or harms, and some pleasures may be inherently illicit, as are those (to take an extreme case) of paedophilia.

This leads us to the claim that there is something intrinsically bad about gossip that may preclude consideration of the good outcomes (if any) or at least may need to be weighed against them. Here, we should consider two of the issues raised earlier. First, there is Holland's claim that "It is characteristic then of gossip to fail to give matters their due regard; gossip often involves a mismatch between the tone and substance of the discussion. Such a mismatch may simply reveal superficiality or it may constitute a failure of empathy and moral understanding." Gabrielle Taylor makes a similar claim, though less forcefully. "Gossipers", she says, "trivialize experience by ignoring the impact with which the author of the experience will in some way have to cope. Thus they distort and belittle that person's experience" (Taylor 1994: 46). On the face of it, both claims seem excessively high-minded. Gossip is not always concerned with matters of moment, and, even where it is, the requirement that tone should match subject matter smacks of puritanism. The idea that serious subjects should only be addressed in a solemn tone of voice presents an affront to the complexity of human communicative intercourse, especially to the dimensions of humour, irony, satire, and playfulness that are rightly characteristic of much of it. Of course, tone may reprehensibly mismatch content, as with some sneering discourse, and this may well exhibit superficiality or moral failure of some sort. My only point is that, contrary to Holland, the tone characteristic of much gossip need not display moral fault, nor need it trivialize what should not be so treated.

Second, there is the issue, already briefly discussed, that gossip is standardly unwelcome to the gossipee. It is natural to think that this shows it to be in violation of respect for persons, and hence immoral. As mentioned above this depends to some degree on why the conveying of the information is unwelcome. There is no absolute right that information about oneself be withheld from others. Respect for privacy cannot reach that far. Perhaps my not wanting facts about myself to be made known to others creates some presumption against doing so, but it may be rebuttable in a variety of circumstances. Nor need these circumstances require some very great good to rebut the presumption. To give a personal example. I was once in a group of philosophers who were criticizing another more famous philosopher in ways that seemed to me to impugn his character as well as his philosophical standing. I had discovered from his publisher that the author under attack had actually assigned all his royalties from a very successful book to charity and proposed to do so again for the second edition. When I mentioned to the author my knowledge of this fact and my respect for his decision, he asked me not to tell anyone about his altruism. But in the company of his somewhat carping critics, I thought it right to do so and did. I think I was justified in acting in this way, and, if so, the example shows that the gossipee's desire to keep the matter secret need not be determinative of the moral status of the gossip. It also shows that Bertrand Russell was wrong to claim that "no one gossips about other people's secret virtues" (Russell 1994: 50). It further suggests that it does not require the prospect of some overwhelming good to validate the gossip transaction, since the author in question is fairly unconcerned with what people think of him.

Another interesting phenomenon is that of what might be called remedial gossip. By this I mean that phenomenon where B gossips about A to C, D, and E and then E tells A that B has been telling them about A. We might be reluctant to call E's transmission "gossip" because it is aimed at alerting A to the gossip about him or her. But it may well be offered in the characteristic tone of gossip and E may be well aware that B, C, and D would be unhappy to have the matter relayed back to A. Nor need E's motives be particularly noble.

I said that gossip is usually conveyed by those who believe it to be true and who may well be justified in their belief. This feature makes it seem that gossip is not, from the point of view of epistemology, a "pathology" of testimony at all. This idea is worth closer examination. One problem with it is that some of the motives typical of gossip may be fragile with respect to truth-transmission. The desire to titivate, or to show one's "insider" status as someone with access to otherwise unavailable information is not the sober background we expect of solid testimony. Bertrand Russell is thinking in this way in the section from which the earlier quotation was taken. He says, "The widespread interest in gossip is inspired, not by a love of knowledge but by malice: no one gossips about other people's secret virtues, but only about their secret vices. Accordingly most gossip is untrue, but care is taken not to verify it. Our neighbour's sins, like the consolations of religion, are so agreeable that we do not stop to scrutinise the evidence closely. Curiosity properly so-called, on the other hand, is inspired by a genuine love of knowledge."

I have argued that gossip is not necessarily malicious. If it were, then the epistemic objection would carry some weight since an informant who is inspired by malice will be seeking to put another's behaviour in a bad light and this may well bias their testimony. But even gossip that conveys negative information about a person need not be inspired by emphatic malice; it may be mere excitement at discovering the faults or follies of another and an interest in being the one to know and convey such stuff. Curiosity can be as lofty a disposition as Russell claims, but it need not be. It can be more earthy without becoming positively malicious and it may still retain an orientation to knowledge. Leaving aside malice, a disdain for other common motives for gossip faces two problems. One is that various forms of legitimate testimony, even of formal testimony in courts, may be subject to similar motivations. Witnesses conveying information that has no taint of violation may nonetheless be moved by the desire to cut a figure in great events and may delight in the excitement their news will create. They may also be moved by a concern to get things right—any account of what inspires reliable testimony must allow for the existence of mixed motives. Second, even if the motivations associated with gossip are not of the loftiest, they need not be destructive of a concern for the truth. The desire to impress may indeed make one *more* scrupulous in conveying accurate information since one's status as a reliable informant may be crucial to the positive appreciation one seeks.

Another epistemic objection to gossip is that it excludes by its very nature an important source of epistemic reliability, namely, confirmation, falsification, or correction by the subject of the gossip.[6] If we accept that absence of the subject is a necessary concomitant of gossip then it is indeed true that the gossip situation deprives the gossipers of an additional direct checking resource for the information. But I doubt that this is as drastic an epistemic flaw as it initially seems. In the first place, where the information originates from the subject, and our informant is known to be close to the subject and a generally reliable witness who has no particular stake in lying, it may simply be redundant, verging on the neurotic, to insist on checking with the subject. (Consider the parallel with those in the grip of mild obsessive-compulsion who need to return home to check by perception their firm memory that they have turned off the iron or locked the back door.) There are always further checks one can do on testimonial information, just as there are with observational or remembered information, but it is epistemically redundant to do so in many cases. In the second place, there will usually be little reason to believe that the subject of the gossip can be relied upon to provide valuable confirmation or disconfirmation. After all, since the subject does not want the information spread at all, he or she is most likely to deny it or refuse confirmation, whether the facts are as reported or not. In the third place, where the gossip does not originate from the subject, it may well be that the subject is in no position to confirm or deny the information. There is an interesting range of cases here. Consider the case where information is that you are to be awarded some honour and the source is an "insider" in the conferring process. You may know nothing of the fact at the relevant stage, or you may know only that there is some prospect of the honour. So your exclusion from the gossip circle creates no epistemic problem for the reliability of the information.

This example is also interesting as a problem for the unwanted criterion of gossip since it is presumably the people in the honouring process (or most of them) who don't want the information spread, even though it is information about you. Nonetheless, you are likely to want to know about it before the gossiper and audience get to hear about it. If, however, you are so unusual as not to care about that, then you would not be discomforted at being present during the gossip session. This, I take it, counts strongly against the transmission being gossip, at least about you—it may count as gossip about the honour process and honour bestowers.

I conclude that this epistemic objection to gossip fails as a general objection, though there may indeed be occasions on which closing off access to the subject's own testimony has epistemological disadvantages. More generally, gossip as I have defined it is not a pathological form of testimony but a normal form of it. Whatever its moral standing, and I have argued that this may be less dismal than usually thought, its intellectual status is reasonably respectable. In epistemic terms it may be likened to whispered information rather than openly spoken word of mouth.

RUMOUR

Gossip and rumour are often run together in social science treatments, but they are basically different in kind though there are some areas of overlap. At any rate, I shall treat them as differing in the way suggested at the outset, namely with respect to the justificatory base of the information conveyed. Gossip may be true and known or justifiably believed to be so, rumour has by (my) definition no strong justificatory base. The typical way to introduce a rumour is to say, "Have you heard . . .?" whereas the typical introductory mode of delivering gossip is, "Did you know . . .?" The gossiper may, of course, convey false information and be mistaken about the strength of the justification he has for the information. But he must present himself as being in an authoritative position with respect to the information. Must he always believe that he is telling the truth and in an epistemic position to do so? Can't there be deliberately deceitful gossip? Sissela Bok thinks so, indeed she lists "gossip that is known to be false", as one of the three main categories of gossip (Bok 1983: 98). But she, like many others, makes no real effort to distinguish gossip from rumour. To my ear, the phrase "lying gossip" does not ring true; the more accurate description of the activity is just "spreading lies". In any case, it is untypical of gossip. Rumour-mongers, by contrast, may well deliberately create false rumours. In wartime, the spreading of false rumours can be a crucial political weapon, as can be the combating of damaging rumours. Moreover, rumours may well begin in sheer speculation, though they will usually mimic testimonial transmission by conveying the idea that *someone* somewhere is a witnessing source.

A further difference is that rumour is not restricted by topic to the personal. It may be about institutional, political, religious, or physical events. You can spread a rumour about an earthquake but you cannot gossip about it. A further difference is that gossip is normally quite restricted in its circulation. A small group may get together to gossip about a colleague or a boss or whomever, but have no desire to spread the information further. (Gossip columns in newspapers are an exception to this, though even here there lingers some element of the closed group point, inasmuch as the readers of the column are meant to have a sense of being inducted into a privileged, if rather large, group.) Rumour, however, seems essentially prone to run abroad, "to spread like wildfire". Of course, one area of overlap is that something that begins as gossip may well continue as rumour. This is probably one of the reasons for the widespread failure to distinguish between the two.

Given rumour's indifference to a secure basis for its reports, can anything positive be said on its behalf? Even raising this question may seem perverse, in the face of the bad reputation so widely enjoyed by rumour. But it should be remarked that the enemies of rumour sometimes have an agenda that is not itself entirely respectable. I mentioned earlier the attempt to control and counteract rumours during wartime. The American psychologist Gordon Allport, for instance, was one of those who set up rumour clinics to help curb the spread of rumours in Massachusetts during World War II. He was later the co-author of an influential study of rumour (Allport and Postman 1965). Allport was helped in the anti-rumour campaign by his doctoral student Robert H. Knapp who defined rumour as "a proposition for belief of topical reference disseminated without official verification" (Knapp 1944: 22). This definition would count every newspaper exposé of government misdeeds or secrets that met with official silence or denial as rumour even if they were true and thoroughly justified. This makes nonsense of our ordinary understanding of rumour and reflects an ideal of official control of information that is, to put it mildly, undemocratic. It is not surprising that it might arise in a climate of war, but those of us who believe that war is frequently unjustified can hardly take consolation from this. Where governments are bent upon the suppression of information, for whatever reason, then "propositions for belief" unendorsed by the authorities will assume greater significance.

One thing that might be noted as an epistemic merit is the power of rumour in providing hypotheses for further exploration. By itself a rumour may be poor epistemic coin, but investigating it may lead to expanding one's knowledge in direct and indirect ways.[7] The direct route is that of confirmation or falsification of the rumour's contents. The indirect route may be the discovery of interesting information that explains the rumour's genesis, or it may be the discovery of a genuine truth that the rumour misleadingly presents. So we may discover that a rumour to the effect that a rogue politician is selling nuclear secrets to North Korea against his own government's policies and desires is false, but also discover the related truth that a respected senior scientist is selling the secrets with his own government's connivance. Dismissal of reports because they are "mere" rumours can sometimes block opportunities for discovering important truths. One of the most striking instances of this was the rumour emanating from Tokyo in 1941 concerning an impending attack on Pearl Harbor. The US Ambassador Grew reported in January 1941 from Tokyo a rumour that the Japanese Navy was planning a surprise attack on Pearl Harbor. It was attributed to the Peruvian Embassy which was regarded by the ambassador and others as "a not very reliable" source. The rumour was dismissed by one and all, including the Ambassador, as fantastic. As it turned out, the date the rumour began coincided with the inception of the Yamamoto plan for bombing Pearl Harbor (Shibutani 1966: 73–4).

In light of these positive aspects to rumour, it might be claimed that those who spread a rumour are not so dastardly as they are usually thought to be. Indeed, with all its faults, the poor coinage of rumour may often be the only information currency available. Some social scientists exploring rumour argue that it commonly arises in response to alarming situations where reliable information is cut off, either deliberately by censorship or repression, or accidentally by confusion or disaster. In such situations, rumour tends to be a focus of high social interaction. The "news" conveyed is not simply passed on from one voice to another, like the passage of a "brick" of information. The item is often speculated upon, criticized, amplified, compared with other related items of rumour, and with what pieces of hard news or testimony are available. In addition the originator of the rumour, if indeed there is only one such source, need not have had anything like observational access to the supposed fact that is spread. He or she may have produced the information as a speculation in the absence of any reliable testimony or observation. Even so, the rumour mill will usually present the rumoured facts as something that is somehow sourced in someone's observations, though it will usually be vague about who that is. Shibutani's discussion of the World War II rumours about the reduction in training and furlough time for US troops in Georgia in late 1944 exhibits this sort of pattern. The rumours were fuelled by the hard news of the increased German counter-offensive in Europe and the absence of any real information about the effect this might have on these newly inducted troops (Shibutani 1966: 9–14).

Psychological investigations of rumour tend to divide between those with an individualistic and rather static picture of transmission and social psychologists, like Shibutani, who see the picture in more dynamic and social functionalist terms.[8] The former tend to be hostile to rumour and the latter more sympathetic. The former proceed by setting up highly artificial experimental scenarios in which a piece of information is to be passed on to specified others (often the experimenter) and changes in the literal form of the message are noted for inaccuracy. This way of proceeding is open to a number of objections, some of which I have raised elsewhere (Coady 1992). The artificiality of the experimental situations rules out many of the standard ways of confirming, sifting, and interpreting the original informational setting; the emphasis on the literal preservation of a sentence or set of sentences is an unnecessary restriction on the conveying of information; the message in question often has little significance for the witness, and so on. By contrast, the social psychologists emphasize the fluidity of real life situations, the need for information in information-starved settings, the relation of rumour to practical thinking and decision-making rather than speculative reason and abstract truth. Indeed, they are inclined to minimize the issue of truth. So Shibutani says: "rumor is not so much the dissemination of a designated message as the process of forming a definition of a situation" (Shibutani 1966: 9). The cultural historian Hans-Joachim Neubauer describes it as "a mirror in which society catches sight of its hidden self" (Neubauer 1999: 174). These emphases are no doubt important for the empirical study of rumour, but it should be recognized that the dissemination of a designated message is perfectly compatible with forming a definition of a situation or mirroring social psychology. The interest in realistic social settings should not be seen as excluding the concern for the relation of rumour to truth or to epistemic justification.

So is rumour pathological testimony? It seems that it *is* a form of testimony because it involves the transmission of propositions from one or more persons to others, but it often lacks what I have elsewhere claimed to be definitive of testimony. There are sometimes no original sources in even the attenuated senses that I noted in my book since rumour can arise from the merest speculation. Furthermore, the speaker of rumour will often have no competence with regard to the "information" conveyed and may be well aware of that. If we think some degree of authority or competence, no matter how minimal, is a precondition for giving testimony then quite a lot of rumour will be disqualified as testimony. There is a very amusing Australian radio show called "The Coodabeen Champions" in which several witty and very well-informed people comment on sporting events, especially Australian Rules football. In one segment of the show there is a "talk-back" session in which members of the public (in fact, the commentary team with disguised voices) raise topics for discussion. One regular always rang with a rumour, this being the show's acknowledgement of the fact that sporting culture is rife with rumours about secret injuries, the sacking of coaches, the transfer of players, and so on. "Tony, have you heard the rumour", he would begin. When pressed on his credentials, it would emerge that his brother's wife's uncle knew a bloke who had a neighbour who heard someone in his dentist's waiting room say he thought he'd heard that if St Kilda suffered one more loss, the coach would be sacked. With credentials as thin as this, we may well want to treat such rumours as not testimony at all.

Nonetheless, they have at least the superficial appearance of testimony. They are not completely unrelated to it, so if we decide that rumours are not *really* or *fully* forms of testimony we will be treating them as what J. L. Austin called "misfires" rather than "abuses" of the speech acts of testifying. Austin's early discussions of "performative utterances" identified a range of infelicities to which they could be prone in contrast to their failing to be true or false. The idea of infelicities carried over to his more sophisticated discussion of illocutionary and other speech acts. The concepts of misfires and abuses were forged to show different ways in which speech acts could be infelicitous. Misfires make the purported speech act go wrong in a way that nullifies it, whereas abuses constitute real but irregular performances of the act. To use one of Austin's examples, it is a plausible precondition of successfully marrying that there exists an institutional framework within which the words "I do" serve to effect a marriage. But if, for example, you are already married (in a monogamous society) or the officiating officer is not really a licensed clergyman or appropriate civil official then you have merely gone through a form of marriage. The act has misfired, the marriage is void (Austin 1961: 223–8). By contrast, if you utter the vows of fidelity in the appropriate circumstances with no intention of keeping them you are still married, even if you are a genuine cad and the marriage hardly a paradigm of what it should be. Similarly an insincere promise may not be the best sort of model for promising, but it is still a promise and your commitment can be held against you when you fail to perform. Later, in *How to Do Things with Words*, Austin elaborated the distinction and produced sub-groups within misfires and abuses. Similarly, we might say that the rumour-monger's lack of credentials makes his testimony void, as testimony, but he has nonetheless gone through a form of testimony; compare the marriage ceremony performed by a bogus clergyman or official. This case of misfired testimony would count as a misinvocation in Austin's terms (Austin 1962: 14–20).

This gives us grounds for treating rumour as a pathology of testimony and giving a more precise sense to what that means.

URBAN MYTH

Urban myths have much in common with rumours. Indeed, in many respects, they could be seen as a type of rumour. But they have many distinctive features that make it plausible to treat them separately. They have, for instance, much higher levels of narrative complexity. The "testimony" they offer is presented in the form of a fully fledged story where a rumour is usually rather less developed or embellished. A further difference is the abiding nature of the urban myth. Urban myths tend to survive their implausibility and even refutation in specific cases, and re-emerge, sometimes in slightly different dress, at another time and often place. Quite frequently, they have a kind of moral lesson attached to them, like Aesop's Fables though not as explicit, and their revival is often triggered by issues of contemporary interest. In December 2002 there was an interesting episode in Tasmania, Australia, where it was widely reported that a truck driver had given a lift to a man of Middle Eastern appearance who left his wallet in the cabin after alighting in the capital city, Hobart. The honest truck driver called after the man who said to him in a rush of gratitude, "Don't go near Salamanca Place on Saturday." Salamanca Place is a popular market area near the waterfront and is always crowded on Saturday mornings. There was an American naval ship in the harbour. My son, David Coady, a philosopher at the University of Tasmania, was contacted by the media for comment and pointed out that this was a classic urban myth that had already surfaced elsewhere in slightly different forms. His view was publicized widely, panic was averted, and (fortunately for him and the reputation of philosophers) nothing alarming happened on the morning in question. The truck driver story combines a moral element of virtue rewarded with a more general threatening element.

Then there are the many instances of humorous tales of vindication or revenge. A classic is the one that the avid collector of urban myths, Jan Harold Brunvand, has christened "the $50 Porsche" though the type of car varies with different national and cultural settings (Brunvand 1999: 77; 1981). One version of the story (in bare bones) goes as follows: Someone is reading the newspaper ads for used cars and sees an ad for a very recent model Mercedes (Porsche, Rolls Royce . . .) available for sale for $50. He rings the number and a woman answers and says that it is truly available at the price. He goes to the address given and a beautiful woman comes out of an expensive house and shows him a spotless, perfectly maintained Mercedes only two years old. As he hands over the cheque, he asks how it could possibly be sold at such a price. She replies that her husband has recently left her for a younger woman but contacted her just the other day, in a spirit of "surely we can still be friends", to ask her to sell his posh car since he needed an injection of funds, and to send the money on to him. This she was now doing!

There are other tales that build on primal fears. One is the spider's eggs myth. Invariably the victim in the story is a woman. In basic outline the story goes that she has gone far off for a holiday, but before (or during) the holiday notices a small sore or lump on her face. At some time on the holiday, the sore swells and bursts, and a whole lot of baby spiders come out. Various embellishments concern whether she knows she was bitten by a spider or it happened while she was asleep, etc. Sometimes she dies of a heart attack. This story seems to have begun in Northern Europe as late as 1980, but spread to venues in North America and elsewhere.

The field of stories that are called urban myths is very wide and contains much variation, but I shall take it that what I call "urban myth" is invariably false and ill-founded, though commonly enough believed to be true. One qualification that is needed to this is that a true but dramatic and surprising story, based on reliable testimony, may transmute into an urban myth with a life of its own. A case in point is the mathematician's story: "The Unsolvable Math Problem". The original true story concerned an episode in the career of the mathematician George B. Dantzig who, as a student at Berkeley in 1940, arrived late for a class given by Jerzy Neyman and noticed that there were two problems on the blackboard. Thinking they had been assigned for homework, he copied them down and went away and worked on them for several days. He then returned to his professor and apologized for taking so long, but they had been rather hard. He asked whether his teacher still wanted them and was told to put them on the desk. Six weeks or so later, he and his wife were awakened by banging on his door early one Sunday morning. It was Neyman saying that he had just written an introduction to the homework and wanted Dantzig to read it so he could send the lot off to a journal for publication. The homework had in fact been put on the board merely to show the class two famous, unsolved mathematical problems in statistics. Various versions of the true story were then in circulation for years afterwards as, for instance, the subject of sermons showing something or other about God or human character. In the course of this, they changed shape in all sorts of ways, even appearing in the film "Good Will Hunting". So this is a case of numerous fictional accounts having sprung from one apparently genuine happening faithfully recorded by Dantzig and, in part, easily checkable against the publication by Datzig of his solutions.[9] Another form of truth for urban myth might be provided by life imitating fiction, if, for example, some deserted wife found herself in the advantageous position described in the "$50 Porsche" story and took instruction from it! But with these exceptions noted, it is part of qualifying for the title "urban myth" that the tale is false, though for any given story we may not know on hearing it whether it is urban myth or not. Being familiar with a number of urban myths, however, is a good recipe for recognizing others. This is partly because many of them merely ring changes upon the familiar ones, but also because there is a certain narrative style common to many urban myths. I have mentioned Aesop's Fables and another analogy is with biblical parables except that they are not intended to be believed as historical accounts and are often prefixed by phrases that indicate as much, such as "the kingdom of heaven is like . . ." Often, urban myths play upon certain widespread fears or phobias, and there are some types of myth that invoke the wildly improbable or supernatural. Like rumours, it is usually quite unclear how one could check on the sources of the story. Where there are links in the chain of apparent testimony they quickly come to a halt well short of a reliable witness.[10] Is urban myth a pathology of testimony? Well, that depends on the degree to which it is presented as testimony or as fiction. Usually, the stories will be told as if true and based somehow on report, but sometimes they flourish merely because they are a good story. So, urban myth is a pathology of testimony in much the same way as rumour, though perhaps closer to fiction.

What general lessons should be drawn from this discussion? The first is that whether some communication is a degenerate form of testimony cannot be simply read off from the form or content of its telling, though either may give clues to this fact. A communication may have the usual hallmarks of an urban myth, for instance, and we may be wise to treat it as such, but it may turn out to be a case where truth is stranger than fiction and there is a reliable testimonial path to that truth. It seemed like an urban myth but it wasn't. The second is that a pathological testimony need not be altogether worthless. The communication may rightly be judged unreliable but turn out to be true, as with certain rumours or lies. Liars can accidentally say what is true while meaning to say what is false and our knowledge of the background to the liar's performance may enable us to spot this and profit from it. Somewhat similarly, a rumour-monger can hit upon the truth without being entitled to any confidence that it is true. This may indeed have been the case with the rumour emanating from the Peruvian Embassy about the planned attack on Pearl Harbor; the ambassador could have been right in his assessment of the general reliability of sources in the Peruvian Embassy. On the other hand, it might have been his assessment of their credibility that was at fault and the communication may not have deserved the title "rumour". Once we have reason to characterize some communication as rumour, then equally we have reason to treat it as lacking credibility. It may, nonetheless, deserve further investigation, if the stakes are high enough, just in case it is true, or with the prospect of discovering some truth that it distorts. Once we establish that some communication is urban myth then we can be sure that it is false (with the minor qualifications noted earlier) but it remains possible that it is a revealing fiction. The matter is different with gossip. Once we have established that some communication is gossip, the question of its reliability and truth is (*pace* Russell) much the same as that of any other piece of testimony.

REFERENCES

Allport, Gordon W., and Postman, Leo (1965), *The Psychology of Rumor*, 2nd edn. (New York: Russell & Russell).

Austin, J. L. (1961), 'Performative Utterances', in his *Philosophical Papers* (Oxford: Oxford University Press).

—— (1962), *How To Do Things with Words*, lecture II (Oxford: Oxford University Press).

Ben-Ze'ev, Aaron (1994), 'The Vindication of Gossip', in Robert F. Goodman and Aaron Ben-Ze'ev (eds.), *Good Gossip* (Lawrence, Kan: University Press of Kansas).

Bok, Sissela (1983), *Secrets* (New York: Vintage Books).
Brunvand, Jan Harold (1981), *The Vanishing Hitchhiker: American Urban Legends and their Meaning* (New York: Norton).
_____ (1999), *Too Good To Be True: The Colossal Book of Urban Legends* (New York: Norton).
Coady, C. A. J. (1992), *Testimony: A Philosophical Study* (Oxford: Oxford University Press).
Darnton, Robert (2003), *George Washington's False Teeth: An Unconventional Guide to the 18th Century* (New York: W. W. Norton and Co.).
Holland, Margaret G. (1996), 'What's Wrong with Telling the Truth? An Analysis of Gossip', *American Philosophical Quarterly*, 33/2.
Knapp, Robert H. (1944), 'A Psychology of Rumour', *Public Opinion Quarterly*, 8.
Neubauer, Hans-Joachim (1999), *The Rumour: A Cultural History*, trans. Christian Braun (London: Free Association Books).
Rosnow, Ralph L. (2001), 'Rumour and Gossip in Interpersonal Interaction and Beyond: A Social Exchange Perspective', in Robin M. Kolwaski, (ed.), *Behaving Badly: Aversive Behaviors in Interpersonal Relationships* (Washington, DC: American Psychological Association).
Russell, Bertrand (1994), *On Education: Especially in Early Childhood* (London: Routledge) (first published 1926).
Shibutani, Tamotsu (1966), *Improvised News: A Sociological Study of Rumor* (New York: Bobbs-Merrill).
Sousa, Ronald de (1994), 'In Praise of Gossip: Indiscretion as a Saintly Virtue', in Robert F. Goodman and Aaron Ben-Ze'ev (eds.), *Good Gossip* (Lawrence, Kan University Press of Kansas).
Stern, William (1902), 'Zur Psychologie der Aussage', *Zeitschrift für die gesamte Strafrechtswissenschaft*, 22.
Suls, Jerry, and Goodkin, Franklin (1994), 'Medical Gossip and Rumor: Their Role in the Lay Referral System', in Robert F. Goodman and Aaron Ben-Ze'ev (eds.), *Good Gossip* (Lawrence, Kan University Press of Kansas).
Taylor, Gabrielle (1994), 'Gossip as Moral Talk', in Robert F. Goodman and Aaron Ben-Ze'ev (eds.), *Good Gossip* (Lawrence, Kan University Press of Kansas).
Thomas, Laurence (1994), 'The Logic of Gossip', in Robert F. Goodman and Aaron Ben-Ze'ev (eds.), *Good Gossip* (Lawrence, Kan University Press of Kansas).

NOTES

1. Tom Campbell tells me that there is a Glaswegian phrase for this: "having a good hing".
2. A few are positively euphoric about the merits of gossip, most notably Ronald de Sousa (1994: 25–33). He seems to me far too dismissive of the downside of gossip and he exhibits a sort of romantic exaggeration of its benefits. He says "If all truths became public we would approach utopia" (1994: 31). This blatantly defies the fact that there is sometimes a significant value in privacy and confidentiality.
3. What I am calling the "unwelcome" aspect of gossip might be captured in other ways. It might be thought that my criterion turns too much on the psychology of

the gossipee or on what the gossips know of that psychology. David Rodin suggested instead that the information should be "unauthorized". That might do, though there are then problems about who or what does the authorizing. I prefer to stick with "unwanted" and I note in the text and try to deal with some of the difficulties this choice raises. I suspect that there may be other ways of making the transgressive point that would demarcate a closely similar conceptual territory for our discussion.

4. This objection was put to me by Margaret Coady.
5. I owe this point to Ruth Zimmerling.
6. I owe this perceptive objection to John O'Neill of Lancaster University.
7. Somewhat similar points could be made about ordinary lies.
8. For the more static picture see William Stern 'Zur Psychologie der Aussage', in *Zeitschrift für die gesamte Strafrechtswissenschaft*, 22 (1902) discussed in Neubauer (1999: 157–8) and see also Allport and Postman (1965).
9. According to Brunvand, one of them is in the *Annals of Mathematical Statistics*, 1951. See Brunvand (1999: 452–6) for the full details of what he has christened, in a slightly misleading way, "The Unsolvable Math Problem".
10. An exception is the virgin birth tale from the American Civil War (see Brunvand (1999: 469–72) where the story is called 'Bullet Baby') but it originated in an ingenious hoax by a reputable medical practitioner and is therefore not a typical urban myth.

12

Getting Told and Being Believed

Richard Moran

Recent interest in the epistemology of testimony has focused attention on what justification we may commonly have in the vast areas of life where we are dependent on what other people tell us. This dependence is not restricted to what we are told in face to face encounters, for we also take ourselves to know all sorts of things that only reached us through a long chain of utterances and documents, whose evidential status we have never investigated for ourselves and which we will never be in a position to investigate. And the content of such knowledge is not confined to the arcana of specialized studies, but includes such mundane matters as the facts of one's own birth and parentage, the geographical and institutional facts of one's immediate environment, and the 'general facts' that make up one's basic sense of what the world is like.

In part it is the enormity of this dependence that makes for the interest in the subject of testimony, combined with the apparent clash between the kind of epistemic relations involved here and the classic empiricist picture of genuine knowledge basing itself either on direct experience of the facts, or on working out conclusions for oneself.[1] It isn't just that the bulk of what we take ourselves to know is so highly *mediated*, as even knowledge gained through a microscope or other scientific instrument must be; rather it is that the vehicle of mediation here—what other people say—seems so flimsy, unregulated, and is known in

This paper has a long history and I have accumulated more than the usual share of debts along the way. In presenting both this and related material, I have benefited from responses of audiences at: Wake Forest University, Arizona State University, University of Wisconsin, Milwaukee, New York University; the Center for Human Values at Princeton University, Vassar College, University of Connecticut, Storrs, Rice University, Johns Hopkins, Stanford University, Macquarrie University, Sydney, University of Pennsylvania, Amherst College, University of Virginia, Columbia University, University of Chicago, and the University of Minnesota. Earlier versions of this material were presented at the Third Italian American Philosophy Conference, Rome and Frascati, June 2001, and at the Instituto de Investigaciones Filosóficas, UNAM, Mexico City. I am grateful to my hosts on those occasions.

I also received very helpful comments from Jonathan Adler, Tyler Burge, Kate Elgin, Paul Faulkner, Luca Ferrero, Amy Gutmann, Paul Harris, Pamela Hieronymi, Karen Jones, Adam Leite, Wolfgang Mann, Peter de Marneffe, Ed Minar, David Owens, Connie Rosati, Angus Ross, Nishi Shah, Martin Stone, David Sussman, Michael Thompson, David Velleman, Jonathan Vogel, Matthew Weiner, Daniel Weinstock, as well as the comments of two anonymous referees.

I am grateful to the editors of *The Philosopher's Imprint* for permission to reprint.

plenty of cases to be unreliable, even deliberately so. People do lie, get things wrong, and speak carelessly. And while we may realistically hope for continued improvement in the various technical means of epistemic mediation (advances in scientific instrumentation are part of the history of scientific progress, after all), there is little reason to expect that the fallibility and mendacity associated with human testimony will one day be overcome. So in this light, reflecting on just how much we rely on the word of others, we may conclude that either we are very careless believers indeed, with no right to claim to know more than a fraction of what we think we know, or some great reductionist program must be in the offing, tracing this chain back to something resembling the classic picture of knowledge by acquaintance.[2]

Hume's famous discussion of the believability of reports of miracles is the *locus classicus* for attempts to understand the epistemic status of testimony as ultimately the same as any other reliable evidence.[3] And part of what is meant by this claim is that the basis we may have in any given case for believing what we hear can only be an *a posteriori* judgement to the effect that in this case there is a reliable evidential correlation between the statement we are being offered and the facts themselves. Several recent writers, most notably C. A. J. Coady in his book *Testimony*,[4] have argued that the Humean picture cannot succeed in reconstructing our actual basis for believing what people say, and that our entitlement to believe what we are told must have, in part, an *a priori* basis. Somewhat lost in much recent discussion, however, is attention to the basic *relationship* between people when one person tells a second person something, and the second person believes him. This is the primary everyday occurrence, and it is the basic way knowledge gets around. Or at least, so we say. For normally (though not without exception) we take it to be sufficient for bringing someone to know that P that they were *told* by someone who knew, and they believed him. And now, of course, if this second person is taken to *know* that P, he may tell another person, and so on. This may seem absurdly simple and unreflective, and to be at odds with an earlier picture of genuine *knowledge* as being more of an achievement lying at the end of an arduous path from belief or opinion. My concern in this paper, however, is not so much with the conditions for knowledge as with the nature of the two sides of the relationship described here. One person *tells* the other person something, and this other person *believes him*. I want to understand what 'telling' is, especially as this contrasts with other things done in (assertoric) speech such as persuading, arguing, or demonstrating; activities which may also lead to belief or knowledge for the interlocutor, but in importantly different ways. And primarily I want to examine the relation of believing where its direct object is not a proposition but a person. For in the basic case described above, it is the speaker who is believed, and belief in the proposition asserted follows from this. These are different epistemic phenomena. For the hearer might not believe the speaker at all, taking him for a con man, but yet believe that what he has said is in fact true. Whereas when the hearer believes the speaker, he not only believes what is said but does so on the basis of taking the speaker's word for it. I don't mean to suggest that this distinction has been wholly ignored in the literature of testimony, and I will soon come to discuss what I think is the best recent discussion of it. But both it and the distinction between the speech act of 'telling' and other things done with assertion have not been given a central place in the discussion of what is distinctive about the epistemic dependence on testimony. Specifically, I wish to argue that any account of testimony that seeks to resist the (Humean) assimilation of its epistemic status to that of an evidence-like correlation between one set of phenomena and another will have to give a central place to the distinctive relation of believing another person.[5] Only in this way can we account for what is distinctive about acquiring beliefs from what people *say*, as opposed to learning from other expressive or revealing behavior of theirs. The hope is to show that the paradigmatic situations of telling cannot be thought of as the presentation or acceptance of evidence at all, and that this is connected with the specifically *linguistic* nature of the transfer of knowledge through testimony (which will take us through an epistemological reading of Grice's original account of non-natural meaning).

EVIDENTIAL RELATIONS AND THE A PRIORI

It is in part due to the epistemological context of recent discussion of testimony, that argument has focused on the question of the *a priori* or *a posteriori* status of our justification for beliefs acquired in this way. In recent work, both C. A. J Coady and Tyler Burge have argued against a broadly Humean picture, by attacking the idea that we could only have *a posteriori* justification for believing what others tell us.[6] Coady presents more than one argument against the Humean idea, but several of them begin with the following strategy. If we can only have *a posteriori* grounds for taking what people say to be a reliable guide to the facts, then on such a view it must be conceivable for there to be a community of speakers whose assertions bore *no* reliable relation to the facts. If we are to be in a position to deploy an *a posteriori* argument for the existence of such a correlation, it must be possible for us to begin confronting the linguistic evidence without begging that very question. Coady presents a powerful and connected set of arguments for the conclusion that this is not, in fact, a coherent possibility. Not only would the practice within the community of making or accepting assertions soon break down on such assumptions, but from a perspective outside the community there are deeper reasons connected with the interpretation of speech which prevent the Humean scenario from being realizable. For assigning *content* to the utterances of the hypothetical speakers requires, for familiar reasons, regular correlation between assertive utterances and the conditions under which they would be true. Massive disparity between the content we assign to utterances and their truth or rationality would oblige us as interpreters to revise our original assignments of content to them. So there is, in fact, no genuine possibility of a community of speakers whose assertions failed, as a general rule, to correlate with the facts. And thus, contrary to the Humean picture, our general justification for believing what people say cannot be a purely empirical, *a posteriori* one.[7]

Both arguments direct themselves against the idea that we have, at best, empirical, inductive grounds for believing what people say. I don't dispute this general point or the particular way it is argued for in these two instances, but do want to point out that this general form of argument describes no particular role for the notions either of a speaker *telling* someone something, or of *believing* that speaker. What the generality of such arguments provides is a defeasible *a priori* warrant for believing that what other people say will normally be true. But any argument pitched at that level of generality will leave untouched the question of whether believing the person (as opposed to believing the truth of what is said) is a legitimate, and perhaps basic, source of new beliefs. For we might well have an *a priori* defeasible warrant for accepting the beliefs we gain through observing the behavior of others (verbal and otherwise) without this warrant involving the concepts of 'saying' or 'telling' at all. By itself, such a justification is no different from the presumptive right we may have (*ceteris paribus*) to rely on the deliverances of the senses or of memory. At this level of argument, the speech of other people could still be something which is treated as *evidence* for the truth of various claims about the world, the difference would only be that here we may have some non-empirical right to treat this phenomenon as evidence, perhaps even very good evidence.[8] This general line of thought begins, then, to look more like a non-skeptical *version* of the basic Humean view, and less like a vindication of testimony as a distinct source of beliefs, one not reducible to a form of evidence. And yet it is the special relations of telling someone, being told, and accepting or refusing another's word that are the home of the network of beliefs we acquire through human testimony. And these relations, I hope to show, provide a kind of reason for belief that is categorically different from that provided by evidence.

Another way of putting this criticism would be to say that arguments of the generality of Coady's do not address the question of what is distinctive about acquiring beliefs from what people *say*, as compared with other things people do. At bottom, the epistemological role of communicative speech is not seen as essentially different from that of other behavior. But the observable behavior of other people may be a source of true beliefs in all sorts of ways, which need have nothing to do with believing the other person. I may look out my window on a sunny day and see people bundled up against the cold, and then reliably conclude from this that it must be colder outside than it otherwise looks. This transition in thought is not essentially different from the picture according to which I observe the verbal behavior of some exotic community, and in seeking to understand what it means, I necessarily rely on various assumptions about their rationality and general awareness. And here one could point out that the same 'rationalizing' or charitable constraint on understanding what these people say also provides a defeasible warrant for taking *what* we understand them to say to be *true*. This is because we take their speech normally to express their beliefs, and we take their beliefs (as interpreted by us) normally to be true. This familiar, general scheme applies in the same way to the behavior of the people I see bundled up against the cold, and to the verbal behavior observed by the Radical Interpreter. Pictured in this way, one's relation to the exotic speech community does not involve being *told* anything at all, or believing *them*, any more than it does in the case of the people observed from the window. In both cases it is just a matter of an inference from behavior which is seen as rational to some conclusion about the state of the world. So nothing along these lines, justifying the beliefs we acquire from other people, can count as a vindication of our reliance on *testimony*, since it is not a vindication of what we learn through believing other people.

This is, of course, the familiar role of speech and its relation to belief in contemporary philosophy of mind, and it should not be surprising to see it exerting a degree of control over the recent discussion of testimony. Within this discourse, speech is seen as a kind of interpretable human behavior like any other. When we interpret such behavior, we seek to make it understandable within the rational categories of what is called 'folk psychology', and ascribe beliefs and other attitudes which will be reasonable approximations to the True and the Good. And this picture of our relation to the speech of other people leads almost imperceptibly into a view about testimony. For we can argue from here: when we interpret the speech of another we do not only learn about the speaker, we also learn about the world. Most obviously, when someone makes an assertion we may not only learn about what he believes, but if the assertion is *true*, we may also learn the truth of what is asserted. And if our interpretation is guided by principles of charity, we will indeed take most of what people say to be true, even in cases where we have no independent reason for thinking it true. In this way, the fact of the other person's belief (as interpreted by us) may function as *our* reason for believing the same thing. We thus gain true beliefs about persons as well as about the world they are talking about.

PERVERSITY, DEPENDENCE, AND RISK

What this general scheme provides us with is a presumptive right to share the beliefs we take the speaker to have. But, other things being equal, we would have the very same right *however* we learned of that person's beliefs.[9] This epistemic warrant described in this scheme need not involve a dependence on speech any more than it did when I learned about the weather by seeing how people outside were dressed. Speech, of course, can be an especially revealing and fine-grained basis for belief-ascription, but from this perspective it is but a particular instance of the more general scheme of interpreting behavior.

Since it is knowledge of the other person's beliefs that is doing all the epistemic work on this picture, we should note that while speech is in some obvious ways a privileged route to such knowledge, it is also one which subjects the interpreter to special risks which are not shared by other possible ways of coming to this same knowledge. When I learn of someone's beliefs through what they *tell* me, I am dependent on such things as their discretion, sincerity, good intentions—in short, on how they deliberately present themselves to me—in a way that I am not dependent when I infer their beliefs in other ways. People are known to lie, exaggerate, and otherwise speak in ways that do not express their genuine beliefs. Thus, in relying on what a person says, I am incurring an additional risk that the behavior he is manifesting may be deliberately calculated to mislead me as to what he believes. I am here dependent on *him*, and his intentions with respect to me, and not just on my own abilities as an interpreter of the evidence. This source of error is a much more remote possibility in the case of inferences drawn from the private observation of someone's behavior. The people bundled up against the cold *could* be dressed up like that just so as to fool me, but this is hardly the everyday occurrence that lying and misrepresentation is. And that risk of error is not a possibility at all for those ways, real or imaginary, of learning someone's beliefs directly and without the mediation of voluntary expression or behavior at all (i.e., whatever is imagined in imagining the effects of truth-serum, hypnotism, or brain-scans). If the epistemic import of what people say is at bottom that of an indication of what they believe, it would seem perverse for us to give any privileged status to the vehicle of knowledge (speech and assertion) where we are most vulnerable, because most dependent on the free disposal of the other person. And if we are considering speech as evidence, we will have eventually to face the question of how recognition of its intentional character could ever *enhance* rather than detract from its epistemic value for an audience. Ordinarily, if I confront something as evidence (the telltale footprint, the cigarette butt left in the ashtray), and then learn that it was left there deliberately, and even with the intention of bringing me to a particular belief, this will only discredit it as evidence in my eyes. It won't seem *better* evidence, or even just as good, but instead like something fraudulent, or tainted evidence.

Insofar as speech does occupy a privileged place in what we learn from other people, this sort of view seems to picture us as perversely preferring to increase our epistemic exposure, by placing ourselves at the mercy of the free disposition of another, according a privileged place to human speech, which is here construed as a kind of evidence that has been deliberately tampered with. On the 'evidential' reconstruction of testimony, speech functions as no more than a very possibly misleading way of learning the speaker's beliefs. Other things being equal, some more direct way of learning would be better; and *in particular* we should prefer any way of learning the speaker's beliefs that was not wholly dependent on his overt, deliberate revelation of them. Anything that necessarily involved his free action in this way, and thus brought with it the possibility of deliberate deceit, could only be a *less* reliable way of learning his beliefs than some otherwise comparable way that involved going behind his back (mind-reading, brain-scans, private observation of his behavior). If speech is seen as a form of *evidence*, then once its intentional character is recognized (that is, not just as intentional behavior, but intentional with respect to inducing a particular belief) we need an account of how it could count as anything more than *doctored* evidence.

ASSERTION AS ASSURANCE

Let us contrast this view with another picture of how what another person tells me may contribute to my belief, a picture that *will* give central place to the act of saying something and the response of believing or disbelieving the person. On a genuinely non-Humean account, when someone tells me it's cold out I don't simply gain an awareness of his beliefs, I am also given his *assurance* that it's cold out. This is something I could not have gained by the private observation of his behavior. When someone gives me his assurance that it's cold out he explicitly assumes a certain responsibility for what I believe. What this provides me with is different in kind, though not necessarily in degree of certainty, from beliefs I might have read off from his behavior, just as what I gain from his declaration of intention differs from the firm expectation I may form from knowing his habits. On the evidential picture, by contrast, the speaker's assurance as such just clouds the issue, since all the verbal expression of assurance can do is interpose an additional piece of (possibly misleading) evidence between me and what I really want to know. I now have some more behavior to interpret, verbal this time, which brings with it special new possibilities for being misled. From my role as interpreter of others, my ultimate destination is the truth about the world, but often I must pass through the beliefs of another person as my only (fallible) access to this truth. And now relying on what he deliberately *says* provides me with at best a distinctively fallible way of learning what his beliefs *are*.

On both views, when I take someone's word for something I am peculiarly dependent on the will or discretion of the speaker, in a way that I would not be in the situation of interpreting the evidence of his behavior. But they view this dependence differently. On the Assurance view, going behind his back to learn his beliefs would not be better, or even just as good. Rather, it is essential to the distinctive reason for belief that I get from assertion that it proceeds from something freely undertaken by the other person. Only as a free declaration does it have that value for me. Evidence, by contrast, is not dependent on presentation in this way. A phenomenon will count as evidence however it came about, whether by natural causes or by someone's deliberate action, or just as easily by his inadvertence or carelessness. But nothing can count as someone's assurance that was not freely presented as such, just as talking in one's sleep cannot count as making an assertion or a promise.[10] The two views, then, oppose each other most directly over this issue of the role of the speaker's freedom, and the hearer's dependence on it. On the evidential view, dependence on the freedom of the other person just saddles us with an additional set of risks; now we have to worry not only about misleading (natural) evidence, but deliberate distortion as well. On the assurance view, dependence on someone's freely assuming responsibility for the truth of P, presenting himself as a kind of guarantor, provides me with a characteristic reason to believe, different in kind from anything provided by evidence alone.

In the remainder of this paper, I want to sketch out a defense of the alternative picture above, and explore the case for denying that human testimony should be thought of as providing the same sort of reason for belief that ordinary evidence does. A guiding question will be: As hearers faced with the question of believing what we are told, how are we to understand the nature of our dependence on the free assertion of the speaker, and how does this dependence affect the question of whether our epistemic relation to what is said is ultimately an evidential one?

In a ground-breaking paper on the central questions of testimony, Angus Ross (1986) begins by raising the question of whether it makes sense in general to treat what people say as a form of evidence, and he explicitly relates this question to the fact that speaking is a voluntary act. I have some differences with how he understands this relation, but the general line of thought seems to me deeply right and worth developing. Let me begin with a moderately lengthy quotation from the early pages of Ross's article.[11]

The main problem with the idea that the hearer views the speaker's words as evidence arises from the fact that, unlike the examples of natural signs which spring most readily to mind, saying something is a deliberate act under the speaker's conscious control and the hearer is aware that this is the case. The problem is not that of whether the hearer can in these circumstances see the speaker's words as *good* evidence; it is a question of whether the notion of evidence is appropriate here at all. There is, of course, nothing odd about the idea of deliberately presenting an audience with evidence in order to get them to draw a desired conclusion, as when a photograph is produced in court. But in such a case what is presented is, or is presented as being, evidence independently of the fact of the presenter having chosen to present it. If a speaker's words are evidence of anything, they have that status only because he has chosen to use them. Speaking is not like allowing someone to see you are blushing. The problem is not, however, that the fact of our having chosen to use certain words *cannot* be evidence for some further conclusion. Our choices can certainly be revealing. The difficulty lies in supposing that the speaker himself sees his choice of words in this light, which in turn makes it difficult to suppose that this is how the hearer is intended to see his choice. (Ross 1986: 72)

First of all, it should be noted that Ross's target, like mine, is not the class of all speech acts, nor even the class of all *assertoric* speech acts. Not everything done in speech, not even everything done with sentences in the declarative mood, involves the specific relations of telling and being believed. Assertions are also made in the context of argument and demonstration, for instance, where there is no assumption within the discourse that the speaker is to be believed on his say-so.[12] In such a situation the speaker is not expecting to be *believed*, but is attempting to provide independent convincing reasons for the truth of his view, or laying out the steps of a proof. *Telling* someone something is not simply giving expression to what's on your mind, but is making a statement with the understanding that here it is your word that is to be relied on. It is a common enough understanding, and commonly justified, but it is not one in place in such contexts as persuasion, argumentation, or demonstration. For different reasons it is also not the understanding of the speech of a person in the context of therapeutic treatment, in the oral examination of a pupil, or in the police interrogation of a suspect. Such discourses will contain *statements* of various kinds, but they may be received by the interlocutor in a very different spirit, as evidence for truth of a very different kind from the overt subject of the subject's statement. This again is quite different from the exchange of information through telling and being told in everyday life. (And on the picture of speech to be developed here, these other discourses emerge as ultimately dependent on the central discourse of telling.)

Having said that, however, how is seeing one's own utterance as evidence supposed to be incompatible with seeing my utterance as a voluntary act of mine, in Ross's words seeing it as up to me what I shall say? He notes that there is nothing in the idea of evidence itself which is inconsistent with a person's deliberately presenting something as such, as when a photograph is introduced as evidence. And, it should also be noted, an item like a photograph can serve as good evidence even when it was not only deliberately *presented*, but also deliberately *produced* so as to lead one to a particular conclusion. So why cannot the speaker have essentially the same relation to his own words, as something he deliberately produces and presents to serve as evidence for some conclusion (and hence to bring the hearer to some desired belief)? Part of the answer Ross gives lies in the following view. Seeing the utterance as evidence would involve seeing it as the outcome of some general empirical law, the sort of 'reliable correlation' Hume has in mind, connecting the making of the statement with the obtaining of the facts in question. Ross acknowledges that I may see the words of others or my own *past* words in this light, but

> What I cannot do is see the words I now choose to utter in that light, for I cannot at one and the same time see it as up to *me* what I shall say and see my choice [. . .] as determined or constrained by facts about my own nature. (Ross 1986: 73)

Such a stance toward one's own utterances may be barely possible, he says, but it is hardly compatible with taking responsibility for those acts. While the emphasis on responsibility is important, I don't think this part of Ross's response leads in the right direction. For, as far as 'reliable correlations' go, why could I not see my own utterance as securely linked with the truth, not in virtue of my being determined by the facts of my own nature, but in virtue of my own free but unswerving commitment to the truth? The sort of reliability my Humean interlocutor wants to count on does not abolish my freedom. I can present myself to myself and others as *reliable* in various ways, without that meaning that my reliability is a *constraint* to which I am passively subject. My utterance is a voluntary act of mine, something I take responsibility for, and *part* of what I take responsibility for is its correlation with the truth. So it seems it cannot be because I see my utterance as freely chosen that it cannot be taken either by myself or my audience as evidence for the truth.

However, there is another strand in what Ross is saying here that clarifies the role of the speaker's freedom and its clash with the idea of evidence. In the first passage quoted he says that something like a photograph will be evidence independently of the fact of the presenter having chosen to present it; whereas by contrast,

> If a speaker's words are evidence of anything, they have that status only because he has chosen to use them.

Strictly speaking, this last statement is not quite right, as we've already briefly seen. If we've agreed that in various contexts a person's words *can* be treated as evidence, then this need not be dependent on the speaker's having *chosen* to use them. If my analyst can adopt a symptomatic stance toward my more conscious and deliberate statements, then he may make similar revealing inferences from my botched utterances, slips of the tongue, as well as the words I may utter under hypnosis, or while talking in my sleep. Speaking *is* a form of behavior, after all, and human behavior is infinitely interpretable, infinitely revealing, in ways that are not at the disposal of the person to determine their meaning. One's words can be evidence when not *chosen* at all, revealing like a cry of pain; or they can be evidence against one's intent, as when someone's tone of voice reveals that he's lying. What *is* true, however, but still in need of defense here, is that a statement only provides the kind of reason for belief that *testimony* does if it is understood to be something freely and consciously undertaken by the speaker. It is with respect to *this* sort of reason for belief that we, as hearers or readers, are *essentially* dependent on the free disposal of the speaker or writer. Thus, if the idea is that something is evidence, or is being treated as evidence, when it is a reason for belief independently of whether it was intentionally produced or presented as such, we need a fuller characterization of the kind of 'independence' that pertains to the category of evidence, and defense of the idea that testimony as such provides reason for belief that is *not* independent of assumptions involving the freedom of the speaker.

PHOTOGRAPHS AND STATEMENTS

It is here that Ross's passing contrast between our epistemic relations to photographs and speakers is worth developing in some detail. There are many ways in which what we see and what we believe may be dependent on what others do, say, or show to us. In my direct experience of a footprint, I may be dependent not only on the person who made it, but also perhaps on someone who drew it to my attention. And when my epistemic relation to it is mediated by another person in these ways, I am subject to the ordinary risks of distortion, since in principle any evidence may be tampered with. But even with these particular risks and dependencies, my relation to the footprint is still a perceptual one, and does not involve me in the specific relation of believing another person. And this is so even if my perception of it is technologically mediated in ways that involve the doings and expertise of other people. In discussing the nature of photographic realism, Kendall Walton (1984) compares what we see in photographs with what we see through a microscope or in a mirror, to argue for the claim that in all three cases we actually *see* the thing in question, even though this seeing is mediated in various ways, and even though photographs can be doctored in various ways.[13] Real *experience* of a thing may also be mediated or subject to various epistemic risks, without that abolishing the difference between being told about it and experiencing it oneself. As Walton points out, what I see directly when someone points out the window may also be altered in various ways to deceive, but that doesn't transform the situation from perception to depiction. In Walton's terms, a photograph can be 'transparent' to the scene it depicts in part because, unlike the case of a drawing, what we see here is not essentially dependent on what the photographer thinks is there in the photograph. As with a telescope, we may 'see through' the photograph to the scene itself.

In this regard, consider the case of the photographer in Antonioni's movie *Blow Up* (1966). He takes some pictures in the park of a woman and a man, and then later discovers that one of his shots apparently shows the man's corpse lying in the bushes. This is not what he saw or believed at the time, but it is what he sees now. Still, the photograph he took is evidence, of the most ordinary kind, for the fact that this man has been killed. And it is evidence for this regardless of the photographer's beliefs about the matter. That is, it would be evidence even if he positively *dis*believed what it shows, or even if he took the photograph and showed it to someone with the deliberate intent to deceive. Its status as evidence is wholly independent of his beliefs or intentions. And it is for that reason that his *own* relation to the photograph can be an evidential one, like a detective or other investigator. When he gets home he crops and enlarges and studies his photograph in order to see more deeply into what it shows, to convince himself that the corpse on the grass is really there. In this way his own epistemic relation to the photograph he took is the same as that of the friend he shows it to later. They can both learn from it, or doubt what it shows. The situation would be quite different if he were to have made a sketch of what he saw in the park, or taken some notes on what he observed there. It would be absurd for him take his sketch home and blow up *it* to examine more closely what it shows about the man in the park. And were he to show his sketch or his notes to another person to convince him about the man in the park, he would be offering him a very different kind of reason to believe what happened. If he shows his friend a sketch of a corpse lying in the grass, and this is to be a reason for him to believe there *was* such a corpse, his friend has to assume such things as that the sketch was not made with an intent to deceive, that the person who made it was observing things accurately and not liable to error, and even that the aim of the sketch was an accurate picture and not an imaginary scene, etc. In short, the beliefs and intentions of the person who made the sketch are crucial for its status as a reason to believe anything about what was there in the park. Without those assumptions, the sketch does not become *poorer* evidence; it ceases to be evidence of any kind, or any other reason to believe. It's just a piece of paper, and any correlation with the facts in the park could only be by the merest chance.

So how does the issue of freedom figure in here, in a way that distinguishes the case of verbal testimony? After all, the photographer freely takes his picture, and then may freely present it to another person as a reason for believing a man has been killed. How is this different from his friend's relation to his verbal report of what he saw? So far we have seen the following difference. The status of the photograph as a reason to believe something does not depend on the photographer's own attitude toward it as evidence. It depends only on the camera's ability to record the scene, which need not involve any choice or consciousness on the part of the photographer at all. (The exposure could have been made by a remote timing device.) As such the photograph can serve for him as an independent correction of his impression of the scene, in a way that his drawing cannot. It is for this reason that when he looks at his photograph with his friend, they both stand in the same epistemic relation to it; confronting it as independent, public, evidence, and trying to discern its import.

By contrast, the *speaker's* choice enters in essentially to the fact that his utterance counts at all as a reason for belief. The point is not that his utterance is voluntarily produced, for that in itself has no epistemic significance, and does not distinguish the case from that of the photographer. Rather the point is that the speaker, in presenting his utterance as an *assertion*, one with the force of *telling* the audience something, presents himself as *accountable* for the truth of what he says, and in doing so he offers a kind of guarantee for this truth. This shows up in the fact that if we are inclined to believe what the speaker says, but then learn that he is *not*, in fact, presenting his utterance as an assertion whose truth he stands behind, then what remains is just words, not a reason to believe anything. We misunderstood the intent of Professor Higgins when we heard him say something about the rain in Spain, and now upon realizing this, the utterance as phenomenon loses the epistemic import we thought it had (whatever knowledge we may indeed take him to have about such matters). By contrast, if we learn that the photographer is not, in fact, presenting his photograph as true record of what occurred in the park, the photograph as document retains all the epistemic value for us it ever had.

THE IMPORTANCE OF BEING NON-NATURAL

Still, one might ask, why speak of the audience's dependence on the freedom of the speaker, rather than simply refer to their dependence on what the speaker has (freely) *done*? The reason is that the relevant speaker's responsibility is not simply his responsibility for the *existence* of some phenomenon, in the sense that he is the one who deliberately produced these spoken words. Rather, he is more centrally responsible for those words *having* any particular epistemic status. What is the difference, then, between the speaker's role in *providing* something (his utterance) with a particular epistemic status, and the role of someone like a photographer who *produces* something *with* a certain epistemic import?

It is here, I think, that a consideration of Paul Grice's original 1957 paper 'Meaning' proves helpful. The relation of evidence, one phenomenon's being an indication of something else, is the central form of what Grice calls 'natural meaning'. Natural meaning is not something at the disposal of the speaker to confer or revoke, but is a matter of the independent obtaining of causal relations in the world (e.g., the way smoke means fire, or doesn't). Nonetheless, persons belong to this same natural world and may thus produce or exhibit various evidential phenomena, and employ them to get some point across (e.g., pointing to the smoke pouring out of the oven). But spoken words typically bear a different relation to the facts. In his 1957 article, Grice is primarily concerned to delineate the conditions for something he calls "non-natural meaning", or MeaningNN. This project famously evolved into an attempt to ground the notions of the meaning of an expression in a language in the complex intentions had by utterers of expressions on occasions of use; and, presented as a non-circular account of either word-meaning or sentence-meaning, it was progressively refined into baroque complexity under the pressure of counter-examples. However, the interest and importance of the original account of non-natural meaning is not exhausted by the prospects for an intention-based semantics of the sort he proposed. What he isolates under the title of 'non-natural meaning' is a central form of intersubjective dependence, one that is indeed paradigmatically linguistic, but not restricted to linguistic communication.

A striking thing about the essay is how the technical notion of non-natural meaning is introduced by contrast with natural meaning, as if this were an antecedently intuitive notion, one whose definition we could progressively refine by consulting our intuitions about a series of well-crafted cases and asking ourselves whether we should call *that* a case of non-natural meaning. We are given hints, of course, by way of both similarity and contrast with more familiar notions like that of conventional meaning, but Grice's target notion only emerges through the consideration of the cases devised and presented. The cases themselves all have a similar form in that in all of them one person does something which either succeeds or not in inducing another person to some belief P. This common *telos* to the cases invites two related questions. Since the end-point of each of these encounters is that one person ends up with a new belief, we might look at the progression of cases from an epistemological point of view and ask what it is that brings the person at the receiving end to this new belief, what reason he may take himself to have been given for adopting it, and why the particular kind of reason Grice's account of non-natural meaning zeros in on should be of special significance, either epistemologically or otherwise. It is not, of course, as if the other ways of inducing belief, disqualified as candidates for the non-natural, are thought to be insufficiently grounded. Salome certainly acquired justified belief about the fate of John the Baptist by seeing his head presented on a charger, however this may fall short as a case of non-natural meaning. Rather, the target notion of non-natural meaning is meant to capture a *way* of gaining a reason to believe something that is importantly different from others and that we have special reason to be concerned with, both as purveyors and receivers of such reasons. So the first question is: what is special about the reason for belief associated with non-natural meaning? And secondly, as the proposed definition of non-natural meaning is progressively refined in Grice's essay, what pre-theoretical notion is supposed to be guiding our intuitions along the way, so that we can feel conviction about a range of cases that seem to fall more or less squarely in the category? Here Grice is more explicit, since by way of explaining the distinction that matters to him, and why something like the case of Herod's presentation to Salome does *not* count as non-natural meaning, he says, "What we want to find is the difference between, for example, 'deliberately and openly letting someone know' and 'telling' and between 'getting someone to think' and 'telling' " (Grice 1957, in Strawson 1967: 44). So it is the ordinary notion of *telling* someone something, *that* way of inducing belief, that is to play a guiding role in determining which cases satisfy the philosophical notion of non-natural meaning, and Grice's distinction between natural and non-natural meaning can be seen as motivated by a concern with the difference between *telling* a person that P and other ways of bringing him to that same knowledge, such as providing him with evidence for P (evidence that may be accidental or contrived, openly displayed or inadvertently revealed).

As examples of 'deliberately and openly letting someone know' some fact, Grice cites such cases as that of showing someone a compromising photograph, or leaving the china my daughter has broken lying around for my wife to see.[14] In these cases, the phenomenon in question has some independent evidential significance, even though the person may be responsible either for drawing attention to it (the broken china), or actually producing it (the photograph). Their independent significance shows up in the fact that the photograph or the china would have functioned as a reason for the belief in question without anyone's intervention or presentation, even if only stumbled upon accidentally.

By contrast, in cases of 'telling' or 'non-natural meaning', the person (hereafter the 'speaker') plays quite a different role in bringing his audience to believe something. Here, as is well known, a crucial role is played in Grice's account by the recognition of the speaker's intention. Examining this role will help clarify the specific 'dependence on the freedom of the speaker' that I'm claiming is characteristic of the relation of testimony, and which distinguishes it from a relation of evidence.

Following Grice's progression then: a handkerchief left at the scene of the crime may throw suspicion on someone and perhaps lead to genuine belief in his guilt. But as a piece of evidence it would induce that belief whether or not it were left there intentionally, and non-natural meaning (and 'telling', surely) must at least be the upshot of something intentionally done. Further, it should be part of non-natural meaning that the intention to induce a particular belief is *manifest* to the person on the receiving end, and not like artfully planted evidence designed to steer him toward the desired conclusion. Further still, this belief-inducing intention must not simply be *known* to the audience, something he pieces together despite the speaker's best efforts at concealment; rather the speaker must fully expect and intend that his intention will be manifest to his audience. In this way, the audience can appreciate that another person is openly playing a role in directing him to learn something, by presenting a piece of evidence for them both to see and assess. This makes this knowledge, or at least this awareness of the evidence, 'mutual' between them, and hence available as an object of cognitive and communicative cooperation between them. However, this is not yet non-natural meaning, since these conditions are fulfilled when Herod presents the head of St John to Salome, or when the compromising photograph is flourished. Here, although the audience has been directly and openly led to some belief, she has not been *told* anything. Rather, Salome has been shown something and reliably left to draw her own conclusions. Herod manifests a definite intention in bringing her this news, and he bears an obvious responsibility for Salome's altered state of belief. But there is yet another responsibility he does not assume here, which marks the difference between " 'deliberately and openly letting someone know' and 'telling' ", and this is shown in the fact that, while his intention regarding her belief is indeed manifest, it is inert as far as Salome's belief is concerned, just as it is when the person is shown a compromising photograph. It isn't doing any epistemological work of its own. Both people would draw essentially the same conclusions whether the evidence in question were deliberately and openly displayed to them or not. So we might say that Herod's epistemic responsibility for Salome's belief is merely contingent, like that of the person showing the photograph. In these cases they play a role in making a piece of evidence available to another person, but they are not responsible for it having the epistemic import it has.

For Grice, however, nothing can count as a case of non-natural meaning if the relevant belief could be expected to be produced whether or not the intention behind the action were recognized. The speaker must not only intend that the audience recognize his intention, but this recognition must itself *play a role* in inducing the belief in question, and that means that the recognition of the speaker's intention must not just as a matter of fact help to bring about the relevant belief, but must be *necessary* to its inducement. In this way we arrive at Grice's original formulation of non-natural meaning in his 1957 paper:

> A uttered x with the intention of inducing a belief by means of the recognition of this intention. (Grice 1957, in Strawson 1967: 45)

If the audience could not be expected to arrive at the intended belief *apart from* the recognition of the speaker's intention regarding that belief, the speaker must take upon himself the role of providing something with a particular epistemic import that it otherwise would not have, and in this way Grice sharply distinguishes non-natural meaning from the presentation of evidence. For any phenomenon with some independent evidential import will naturally be one which might well be expected to induce belief without the recognition of anyone's intention. That's just what it is for a phenomenon to be ordinary evidence for something else. To count as an instance of telling someone something, however, the speaker must present his action, his utterance, as being without epistemic significance apart from his explicit assumption of responsibility for that significance. In this way he announces that the reason for belief offered here is of a different kind from that stemming from externally obtaining evidential relations.

As Ross points out (1986: 75), from the point of view of the audience, considered as a reason for belief, the role of the recognition of intention is left somewhat mysterious here. The question is: just how does my recognizing that this speaker intends that I should believe P play a role in actually *getting* me to believe that P? If we compare this case with that of other things someone may want me to do it's clear that the mere recognition that he wants me to do X does not, in general, provide me with much of any reason at all for complying. Why should we be so much more compliant when we recognize that someone wishes us to *believe* something? How can the mere recognition of someone's intention be expected to induce belief?

When looked at in this way, recognition of the speaker's intention may seem inadequate to induce belief. It may also seem pointless, adding nothing of epistemic value to what the audience already has. Again, compare this with the picture of radical interpretation, according to which the epistemic significance of speech is that of an indication of the speaker's beliefs. Once I employ this scheme of interpretation to learn what the speaker believes, I am then in possession of knowledge of a certain set of facts, viz. the speaker's state of belief, which *does* have straightforward evidential value for me, quite independently of how or whether the fact of his believing is explicitly presented to me. The speaker's state of mind is phenomenon, which has the same independent evidential import for me, regardless of how I may have learned of it, and regardless of whether it was manifested deliberately or inadvertently. And, as we saw, this same scheme of interpretation can provide a basis for me to infer the likely *truth* of these beliefs, and so come to share them myself. I ascribe beliefs on the basis of his verbal behavior as I would from any other behavior, and in neither case do I rely on recognition of any *intention* to manifest his states of mind. And indeed, what could be the epistemic interest for me in learning of any such intention on his part? By hypothesis, I already know what he takes to be true, and I can now make of this knowledge what I will, deciding for myself whether this adds up to good reason for *me* to take his belief to be true. If his verbal behavior is evidence for his beliefs, then it doesn't *add* to my evidence as interpreter to learn that, in addition to his believing P, the speaker also has the intention that *I* should believe P too (and come to this belief on the basis of recognition of that very intention, etc.). From my side, either learning of his belief is, on balance, sufficient for me to believe P too, or it is not. Nothing further about his intentions, or just *how* he would like me to arrive at this belief, will be evidentially relevant for me at all. Or else, as before with the tainted evidence, learning that his belief was deliberately manifested now casts doubt on my ascription, because the evidence of his behavior is now contaminated by its aspect of performance.

What is needed is more direct focus on the speaker's *explicit presentation* of himself as providing a reason for belief. For it is *not*, in fact, the audience's mere *awareness* of the speaker's intention that is to provide a motivation for belief. If I simply *discovered* on my own that this person had the intention that I believe P, this need not count for me as a reason for belief at all. (Why cooperate with his designs on me, however benign?) The conditions given so far still have not accounted for any special importance to the overt act of *saying*, the explicit manifesting of one's intention, as opposed to simply doing something that allows one's intention to become known. If, unlike a piece of evidence, the speaker's words have no independent epistemic value as a phenomenon, then how do they *acquire* the status of a reason to believe something? It seems that this can only be by virtue of the speaker's there and then explicitly *presenting* his utterance as a reason to believe, with this presentation being accomplished in the act of assertion itself. The epistemic value of his words is something publicly conferred on them by the speaker, by presenting his utterance as an assertion. And indeed, it is *because* the speaker's words have no independent status as evidence that their contribution to the audience's belief must proceed through the recognition of the speaker's intention. Further, the intention seeking recognition must not simply be that the audience come to believe something, but must include the intention that the audience recognize the speaker's act of asserting as itself constituting a reason for belief. If it seems difficult to see how anything, even someone's words, could acquire some epistemic value through something like *conferral*, perhaps because this suggests something too arbitrary or ceremonial to constitute a genuine reason for belief, it should be remembered that for both parties this conferral is by its nature an overt assumption of specific responsibilities on the part of the speaker. This is no more (or less) mysterious than how an explicit agreement or contract alters one's responsibilities, actions which are also within the capacities of ordinary speakers. The speaker's intent then, is that for the audience, the very fact that this speaker is freely and explicitly presenting P as worthy of belief constitutes his speech as a reason to believe that P.

Of course, as with any public assumption of responsibility, the appropriate abilities and other background conditions must be assumed to be in place for it to amount to anything. For the speaker to be able to do this it must be assumed by both parties that the speaker does indeed satisfy the right conditions for such an act (e.g., that he possesses the relevant knowledge, trustworthiness, and reliability). These background conditions can themselves be construed as evidential, or at any rate not at the behest of the speaker to determine, but they are not themselves sufficient for giving any epistemic significance to the speaker's words, for the relevance of these conditions only comes into play once it is understood that a particular speech act is being performed with those words (i.e., an assertion or promise rather than something else). The speaker has to constitute his utterance as having this or that illocutionary force before the empirical background conditions can contribute anything to its epistemic significance. Hence the idea is not that the speaker's word's "all by themselves" should count as a reason for belief, or that the speaker's authority over the constitution of the particular speech act he is performing (e.g., as assertion rather than recitation), shoulders the epistemic burden all by itself. As with the explicit assumption of responsibility that goes with making a promise, its success will depend on the various conditions that go into the speaker's being in a position to take on any such responsibility, and which make for his public assumption's being anything for another person to count on. But in considering the speaker's words, the audience's belief in his knowledge and trustworthiness do not do him any epistemic good if it is still left open just *what* kind of action (if any) the speaker is presenting his utterance as. As far as relating to his words goes, the speaker's knowledge and trustworthiness is epistemically inert for the audience until the question of the particular speech act or illocution is settled. Determining his utterance as an assertion is what gets the speaker's words into the realm of epistemic assessment in the first place (or at least epistemic assessment of the sort that is relevant to testimony: we may indeed make evidential use of the words or inarticulate sounds made by someone asleep). And in this matter, the speaker and his audience are in essentially different relations to the epistemic import of the speaker's words. The speaker does not relate to the question whether his utterance is a committed assertion or not as something to be settled by evidence, because as a speaker of the language he plays an essential role in making it the case that his utterance is an assertion or not.

Hence Grice's original formulation needs some further refinement. The speaker intends not just that the recognition of his intention play a role in producing belief that P, but that the particular role this recognition should play is that of showing the speaker to be assuming responsibility for the status of his utterance as a reason to believe P. This addition is necessary since in principle there are all sorts of ways in which the recognition of intention could 'play a role' in producing belief, ways that would not capture what is meant by 'telling' or 'non-natural meaning', or the correlative notion of believing the speaker. One such way would be manifested in the familiar situations of 'double-bluffing' where, e.g., I tell you I'm traveling to Minsk, knowing you'll take me to be lying and attempting to conceal my plans to travel to Pinsk, and hence meaning to deceive you about my genuine plans to go to Minsk after all. Knowing all this about me, however, you see through the ruse and conclude that I'm indeed going to Minsk, just as I told you. Here the recognition of intention does indeed play an essential role in the belief arrived at, and the audience comes to believe that what I say is true, but this is not a case of believing the speaker.[15] And there are other possible ways in which the recognition of intention might play a role, even a necessary one, but of the wrong sort.

Grice is sensitive to an incompleteness here, when he suggests toward the end that it should somehow be built into the definition that the intended effect must be something which in some sense is within the control of the audience, or that in some sense of 'reason' the recognition of intention behind X is for the audience a reason and not merely a cause (Grice 1957 in Strawson 1967: 46). It is not the speaker's aim that the belief in question be produced by the audience's simply being so constituted that his awareness of the speaker's complex self-referential intention somehow produces the belief in him. That would fail in another way to describe the nature of the dependence on the person as such and the importance of mutual recognition. For the audience must not simply respond with belief, but must *understand* what the speaker is saying, and must understand what the speaker is *doing* in saying P, which is to say, purporting to present him with a reason for P. And the audience must believe P *because* he understands what the speaker is saying and what he is doing in saying it. In addition, and crucially, the audience must take this entire understanding to be *shared* by himself and the speaker. That is, he takes himself to be responding to just the kind of reason for belief that the speaker is presenting himself as offering (which is why cases of "double-bluffing" are not cases of believing the speaker).

Any of the 'proto-Gricean' ways of producing belief, the cases leading up to the full definition of non-natural meaning, provide us with something mediating between the audience and the speaker, something other than the person as such that is being depended on. Believing the speaker, on the other hand, involves accepting the offer to rely on *him*, and not something connected with him or as a consequence of what he has done. This direct dependence on the speaker's offer of responsibility is what is expressed in the 'hereby' that is implied, and sometimes explicitly stated, in illocutions such as 'telling', 'warning', or 'accepting', for it is in this very presentation of himself that the speaker assumes responsibility for the audience's belief.[16] The implied 'hereby' is thus also an expression of the self-referentiality of the Gricean formula, for it declares that it is dependence on the person as such, and not on something else he might point to, that is solicited in saying that he *hereby* tells his audience that P.[17] In this way we can see the progressive refinements of Grice's definition of non-natural meaning as each aimed at laying bare the reliance of the audience on the other person as such. The belief is to be produced not simply by the speaker's action, or by his intention, or by the audience's awareness of his intention, or anything else outside their encounter. Just as the audience could treat the handkerchief or the photograph as evidence for P, and thus without trusting the speaker for the truth of P, so he could treat the speaker's action or intention as a similar kind of evidence without trusting the speaker, without his belief that P involving dependence on the person of the speaker as such.

When Grice says that the belief in question should be "something which in some sense is within the control of the audience", or that it should function as a reason for him and not a mere cause, this is not meant to suggest that the audience complies with the speaker's intention as a kind of favor, adopting the belief on request (as Ross notes, 1986: 74). But it does serve to clarify the kind of role that is to be played by the mutual recognition of the speaker's intention, how that can matter epistemically to the audience in the way suggested by Grice's progressive refinements of the account of non-natural meaning. The account of this role suggested by the Assurance view is that the mutual recognition of intention can play the role for the audience of providing him with a reason for belief, because he sees the speaker as presenting himself as accountable for the truth of P, and asking, through the recognition of his intention, that this offer of his assurance be accepted. And it is understood by both parties that this acceptance is something which the audience is free to give or refuse. The speaker is asking that a certain authority of his be acknowledged; the authority to invest his utterance with a particular epistemic import, and this investment occurs by his explicit assumption of responsibility for his utterance's being a reason for belief. This is the role for the recognition of intention that the speaker is asking for. And, I would argue, it is *only* such a role that could account for how, in the case of speech, the recognition of intention *enhances* rather than detracts from the epistemic status of the phenomenon (utterance), reveals it to be something other than doctored evidence.

The idea of assertion as providing reason for belief through the explicit assumption of responsibility for the truth of what is said accounts for a number of contrasts between belief through testimony and belief through confronting evidence. It points the way to understanding how the recognition of intention can play a positive role, rather than see it as something that is either epistemically irrelevant or undermining to the evidential value of the utterance. Further, a specific assumption of responsibilities is essentially an expression of a person's freedom, something that only makes sense as consciously assumed. It is for this reason that words spoken during sleep, or under hypnosis, do not have the value of testimony, because they do not count as *assertions*, whatever expressive psychological value they might still retain as evidence. Like a promise or an apology, something only counts as a person's assertion when consciously presented as such by him.[18]

Promises and apologies, like acts of telling someone something, can be more or less reflective, more or less deliberate, done more or less voluntarily or under duress. Reference to the speaker's assumption of responsibility for the truth of what he says is not meant to deny that much of our speech is spontaneous and unreflective, or that much of what we acquire from the speech of others is more or less passively absorbed. 'Telling' also includes telling something by mistake, to the wrong person, or just blurting something out when we meant to keep silent. We express our freedom not only in our considered actions, but also in the actions that go wrong, or are forced upon us, and the outbursts that we immediately regret. Blurting something out when you meant to keep silent is still a different matter from either talking in one's sleep, or having the utterance of those words be produced by electrical stimulation of the cortex. And the epistemic significance for the audience is entirely different in the two kinds of cases: in relating to the words produced by electrical stimulation we *may* learn something, but what we learn need not be dependent on such assumptions as, e.g., whether the person had any understanding of the words themselves, or any sense that he was providing anyone with a reason to believe something. These assumptions, however, are still indispensable to the understanding of the words that escape us or are forced from us, and they express the role of the person as such in providing a reason. This is confirmed by the fact that both speaker and audience relate to the blurting out differently than they would to the cases of talking in one's sleep or through electrical stimulation. In the latter case, the speaker would not *regret* what he said or try to make amends; in a sense what happened didn't involve *him* at all.[19] And for that matter, a person may also *lie* spontaneously or out of panic as well as tell the truth. But surely the description of a person telling a lie makes reference to such things as the intention, whether conscious or not, to exploit the trust of one's audience and present oneself as providing them with a reason for belief. At the same time, it is consistent with the Assurance view to think of assertions and tellings as something like the default assumption for indicative sentences in the declarative mood. It requires more, rather than less, sophisticated intentions to utter 'The rain in Spain falls mainly on the plain' and *not* mean it as an assertion. And so, barring any special reason to think otherwise, we may be entitled to treat an utterance of an indicative sentence as an assertion of it.[20] But in a given case we may be wrong about this, and it remains true that what settles the question about the status of the utterance is whether or not the speaker is presenting it as true.

THE SPEAKER'S CONFERRAL: HAVING YOUR SAY, GIVING YOUR WORD

We are now in a position to clarify the problem Ross suggested with the idea of a speaker presenting his utterance *as* evidence for his audience. The problem is not that the speaker's words could not be *taken* as evidence by his audience. In principle, anything said or done by the speaker can be given a symptomatic reading. Nor is it true that the speaker could not privately *intend* that his words be taken as evidence. This would be the intention for many cases of deceit or more everyday manipulation, for instance. In a given case, my primary aim may be for my listener to draw the conclusion that I'm being scrupulously candid or self-revealing, and I accomplish this by confessing some minor fault of mine. Here, I am not *telling* anyone of my candor, giving my word on it (whatever good that would do), but rather doing something (in this case: saying something) that I hope will be taken as evidence for it. When it is a question of *non*-natural meaning, by contrast, the speaker is not relying on evidential relations alone to get his point across, but rather is counting on the explicit presentation of his intention to be the very thing which *makes* his words a reason for believing something in the first place. The recognition of his intention could only function this way if it was seen to be his assurance of the truth in question, his explicit assumption of responsibility for the truth of what he says. By contrast, the presentation of his utterance *as* evidence would be an implicit denial of this responsibility, breaking the link between the proposition he is giving his backing to and the belief he is hoping to induce, in which case there's no question of believing *him*. Thus for the speaker to present his word *as* evidence would be for him to present it as a reason to believe, while suspending the guarantee that gives it the epistemic significance of testimony in the first place. This is the problem Ross is pointing to.[21]

And as we have seen, to present something as evidence is to present it as having its epistemic value independent of one's own beliefs about it, or one's presentation of it, or the conferral of some status upon it. To offer some phenomenon as evidence is to present it as belief-worthy independent of the fact of one's presenting it as belief-worthy. When we present something as evidence for someone, we are inviting that person to 'see for himself', to find it convincing as we do. And we are prepared to offer reasons why it should be convincing, reasons independent of our simply *claiming*, once again, that it is belief-worthy. To present something as evidence is to be in a position to *report* that it is a reason for belief, and to be in this position one must be presenting that claim of belief-worthiness as having a basis in fact that is independent of one's reporting itself. A photograph has such an independent epistemic basis, independent of anyone's conferral. As a phenomenon, it counts as a reason for belief independently of anything concerning how the photographer may conceive it or present it. Because of this independence, its epistemic status is something the photographer himself may *discover* about it, or speculate about. His relation to this question is in principle no different from anyone else's. He may, of course, happen to know something about how it was produced that we don't know, and which may affect its epistemic status. But he may not know anything of the sort, and conversely we might know more about it than he does. He marshals the same kinds of reasons as any other viewer in considering the question of what beliefs the photograph may provide a basis for.

But the speaker's relation to the epistemic status of his own assertion *is* different from anyone else's. For the speaker, it is not a matter of observation or speculation whether he is indeed presenting his utterance as something with the force of a committed assertion, and were he somehow unclear about this, then to that degree his utterance would be something less than a committed assertion. He may inquire into his own reliability, truthfulness, and command of the facts, but the status of his utterance as assertion is a matter of what he is then and there prepared to invest it with. It has been noted by more than one philosopher that the relation of 'believing someone' does not have a reflexive form; it is not a relation a person can bear to himself.[22] The problem with this, we can now say, is the problem with the idea of a person offering and accepting an epistemic guarantee from himself, which would require him to be simultaneously in command of and at the mercy of his own freedom. This is another basic feature of testimony not captured by an evidential perspective on it. Speaker and audience do not confront the utterance as a phenomenon with an independent or natural epistemic status which they could assess in the same spirit, for the speaker does not confront his own assertion as a *phenomenon* at all, but as an issue of his commitment. To speak of 'conferral' of epistemic status is intended to register the fact that to count an utterance as, e.g., an assurance or a promise just is to count it as something presented with a particular epistemic status, the status of a reason for some belief (as contrasted with the status, say, of recitation or ironic mimicry). To count as a competent speaker of a language is to be recognized as having definitive 'say' over which illocution one's utterance counts as, whether as informative assertion, or as promise or apology, whether as a mere recitation or as a claim expressing one's commitment. An utterance counts as an assertion or an apology just in case the speaker presents it as such to his audience, in the appropriate context where his audience can be expected to recognize what it is being offered. The speaker cannot count as having promised or asserted something if he had no such intention, or if he did not present his utterance to be seen as a promise or assertion, whereas the evidential import of what he says and does is independent of such conditions.

The speaker's authority to determine the illocutionary status of his utterance is the authority he has to present himself as accountable for the performance of some speech act. This is not a matter of discovery for the speaker, something he could investigate or report on, as he might with respect to the evidential status of something. When it is a question of the evidential status of something, even something the person himself has done, he and his interlocutors are on an equal footing with respect to establishing its standing as a reason for belief. A person does not speak with any special authority about the evidential significance of his actions, including his verbal ones. By contrast, the authority to present oneself as 'hereby' assuming certain responsibilities in speech makes the speaker's epistemic position irreducibly different from that of his audience. For him the import of his words is not an independently obtaining fact, something he has his own opinion about, but is directly dependent on the import he is then and there prepared to invest them with. And it is internal to the notion of the speaker's authority to confer illocutionary status on his utterance that he also has the exclusive authority to cancel or revoke such status. Words can be retracted, apologies or warnings taken back, but only by the speaker himself. At the same time, he has no authority to determine, much less cancel, the evidential import of anything he has said or done, not even of his retraction itself.

When all goes well, in testimony a speaker gives his audience a reason to believe something, but unlike other ways of influencing the beliefs of others, in this case the reason the audience is provided with is seen by both parties as dependent on the speaker's making himself accountable, conferring a right of complaint on his audience should his claim be false. Whether this counts as a good or sufficient reason for belief is *not* a matter of the speaker's illocutionary authority, but will depend both on his sincerity and on his having discharged his epistemic responsibilities with respect to the belief in question.[23] But his presentation of his utterance as having this particular illocutionary force *is* what makes it candidate for epistemic assessment in the first place, and determines what kind of reason for just what proposition his audience is being presented with.

This way of looking at testimony makes much of the fact that in its central instances speech is an action addressed *to* another person, and that in testimony in particular the kind of reason for belief that is presented is one that functions in part by binding speaker and audience together, and altering the normative relationship between them. It doesn't follow from this, however, that someone outside that normative relationship can't avail himself of it and thereby acquire a reason to believe the same thing. If one person gives his word on something to another, whether as promise or assertion, someone overhearing this may derive a sufficient reason to believe, say that the speaker will in fact do what he promised or that what he asserted is true. And the overhearer improves his epistemic situation in this way, without entering into the altered normative relationship of the two parties involved in giving and accepting of words. He has not himself been *told* anything, much less promised anything, and no right of complaint has been conferred upon him.[24] To say this much, however, does not provide a reason to assimilate his situation to that of someone confronting a piece of evidence, or suggest that the speaker's illocutionary and epistemic responsibilities aren't playing a genuinely epistemic role here. For even though the statement was not addressed *to him*, the overhearer is still in a different position from that of someone confronting a piece of evidence like a photograph or a footprint. It still makes a difference to his epistemic relation to the overheard report that he is responding to something whose epistemic significance is not independent in the way of a photograph or footprint, but is inherited from the speaker's assuming responsibility for the truth (and meaning) of what he says. This is so even if, as we might say, that responsibility was undertaken with respect to another person and not himself.

Naturally there is a certain vagueness as to just what situations will count as overhearing, and in a given case the addressee may be a group of people. Nonetheless, while the overhearer may get a reason to believe without having the right to complaint that is conferred on the addressee, the fact that the overhearer of the assertion acquires any reason to believe from listening to these words is dependent on them being addressed to someone, with the force of assuming responsibility and thereby conferring a right of complaint. The overhearer of testimony is not in the same normative relation to the speaker as the addressee is, but his gaining any reason to believe is dependent on such a conferral having been given to someone. Without that, the question of what speech act, if any, is being performed with these words would not be settled, and hence the overhearer could not get started on assessing their epistemic significance. (Imagine overhearing someone say "The rain in Spain falls mainly on the plain". Until you know what speech act, if any, is being performed here, you don't know if considerations of reliability or trustworthiness are even relevant to the status of the words as source of knowledge about the weather in Spain.) So, while in both cases (promising and telling), the overhearer can gain a reason to believe something without entering into the normative relation of promisor-promisee or teller-believer, in the overhearing of testimony he only gains a reason to believe something because such a relationship *has* been established by the original speaker and addressee.

This, then, is how I suggest we understand Ross's claim that the evidential view is inconsistent with the kind of reason for belief offered in everyday human testimony. In telling his audience something the speaker does not present his utterance as something with the force of evidence because that would be to present his words as having their specific epistemic import apart from his assurance, and the responsibility he thereby assumes. And in obscuring the speaker's responsibility, such a stance would also obscure the nature of the audience's dependence on him. For if it were a matter of evidence then in principle we would both be on an equal footing with respect to establishing its epistemic import. But this equity does not obtain with respect to someone's words, where it is up to the speaker alone to determine whether they are to count as an assertion or other committed speech act.

EVIDENCE AND DISHARMONY

The two broad views about testimony which I've been calling the Evidential View and the Assurance View are in no disagreement over the status of an assertion or a promise as essentially the action of a free agent. Both views are clear that speaking is a voluntary activity, and that the speech of others has *that* kind of significance in our lives. Where they differ is in how that freedom is related to the status of the utterance as a reason to believe. For on the Assurance view, it is not just that a particular free action is seen to have some epistemic import, but rather that the epistemic import of what he does is dependent on the speaker's attitude toward his utterance and presentation of it in a certain spirit, whereas by contrast, it is in the nature of genuinely evidential relations that they are not subject to anyone's conferral or revocation. It might still be asked, however, whether it doesn't still all come down to evidential relations in the end. The following reconstruction may be offered: Yes, the speaker freely assumes responsibility for the truth of what he asserts. But now this very act of assurance is a *fact*, which the audience confronts as evidence (of some degree of strength) for the truth of what has been asserted. Speech is acknowledged to be importantly different from other (indicatively) expressive behavior, but the audience's relation to it, as a reason to believe something, can only be evidential.

The claim of the Assurance view, however, is not that an assertion could not be treated purely as evidence. It is always possible to treat anything a person says or does as constituting further evidence for one thing or another, and there is no level at which this somehow becomes impossible. The point instead is that refusing to acknowledge any epistemic stance toward the speaker's words other than as evidence means that speaker and audience must always be in disharmony with each other, for in the contexts of telling, promising, and apologizing the speaker is not *presenting* his utterance as evidence. And it is internal to the speech acts of, e.g., telling or thanking that they are not presented as evidence for one's belief or gratitude. To present one's utterance as evidence would be to do something other than to tell, promise, or apologize.

This claim may seem paradoxical. On the Assurance view, the making of an assertion can be treated as evidence, can properly *be* evidence for various things, but the practice cannot coherently be described as the *offering* of evidence. But how could this be? If the speaker recognizes that his asserting can be, or even just *is*, evidence for the truth of the very proposition asserted, then how could there be anything amiss with him presenting it *as* something (viz. evidence) that he sees it legitimately *is*? But this general possibility for self-defeat should not be surprising. To allay the sense of paradox here, compare the assurance given in a *promise* with that of an assertion, and consider the incoherence or self-defeat in saying something like, I promise; but of course I might change my mind, or forget, or cease caring. Here as well, the speaker is only saying something that both parties know to be true, about himself and about promises in general. But to say so is, at the very least, contrary to the spirit in which a promise is made, contrary to the very point of making a promise. And what makes for this self-defeat is precisely the presentation of it in an evidential spirit. For notice: for someone to say 'I promise, but I might change my mind' is to refer to his promise as a fallible indication of future performance. That is, it is to present it as a kind of defeasible evidence for what he will do. And, of course, insofar as a promise is seen as evidence at all it can only be seen as *defeasible* evidence. Hence for the speaker to offer his promise as evidence means he must be offering it as, at best, defeasible evidence, with respect to which the promisee is on his own. And to do so is contrary to the point of making a promise, which is assurance.

The disharmony between speaker and audience entailed by the Evidential view comes out in the consideration of two possible responses to receiving a promise. If someone promises to mail a letter for me, one thing I might do is accept his promise, placing myself in his hands and taking myself to now have sufficient reason for believing that he *will* mail the letter. If it turns out he *doesn't* mail the letter, either through carelessness or because he never really intended to, then I will feel aggrieved and let down. This is the ordinary expectation and liability to disappointment. I might, however, opt for another kind of response altogether. Here I don't *accept* the promise; I simply don't go in for that sort of thing, as I may not accept promises from a small child or (for different reasons) from someone I despise, but in another way I do take seriously the fact that he made one to me. In this spirit I may reason: 'He is unlikely to make a promise he won't fulfill, since that would discredit him as a future promisor, and there are great and obvious advantages in remaining someone whose promises are accepted. Therefore, the fact that he made this promise to me makes it probable that he will in fact mail the letter. So I believe he will.' If, on this second scenario, I later discover that he did not mail the letter after all, my reaction will be different. I will be disappointed, of course, and I will be surprised that he would discredit himself in this way. But I can't confront him with my complaint or my resentment because I never accepted the promise in the first place. My relation to this person's promise is similar to my relation to the person I suspect of 'double-bluffing' me. I don't believe him; there's no question of that. But nonetheless his statement that he's traveling to Minsk functions as my reason for believing that this is what he will do. In both cases the speaker has made me a free declaration which I then make evidential use of to infer to the truth of what he says. On the Evidential view, this second type of response to promises and assertions would have to be the only epistemically legitimate one, and yet such a reconstruction would yield an incoherent description of the practices of telling or promising. It would be incoherent because on such a view the speaker would have to be in the position of offering assurances that are never accepted, and which he knows are never accepted, and the audience would nonetheless be relying on the continued offering of such free assurances to serve as his evidential base.

The issue of harmony between speaker and audience goes deeper than this, however, and helps to delineate the relationship between the speaker's authority to determine the illocutionary status of his utterance, and its actual epistemic import. In asserting that P, where the context is one of 'telling', the speaker is not in a position to constitute his utterance as a good or sufficient reason for P, since that will depend on his credentials and success as a knower, as well as his honesty. But in the act of telling his audience that P, he does claim definitive 'say' in determining that his utterance is being presented as a *reason for belief*, rather than, say as a speculation or grammatical example, as well as determining just *what* it is that he is giving his word on. From the speaker's perspective both determinations matter to the alignment of speaker and audience that he sees himself as aiming at. From a purely evidential perspective, however, it shouldn't matter to the audience whether the route from the speaker's words to a true belief involves the loop in double-bluffing or not. And just as clearly in such a case there would be failure of correspondence between the spirit in which the statement is made and that in which it is received. The speaker who asserts P is *not* indifferent to whether he induces belief in his audience through the loop of double-bluffing. His assertion is asking for belief in the *very* proposition stated and for the *very* sort of reason that he is then and there presenting to him. And *that* sort of reason is bound up with his presenting himself as accountable for this truth. In double-bluffing, the reason for belief taken by the audience is different from the reason the speaker offers. What 'telling' aims at, by contrast, is that there be a correspondence or identity between the reason the speaker takes himself to be offering and what the audience accepts as a reason. So we might say, in telling his audience that P, the speaker asks that his authority be acknowledged to determine what sort of candidate reason for what belief is up for consideration. This is the spirit in which his statement is made, and it is this that is denied by treating his utterance in a wholly evidential spirit, in which the question of what is being considered a reason for what is anybody's business, and is not tethered to the speaker's awareness or intent. Conversation may of course move into and out of this dimension of assessment, but for purposes of either agreement *or* disagreement it cannot begin there.

In the speech act of telling, the speaker commits himself to his audience with respect to a particular proposition, and with respect to the kind of reason being presented. This follows from the difference between doing something that *has* a certain epistemic significance (as with taking or showing a photograph) and being responsible for something's *having* the epistemic significance that it has (as with a speaker and his words). In telling his audience something, the speaker aims at being believed, an aim which is manifest to both parties, and which binds the speaker and audience together with respect to a norm of correspondence between the reason offered and the reason accepted. When an act of telling completes itself, speaker and audience are aligned in this way through their mutual recognition of the speaker's role in determining the kind of reason for belief that is up for acceptance, so that when the speaker is believed there is a non-accidental relation between the reason presented and the reason accepted. The speaker says, in effect, "The kind of reason for belief you gain from my statement is precisely the kind of reason for belief I am hereby presenting myself as offering you. Insofar as there is a disparity between the two, I disavow responsibility for whatever belief you may derive from my assertion." Presenting his utterance that way is a kind of declaration of transparency to his audience: the kind of reason overtly presented is precisely the reason that is meant to count for you. When the background of the speaker's knowledge and sincerity can be assumed, and the speaker is in fact believed by his audience (a common enough occurrence, after all) the two parties are in sync with each other in a way that they would not be if the audience were to take the utterance either as a reason for some other belief rather than the one stated, or a different kind of reason for that belief (as with double-bluffing). Taking the utterance as evidence detaches the reason-giving significance of the utterance from the speaker's authority to determine what he is thereby committing himself to.[25] From an evidential perspective it may function as evidence for any number of things, for which the speaker's competence or responsibility may be irrelevant. This is manifestly not the speaker's perspective on the epistemic significance of his statement, which he sees in terms of the nexus of a specific responsibility assumed and a specific entitlement conferred.[26]

For the act of telling to complete itself there must be a correspondence between the reason being *presented* by the speaker and the reason *accepted* by his audience. This is the nexus that is aimed at in the self-reflexive aspect of the Gricean formula, wherein the speaker asks that the very reason he is thereby presenting be the reason that the audience thereby accepts (i.e., through recognizing that very intention). Telling aims at being believed, which proceeds, via the speaker's overt assumption of responsibility, by joining together the particular belief proposed for acceptance, the kind of reason being presented for it, and the reason accepted by the audience. An evidential stance, by contrast, de-couples all of these from each other, to be reassembled as the observer thinks best. But such a stance is contrary to the speaker's perspective on his action, insofar as it pictures his presentation of himself as meaning, in effect, that as far as reason-giving force goes, the audience is on his own; as if the meaning of his utterance were "Now I have spoken; make of it what you will", rather than "Take it from me".

More is conveyed in our ordinary assertions that the specific proposition asserted, and more is often *intended* to be conveyed by the speaker, and much of this will be picked up in an evidential spirit. All of which is to say that not all, not nearly all, speech takes the form of one person telling something to another, testifying to its truth. Not everything we need to convey is best conveyed by being *told* to another, in part because not everything we need to communicate is something we could sensibly ask to be relied on for, present ourselves as accountable for, or ask to be accepted on our say so (e.g., the occasional comedy or tragedy in someone asserting his own dignity or probity). Nonetheless, it is clear enough what Anscombe means when she speaks of the insult and injury in not being believed.[27] And the offence remains even when the speaker's audience takes his having made the statement to count as evidence for its truth, just as above he may take the speaker's having made the promise to make it more probable that he will do the thing in question. The offence lies in his refusing to accept what the speaker freely and explicitly offers him, in favor of privately attending to what the speaker's action passively reveals, just as someone might refuse an apology while still taking it in this case to be a reliable indication of remorse. What makes sense of such refusals is the fact that acceptance of an assertion or an apology doesn't just put one in a different epistemic position with respect to the facts, but brings with it certain vulnerabilities and responsibilities of its own. Accepting an apology, for instance, brings with it the responsibility to put away one's resentment, and makes one vulnerable to a particularly bruising possibility of deceit. These risks are avoided by simply taking the apology as more or less good evidence for remorse, and then making of it what one will.

The Evidential picture puts speaker and audience into disharmony with each other in mislocating the connection between what the speaker does and the fact that it provides a reason for belief. From the speaker's point of view, it is not a matter of what his behavior passively indicates, but a matter of what he then and there presents himself as assuming responsibility for. Unlike an evidential relation, the connection between the speaker's words and what he asserts or what he promises is entirely at his disposal to declare or to retract. The possibility of such retraction is central to the meaning of speech acts of assertion, promising, and the like, and shows how different they are in meaning and consequence from other actions. The speaker alone has the authority to bestow such epistemic import on his words, or cancel it; whereas he speaks with no such authority over the evidential import of anything he does or says.

Speaking of course, *is* an action; something with consequences in the world like other actions, and which leaves behind evidence of itself. But the exclusivity of the speaker's authority shows that retracting one's words is not to be confused with undoing the consequences of an action that went wrong. Often enough, another person could in principle clean up after the mess I made as well as I. But no one else can take back what I said. And, of course, taking back what I said does not make it as if it never happened. After I've taken back what I said it may still take a long time for me to undo the damage my hard or thoughtless words have caused. But that doesn't mean that taking them back doesn't accomplish anything, that I might just as well not have returned to them. There's still an important difference in the situations before and after the angry words are retracted. Indeed, taking them back was a prior condition for the more practical (or consequential) work of starting to try to undo the damage they caused. And that's a different kind of task. I cannot *'hereby'* undo the damage, the hurt feelings I caused; that takes consequential work, which may fail in unforeseen ways, like any other action. But again, that doesn't mean that the sort of thing I *can* accomplish 'hereby' is something I perform magically or effortlessly, or that it may not be something I can only manage with great difficulty. It will, however, be a different kind of difficulty from that involved in repairing the actual damage. If I try and fail here, at the level of retraction or apology, it will not be for reasons of unforeseeable accidents, or the general resistance of the world to our wills.

REFERENCES

Anscombe, G. E. M. (1979), 'What Is It to Believe Someone?', in C. F. Delaney (ed.), *Rationality and Religious Belief* (Notre Dame, Ind.: University of Notre Dame Press).

—— (1981), 'Faith', in *Ethics, Religion and Politics: Collected Philosophical Papers, Vol. III* (Minneapolis: University of Minnesota Press).

Austin, J. L., (1962), *How to Do Things with Words* (Cambridge, Mass.: Harvard University Press, 1962).

—— (1979), 'Other Minds,' in *Philosophical Papers* (Oxford: Oxford University Press).

Brandom, Robert (1994), *Making It Explicit* (Cambridge, Mass.: Harvard University Press, 1994).

Burge, Tyler (1993), 'Content Preservation', *Philosophical Review* (Oct.).

Cavell, Stanley (1979), *The Claim of Reason* (Oxford: Oxford University Press).

Coady, C. A. J. (1992), *Testimony: A Philosophical Study* (Oxford: Oxford University Press).

Darwall, Stephen (forthcoming), *The Second-Person Standpoint: Morality and Accountability.*

Grice, H. P. (1957), 'Meaning', *Philosophical Review*, 66: 377–88; repr. in P. F. Strawson (ed.), *Philosophy of Logic* (Oxford, 1967), 39–48.

Harman, Gilbert (1986), *Change in View* (Cambridge, Mass.: MIT).

Holton, Richard (1994), 'Deciding to Trust, Coming to Believe', *Australasian Journal of Philosophy*, 72: 63–76.

Hume, David (1977), 'On Miracles', in *An Enquiry Concerning Human Understanding* (Cambridge, Mass.: Hackett).

Leite, Adam (2004), 'On Justifying and Being Justified', *Philosophical Issues* (a suppl. to Nous), 14., *Epistemology*, 219–53.

Locke, John (1975), *Essay Concerning Human Understanding*, ed. Peter Nidditch (Oxford: Clarendon Press).

Moran, Richard, 'Problems of Sincerity' (2005), *Proceedings of the Aristotelian Society*, 105/3: 341–61.

Quine, W. V. O., and Ullian, J. S. (1970), *The Web of Belief* (New York: Random House).

Ross, Angus (1986), 'Why Do We Believe What We Are Told?', *Ratio* (June).

Stone, Martin (2001), 'The Significance of Doing and Suffering', in G. Postema (ed.), *Philosophy and Tort Law* (Cambridge: Cambridge University Press).

—— (1996), 'On the Idea of Private of Law', *Canadian Journal of Law and Jurisprudence*, 9/2 (July) (repr. in E. Weinrib (ed.), *Tort Law, The International Library of Essays in Law and Legal Theory*, 2nd ser. (Aldershot: Ashgate Publishing, 2003)).

Strawson, P. F. (1974), 'Freedom and Resentment', in his *Freedom and Resentment* (London: Methuen), 1–25.

Thompson, Michael (2004), 'What Is It to Wrong Someone? A Puzzle about Justice', in R. J. Wallace, Philip Pettit, Samuel Scheffler, and Michael Smith (eds.), *Reason and Value: Themes from The Moral Philosophy of Joseph Raz* (Oxford: Oxford University Press).

Traiger, Saul (1993), ' Humean Testimony', *Pacific Philosophical Quarterly* (June).

Walton, Kendall (1984), 'Transparent Pictures: On the Nature of Photographic Realism', *Critical Inquiry* (Dec.).

Watson, Gary (2004), 'Asserting and Promising', *Philosophical Studies*, 117.

Weinrib, Ernest (1995), *The Idea of Private Law* (Cambridge, Mass.: Harvard University Press).

Welbourne, Michael (1986), *The Community of Knowledge* (Aberdeen: Aberdeen University Press).

Williams, Bernard (2002), *Truth and Truthfulness: An Essay in Genealogy* (Princeton: Princeton University Press).

Williamson, Timothy (1996), 'Knowing and Asserting', *Philosophical Review*, 105/4. (repr. in his *Knowledge and Its Limits* (Oxford: Oxford University Press, 2000)).

Wittgenstein, Ludwig (1980), *Remarks on the Philosophy of Psychology*, vol. i, trans. G. E. M. Anscombe (Oxford: Blackwell).

NOTES

1. Cf. Locke: "For, I think, we may as rationally hope to see with other Men's Eyes, as to know by other Men's Understandings. So much as we ourselves consider and comprehend of Truth and Reason, so much we possess of real and true Knowledge. The floating of other Men's Opinions in our brains makes us not a jot more knowing, though they happen to be true." (Locke 1975: 1, 4, 23.)

2. Or back to observation sentences: cf. Quine and Ullian (1970: 33–5), which makes explicit comparison of testimony with the 'extension of the senses' provided by telescopes and radar.

3. 'On Miracles' (Locke 1975).

4. *Testimony: A Philosophical Study* (Oxford: Oxford University Press, 1992).

5. I follow other recent writers in characterizing this as a Humean position, but I don't argue for the attribution. For a dissenting view, see Saul Traiger (1993).

6. Coady (1992) and Burge (1993).

7. Burge's argument is very different, and I will not be examining its details here. In particular, unlike Coady as we will see, his account does not appeal to a principle of charity in the situation of radical interpretation. What it shares with Coady's argument is the aim of providing some *a priori* warrant for believing what is said. Burge argues for what he calls the Acceptance Principle, which states that: A person is entitled to accept as true something that is presented as true and that is intelligible to him, unless there are stronger reasons not to do so (Burge 1993: 467). He states that this is not an empirical principle (1993: 469). And the general form of justification associated with it is meant to apply equally to our epistemic dependence on other *people* ('rational sources') and to our dependence on certain *capacities*, what

he calls 'resources for reason', such as memory and perception (1993: 469–70). By contrast, for my purposes the difference between our dependence on memory and perception and our dependence on other people is all-important for the understanding of testimony.

8. Summarizing his line of criticism of one version of the reductionist thesis associated with Hume, Coady says "The difficulty consists in the fact that the whole enterprise of RT" in its present form requires that we understand what testimony is independently of knowing that it is, in any degree, a reliable form of evidence" (Coady 1992: 85).

9. With some obvious exceptions; for instance, if I learned of his beliefs from the bragging admission of the person who deceived him. But these sorts of cases are just what is taken to be excluded by speaking of 'other things being equal'.

10. When in the course of a discussion of Moore's Paradox and the idea of "two people speaking through my mouth", Wittgenstein asks, "Where is it said in logic that an assertion [*Behauptung*] cannot be made in a trance?", I understand him roughly to be saying: Logic (on some conception of it) may well say nothing about the speaker's awareness of what he is doing in making an assertion, just as the same conception of logic permits statements of the form 'P, but I don't believe it', but both possibilities are contrary to the point and hence the meaning of assertions (Wittgenstein 1980, §818).

11. I should add that I'll only be discussing a part of Ross's argument, focusing on his criticism of an evidential view of testimony, and not his positive account of how assertion contributes to belief. Michael Welbourne's account of testimony in his monograph, *The Community of Knowledge* has various affinities with Ross's, including the denial that an act of telling is presented by the speaker as evidence, and an emphasis on believing the speaker as the target notion for an understanding of testimony (and the concept of knowledge itself on Welbourne's view).

12. And if we take it that assertions are made in the course of following out a proof, or in *ad hominem* argument, then it's clear that their role in providing reason for belief needn't even depend on the assumption that the speaker believes what he says. See Moran (2005).

13. For purposes of the account of testimony developed here, we need not of course follow Walton in his claim that the object itself is in fact seen in the photograph, for it is precisely the differences between photographs and assertions that concern me here.

14. Grice (1957), in Strawson (1967: 44). Ross discusses natural vs. non-natural meaning at p. 74.

15. At the end of her paper, Anscombe (1979) points out that it is a requirement of any successful account of the phenomenon that it explain why we only speak of believing someone when we take them to be both right about the facts and truthful in intent.

16. Austin (1962: 57).

17. Here I agree with Harman (1986: 88) in seeing as mistaken Grice's later attempts to eliminate the self-referentiality in his original formulation for non-natural meaning. ("Much of this complexity is artificial and due to Grice's refusal to stick with the original analysis and its appeal to a self-referential intention.")

18. Coady (1992: 45–6) distinguishes genuine testimony from the situation of someone who has been hypnotized specifically to say something, perhaps even with the expectation of being believed. But his reason for excluding this case is different from mine. For Coady, this cannot count as 'testifying' because it fails to satisfy the condition that the speaker has the relevant competence, authority, or credentials to state truly that P (1992: 42), since the words have more or less been 'planted' in the subject. This focus on epistemic authority seems misplaced, however. For the speaker in this case *could* after all also happen to have the requisite competence and authority on the subject. Instead, the reason this doesn't count as testimony is that, in his present condition, he is not presenting himself as responsible for P's being true.

19. Holton (1994) provides an illuminating focus on the role of what Strawson refers to as the Participant Stance and the Reactive Attitudes, especially with regard to the distinction between belief through trust and belief through reliance. Holton says of the latter case, "Seen in this way, a person is like a measuring device: they respond to the environment in various ways, and we infer from their response to what the environment is like" (1994: 74).

20. Something like this assumption is expressed in Bernard Williams's idea of assertion as the "direct expression" of one's belief (Williams (2002: 74 *passim*), which I discuss in Moran (2005: 347–50)).

21. "No abandonment of the agent's perspective, no abdication of responsibility for one's actions, is involved in seeing those actions as generating entitlements and obligations, either on the part of ourselves or on the part of others. (Compare the case of promising or issuing a command.) There is on the present account no difficulty in seeing the hearer as taking the speaker's words in the spirit in which they are honestly offered" (Ross 1986: 79).
    See also Robert Brandom's richly developed account of assertion in terms of the constellation of entitlements and obligations (Brandom 1994: ch. 3).

22. After a 'preamble', Anscombe *begins* her essay with the statement " 'Believe' with personal object cannot be reflexive" (1979: 144). See also Cavell: "A striking exception to the thought that I can stand in any relation to myself that I can stand to others is that of belief. Why apparently can I not, in grammar, believe myself?" (Cavell 1979: 393).

23. Cf. Williamson (1996): "To make an assertion is to confer a responsibility (on oneself) for the truth of its content; to satisfy the rule of assertion, by having the requisite knowledge, is to discharge that responsibility, by epistemically ensuring the truth of the content. Our possession of such speech acts is no more surprising than the fact that we have a use for relations of responsibility."

24. For further discussion of the assertions and promises, emphasizing their differences as well as similarities in their relations to the speaker's responsibilities, see Watson (2004).

25. That the directness of the audience's dependence on the person of the speaker as such is related to the directness of the speaker's own relation to the reasons on which he *bases* his belief is something I have been helped to see by Leite (2004). Because the speaker's statement of his reasons is not a hypothesis he makes about the origin of his belief, his assertion makes *him* (and not, e.g., something inside him) directly accountable for the truth or believability of his claim. Leite puts it the following

way: "Suppose that you consider reasons for and against a claim, find that certain reasons decisively support holding it, and sincerely declare that you believe the claim for those reasons. In the usual case, you thereby directly determine what the reasons are for which you hold the belief. Moreover, in declaring your reasons you both open yourself to epistemic evaluation or criticism on account of those reasons' inadequacy and incur certain obligations—in particular, an obligation either to give up the belief or to seek better reasons, should those reasons prove inadequate. A minimal adequacy condition for an account of the epistemic basing relation is thus that it allow (1) that the reasons for which a belief is held can be directly determined in this way, and (2) that one sometimes directly opens oneself to epistemic criticism and incurs further justificatory responsibilities by sincerely declaring that one holds one's belief for particular reasons" (2004: 227–8).

26. Putting it this way describes the relationship of speaker and audience in terms of an essentially correlative or "bi-polar" normativity, of the sort that has recently been explored by a number of philosophers. By contrast, the non-personal nature of evidence, the independence of its epistemic force from its being presented as a reason *to* another person, expresses the "monadic" character of its normativity. It was only at a late stage of working on this paper, that I began to see the direct relevance to these issues concerning testimony of the work on "correlativity" "bi-polar normativity" and private law by Ernest Weinrib (1995), Martin Stone (1996 and 2001), and Michael Thompson (2004); as well as Stephen Darwall's work (forthcoming) on the second-person standpoint, all of which will repay further study in thinking about speech and testimony.

27. Anscombe, (1979: 150). See also Austin (1979: 100).

Index